Flat Aesthetics

Flat Aesthetics

Twenty-First-Century American Fiction and the Making of the Contemporary

Christian Moraru

BLOOMSBURY ACADEMIC

NEW YORK · LONDON · OXFORD · NEW DELHI · SYDNEY

BLOOMSBURY ACADEMIC
Bloomsbury Publishing Inc
1385 Broadway, New York, NY 10018, USA
50 Bedford Square, London, WC1B 3DP, UK

BLOOMSBURY, BLOOMSBURY ACADEMIC and the Diana logo are trademarks of
Bloomsbury Publishing Plc

First published in the United States of America 2023

Cover design: Eleanor Rose
Cover image: The Nest, 2016, by Rebecca Darlington. Photo: Michael Dale Nelson.
Size: 14″ × 9″ × 3″, Medium: Bird's Nest, Resin, Bronze, Iron.

Library of Congress Cataloging-in-Publication Data
Names: Moraru, Christian, author.
Title: Flat aesthetics : twenty-first-century American fiction and the making of the
contemporary / Christian Moraru.
Description: New York : Bloomsbury Academic, 2023. | Includes bibliographical references
and index. | Summary: "A literary-historical study that deals chiefly with post-1990 American
fictional prose and argues that David Foster Wallace's phrase, "après-garde" (the opposite
of avant-garde), encapsulates an aesthetic that is applicable to much of the past thirty-odd
years of American literature"– Provided by publisher.
Identifiers: LCCN 2022025097 (print) | LCCN 2022025098 (ebook) |
ISBN 9781501355271 (hb) | ISBN 9798765101117 (pb) | ISBN 9781501355288 (eBook) |
ISBN 9781501355264 (ePDF) | ISBN 9781501355295
Subjects: LCSH: American fiction–21st century–History and criticism. |
Contemporary, The, in literature. | Aesthetics in literature. |
Postmodernism (Literature)–United States. | LCGFT: Literary criticism.
Classification: LCC PS374.C596 M67 2023 (print) | LCC PS374.C596 (ebook) |
DDC 813/.609—dc23/eng/20220921
LC record available at https://lccn.loc.gov/2022025097
LC ebook record available at https://lccn.loc.gov/2022025098

ISBN: HB: 978-1-5013-5527-1
        ePDF: 978-1-5013-5526-4
        eBook: 978-1-5013-5528-8

Typeset by RefineCatch Limited, Bungay, Suffolk
Printed and bound in Great Britain

To find out more about our authors and books visit www.bloomsbury.com
and sign up for our newsletters.

Always think of the objects.
                    —Ben Lerner, *Leaving the Atocha Station*

. . . the irremediable thingness of the world.
                    —Giorgio Agamben, *The Coming Community*

Contents

Preface and Acknowledgments

Oh, chatty things! They pester you
With steady whispers in your ear,
Bronze, velvet, wood, or silk—you hear
Them talk to you like people do.

You think they're dead, yet they live too
Scattered both far and near—
Oh, chatty things! They pester you
With steady whispers in your ear.

Stories galore—true and untrue—
Those hermits tell you and appear
To tempt or torment you, anew,
With your soul's snows of yesteryear.

Oh, chatty things! They pester you.
—Alexandru Macedonski, "The Rondel of Things"[1]

The world is flat, after all. Not in a flat-earther's sense, of course, and it turns out, not in Thomas Friedman's either.[2] The world is flat not because its unevenness has been corrected by a presumably egalitarian post-Cold War globalization. As has been suggested, the world is flat ontologically, and, I propose in this book, the world is flat aesthetically too. I also argue that to understand contemporary American fiction and contemporaneity broadly, my main goal in these pages, one needs to come to grips with this flatness. Admittedly, this concept is somewhat counterintuitive. But then so are many of our thought-provoking notions. In any case, I adopt it as a loose descriptor of material beings—existents, things, or with the most popular term in this sometimes synonymous series, objects—although I employ it as often with reference to entities such as numbers, words, and philosophical categories, which we ordinarily consider neither flat nor concrete, or at least not concrete in the way we think fruit and curios are.

As one might suspect, in so doing, I take my cue from flat ontology. But I take a few liberties with its axioms too. Since the book's introduction details my qualified indebtedness to object-oriented ontology (OOO), speculative realism, and new materialism, suffice it to say for now that one idea making deeper and deeper inroads into these and other fields and setting twenty-first-century critical consciousness apart from past eras' defining *Weltanschauungen* is that all things surrounding, making, and preoccupying us *are*. To paraphrase Ian Bogost, *everything* is. Full stop. And everything follows in *Flat Aesthetics* from this stop, as it were.[3] But, as Bogost also writes emphatically, "*[a]ll things equally exist, yet they do not exist equally.*"[4] So the stop is not entirely full—it is a "Hoosier stop," as the joke goes in Indiana; drivers do stop at stop signs ontologically, but their Silverados keep moving politically, "messing things up."

Born ontologically free, things are everywhere in chains.

It is the growing and intolerable asymmetry between things' existence and their status or "eminence"—political, aesthetic, and so forth—over the last decades that has prompted my new monograph.[5] Like others, I have come to realize that, today more than ever, what is *presents itself* most powerfully regardless of what it is. As I clarify in the introductory section, there is nothing metaphysical about this historically unmatched show of presence, about the world's objects stepping forward instead of "withdrawing";[6] nor is, I stress, this presentation done for human benefit. More importantly, this presence finds itself nowadays threatened with overuse, contamination, depletion, and annihilation, processes that have dramatically accelerated and expanded during the Anthropocene and its late-global avatar. As a consequence, human and nonhuman, "sentient" and "insentient" beings have entered an era of ontological precarity in which they are radically besieged, teetering on the brink of non-being. Exploited, diminished, endangered, and underappreciated as they stand, they are all nevertheless present and lay the same claim to presence, to *being-there*. Thus, "flat" is an ontological datum; it is something that characterizes all that exists, the "world," another slippery notion I decline to discard although I agree with those object-oriented ontologists who remind us that the world *is* the objects, not their container. At any rate, flatness can be put to meaningful critical use. I try to do so here by taking steps toward a literary aesthetics that strives to place *all* objects on the same level.

Flat Aesthetics carries on an inquiry begun in my previous books, principally in *Cosmodernism, Reading for the Planet*, and the *Bloomsbury Handbook of World Theory*.[7] Like those, this one builds a many-sided argument. The most important sides are critical-theoretical, political, and historical. To reiterate, my central objective is to get a more granular, ontologically "demotic" handle on the ever-elusive contemporary in

American fiction. I approach contemporaneity as something things of all sorts have been making for a while, as some-thing produced by them "out there" in the world and whose production is variously reproduced and restaged by the body of literature under scrutiny here. In this sense, this corpus itself participates in the making of the contemporary. In any event, as I repeat throughout, the contemporary is *manufactured*, and *things make it*. I further contend that it preexists neither to objects nor to the novels featuring them. It is not their "background." It does have a historical dimension—we talk about the "contemporary era" for a reason, if often by virtue of habit. But, as the introduction also insists, the contemporary is not to be viewed, or not primarily, as a temporal category, let alone as the "present." As objects present themselves *in* this present or "now," they engender certain thing-configurations that together make up the form of—and more basically just make—the contemporary. This is the present's cultural signature, as I call it.

This signature is not indecipherable. Complex as it is—a lattice of forms—this form is nonetheless distinct. It is *our* contemporary and in that largely different from previous contemporaneities. Like its sub-configurations, this form or formation is not only typical of, and defining for, our point in history but also the backbone of the *Zeitgeist*. It is complex and confusing but not pure chaos, a cultural "brouhaha," as some would have us believe.[8] There is a shape and consistency to *this* contemporary, an individualizing texture to it. A pivotal gambit of *Flat Aesthetics* is that this texture, this material fabric, obtains and presents itself in and through objects. The introduction develops a framework to account for the new aesthetics or ontoaesthetics, as well as for the new epoch things' self-presentation has spawned, as I submit, after the fall of the Berlin Wall. The framework is thus theoretical as it is cultural-historical in a reluctantly "epochalist" sort of way. It integrates considerations of ontology and aesthetics and defines the unprecedented rise into presence of the world's "thingness" as a post-Cold War or, more specifically, post-2000 development that accelerates the shift away from postmodernism and the dawn of a new paradigm: the contemporary.

To shine light on this epoch-making process, this book offers a cross-sectional reading of postmillennial American fiction, with particular attention to what I deem highly representative, emerging, or recognized contemporary classics. *Flat Aesthetics* discusses solely twenty-first-century works by writers who have also established themselves over the past two decades or so. They range from the Jewish-Americans Nicole Krauss, Michael Chabon, and Ben Lerner to the Pakistani-British-American Mohsin Hamid, the Turkish-Irish-British and, lately, American Joseph O'Neill, the African-American Colson Whitehead, and the Canadian-American Emily St. John Mandel. In this group, O'Neill, Chabon, and Whitehead are the only ones who published books in the previous century (Whitehead's debut novel, *The Intuitionist*, came out in 1999). All these authors are contemporary twice: aesthetically and historically. Their output, I claim, bears witness to the onset of a new aesthetics in American letters after the Cold War, especially after September 11, 2001. This aesthetic constitutes, I also maintain, a reaction not only to postmodernism but also, if sometimes ambiguously, to a wider, U.S. and international, sociopolitical, geopolitical, and environmental situation. Thus, the aesthetic realignments I uncover are symptoms of a bigger context. In *Cosmodernism* and its sequel, *Reading for the Planet*, I pursued chiefly the cultural dimension of that context. The analysis there did not ignore "the secret life of things," nor did it skirt issues of materiality playing out in the open.[9] Far from it. But, by design, the discussion in essence orbited the human, dwelling on the discursive-cultural packaging of objects and otherwise attending to them insofar as they were relevant to us, humans. I do not ditch that anthropocentric baggage completely either—no one could or, as some new materialists emphasize, should. I do try hard to level the playing field by reframing materiality, objects, and their analysis away from their traditionally human-oriented meanings and concerns.

Unlike some prominent object-oriented thinkers, I have been and remain keen on relations. This book too is about them and their creative force. But what goes on in these object "entanglements," as Karen Barad refers to them, no longer revolves in *Flat Aesthetics* around human agents, *their* sense of cultural alterity and relatedness, and the like.[10] In fact, I "flatten" these webs as much as possible, examining chiefly their nonhuman element, the relational or energetic dynamic *they* initiate and sustain among *relata* human and nonhuman. There is no "correlationism" systematically privileging a knowing subject here but a lateral "interrelationism" of objects and the object montages derived from it according to a range of "onto-logics." For this reason, what takes place inside such object circuitries differs from what my previous books describe. Generally speaking, what intrigues me is how objects, which populate Quentin Meillassoux's "great outdoors" already, with or without "us" out there to pay heed to them, acquire, when their ability or "willingness" to be useful to us fails or is in question, intensities that make them "hyperpresent."[11] Those are moments, I propose, when they challenge their own instrumentality as well as the surrounding "exchange regime," as I call it. Not exchangeable for something other than themselves anymore, hyperpresent objects boost and signal, not necessarily to us, their *form* rather than their "content," handiness, or whatever practical value they may have—again, to us. This formal vibration or "insistence" translates into an energy upsurge, which allows them to engage in all kinds of ways with other objects to com-pose and present, to put together inside the seemingly incoherent present another form—the form of contemporaneity and sometimes even formal anticipations of the future.

I am not committed to solving here endlessly debated issues of animal and "inanimate" rationality, agency, intentionality, causality, or subjectivity for that matter—one more reason to gladly accept that we are all objects and at the same time wonder, as the scare quotes in this sentence hint, if our understanding of life need be biologist or organicist. I am not obsessing over what things "really" are either, over what their "substance" may be and where—in plain sight? Concealed?—although I have my own answers to these questions, as the reader will discover. But I pose them to the extent they bear on my project. Otherwise, I feel compelled to rehash neither the commonplaces nor the controversies swirling around, say, the aporias of correlationism, Actor-Network-Theory, or vitalism. My priorities are to acknowledge what objects *do* and to grasp what their doings' outcomes are. I am interested, that is, in how objects discharge and channel their energies across the postmillennial storyworlds, in the resulting object clumps and mazes, and ultimately in the aggregate they all combine into—the coarse-grained but not illegible "system" of the contemporary. To that effect, I screen a narrative corpus, and within it, I curate various sets of objects that allow me to uncover certain configurations of contemporaneity *from inside out* and show how recent fiction itself constructs, quite literally, the contemporary.

Needless to say, I assume responsibility for the construct, for this quasi-Latourian "com-position" of objects, as I often say in this book. Key to "flat reading," *Flat Aesthetics*' primary instrument, is an effort, itself compositional, to locate and set out object com-positions. This descriptive operation can be seen as an exercise in "thing-mapping." There is nothing arbitrary about this compositional exercise even though the chapter titles may leave this impression as they invariably list, a bit playfully and alluding to Latourian object "litanies," no more and no less than three things.[12] On the other hand, a different "compositionist," with his or her own agenda and philosophical compass, may pick up on different items while canvassing the same territory. So may somebody working from a different list of post-2000 U.S. fictional narratives such as, say, Native American—which, incidentally, would reveal fascinating visions of ahuman thingness and thing-spirituality—or graphic novels, typographically experimental metafiction à la Mark Z. Danielewski, new-, mixed-media, born-digital, and related, electronic and "post-electronic" literary creations by Steve Tomasula and others and attesting, no doubt, to an entire rebirth of "book presence in a digital age," to quote an important volume on the subject.[13] Should one deal with such material, which I do not take up here, one may well produce different maps—but, I submit, not *wholly* different from what I am drawing in *Flat Aesthetics*.

That difference would also stem from an object definition not at play in these chapters. The reader will probably agree that my own definition is not restrictive at all. I do want, however, to own up to my slight "somatist" bias, to borrow Iain Hamilton Grant's term.[14] In other words, I tend to focus on physical or material, corporeal, and discrete entities although I also talk about activities (scuba diving instead of scubas), about words, about imaginary beings twice or thrice removed from "reality" (Whitehead's "skels"), about large, complex "crowds" of things comparable to Timothy Morton's "hyperobjects," such as storms and shipping lanes, and even about Kabbalistic infinity.[15] To make it clear: I consider them all as material and, in a way, as concrete as a lump of concrete in terms of what they can do, how they can bear on other things, including people, as well as in other regards. However, I ordinarily turn to palpably embodied, small- to medium-scale, and easier-to-pinpoint, -visualize, and -identify "stuff" such as cell phones, cereal, and bees.

Even so, thematically, this material is not organized into object categories, which would have rendered, more or less, each book part an intervention into one of the "studies" areas of post- and nonhuman scholarship and theory: environmental, animal, botanical, technological, and so on. *Flat Aesthetics* does share concerns with all of these, as it does with debates around race and gender. Along another axis of foci, my book engages, extensively or tangentially, with "new aesthetics"—from the aesthetics of affect to "everyday aesthetics"—as well as with recent preoccupations of genre (metafiction, autofiction, speculative, the "undead," end-of-times, postapocalyptic).[16] On still another, it is in conversation with criticism on globalization, world-systems theory, World Literature, postmodernism, the transition out of the latter and this process's implications for discussions of literary-cultural history, and especially in the closing chapter of the introduction, periodization and the troubling "period" commonly known as the contemporary. Following the lead of the primary sources, the project's investigations cut across object classes, looking at the ways in which remarkably different things assemble over and over again into arrangements whose formation tells us, as process and structure, something about this momentous shift. I pursue, then, both individual objects and their dynamism; I single out the most active among them—the object "ringleaders"—which are sometimes designated as "Ur-objects"; I record their energetic "upgrade" to form and, accompanying it, the coming to the fore of their "objecthood" or "thingness"; I reconstitute or survey the ensembles they themselves have constituted; and in a more speculative vein, I gloss on what these conglomerates "tell" us about our time and even about times to come.

Thus, part one deals with language as object and with objects of language—or metaobjects, if you will—from words and numbers to speeches and from e-mails and quotes pilfered from classics by aspiring poets to entire poems, "original" or less so. But, as I show, linguistic entities affect and are in turn somehow affected by things such as movies, cereal boxes, uniforms, jewelry, talking parrots, insects, and train cars. These are all fictional objects, featured as such inside the prose discussed here. What happens, I ask, when such language things quit doing their thing? What does their declining to "serve" their speakers, writers, and translators *do*, and in what sense can that be said to be a positive thing? What kind of strength do words and texts draw—because they do—from their failure to mean or from their resistance to meaning, representation, paraphrase, and even critical claim? What combinations do they form, in their "uselessness," insufficiency, and opaqueness, with other forms, and what do those object constellations convey about the present, its cultural hallmark—the contemporary—and the future? The first two chapters of this book section answer these and other questions through marginalia to Lerner's slim but poignant 2016 book *The Hatred of Poetry* and to his most important novel to date, the postmillennial landmark *Leaving the Atocha Station* (2011). The third and last chapter is devoted to Chabon's 2004 novella *The Final Solution*, where I raise similar questions apropos of animal language, the unyielding idiom of digits, and the tragic eloquence of silence.

As its title suggests, part two focuses on object displays. Here, I review museal assemblages and weigh the tensions between patrimonial collecting and the "curating scene" in post-2000 American fiction. The first chapter dwells on Mandel's *Station Eleven* (2014), which has risen to spectacular prominence during the recent pandemic, at the top of a long list of apocalyptic, postapocalyptic, dystopian, and catastrophic novels, some of them exploring specifically viral outbreaks of various sorts and magnitudes. The final chapter goes back to Lerner to revisit *10:04*, which also came out in 2014. Nationally and internationally acclaimed, both novels are central to the expanding contemporary canon of U.S. literature; both boast cataclysmic, multilayered, and metafictional plots; and, typical of the disaster-narrative scheme, both regale us with episodes in which everyday things such as photos, comic books, laptops, typewriters, and ID cards, mostly broken and disused, are salvaged, collected, and then shown off in all kinds of venues. These beings connect in and energize object ensembles alongside mollusks, snow globes, and artworks "proper" such as Donald Judd's "special objects." Mandel, Lerner, and other U.S. authors allow me to comment on a certain "post-conservative," post-transactionalist, and even postcapitalist politics of preservation, another indication that, here and elsewhere in *Flat Aesthetics*, attending to things "on their terms" need not deactivate "critique."

Part three, "Exit," turns to the interface of objects and space and subsequently to what I label, in dialogue with Jacques Rancière and Nelly Wolf, spatial contracts. "Inanimate" things, I point out in this segment's introductory considerations, make up the fine print of those contracts, whereas, predictably enough, the large print has historically been set aside for human signatories. But the fine print becomes writ large in O'Neill and Hamid, the main authors treated in this section's opening and closing chapters, respectively. The former analyzes O'Neill's novel *The Dog* and its spatial sublime; the second wrestles with the paradoxes of migration in Hamid's fiction, principally in his widely read 2017 novel *Exit West*. These "exit narratives," I note, tell us as much as they un-tell or withhold information. They make legible a crisis of post-Cold War Western and non-Western spatial allotment and compacts and by the same token a certain structure of contemporaneity. The components of this structure are objects distributed in space as well as objects of space, "spatial operators" or distributors that afford both the reality and delusion of travel, escape, and self-reinvention. Besides Hamid's famous "doors," they include children's books, diving equipment, and Southeast Asian food.

As I acknowledge at the beginning of the next part, a book about things cannot turn a blind eye to *the* "things" themselves. This portion of *Flat Aesthetics* focuses therefore on zombies, more exactly on what I describe as "zombie pedagogy" or "rhetoric"—on what the undead "communicate" to us in their thing-language. Chapter one of this segment expatiates in detail on the thingness of revenants, discussing how it embodies an extreme "dysfunctionality" or "intransitivity" by comparison to humans and the functions we perform routinely, as a matter of course, in culture. A number of artists, writers, critics, and philosophers have underscored that the sociocultural mechanics of this inertial performance keeps alive—on life support—the American body politic. Whitehead is one of them. Chapter two reads his 2011 masterpiece *Zone One*, listening to what a particular zombie category, the "skels," has to "say" on the political ensemble—the "thing" or Heideggerian *Ding*—also known as the United States. The thing-assemblage by dint of which *Zone One* imagines and, as I accentuate, critiques the government's attempt to resuscitate American polity consists, as the reader should expect by now, in a medley of objects, from magazine illustrations to Halloween party costumes, office furniture, ashes, military gear, ice cubes, islands, and, of course, the zombies themselves. These entities are arranged in a fashion that exposes the pseudo-futurality of the official reset of America.

The fifth part of the book, "Kinship," glosses on Jonathan Safran Foer's "rubbing" metaphor to canvas the ontological and geocultural terrain staked out by what I call the "Kafka family." On one hand, this is a confederation of kindred literary spirits sharing their indebtedness to Franz Kafka and responding to his work and biography though a wide panoply of allusions and rewriting techniques. On the other, this is a family of life forms. Only, "life" pushes here the envelope of the biological, spilling over into the "inanimate" kingdom and bringing together hummingbirds and sheep, Torah leaves and typewriters. As this part's first chapter demonstrates with references to Bruno Schulz, Max (M.) Blecher, and Foer himself, the two family branches splice up, cross-pollinate, and wrap around each other, as do texts and beings, Lurianic Kabbalah-inspired transmission and innovation, old and new, what is there and what surges forth in the very place of what is not. As in other works, absence is form-heavy, a springboard of unforeseen potentiality. Chapter two turns to another classic in the making, Krauss's 2017 novel *Forest Dark*, to illustrate this formula of paradoxical, vitalist creativity.

In closing, I offer my final laundry list of things—a list of things contemporary. This is a surely incomplete but plausible enumeration of traits, patterns, and tendencies that, to my mind, characterize postmillennial American fiction and contemporaneity overall. The novelty of the contemporary as object configuration and, following from it, as form or style—and by implication the distinctiveness of the contemporary as "epoch"—is, I posit, an actual "thing," and this thing comes into view as an increasingly clear, sometimes polemical departure from postmodernism's aesthetics and, especially, ontology. The ongoing if frequently ironic reliance of Lerner, Mandel, Chabon, Whitehead, and other recent American authors on the tricks of the postmodern trade suggests that postmodernism has become, several decades after its high noon, a historical category and dependable repertoire of techniques.

I worked on this book through the devastating spread of Trumpism and Covid-19. As I was finishing it, Ukrainian civilians were stepping barehanded in front of Russian tanks. Writing *Flat Aesthetics* turned out to be a form of survival when survival was not enough, as one of Mandel's characters reminds us, and as people the world over have realized these years again and again. My family has been no exception. Amid worldwide death and loss, we lost one of us too, but we managed to regroup and push on, with my wife at the helm, coming back at night from what is now known as the pandemic "front line" and asking me, with a smile, how many pages I had done that day. So thank you, Camelia. You and I have been through another book. We have made it, it seems.

I am also grateful to what I would like to think of as my expanded families, at least professionally speaking. One is named Bloomsbury. You do become family in this line of business, I suppose, when you work so closely with one another. *Flat Aesthetics* is my fifth book, authored or coedited, to come out from this press in four years. Once again, I am thankful to Editorial Director Haaris Naqvi for his friendship, patience, and steady guidance. Editorial Assistants Amy Martin, Rachel Moore, and Hali Han have been of great help also. So have been their colleagues from copyediting, production, and marketing, as well as Bloomsbury's anonymous outside readers.

The other family in this category is University of North Carolina, Greensboro, where I would like to recognize the following entities, programs, and individuals who have provided various forms of assistance: UNCG's Class of 1949 Distinguished Professor in the Humanities Endowment for the resources it has made available to my professional undertakings; Chancellor Franklin D. Gilliam, Jr., and Provost Debby Storrs for their support of advanced research; the College of Arts and Sciences, whose help extended far beyond the travel grants and the fall 2021 research assignment leave awarded by Dean John Z. Kiss; the Atlantic World Research Network and its Director, Professor Christopher Hodgkins; the Office of Research and Economic Development and its Vice Chancellor, Dr. Terri L. Shelton; Associate Provost Maria Anastasiou and the International Programs Center for recent stipends and administrative support; the University's Walter Clinton Jackson Library staff; the English Department's former and current Heads, Professors Scott Romine and Jennifer Feather for their leadership and commitment to an authentic culture of scholarly creativity among faculty. I am also grateful to my students in the literature and theory classes where, in recent years, we have discussed some of the authors and issues *Flat Aesthetics* deals with.

Also acknowledged are the support, kindness, and friendship of the following individuals: Henry Sussman, Brian McHale, Jeffrey Williams, Patrick O'Donnell, Stephen J. Burn, Bruce Robbins, Jean-Michel Rabaté, Wai Chee Dimock, Bertrand Westphal, Raoul Eshelman, Zahi Zalloua, Nicole Simek, Keith Cushman, Karen Kilcup, Stephen Yarbrough, Noel Cox, Mircea Martin, Andrei Terian, Mihai Iovănel, Ştefan Baghiu, Alex Goldiş, Doris Mironescu, Alex Matei, Magda Cârneci, Rene Marzuk, and Radu Ţurcanu. As I was finishing the book, Simona Popescu, distinguished poet and critic, was kind enough to share her thoughts about plants, animals, humble things in Parnassian poetry, Sy Montgomery's octopus book, and more. Jayshri Shelat told me what Nadeem Aslam's *ravann* was. Jeffrey R. Di Leo, old friend, comrade in arms on the ever-advancing theory front, and coeditor of the 2022 *Bloomsbury Handbook of World Theory*, has been of great help. I also thank the Alexander von Humboldt Foundation for its ongoing generosity and Rebecca Darlington for allowing me to reproduce her 2016 painting *The Nest* on the cover.

Portions of the book have been presented as lectures at Yale, University of Pittsburgh, University of Tampere (Finland), University of Pisa (Italy), University of Glasgow (UK), Goldsmith College (UK), Sheffield Hallam University (UK), University of Montreal (Canada), University of Limoges (France), University of Amiens (France), University of Bayreuth (Germany), University of Alicante (Spain), and Romanian higher-education institutions such as Babeş-Bolyai University (Cluj-Napoca), Transylvania University (Braşov), and University of Bucharest (Romania). I am thankful to my hosts there, as I am to the editors who have let me reprint, in substantially altered form, segments from the following articles and book chapters: "Objecthood, Flat Form, Political Formalism: OOO and Ben Lerner's *Hatred of Poetry*," *Metacritic* 7, no. 1 (July 2021): 16–39. https://doi.org/10.24193/mjcst.2021.11.02; "Periodization," *The Encyclopedia of American Fiction, 1980–2020*, edited by Patrick O'Donnell, Stephen J. Burn, and Lesley Larkin (Malden, MA: Wiley Blackwell, 2022, vol. 2, 1053–62); "Topodemocracy: Joseph O'Neill and the Spatial Sublime," *Études britanniques contemporaines* 57 (December 2019), https://journals.-openedition.org/ebc/7789; "Embedded with the World: Place, Displacement, and Relocation in Recent British and Postcolonial Fiction," *Études britanniques contemporaines* 55 (December 2018), http://journals.openedition.org/ebc/5054; "Crossing the Kafka Network: Schulz, Blecher, Foer, and the Repositioning of the Human," *Echinox* 34 (2018): 101–16; "World History, Literary History: Postmodernism and After," *Studia Universitatis Babeş-Bolyai Philologia* 3 (2022), forthcoming at the time of writing; and "Zombie Pedagogy: Rigor Mortis and the U.S. Body Politic," *Studies in Popular Culture* 34, no. 2 (Spring 2012): 105–27, http://libres.uncg.edu/ir/uncg/f/C_Moraru-_Zombie_2012-.pdf. Unless otherwise specified, all translations are mine and the italics in texts quoted in this book belong to the original.

INTRODUCTION | The New Aesthetic, the Contemporary, and Compositional Criticism

An artistic event is always the accession to form, or the formal promotion of a domain that has been considered extraneous to art.

—Alain Badiou, *Philosophy and the Event*

Only the flat golden disks around their heads were strangely static. Why did they insist on painting halos like that? Why, when they had already discovered how to create the illusion of depth, did they always revert, in this instance alone, to a stubborn flatness? And not just any instance, but the very symbol of what, drawn close to God, becomes suffused with the infinite?

—Nicole Krauss, *Forest Dark*

Objects, Graham Harman ruminates on a Heideggerian tone, "are sleeping giants holding their forces in reserve, and do not unleash all their energies at once."[1] Harman also tells us that those energies are released, and so objects manifest themselves, call attention, stir other objects, and generally act whether humans are around or not.[2] Made in recent years by OOO proponents, claims like this have perplexed. To me, however, the picture they draw is business as usual on a planet that has been signaling more and more distressfully not just its being there, but also that its presence, far from being predicated on ours ontologically or cognitively, may in fact be jeopardized by it.

If this is true, then, *pace* Harman, Manuel DeLanda, and other OOO advocates, the notion of an art "autonomous from humans" and even of an aesthetic "world without us," while bringing us down a peg, is neither farfetched nor undesirable.[3] Entertaining this spreading, non-"correlational" hypothesis, my book argues that something like the energy outbursts described by the American philosopher fires up a flat kind of aesthetics, and that this aesthetics not only marks the fiction of the contemporary era but also *makes* the contemporary, composing and displaying distinctive structures of contemporaneity across this narrative corpus.[4]

With a nod to flat ontology, I refer to this aesthetics as flat to set it apart from an activity and discipline whose accounts, if not necessarily its phenomenology itself, have historically given pride of place to humans. An aesthetics is not flat when it is tilted to some of its possible actors, and aesthetics as we know it has been largely lopsided, that is, theorized and practiced as a human prerogative. By contrast, flat aesthetics is not anthropocentered and even aims at not being biocentered either even though it never leaves the anthroposphere completely. It obtains both inside and outside the human domains of art creation, distribution, and appreciation.[5] It is an *ontoaesthetic*—an aesthetic of things that "are" (*ta ónta*, in Greek), of what exists, of what is present and, in that, presents itself, regardless of what it is; and it is a particular kind of ontoaesthetic, for it recognizes the aesthetic quality and capacity of *all* objects irrespective of what they are and whether they lie within or beyond the "artistic" and the humanmade. This aesthetic democracy rests, of course, on an ontology of equal-footing objects; evenly distributed aesthetic status or potential follows from a uniformly apportioned ability of objects to *be there*, to present themselves. Flat aesthetics is then an aesthetics of equal presence that accepts aesthetics ontology as first philosophy, although, as we shall see, the aesthetic and the ontological reinforce each other in fascinating and complicated ways.[6]

Flat Aesthetics: Things, Forms, and Exchange Regimes

Aesthetics involves feeling an object for its own sake, *beyond those aspects of it that can be understood or used.*

—Steven Shaviro, *The Universe of Things*

Back in the critical spotlight once the postmodern statute of limitations began to run out in the early 1990s and indicative, some say, of a "new paradigm,"[7] this presence, as far as I am concerned, has nothing mystical, preternatural, or metaphysical to it. Very basically, it comes down to what objects present, to the presentation they make and what it does through their sheer *being-there*, in specifically configured material embodiments and contexts. Explicitly echoing Jacques Derrida's anti-logocentrism and, more broadly, poststructuralism's absence-based model of meaning and being, thinkers like Bryant speak of "ontologies of presence *and* transcendence" (emphasis mine) in the same breath.[8] I do not, and I go to great lengths to keep presence and the transcendent separate throughout, including in the book's part five, where issues of "transcendence" seem impossible to tiptoe around. Granted, the vocabularies surrounding the two concepts have historically been entangled, but their contemporary meanings need not be. Along the same lines, Bryant also talks about "*presence* or the fullness of being,"[9] but what matchboxes, flower bulbs, marine creatures, and other objects present to each other, to us, or in our absence is not necessarily, although it may be too, the "fullness" of what they are or can be, ever a quasi-unquantifiable entity anyway. Admittedly, this self-presentation can be powerful and can reach a certain plenitude both ontological and aesthetic *qua* presentation, and yet there is nothing "ontotheological" about it, nor do *we* have access directly to what is being presented.[10] Presence does not entail access thereto. As the literary corpus analyzed in these pages suggests, exactly what things "really" are and how much of Harman's "real objects" or "things" comes through in things' presentations are not the main point although, I maintain, such presentations are or can be strong and therefore relevant ontologically.[11] In them, it is not just "certain qualities of the thing" that "affect" us, but much more, possibly yet not necessarily "its total and irreducible existence."[12] Be that as it may, what counts is the presentations themselves, their "thereness" and how it affects other objects. More significantly still, I reject the notion that human presence is the predicate—the subject-predicate, as it were—of other presences. Much like these presences are not premised on our own, their aesthetic reverberations do not necessitate our proximity or feedback either.

   While "our" being-there, as humans, is no precondition to nonhuman objects' existence as well, how we conduct ourselves around them when they discharge their energies matters—how we react to objects' immanence or objecthood, in other words, how we handle them *qua* objects, as they are, as formed or more simply yet, as form. How we relate to objecthood or form is pertinent not because what objects are, mean, and express hinges on humans' response to them—the anthropocentric presumption of one modern school of thought and criticism after another—or because, as Harman also contends in a similarly Kantian vein, the human actor somehow winds up filling in for objects courtesy of his or her unique knack for working through metaphors.[13] Needless to say, a molehill or a painting does appear in a certain way to us, or ways rather, depending on circumstances, on who "us" is, and so on. But, and this is paramount, molehills do not morph into mountains in the absence of a human onlooker, nor does Flemish master Rogier van der Weyden's *Descent from the Cross* quit being the artwork it had been before Adam Gordon's visit to the Prado in *Leaving the Atocha Station* and, regardless of the hero's "experience" at the museum, will continue to be after that. How we behave around objects as form makes a huge difference not only in museums and art galleries but also outside them. If there is an object-oriented ontology, then there is implicitly, and there should be explicitly, according to Bruno Latour, an object-oriented politics that would "oblige" political concerns about today's world to "curve" around ontological facts.[14]

This world is one of objects, with some of them—usually us—enjoying more leverage than others. And this is precisely the problem, namely, the "political" asymmetry skewing, with devastating effects in modernity and especially in the Anthropocene, world ontology. In this planetary domain of being, hardly everything that is is also acknowledged and treated as such. What has been presenting itself for ages in this arena or has just come into existence is not afforded the rights, the care, and the protection warranted by its being-there. Whether a given or "controversial"—the being-there of the Roger Federer poster on my wall is not up for debate whereas climate change, some think, is—ontological *state* constitutes no guarantee of political *status*, i.e., of the basic recognition from which other realizations, understandings, mentalities, and attitudes might follow, and with them, one hopes, more responsible policies and behaviors pertaining to Alpine ecosystems, endangered species, dying languages, responsible tourism, sustainable consumption, recycling, and so forth.

This needs to change. We need to make all this worldscape "flat," as Latour would advise.[15] As a critic, I submit that one way to kick-start this change is to recalibrate aesthetically our engagement with world existents. To be sure, one might prioritize those whose recognition seems environmentally, geopolitically, or epidemiologically urgent, and entire disciplines, critical directions, and methodologies have been doing just that. But, in the spirit of flat aesthetics itself, this readjustment of our dealings with the world should include all ontological players, all objects, be they central to the welfare of world-systems or not. Key, to my mind, is forging in humans a new relationship with objects, and this relationship would be new and world-transforming if it were one with *all* objects, that is, if we learned to see and honor presence wherever we came across it. Once we have become attuned to objects' objecthood, to how intensely they are there regardless of what, who, and where they are, we ourselves may awaken not only to their presence but also to what this presence requires from us.

The issue, then, and one of the major questions raised in this book, is ultimately not how "beautiful" all objects are, even though avant-garde after avant-garde keeps rediscovering this simple truth, but what to do when we are presented with objects in the strong sense of this presentation, how to act on their inherently beautiful *thereness*, how to respond to the setting forth of the presence whose vehicle this presentation is. This is also the question of the contemporary, twice: first, because, as the writers discussed in this book tell us again and again, our time is one of deep crisis, a time itself in question and therefore demanding immediate and radical action on a number of fronts; second, because the contemporary, that notoriously volatile category that "make[s] lexicographers and cultural historians weep," is a question itself, and no action can be taken unless this question has been answered.[16] In my view, objects give us an answer as they present themselves in particular fashions and combinations—as they aggregate the contemporary, crafting it and defining it for us. Recent U.S. fiction bears witness to this process.

Myriad such objects have been there all along, sometimes fully and other times holding back, throbbing in the mode of an idle ontology of sorts and yet no less involved for that in the building and maintenance of various "animate" and "inanimate" assemblages, networks, and systems of existence. Trees forever falling in the world's forests, objects have been, and have been active and even active aesthetically, while or without being contemplated and perchance "enjoyed" by Harman's human "beholder."[17] There are moments, however—"kairotic" milestones in the course of their lives—when they become present with a new intensity, as Gilles Deleuze and Félix Guattari would say.[18] *Flat Aesthetics* records some of these moments in post-2000 fiction as they grab my attention. These instances, these flickers of life, matter, and culture, make up the chrono-structure of contemporaneity. Powered by this new intensity, objects "light up" ontologically and by the same token aesthetically.

When that happens, their presence swings into what I determine as *hyperpresence*. This is an intense presence we may feel and are actually enjoined to take in and answer to as soon as we cross into things' energy field—into their *strong ontology*. I call this ontology strong because their thereness is independent of our thought and flatly distributed in the being realm.[19] It is also strong, or stronger today than in the past, given the historically unequaled force with which it makes itself felt. Energetic in a heightened but self-collected and understated kind of way, intensive or hyperpresent entities need not change visibly or move physically in order to move us, nor is affecting us their rationale. But if we are there when objects let their energies loose with escalated force, and if we are not impervious to the event, for an event it is, we may get the impression that objects turn to face us; they have been facing the world, but now we may sense that they are facing us. As Harman comments with a direct reference to Michael Fried's 1967 essay *Art and Objecthood* and obliquely to Emmanuel Levinas, we are confronted then by objects' "facingness," and so we too are facing their faces.[20] Quite ad litteram in that regard, their factual presence becomes or should become our con-cern, visually and in many other ways. And, if their hyperpresence truly concerns us—if we genuinely pay attention to it—then we ourselves face, and must face up to, what makes that hyperpresence hyperpresent, namely, its particular material texture or form. In that, the above-mentioned event is quintessentially formal, has to do with form.[21]

This is a challenge, no doubt. For the hyperpresent object typically animating flat aesthetics hardens into a materiality even more difficult to sidestep sensorially and transcend interpretively than before, an objectuality that advertises its self-indexing opaqueness as well as its position, its being-there—or perhaps *being-here*, acutely and *immediately* present—in the bigger ensemble the object in question is part and parcel of. The same power spike that triggered the object's rise into a thing impossible to explain away, rationalize, instrumentalize, and substitute with "clarifying" meaning, "depth," "worth," and other values assigned hermeneutically—ideologically, politically, morally, commercially, and in other regimes of analysis and assessment— brightens up the circuitry to which the object belongs, making other objects and, in some cases, the entire objectual motherboard more visible or perhaps discernible for the first time. In fact, the object system's newly acquired brightness and what this salience affords us existentially, aesthetically, cognitively, and politically flow from the higher intensity with which the individual object, the system's building block, exists, or in-sists rather, from its quiet insistence to be and to be what it is instead of what it putatively *is* a representation, outgrowth, designation, instrument, or conduit of.

These affordances derive from the wordlessly eloquent resolution with which the object stops short of fulfilling a predetermined role and vanishing in the latter's exercise by standing in for an *objective outside the object*, for an elsewhere, a beyond, a critical conjecture, a convenient "alternative," or other human projection that places things' center of ontological gravity, so to speak, outside themselves. To be clear, things are not ugly while doing their assigned chores, nor do they get automatically beautiful as they become dysfunctional. The "fall" out of functionality, out of ontological transitivity, as I say below, "intensifies" them and escalates their presence, making possible their presentations as forms. These forms may or may not be beautiful or good either. Beauty, or beauty commonly thought of, is not the point here. The aesthetic is present in "natural" and "cultural," crafted and un-crafted, "artistic" and "everyday" objects alike at all times but especially when their *raison d'être* is not to "channel" anything other than themselves. When objects no longer serve in their preordained roles and meanings, they still mean something, and so does their system. But meaning here is a function of their being-there, of their presence, so what objects and their energies and networks signify and spark—good or bad, beautiful or less so—neither preexists nor takes place outside the object and the other objects it is associated with.

Shaped by emotions, history, politics, and production modes, the object does remain visibly "constructed" by them, as it also stands oriented—and thus poised to affect other objects—affectively, historically, politically, and economically; it lies and stems from a palpable world and has no less palpable effects.[22] The object declines, however, as Harman would put it, to be "literalized" by design, use, and interpretation into their affective, historical, political, and economic accessory, to exist or rather subsist extraneously as their mere epiphenomenon, index, or implement. In this respect, flat aesthetics is not one of instrumental subsistence but insistence. It is one of objects insisting in a revved-up, high-density, and uncircumventable presence. Whether "total" or not, this presence asserts itself as it rubs up and ordinarily pushes against their time's *exchange regimes*. These are entire socioeconomic, symbolic, and political apparatuses that not only organize the value and valuation systems of a culture but also set it up as an environment in which things are continuously substituted, transacted, swapped, and "redeemed" for a wide spectrum of uses, applications, monetary values, meanings, and so on. Unlike Harman and alongside Steven Shaviro and others, I think that while endeavors to "literalize" objects do threaten to "replace" them by "disappearing" their objecthood into this or that uptake, "explanation,"[23] or "assessment," commercial or otherwise, objects do not "withdraw" by hiding their "reality" in the world's chiaroscuro.[24] To the contrary, St. Elmo's fires, scratch-off lottery tickets, and even Martin Heidegger's fabled hammer step forward and show themselves more saliently as they "fail," with characteristic "composure" and not infrequently with mute "deliberation," to do their job self-effacingly, "transparently," as crutches, tools, commodities, clues, symptoms, and other vehicles, metaphorical or not, for concealed or remote actors, tenors, rationales, and ends.

It should be obvious by now, this show, this self-presentation of objects, implies a presence concept and underwrites a presentation praxis only in part chiming in with the presence notion deployed in Heideggerian, post-Heideggerian, and most object-oriented approaches to "tool-objects" and instrumentality. While the ontological dialectic of absence-presence and being's coming into the open in various symbolic "clearings" (*Lichtungen*) remain constant references in *Flat Aesthetics*, as they do in OOO, the presence in play in *Sein und Zeit*'s ritually and variously annotated distinction between "being-handy," "handiness," or "readiness-to-hand" (*Zuhandenheit*) and "unhandiness" or "presence-at-hand" (*Vorhandenheit*) is not what I have in mind, nor is it the same as objects' presence in the literature to which this book attends.[25] This does not mean that I buy into the "metaphysics of presence," as Heidegger and his followers understand it and are right to critique,[26] and even though the dissociation between objects and things is not important to me, that between handy (useful, utilized by "us") and unhandy (unused or unusable) objects is. But first, in Heidegger, *Vorhandenheit* still entails a presence to "us," a human reference point. And second, what presents itself in the broken, no longer functional former tool—for some-thing does present itself in it—was unavailable, rather than completely inexistent, when the device was in use, "handy," and "taken for granted" as such. It is an "excess of being [that] is suddenly revealed to us"[27] in what becomes present-at-hand, indeed a presence. But, nota bene, this presence is not reducible to the thing's features, which I may consider for the first time, and it is not necessarily absolute, an embodiment of essence, the "real thing," while it may well be just that or, at any rate, a lot, ontologically and otherwise. Once more: whatever it is, it presents itself, and, yes, Harman is right, as it does so, it releases tremendous energies or, writes Shaviro, comes "alive." It is an "uprising" and an "unveiling," a "more-than-present"[28] presence: a hyperpresence.

Thus, at the same time that objects withstand their substitution, erasure, and skirting around through "literalization," as Harman and others view it, objects' vivaciousness of presentation, the hyperpresentation that makes them be and brings out their being energetically, forgoes Harman's metaphorics, whose brief is to reach *behind* the object's sensuousness of presentation and "give us" the "thing in its own right."[29] An interesting role reversal takes place at this point: on one side, hyperpresence affirms the sensual object non-metaphorically, with an impetus that, bordering as it does on the literal insofar as *there are no two ways about the object's "thereness,"* is not limited nor limits the object to one, denotative modality of being and meaning; on the other side, if Harman's metaphorical protocols are tasked with getting *past* the object's concrete "hereness" to retrieve "the infamous thing-in-itself," then they risk enacting, ironically enough, just another kind of Harmanian literalization.[30] Not that the "thing-in-itself" exists, as Harman and others allege repeatedly. But if it did, it would "be there"—or, if you prefer, "here"—and thereby *appear* sensorially, in and via its appearance or form itself, wherein Heideggerian ontological difference would collapse, and so would that between the ontic object one touches, puts in one's pocket, etc. and Harman's "real," absconded object.[31] "Welded inextricably to what things are," appearance is, as Morton emphasizes, inseparable from their essence[32]—in reality, he quickly corrects himself, the two are more than "welded," for "[a]pperance and essence are like two different 'sides' of a Möbius strip, which are also the 'same' side."[33]

This side, *the only there is*, then, is the side of the thing's presentation, where the thing, rather than receding, at once is and appears. "Appearance" should then not be understood here as impression, let alone semblance or false front. This does not mean that whatever appears is or means exactly what it is or seems ("appears" to be or mean) either, hence the persisting import of careful examination, interpretation, and criticism in *Flat Aesthetics*. Appearance can be but is not by necessity illusion or disguise. In appearing, the "thing in itself" can show itself in, and can be one with, the object as *form*, more to the point, with the object's form as this form itself performs its sometimes "tactical" dysfunctionality, at the very moment of its misfiring or failure *as* form, vehicle, message, expression, or equipment. As such, from a formal standpoint, form can be and is perhaps inevitably imperfect; form's self-presentation never is, for the form "as is" is all there, in its coming forward, and that is all that matters. In any event, whether in its inexorably formal and therefore *formally* constrained ability to achieve an "essence" (idea, meaning, design, intent) or in its calculated refusal to incarnate a reality, context, causality, and concept beyond or in lieu of itself, this very form can be said to have access to or even be, *faute de mieux*, the "thing-in-itself." Less consequential is *our* actual access to this thing, "getting to it" supposedly by peeling off its "sensible" clothes. The garments, its qualities, play out in the presentation, and this is a presentation of this "elusive" thing; the proof for the latter is, one way or the other, in the pudding of the former. As form, for all intents and purposes, the thing itself *is* the thing-in-itself and vice versa; how the object appears—not just how it looks, but what it does overall and how it affects other objects—captures or may even sum up what it is, and its thingness is that or in that. This is *not* idealism, for the issue is not how the thing appears *to me* nor that the thing is *solely* what and how it appears to me. What appears *is*, a priorily. It makes a presentation without a spectator although it can have one or many. Neither phenomenal nor noumenal, form is both, *phenoumenal*, whatever the ratio and wherever may be what may be missing from the picture, if any-thing. The form's self-presentation as form is what counts. Once again, no metaphor and, more broadly, no "meta" either, no transcendental élan invigorate or "disclose" the thing's thingness unless the meta is that of the metonymy, not of metaphor—of the metonymic or, as I also echo Harman below, paratactic logic that has the individual object's crisis flagging the systemic troubles of the bigger ensemble.

A kind of semiotic and cultural thermodynamics drama unfolds here, a script of meaning, reference, and the multiple forces and investments galvanizing them, where the whole action flows out from an entity's ontological vibration, from an object's *existential insistence solidified into form*. I describe that form as flat and intransitive, which, admittedly, is partly redundant. Flat form too points to flat aesthetics and, through it, to flat ontology. Therefore, this form's flatness conveys, on one hand, the aspirational if not effective, non- or post-anthropocentric democracy of existents within a less hierarchical, ideally "flattened" object ecosystem where both human and nonhuman, artistic and non-artistic entities are granted aesthetic status.[34] On the other hand, flat form foregrounds the need to revisit our picture of the aesthetic as a domain of objects whose unrevealed "truth" or "subtext" critics all-too-confidently "bring to light" or "plumb" by "breaking through" or "diving" underneath those objects' "shell," "veil," or "surface." It is in relation to this second sense of form that flatness—flatness as formal attribute—somewhat overlaps with intransitivity. An immediacy rather than an intermediacy, an intransitive object inhibits "drive-through" meaning-making, cavalier reading as transit and bypassing. In other words, this object, this unyielding object *qua* thing, according to critics from Bill Brown to Stephen R. Yarbrough, resists, "wittingly" or not, attempts at passing through, transcending, or circumventing it.[35] Such moves, it appears to me, would compromise its objecthood by causing intellectual and affective energy leaks and losses at the object site, through the object, whether critics and other "beholders" strove to "get to the bottom of it" by reaching the object's "profundity," the seat of and topological analogy to a "profound" comprehension of the object, or they pushed beyond it, detoured around it through its contextual hinterlands, and so on.

Flat Reading: Object Tangles and Criticism without "Us"

But not only does intransitive form safeguard the object's evaluative-interpretive impermeability. It also maintains intensity levels within the wider assemblage, redirects investigative efforts—the common perceiver's or the critic's own cognitive energies—away from itself and toward the system's other existents, warranting their discoverability as system parts one by one and thus elucidating, in all senses, the systematicity of the system. As Bryant reminds us, every object is a "crowd of objects,"[36] which holds even truer of large-scale and composite objects, and which means, naturally, that every object is part of a crowd, of a network of objects also. Another implication is, contra Latour, to whose ANT I am otherwise indebted, that such network is an actual thing too, not just a thing of the mind, a concept or descriptive model.[37] A thing of things, it can be accessed, as I do in *Flat Aesthetics*, through its components. These are its entry points; its materiality—and, to my mind, everything is material and even alive in a network—is its "vulnerability"; its hardness is its weak spot cognitively speaking. It has been postulated that "[y]ou can never directly confront the network, stare it straight in the eye. For it is always somewhere else from wherever you may be looking."[38] This may be true, but I believe so is the reverse: wherever you are, you can look for the network if not directly at it; it is just that you are never going to take in its Realness all at once ("straight") but indirectly, piecemeal. With another Lacanian analogy, while you cannot make out the webbed whole of the ever-elusive *object petit a*, you can put it together *object by object* as your gaze caroms off one after another instead of going *through* them into their (and their network's) metaphysical, political, or semiotic elsewhere. An individual object "allures" us (Harman's term) and so draws us to itself, but its "attraction," Shaviro asseverates, carries us "onward" as well,[39] "tak[ing] us . . . toward [the] object's vital connectivity with the world."[40]

For flat aesthetics is also dialectical insofar as nontransparent, opaque form, form that refuses to mirror something else deeper than or past itself and thus be exchanged for something external and extraneous to itself, generates and focuses meaningful light metonymically, on other, adjacent or faraway objects in its objectual chain, and at times, in an ontologically and rhetorically cognate fashion, even synecdochally, on the bigger whole these objects are affiliated with. Having dodged hermeneutical maneuvers to turn it into a *reflecting* mirror, a representation medium through which "clarifying" energies ooze out into a before, beyond, above, or below, vertically, the object works like a prism. Thus, the thing *deflects*—or, Barad might say, "diffracts"[41]— those energies "paratactically" or laterally, toward the neighboring penumbras and other obscurities, optical or cognitive, of the greater ensemble.[42] I define these prismatic diffractions of thing-energies as life. To my mind, this life subsumes both the organic and the inorganic. Persuaded by some of the more recent vitalist arguments, I tend to think that all matter is—all things are— bios, for the latter inheres in energetic manifestations and ability to affect, as an entire post-Spinozian tradition of thought has contended. Also as in a theorist like Bennett, such manifestations, such releases and diffractions, are what life, or existence, is and does in and through turtles, snacks, or erotic fantasies. Once again, I am interested in what things make happen, and what happens is a puzzlelike world of things and *in things* (*rebus*), in objectual patterns, crystallizations of thing-energy into tangles, bundles, or mosaics multiply, ontologically and culturally relevant to our present—all of them in it and of it but not quite it, as we will see below.

As underscored in the preface, while I have canvassed material networks previously, they have been largely human-centered, and in line with the network theory of the early-internet, late-postmodern years, my treatment of them had to take this into account.[43] Here, I try to level the playing field as far as the distribution of agency among network actors goes, and to accomplish this, I take my cue from Latour's ontologically "democratic" understanding of network actors,[44] as well as from his "refusal" of the Kantian noumenon and of the "thing-in-itself"'s implications for OOO (hence the heat he has been getting from object ontologists).[45] I also follow the French philosopher in his Alfred North Whitehead-inspired pragmatic ontology of things. Begrudgingly, Harman informs us that Latour believes that "a thing simply *is what it does*,"[46] or worse, that "new materialists" such as Barad fancy that "what a thing *does* is even more interesting than what it *is*."[47] In a largely new-materialist vein, I suppose, I think that what *matters* ultimately is what things do, even though the scenarios of their doings can vary considerably, from "arbitrary" to more "logical" juxtapositions and associations, and these all result, accordingly, in thing conglomerates with equally variable coherence and coordination, from "mélanges" and "bricolages" to "lumps," "crowds," "entanglements," "webs," "assemblages," and so on. As I describe them, the ineluctable linearity and flattening operations of critical presentation force me to pull things out of their three-dimensional ensembles and list them one after another in enumerations that may remind the reader of Latour's and Bogost's "litanies."

In hindsight, the oftentimes remarkable intellectual and aesthetic upshots of the deflections, diffractions, and prismatic refractions of thing-energy render, as suggested earlier, intransitive form's imperfection tactical and its failure to play its reflective role ambiguous. For this malfunction of form is routinely a chapter of a larger strategy of spotlighting realities and meanings "surfacial" in their location inside the ensemble yet by no means superficial. There is a profundity to them, but, with an apparent paradox, it lies flat, in plain sight quite literally. This quasi depth attests to the ontological, epistemological, and aesthetic dignity of objects neither reducible nor subordinated to a transcendental realm, objects that are thus significant in and of themselves as well as *relata* in a latticework of relations within which, Harman's worries aside, they are not convertible into or subsumed to each other either.[48] This flat profundity—this profound flatness—is legible.

Flat aesthetics demands, therefore, a flat or, as we have been saying lately, "surface reading." Like flatness—and like flatness in "flat ontology" and "flat aesthetics" also—surface is a serviceable if approximate geometrical trope for how flat reading works. Where "in-depth" reading variously rehearses the old base-superstructure interpretation scheme and so ends up transgressing and even canceling out its object in search of the foreordained "determining" context, flat or surface reading reinstates the object as object, as "sticky" form to be read as *such*. This makes such reading "close," in fact painstakingly close and slow too, accepting and laboriously working through the stickiness of form, as the reader will discover in this book's analytical parts. This reading is closely focused, first *on* the object as form or, more basically, on the object's form, and second on whatever *other* objects may find themselves close *to* the object, i.e., *in relation to it*. But flat reading is "distant" as well, in that it also gets a purchase on objects situated at various distances from that object inside ampler ensembles, whose "viscous" materiality this kind of reading navigates unhurriedly, its "dense" critical *écriture* logging and detailing meticulously one object at a time. Either way, to flat readers like myself context "stinks" too, but not in an ahistorical kind of way.[49] In a sense, there is no, say, "cultural" context to objects, as there is no world around them. They *are* that context or world; they "weave" it as they interface relationally, and so, I might add, and as Bennett stresses in her response to Harman and Morton, addressing object relations is possible, necessary, and makes for a more "balanced" approach to things.[50]

Resisting the structuralist and historicist temptation to explain objects through their relations "exhaustively" remains paramount.[51] In flat-reading practice, objects neither participate in nor are annexed and assimilated by this ensemble as a text is in and by its context and history according to prevailing critical wisdom. For, in all actuality, this ensemble is not a context or superior order to begin with. Or, if it is an order, it is vaster, *not higher*. Counterintuitively as it may sound, it presents itself as a string or flat configuration of equal-footing components. On this ground and within this ontologically "horizontal" constellation of elements, the object is no longer a symptom, a stand-in, or other fungible item to be traded for a revelation, disclosure, ambition, and other kind of subtextual or contextual knowledge, value, or aim, but the agent and site of an "energetic" wink, enlightening and valuable, at other objectual links in the assemblage's chain. This chain-as-chain—the system's own systematicity or objecthood—is itself *on the surface and composes that surface*, that object mosaic, a flat entity itself produced metonymically and for that reason discoverable or readable "laterally."

Not unlike the New Critics before him, Harman suspects that all contextualizations, trades, and conversions displace the object, replacing it with an "account of its components or its effects, *as literary critics have long known*" (italics mine).[52] We have seen that his suspicions, by my lights at least, do not always steer clear of some pitfalls. I do concur, however, with his overall argument, and I also appreciate its added bonus, as he does not just rebuke such misguided "paraphrasing" bids, but he also challenges the same critics to deal with literature in ways owning up to its objecthood rather than de facto voiding it through "overmining" and "undermining" analyses that, separately or in some combination, presume to "explain it in terms of its smaller constituents," histories, properties, effects, and the relations it is enmeshed in.[53] In throwing down the OOO gauntlet, he nonetheless dares us to pick it up *analytically* for, after all, analysis, responding to things descriptively, is not only what critics have long known but also what they have been known to do. Granted, analysis risks "reducing" a novel or poem to what it is not and thus exchanging it for the generic and often-inflated currency of critical interpretations and representations.[54] Such analysis or handling of objects, including linguistic and literary objects, is not, however, the only one imaginable, as Harman has been insisting. What he and other speculative realists have been dwelling on is essentially both the shortcomings and the necessity of commentary and criticism broadly— of a criticism that still does analytical labor and responds to literature, but whose response, apposite to the outflow of the literary object's paratactic energies themselves, should be, as I propose, flat, a flat reading.

Making meaning both in agreement and disagreement with some of the tenets of Harman's position, this kind of reading pursues these energizing currents and tensions horizontally, across the object's larger assemblage instead of swapping their objectual source for something else deeper, higher, elsewhere, in another place, form, or medium. *Flat Aesthetics*, I would like to think, is the outcome of such a pursuit. In that, its modus operandi is constructive rather than deconstructive. For flat reading is geared roughly to enriching rather than debunking, although, as it will become apparent, it can still work as "critique" as well. Anchored as it is in the objects' thereness—or again, "hereness," "in-your-facedness"—mine is an investigative routine honed in on expanding and nuancing the world picture the object is a feature of. Flat reading does not seek, or does not seek primarily, to take the ensemble apart and "expose" its ideological underbelly, and this is *not* because this reading mode is "non-ideological." Far from it. This is because ideology is and works, along with everything else, in broad daylight—not superficially but "surfacially," dispensing with *The Matrix*-like disguises the likes of Slavoj Žižek presume to "uncover" so cleverly. Ideology, a thing, *also presents itself*, and we shall discover that things present it too. Its being modality is exhibitionist. Ob-scene, and ob-jectually so, ideology "throws" itself at us in and as certain objects. Neither above nor below, ideological and non-ideological entities are present, sometimes indisputably, as a matter of evidence and are already on display left and right, hence, again, the laterally inquisitive movements of this reading. Still a critique but quite adept at canvassing and recording a reality "degree zero" and its "facts," flat reading has then little interest in reaching over or beneath spaced-out existents, much as it does not aspire to dismantle these objects individually or the configuration they find themselves in. What it seeks instead is largely the opposite, that is, to acknowledge the object-as-object, its objecthood even, or especially, at a time of crisis and use this reckoning moment as a preamble to a vaster recognition, namely, that of the greater objectual configuration. Latching onto a here-world, flat reading activates a novel, *analogously immanent analytical mode*, one that is not so much dissection, uncovering, transcending, unraveling, and decomposition, but compositional and so comparable to Latour's "compositionism."[55] Naturally a reading for meaning, this reading bears witness, as cultural practice, to a shift away from what Hans Ulrich Gumbrecht identifies as "meaning culture," one in which objects are "traded" for semantic content and evaporate in this cognitive exchange, and a "presence culture" where "the things of the world, on top of their material being, have an inherent meaning (not just a meaning conveyed to them through interpretation),"[56] one "beyond interpretation"[57] and bearing witness to an object "independent"[58] of interpreters. The critic's job, then, is not hermeneutical. The challenge here is not to look deeper but around. The task at hand is not interpretive but ontological: not to discover an unrevealed depth but to acknowledge a presence, what presents itself, is there, and awaits its description in the storyworlds under survey. If that is true, then discovery is probably too assuming a term, a symptom of vestigial anthropocentrism. Should we call it "critical reportage" instead? Critical curating perhaps? After all, the flat critic does work like a collector, a curator of things, and sometimes, more humbly still, as a surveyor of com-positions already there.[59]

What the "things of the world" com-pose, the "graphs" their tangles and aggregates literally—physically—put together, is something like Bogost's "ontographies."[60] To read this worldly thing-*écriture*, flat reading screens literary prose for objects. As it runs into them, it learns that they are arranged in a culturally-historically meaningful way. This meaning, I contend, is essentially "out there." It is principally a matter of *res extensa* and secondarily "my construction." The flat reader is a realistic ... realist, a realist, philosophically speaking, very much aware of his or her human meaning-making reflexes and biases. Because his or her findings are conveyed in the language of things—the only one there is, after all, for words are things too, as part one shows—to articulate those findings, viz., to pursue objects' compositions and especially to formulate critically what these onto-semiotic arrangements do, accomplish, and "express," this reader must "speculate," and sometimes, alas, anthropomorphically so. It is in this sense that flat reading's compositionism is speculative.

Flat reading is compositional or "comparative" spatially and temporally, comparing present objects in the joint etymological spirit of the Latin *comparō* ("set next to," "unite") and *compāreo* ("appear," "be present," "be in existence") and so casting about for objects' presence and for how they are spatialized or positioned with respect to one another in a particular present. On this account, this reading concurrently measures space and tells time—*cultural time*. Better yet, it tells time *for that space* at the very moment it treats and surveys that space, "closely" or from a "distance," as spaced-out objects, thus marking out that here-space's now. In reconstituting and composing that objectual arrangement or system, in configuring the form, meaning, and mutual relationships of presences in that assembling space, this reading effectuates a reverse-engineering of the *present as contemporaneity*, retracing *the production of the contemporary within and by the chaotic, fleeting, non-coinciding present.*[61] For the contemporary is not a temporal container; it is not the present, whether conceived punctually, as a sequence of instants, or as a "stabilized" interval, and it is not a pregiven historical background over and against which existents are and act. True, we do talk about the "contemporary age," the "present age" or moment, or "the present." I do so occasionally too, for one is bound to refer to the contemporary in temporal or historical terms, as "contemporary history," although, to prevent confusion, I prefer to use formulas such as "the present era," "the present moment," "the present," or "now." In that historical sense, the contemporary—or "our" contemporary, as I elaborate in more detail in the next chapter—can be defined as the time elapsed since the end of the Cold War or, more so now than when I wrote *Cosmodernism*, as the post-September 11, 2001 era. But more than anything else, the contemporary is in *Flat Aesthetics* a specific configuration of material culture, a cultural temporality fostered inside a certain historical temporality or interval in history. Thus, for one thing, the contemporary is not only spectacularly *heteronomous* (its objectual matrix consists of things that are prodigiously diverse materially, socially, culturally, ethno-racially, and otherwise) and *heterotopic* (it weaves together existents from "all over the place"). It is also *heterochronic*, bringing together meaningfully a set of temporally discrepant objects (the latest Corvette model, an Inuit soapstone carving, an original

Swiss-made grandfather clock, a dinosaur vertebra). In it, what we are ultimately dealing with is an age of many ages, as we will see throughout the book. For another thing, this is a cultural age, something that may itself be "comparable" to another age (and its own "contemporary") in one or more respects but that can be and, historically speaking, frequently is quite unique because it is produced, *assembled* inside of and by that one-of-a-kind assemblage, through an interplay of objects themselves unique in their insistent presence and in the way they are co-present with one another. If this is the case, then configuring this presence and the panoply of objectual presences constituting it gives us not only the ontological and cultural formula of and the code to the present, to the "now" or slice of time we inhabit, but also to *the present as con-temporary*: as formation, as genesis and defining "structure" of the contemporary understood as existents relating to one another within the space of a certain composition, arrangement, or ensemble, as well as inside the coevalness or time in which they are with each other inside that space. *This objectually orchestrated, materially and culturally shared temporality or co-temporality is the contemporary.* Once more, neither a synonym to the historical now nor a datum nor an inert backdrop for aesthetic, economic, social, or political figures and their various scripts, the contemporary is but an immanent configuration or schema of human and nonhuman actors acting on each other, something *made* by their actions and interactions in the present and whose poiesis is for us to read.

This "comparative" making and the obtaining figure or form may illuminate, to reiterate, an impasse or incompletion, a willful or just unavoidable "failure" to deliver and carry off a formal design, whether we talk about the crisis of a single object as form or about the broader parataxis of interrelated objects. The poiesis in question may then also be the chronicle of a fiasco, of an ontological-expressive limitation of the object as form, as well as of a breakdown of objects or object assemblies. But when they are in play, flaws, incompletion, and whatever the form may be lacking in formally, thematically, and otherwise open up *in* the object, rather than, again, beyond it, a new and productive space—a space itself poietic, where something novel is brewing. This space is an interstice sheltering the "presence of an absence" as Giorgio Agamben defines "potentiality" in his commentary on Aristotle.[62] What Harman and flat ontologists say about qualities certainly can be said about two of this form's main traits, namely imperfection and malfunctionality: neither "exhausts" its ontologically sovereign being-there, its objecthood as form or its formal reality. Quite the opposite: both, if strangely, enhance the object existentially and aesthetically by raising the degree to which it *is* when it stops being in the transitive modality of a surrogate for or shortcut to elsewhere, to a successfully completed task, to a superior, hidden, or metaphorical order—in brief, when the object "just" presents itself rather than re-presenting or presenting a representation, a meaning, a usefulness, or any other exchange possibility. Coming to the fore in the throes of auspicious representational crisis instead of "stepping back," the object's objecthood or the object as form accrues Agamben's potentiality only to release it through intensity upsurges that, in their metonymic sweep, reveal or point, rather, to the assemblage of objects, as DeLanda remarks.[63] In a nutshell, this is what this potential is as an object's feature, or this is what is potential about the object-as-object, about the object *qua* form: neither a transcendent noumenality nor a virtuality it may be able to attain in its beyond, but an immanent, in-built ability to "discover," and thus help us read, "horizontally," left and right, close-by and far-off, the rest of the object system. This potential nests inside the object and therefore inside the actual system of objects—inside the system of actuality also known as the contemporary. Yet again, the uncommonly dense and rich complexity of texture and semantics need not be imagined as depth and thickness, as deep and thick form. In that, the objects populating the storyworlds of contemporary literature and, on another level, this literature itself can be viewed as flat. Nor is this flatness just a misnomer playing fast and loose with geometry or with terminological propriety for that matter. As mentioned earlier, "flat" also is an ascertainment of intransitive form, of a formal consistency or sui generis formalism. Brought to bear on this formalist literary art in terms germane to this art itself, flat reading may be seen as formalist too.

If this reading paradigm is the hallmark of a formalism of sorts, then that formalism—surely a term overburdened by its history—is political. This is where I once again part company at least with, say, mainstream OOO. Emboldening cipher of an otherwise, a futural politics lies embedded sometimes allusively, sometimes clearly spelled out in objects taken separately—given that everything issues forth from their uniqueness or form—as well as in them collectively, in the com-position or paratactic placement, side by side, of the objectual pieces of the contemporary puzzle and, once removed from this system poiesis, in the compositional enterprise of flat reading itself. For this reading sets out not just to rehash analytically the making and makeup of the assemblage so as to work out, à la DeLanda, a *system of presence*, the structure of that which corrals us into the assemblage and the "historical moment" thus assembled. This reading is also keen on what this present *presents but not in its present*, in its now—on the embryonic future or what Morton describes as the "not-yet-ness built into the ontological structure of a thing."[64] Flat reading surmises that this presence harbors another presence and another present altogether, another con-figuration and another time for the objects involved; both absent "for the time being" and pre-figured in its very absence, this is an *other* time. Better still, this is a time for a contemporaneity to come, and yet it can be figured out in the figures—the forms, the objectual tea leaves—of the present contemporary. This time of possible being and largely a time of possibility—

in brief, a future—flat reading must tell. Writers do so in the first place, and flat reading cannot but follow suit.

Little surprise that contemporary American authors dwell persistently on the potentiality of this other to the assemblage and its temporality by taking on the material and symbolic economy of representation, illustration, and exchange that endanger form through reductions to contents and conversions into values that eschew, degrade, or deform form as form. Preceding modern capitalism, this economy became, inside and outside the economic sphere narrowly understood, a mainstay of modernity in market-oriented no less than in central-planning societies such as those of the former Eastern Bloc, as the latter's 1950s Socialist Realist literature's transparent aesthetics, self-flauntingly ideological representationalism, and aggressive anti-formalism go to show. The post-Cold War late-global era, however, has taken the instrumentalizing and transactional logic of modernity to a whole new level. After 1990, deregulatory neoliberalism marked the onset of paroxysmal exchange in and of a world firmly and quasi-entirely shaped, accordingly, on one side by increased treatment and exploitation of beings as resource, raw material, means, auxiliary, and expandable possession of human users, agents, principals, and owners, and on the other, but relatedly, by barter, trade, monetization, and other fungibility protocols keyed to redistributing and regularizing existents into commodifiable series and classifications and translating into lucrative rationalizations, expedient clichés, and "universally accepted" languages, codes, notions, standards, and liquidity. Late globalization has been both vehicle and consequence of a historically unrivaled exchange regime, which subtends a new world-system where, after the crumbling of the Soviet Bloc, few actors operate unilaterally anymore. Global leaders such as the United States itself have been no exception to this worldwide condition of interdependence, and so, more extensively than any other transformative chapters in U.S. history, the post-1990 mutations in America's novel and society have echoed developments unfolding on scales larger than the nation-state, the region, and the continent.

In this already naturalized or "normalized," fast-globalizing geosystem of remunerative transactions, a "new normal" of our exchange condition has also emerged, in which things that *are*, despite their in-sisting in being so, are unconscionably, if profitably, swapped for their ontological double, that is, for what they demonstrably are not: trutherism for truth, conspiracy theories for science, "alternative" facts for actual facts, tribal spin for reliable public-domain information, the January 6, 2021 mob for patriots, reality TV for mere reality, Trumpland for planet Earth, and the like.[65] Having flourished across and beyond the so-called social media, the exchange culture rooted in this cynical transactionalism is hardly endemic to the United States and predates our juncture in history. But today's America has been front and center to this culture's proliferation. It is therefore politically heartening to watch U.S. writers of our time take on this pseudo-reality factory, as it is aesthetically intriguing to see them do so on the very terrain of make-believe and reach to that end into the toolbox of *fiction* writing—of a writing at the same time sophisticated and flat, which, seemingly with another paradox, presses the fictional into the service of truthfulness and its "hard" and hardly disputable ontologies. If this category of writing is flat in the existential and aesthetic sense of the term, then so is this writing's politics. Itself flat, this politics befits the "reality" of things, which has been under siege by quasi-totalitarian forces and in fashions compatible and frequently identical with those driving the broader, economic and political assault on reality by neoliberalism's exchange apparatuses.[66] It is encouraging to notice that these authors respond in kind to this attack and ensuing transgression, depletion, and cashing out of world reality. For they home in, time and again, on the formally dense, incontrovertible and inconvertible objecthood of objects, more exactly, on those moments in which objects up the ante of their being to make an "energetic" stand as intransitive forms significant and valuable in and of themselves.

The story of the coming along of a new exchange system and of a new world-system altogether has been told in various disciplines and lingos ad nauseam. On the whole, its main and oftentimes only characters have been human beings. This book wants to be a story of all things considered. Its goal is to tell of the overwhelming presence all objects bring at this time before "us," with or without "us" there. Nonhuman and nonbiological objects, I argue alongside more and more philosophers and critics, are world-system actors on a par with any others; they too participate in the production of the system. In giving their role its due, *Flat Aesthetics* joins in the ontological turn currently underway in the humanities. Acknowledging once more objects' strong ontology, I add here that what makes it strong is also the system-wide ripple effect of their presence, whose vibrations and prismatic refractions take us and other entities to other things and system areas and sometimes to entire world ensembles of existents and codependencies.

This presence is so impactful that its force is culturally definitional, resetting cultural time in the United States and elsewhere in our interdependent world. Ice floes, toilet paper, and memes assert themselves dramatically, for a whole host of reasons, some of them of their own, still unfathomable, others more obvious at this crucial juncture in the Anthropocene. Whatever the reason or reasons, this is happening because we are facing a planetary crisis. We are all in trouble, but what things do in the era of climate change, catastrophic deforestation, and neo-imperial military aggression—and as a way of *articulating* the ontological proportions of these emergencies—is to affirm their own being-there at the time when disasters, pandemics, shortages, and human excesses of all kinds threaten their being, sometimes with irreversible absence. The resulting and generalized openness of things of all sorts, their coming into the open and our growing realization of "the irremediable thingness of the world,"[67] as Agamben puts it, are increasingly distinguishing the "contemporary era" from previous "periods."

Contemporaneity, Periodization, and the Signature of the Present

By and large, I do not approach the contemporary as a period but as the "signature" of a period—as the thing-configuration or cultural-material watermark or *our* period. Of course, we do refer to the "contemporary period." But does it exist? And is "periodization" of any help still? It seems to me that after the Cold War, the world's "thingness" has ushered America into a new if atypical period. If the contemporary was a period, the decades after the fall of the Berlin Wall and especially after 9/11 would be "our" period—our contemporary period *historically speaking*. Several critics have named it "late-global"; others, less satisfied with the accuracy of the "global" family descriptors particularly in cultural-aesthetic matters, have preferred to talk about the age of "planetarity."[68] Either way, what distinguishes the post-Cold War period is an entirely new, "combined" albeit "uneven" *world setup* into whose grid U.S. circuitries of change got, and have remained, plugged. I decline, then, to throw the period notion out with the bathwater of periodization's recent critiques. By dint of its etymology and common use, "contemporaneity," or "the contemporary," does have an epochal element to it; you do not have to be guilty of "'chronic' ageism" to admit it.[69] Incessantly "drifting"[70] across history and thus flaunting its impermanence as it does, the contemporary nevertheless repeatedly acquires, leaves behind, and gets himself again, and again temporarily, a historical body and, more often than not, an equally well-defined cultural body also—viz., a time span, a "when," and a formal identity, i.e., a "what," "how," or cultural signature. Eventually, they all end up disputed by later commentators, who no longer see nor appreciate what others noticed or liked before them. For, to be sure, the contemporary is always located and assessed as contemporary by observers inhabiting a certain "now" itself in motion, steadily ebbing away from past nows and their own determinations of contemporariness. David Cowart is surely right to describe the "[c]ontemporary," along with "[m]odern" and "[p]ostmodern," as a "moving targe[t and] semantic shapeshifte[r]."[71] Nonetheless, mercurial as the contemporary's appurtenances are, making legible a certain logic of post-1990 and, even more clearly, post-2000 American fiction and historical interval is not beyond our reach. I propose that the logic in question is a thing-logic, that it comes through in objects' presentations, and that its script is embedded in a whole range of recent literary works.

Accordingly, and if we must keep referring to a "contemporary period," I designate as contemporary a "counter-" or, better yet, "paraperiod" that has been slithering across the post-World War II temporal plateau and that—for a while and from *our* perspective—appears to have solidified and to have become *our* contemporary most visibly within the banks of the last two decades or so, also crystalizing, in the process, a number of novelistic structures typical of this moment. The Greek adverb and preposition *pará* signifies, among other things, nearness, being alongside, beside, and next to or in the presence of something or somebody. For one thing, the *para*-morpheme shares in the existential syntax of the *con*-, reaffirming the being-with as the onto-topological marker of the late-global era—"One is not contemporary; one is contemporary to" (*contemporain* de), Martin Rueff reminds us;[72] for another thing, the prefix front-loads the same semantics temporally, working it into the structure and diachronic "behavior" of period itself: we are not just others' *con*temporaries, willy-nilly *beside* them, near them in this "now-" and "with-world" regardless of what the Brexitarians and the Trumps of this world may think or tweet. Contemporaneity itself is, again and again, *pará*, a paraperiod "beside itself," restless, constantly streaming forward, changing places and names. It washes over the post-World War II interval, its schools, movements, and generations of writers, settling in a few decades' riverbed only to brim over and resume its search for its next temporal abode, where it sheds its modernist or postmodern skin only to grow a new one and thus into a new contemporary altogether.

I call this Viconian *corsi e ricorsi* of sorts the cycle of contemporaneity. There have been at least two of them since 1945. The first was the longest and started after World War II. This is, or was, the "old" contemporary, whose axial, twin development was, culturally speaking, the eclipse—partial or total, depending on whom you ask—of modernism and the birth of postmodernism. The contemporary, *this* contemporary, aged precipitously and the world renewed or began to renew itself once again with and at the end of the Cold War. A *world-historical event*, this was a real *American event* too, not just some serviceable "creation myt[h] of the contemporary moment."[73] The 1980s may have got out to a disappointing start, at least for some, what with Ronald Reagan elected to office, but finished with a bang "on or about" November 9, 1989. The bringing down of the Berlin Wall marked the de facto end of World War II (a few anti-periodists would probably agree), of the "short" twentieth century (1914–1989), and of "peak postmodernism."[74] Succeeding what used to be the contemporary for almost half a century—when it culminated with, and passed, one by one, high modernism, the onset of postmodernism in the late 1960s, and the rise of postmodernism's avant-pop spinoff in the mid-late 1980s—is the "new" contemporary period, ours. A post-Cold War affair broadly speaking, its structures become better marked after 9/11, during the postmillennial epoch. Historically and culturally, this is "strong" contemporaneity, and this is what *Flat Aesthetics* basically tackles.

As David Blackburn writes, "[t]he renewed recognition that history occurs in space as well as time has indeed been a welcome development of recent years."[75] This understanding has affected period both as segment of events that came to pass and as model to group and narrate them. "Space-compression" inside and outside the United States also brought about a thickening of time, an acceleration of temporality and a "lateral" accumulation of cultural times within a given temporal slice, hence what looks like an abundance of period—that is to say, of more or less marked-out periods—in the "actual" history of the last decades. Yet again, the broad change they have witnessed has been triggered, signaled, and accompanied by incidents, crises, "breaks," and shifts that include things as diverse as the collapse of European Communism, the consolidation of world markets and their undergirding exchange regime, the birth of the internet, Covid-19, and more plastic bottles floating in the oceans. These and innumerable other instantiations of the world's thingness have been salient and have made a big difference not only in history but also to historians. For many of them, the time passed since 1990 is not just *a* period of transition out of the Cold War, and subsequently out of postmodernism, into "late" or "strong" globalization and its own cultural paradigm, but a chain or, better yet, a pileup of periods and subperiods even, all of them . . . periodically challenged and even "supplanted" by others. Thus, by most accounts, while the post-1990 decades do make up by and large a separate entity with its own structure, what this historical container seems to contain—all puns intended—is history's own motility, a blur of moving milestones and dimensionally fluctuating stretches. Keeping this period machine humming is, inside it, the ghostly theater of transformation. Future historians will likely view the Cold War's twilight and dragged-out aftermath as one cultural-temporal unit, but to many of those closer to the historical canvas, the image is clear *and* fuzzy; it is well delineated, for so is its frame, whereas the painting itself is pointillistic. Epochal and heterogeneously so, the picture looks like an epoch but also like an epochal hub, a crossroads and contest of periods.

The effort to describe and label this interregnum and its historical stratification has yielded clarifications as well as an excess of clarity and all-too-neat delimitations, and the period-based attempts to tell the story of an interval of remarkable change in American and world history has got predictable. No wonder generation after generation of scholars, from Marshall Brown's to the even feistier Victorianist Young Turks a.k.a. the V21 network, have grown increasingly weary of "periodizing."[76] It has become de rigueur, in fact, to deplore the pitfalls of periodization, discrete "epochality," and straight-line chronologies. In the same breath, critics have berated the individual and institutional self-complacencies involved in pressing into service—granted, sometimes mechanically—temporal and cultural categories, divides, "turns," "bookends," and other periodizing accoutrements as if they were already there, carved in history's stone. Gradually, all these have come to be seen as peddling Eurocentric chronopolitics,[77] "ideological" and "hegemonic," skewing rather than laying bare the complex workings of history, and betraying a "dominant," inertial intellectual routine that "amounts to a collective failure of [the] imagination and will on the part of the literary profession."[78]

Such allegations have added insult to older injuries. More ingrained if less aggressive than this relatively recent anti-periodism is an earlier one, which we might call postmodern although it predates historical postmodernism. It holds that the stone metaphor above does not apply, given that both "conventional," *a posteriori* historiography and the Baudrillardian, "*a priori* history"[79] forged by the media presuppose varying degrees and forms of "revisionism." History is not immutable—not that stones, rocks, and any other geological formations really are; it moves in a dizzying array of directions, successively and concomitantly, and morphs into a whole range of new configurations of events and meanings thereof. As an *object*, it is as fluid, full of surprises, and protean as the disciplinary paradigm grappling with it. In that sense, history, *all* history, is contemporary. One need not be Crocean, Borgesian, or a card-carrying postmodern, for that matter, to see all that, although it may help. For the critique of the retrospective manufacturing of the bygones—influences, origins, causality, tradition, Kafka's "precursors," and antecessors generally—and a hyperawareness of the related, provisionally "constructed," and intrinsically evolving nature of the periods and rubrics under which this Grand Narrative sort of parading of the past ordinarily takes place mark postmodernism from forerunners such as Friedrich Nietzsche, Walter Benjamin, T. S. Eliot, and Jorge Luis Borges to its Pynchonian-Lyotardian heyday. These postmodern hallmarks have drawn accusations of "relativism" and even "ahistoricism," charges every now and then brought as a "presentist" indictment.

In François Hartog's classical version, this presentism involves a "regime of historicity" under whose purview "the production of historical time seems to be suspended" while "generat[ing] today's sense of a permanent, elusive, and almost immobile present, which nevertheless attempts to create its own historical time . . . as though there were nothing but the present, like an immense stretch of water restlessly rippling."[80] Neither identical with nor inseparable from the historical "now" in which we live after the fall of the Berlin Wall, this bloated omnipresent present tends, according to Hartog, to dehistoricize history by recreating "historical time," including past times, in its own, presentist, self-obsessed image. In this "anti-periodist" picture, the established periods and their sequential chronology are far less conspicuous than under other "regimes." Like Eric Hayot, Hartog also takes note of the ever-heightening pace of existence and correspondingly progressive abbreviation of production–consumption–reproduction cycles across all spheres of life. In Hayot's opinion, however, this wholesale quickening of cultural rhythms appears to endorse if not fuel another kind of presentism, enacting in and *on* our present the periodist fashion in which we treat "historical" time roughly understood as the "past."

This historiographic approach is presentist because, as pointed out earlier, and as Hartog himself would say, it projects our time's "horizontal," rushed tempo onto the vertical axis of history. Thus applied on the yesteryear mass, the pressure of "now"-rhythms, remarks Hayot, makes "[p]eriods get shorter as we get closer to the present [and] expand as we move backwards."[81] "[T]he decreasing size of periods," the American critic goes on, "is an effect of chronological narcissism, in which the receding and foreshortened past plays Kansas to our Manhattans"—a reference to the "hemispheric vision" of self-absorbed Manhattanites satirized by a 1976 *New Yorker* cartoon magnifying spatially what is immediately adjacent to them (the few blocks separating Ninth Avenue from the Hudson River) while allotting a ridiculously smaller space to the rest of the United States, the Pacific, and the Western hemisphere.[82] What the drawing is getting at is that one sees better, bigger, and more (in) what is adjacent geographically and temporally, but, claims Hayot, this is not an inevitable perspectivism at all, a "natural" optical condition foreordained or warranted by the viewer's physical location. What we are dealing with but are not talking about, he maintains, is a self-induced myopia, proof that "the entire literary profession results from a self-regarding love for our historical present."[83] In brief, this temporal self-centeredness is then presentist, and this presentism is "periodist." It is so, the critic implies, not necessarily because it breaks down the past into periods that get tinier and tinier as they near "our" point in time, but simply because it is period-driven. The analogous, incremental temporal shrinking of scholarly expertise and description—"historical microscopism"[84]—is just a fallout of betting the farm on periodization, period.

Presentism in general and "postmodern" presentism in particular are, then, oddly enough, responsible for both the declining and inflationary use of the period concept. Compounding the inconsistency are those of us who, in the same sentence, have professed to be fed up with periodism and have pronounced the postmodern irrevocably dead, "passé," and "obsolete," either "supplanted" by a new, "post-postmodern" . . . period or sucked back into the modernism from which, ten or twenty years back, it seemed safely and usefully demarcated. It is not always clear what the reason for the anti-postmodern hostility is, although denying postmodernism its period status would relitigate the issue of the modern–postmodern divide (real? a self-serving postmodern fiction?) and bring back the question as to whether modernism has ever ended or subsided. At any rate, one cannot help but notice that, in many revisitations of recent literary-historical periods *and* of period itself, "old" modernism has suddenly overflown its historical banks and has grown into a *longue durée* or "long modernism," a twenty-first-century elephantine backformation eager not just to swallow formerly stand-alone postmodernism whole but also to dehistoricize and ultimately dissolve it by cavalierly reclassifying postmodern aesthetic protocols such as autoironic metafiction and intertextual revision and authors like Gabriel García Márquez as "modernist."[85] Conversely, what seemed for a while to hold as a single cultural-historical age has split, some have suggested, into better-marked "stages." One of them is, for instance, "late postmodernism,"[86] which anticipates the postmodern's more unequivocal, post-2000 "waning" and the mushrooming, under "post-postmodernism," of "metamodernism," "digimodernism," "exomodernism," "performatism," and other "isms" that at least recall if not mirror, at the dawn of the twenty-first century, the similarly avant-garde effervescence of one hundred years ago and by the same movement fold postmodern aftershocks back into the history and aesthetics of modernism. Also revealing their Teflonlike temporality at the hands of literary historians working during and sometimes openly against postmodernism have been periods' own temporal subunits and building material such as decades, centuries (wholes or halves), pivotal years or multiyear epoch-making events like world wars, what with the proliferation of "long" and "short" centuries, the mega-"ageism" of a new player such as the Anthropocene, and the fluidity of past war and interwar dates, which have been changing too.[87]

Historical signposts have shifted but remain in use, and so beginnings and ends of periods and, with them, entire periods themselves have expanded and contracted, vanishing from one place only to pop up somewhere else. They have not disappeared even in the work of anti-periodist hardliners, who, in all actuality, have been engaged in various *re*periodizations, in the fostering of *alternate* periods[88] rather than in *alternatives* to periodization—what is "post-45" if not another period vision of a broadly conceived "contemporary era" after all? As a most thought-provoking anti-periodist such as Susan Stanford Friedman concedes, even "V21 affirms the Victorian period as an entity, and Dimock herself"—who has helped promote neovictorianists' presentist platform—"filters literary history through the discourse of time as the linear chronology of past, present, and future."[89] Thus, "[t]he traditional notion of period," Katie Trumpener has concluded, "may be bankrupt, depleted, a mere placeholder for a truth we know to be more complicated. Yet it is hard to see just how to reorganize curricula, job descriptions, or library cataloging systems using alternative templates."[90]

Mindful of what happens when the rubber of analysis hits the road of history, many have recognized that, at the end of the day, "we cannot not periodize."[91] In certain cases, this admission betokens historicism (old, New, Marxist, etc.), for you cannot be an anti-periodist and also "historicize," thereby depending on periods, ages, and their sometimes teleological pageant. In other cases, this realization is a matter of descriptive pragmatism. A pragmatic historian would have to concede, I suppose, that historiography is description, and that since any descriptive venture requires a language, to wit, a set of conventions subject to a principle of classification, periodizing is nothing else than this categorizing principle in action, historiographic language speaking in periods. Therefore, the same historian would probably agree, talking about historical occurrences represents just specialized talk, a communication mode. In it, cutting up the temporal continuum into logically distinct and meaningfully tagged pieces is as important as is in language broadly the mapping out of reality by the linguistic system into linguistic signs—the historiographer "cannot not" do descriptively on the axis of diachrony what any speaker cannot *but* do conversationally on that of synchrony. We may refocus all we want on said continuum over discontinuities and "watersheds" in genre history, for example, but once more, insofar as literary developments and change overall are concerned, some kind of periodization—more flexible, aware of its shortcomings and conventionality— is bound to come in handy.

But what if it is not "us" who do the periodizing? The *pará* may also accommodate a periodization without "us," I suppose. If so, then how might we envision such "paraperiodization" and possibly a "paraliterary" history, an object-oriented literary history without "us" to boot? However one might go about them, their premise—of necessity a thing-minded one—should be something to the effect that things of all sorts produce history, and therefore the same things fashion literary history also. Further, a literary historian and critic sold on the historical reality and world-transforming, sometimes epoch-making impact of actions and interactions of all imaginable objects would probably find it hard to ignore some striking homologies between post-Cold War and especially post-9/11 American literature and culture, on one hand, and on the other, small- and large-scale object patterns, incidents, and processes that trace a fairly unmistakable shift in "the great outdoors," in things' demeanor "out there." Otherwise put, the post-2000 fiction *Flat Aesthetic* turns to bears witness to a change in the American world and world at large: the stark coming into view of the world's ontological flatness. This mutation is historically "contemporary." It started before 2000 but picks up speed in the third millennium and is still unfolding. Its symptomatology is ordinarily that of crisis. One might call it a postmillennial change. As suggested, it inheres in the spectacular intensification of objects' presence all over the planet, in their loud, clear, and historically unsurpassed hyperpresence in recent decades. This *is* history. Things both orchestrate and present it in and through their actions and interactions. What trees, viruses, and chatbots do is historically performative and "periodizing," and visibly so. Objects' presentations *presence* historicity, articulate the present as historical by giving it a structure: the contemporary. Things do not perform "in" history, much as they are not "in" the world; they forge and are both.

Entities are there with such presencing intensity, and their energetic state of being makes them act and *manifest* themselves such that little of them remains "withdrawn" or "hidden." All there is now lies *on the inside* ontologically speaking, fully exposed within the all-embracing panopticon of being, and everybody is on the inside looking in. Being itself is an "exposed" insideness. Consequently, there are no more places to hide nor out of which to conveniently ignore the presence of a thing-world calling out to us to acknowledge its pain and work with others to alleviate it. "Nature loves to hide," Morton strategically quotes Heraclitus in *Realist Magic Objects, Ontology, Causality*—or, I would reply, nature may have done so when there were still hiding places, an outside.[92] But "there is no outside anymore," as Vija Kinski, Eric Packer's "chief of theory," memorably proclaims in Don DeLillo's 2003 novel, *Cosmopolis*.[93] We are indeed witnessing the "disappearance of the outside," Andrei Codrescu confirms in the title of one of his books,[94] a disappearance that has forced object ontologists, including Morton himself, to "sometimes say 'open' instead of 'withdrawn'—*so in your face that you can't see it*."[95] And because, as a speculative realist such as Shaviro says, "[n]othing is hidden," and so "there are no more concealed depths" either, [t]he universe of things is not just available to us but increasingly unavoidable. The volcano is actual, here and now; we cannot expect to escape its eruption."[96]

The volcano and the polar ice caps are here—or "there," but definitely affecting us all "in here," inside the planetary web of things—and so are we, our Teslas, and the polluting cars we can afford. But even what is not there, or not there any longer, or there only for fewer and fewer of us, what is extinct or in short supply, poisoned, irreversibly damaged, and also what is still there but does not stand out because it never has, and we have got desensitized to its presentations, all the utensils and trinkets we handle, scrap, and bump into day and day out, *all* exude a new kind of vibrancy. We may pay more attention to heat waves than to shoe parts and their all-but-forgotten names—which may be why DeLillo tarries with them in a famous scene of his 1997 masterpiece *Underworld*—but both heat waves and shoelaces, hyper- and micro-objects, the hip and the humble, the "beautiful" and the "ugly," what charms, what hurts, and everything in between are "erupting" these days with new intensities. These intensities and spurts of thingness are relational. What I mean is that through them, at close quarters or across vast distances, objects reach out to one another. They interpellate each other quietly or volubly, with obvious and obscure logics within and without our grasp, to make meaning and not, to give structure to plots and themes and not, to assemble into stories or not, but always to inform present history in ways that both produce it and ensure its "definition," its visibility.

The production is ongoing, apparently and effectively chaotic, unabating and slapdash. The definition or description, what the present is and what characterizes it—its cultural signature—is available in this present, in its relentless ebb and flow. This picture, this descriptive set of characterizations and attendant characteristics, is contemporaneity. Whether the last twenty-odd years are a new period in American history and literature or not hinges on how well contoured this overall picture of thing-eruptions is and on how different this image, this "transparency" of the present, is from similar images of past presents. These energy bursts, weaves, and effluvia run through postmillennial American fiction as they do through any-thing else, but they are also "stabilized" and "arranged" narratively and cognitively, *represented* and made sense of in these works. A com-positional undertaking itself, flat reading follows these texts' lead.

ONE | Language

The silver hourglass does not just lie on my desk but *is* there. So is my Mac. Its manufacturer is not there—I mean not right here, in front of me—but it also *is*, in an overly polluted Asian town, perchance across the street from the desk's maker and not far from the makers of most things surrounding me and, poets intimate, nagging me as I type "as I type." These very words are as well. They assert a presence—they *are* presences, as Ben Lerner assures us in his 2014 novel *10:04*.[1] But they are also co-present in phrases, sentences, and other linguistic and non-linguistic combinations. At various physical distances from the hourglass, the laptop, the Chinese factory, the factory's grossly underpaid workers, and the pine tree drying up in my backyard, they nonetheless are and mean alongside all these objects; they are like them ontologically and with them in ways at once systemic and culturally-historically defining. For the words, the sentences, the paragraphs, this monograph itself, and language generally are more than "about" objects.

They are objects themselves—they are toys sometimes, or weapons, plows, swords, and anything in between, but they are beings more than anything else, instantiations of what *is*.[2] They make worlds and claims about them, but they themselves are worlds. In that, linguistic objects partake of the fundamental, twin propensity of all objects. For one thing, they draw attention to themselves, especially when they are in distress, showing off their form and inviting us to respect it, to *work through it*, wanting, fragile, and imperiled as it may be; for another, they floodlight a whole object ecosystem as they point to their proximate and "remote" neighbors, thus brokering further presentations by introducing more objects to us, the ensemble they all compose, the cultural time they measure, and the new temporalities they sometimes harbinger.

This part of *Flat Aesthetics* zooms in on objects such as language and the discourses grounded in it, including literature. I have labeled the spoken and written word a metaobject, viz. an object naming, indexing, describing, and overall referencing other objects, and I have done so without enthusiasm mostly because, while it may make us think of other objects, a metaobject cannot be reduced to what it is about or for. Its insistence as intransitive form, its objecthood, is at odds with the logic of aboutness and instrumentality broadly. The prismatic deviation of escalating energies toward other presences in the object network and the latter's ensuing discovery, with everything these actions entail cognitively and politically, run counter to this transcendent logic. The paratactic, under whose auspices the system lights up, goes against the grain of paraphrase and metaphor. If there is a "meta" structure to objects at all, its thrust is, as we have seen, metonymic rather than referential or substitutive. An object's formal consistency does not warrant transgressions, rationalizations, reductions, replacements, and other similar trades and the claims usually accompanying them. These are, however, hallmarks of modernity. Amped up under neoliberalism, they have in fact been quasi-officialized of late by the con "art of the deal" and other kinds of Trumpian transactionalism. These developments and the exchange culture they have brought on threaten not only the material world commonly understood but also literature's own, intrinsic materiality—literature *qua* object.

Twenty-first-century U.S. fiction has responded by reaffirming the objecthood of literature and of language largely. Examples are legion. DeLillo, whose relationship with postmodernism would have to be revisited also on account of his obsessive presencing of words, lexicons, and locutory acts, has become even keener on the flatness of words and idioms after *Cosmopolis*, where, making protagonist Eric Packer eerily aware of his presence, poetry "bares the moment" to other objects too, alerting him to "things he was not normally prepared to notice."[3] Along the same lines, the 2020 novella *The Silence* and its "pure film, pure language"[4] evoke, beyond *Point Omega* (2010) and its cinematic and linguistic episodes in which "everything is so intense, what it is,"[5] scenes in pre- and post-*White Noise* works that dwell recurrently on language's mysterious and haunting intensity. Around the same time DeLillo's *Underworld* sang, in Nick's Jesuit "language therapy" and across the novel, a paean to "everyday things" and the "physics of language,"[6] Barbara Kingsolver's anagrams, paronomasias, palindromes, and mistranslations in *The Poisonwood Bible* (1998) also "reverse" the denotative transparency of scriptural rhetoric, de-functionalizing the worn-out language of preaching and restoring its poetic and political vibrancy.[7] Kingsolver's Congo is, mutatis mutandis, Jonathan Lethem's Planet of the Archbuilders, an alien species who evolved a civilization through "viral" technologies. Reconstructed by the Archbuilders, English loses its structure and usage to mutate, via puns and morpho-syntactic permutations, into a new and neo-Joycean form or "assemblage," as it has been aptly described.[8] Intriguing in and of itself, the Archbuilders' creolized English participates in and glosses the biopolitical entanglements into which Lethem's interplanetary Western casts the Marshes, the recently arrived human "pioneers."[9] Back on Earth in Jean Kwok's 2010 *Girl in Translation*, English similarly breaks down in Chinese immigrants' solecisms and coagulates into something starkly present, with a consistency and heft to which native speakers have become jaded. This is the "alphabet soup" whose perpetually recomposing acronyms spell for Kimberly Chang language itself—supreme horizon, responsibility, and value of immigrant life.[10]

While the accentuation of form marks postmillennial fiction as a whole, this section of *Flat Aesthetics*, in particular, deals with prose that punctuates language and the agency of linguistic acts and objects. This emphasis has two intertwined consequences, which both extend and part company with postmodernism's formal self-centeredness. First, the metafictional dimension of the body of work examined here is stronger than in material covered elsewhere in this book. As it presents itself, as it flaunts itself formally, this corpus gives away its workings, what it does and how it does it, more overtly. The poiesis of this prose is therefore on display more vividly and more self-reflexively than elsewhere. Second, so is what I have called the making of the contemporary, an operation that comes under the overall purview of this poiesis. Again, this narrative material is contemporary not because it happens to be written and published during what is colloquially known as "the contemporary era," but because it makes the contemporary. What is more, it does so not in an about mode but as flat form, and that form is flatter here than in other, less metafictional situations. As in those, instead of merely referencing contemporary issues and situations presumably already "out there," awaiting their literary reproduction, fiction *produces* the contemporary itself, effectively piecing it together, and this production, this assembly of disparate objects into a meaningful "constellation," as Lerner's Adam Gordon says, also starts off with the gathering into being of a certain object. Notably, in the works scrutinized in this part of *Flat Aesthetics*, that object is linguistic and subsequently literary. As we will also notice in Lerner,

literature and contemporaneity are intimately bound up with one another
not because the former duly reports on the latter or because the latter is the
shaping context of the former, although both can be true, but because
a poem or a play's composition is part of, brings to light, and offers
systematically insights into the vaster composition—the making and the
resulting makeup, the architecture of the contemporary. To get a better grip
on the intricacies of this compositional process, I turn in this part's first
chapter to Lerner's novel *Leaving the Atocha Station*. In an attempt to do
justice to nonhuman language as well, I attend next to Chabon's novella *The
Final Solution*. I begin with *Atocha* but not before spending some time on
Lerner's poetry criticism because it provides a thumbnail view of what the
novel accomplishes on a bigger scale.

cap'n crunch, planet of the apes, the kingfishers: Ben Lerner and the Uselessness of Poetry

. . . not beauty, but a sublimity of perfect exchangeability . . .

—Ben Lerner, *The Hatred of Poetry*

*. . . that banal but supernumerary sublime of exchangeability. To be a subject here
was to be spread by objects.*

—Ben Lerner, *The Topeka School*

Few contemporary American writers have pushed back against exchange
culture more assiduously than Lerner. A leading postmillennial, he stages
programmatically, across his oeuvre—prose, poetry, and criticism—the
inexchangeability of objects, especially of language, literature, and, we will
notice later in the next chapter, in other arts as well.[11] Laboriously cross-
referencing his works and mixing up fiction and nonfiction, autobiography
and metafiction, realism and lyricism, candor and pose, and irony and self-
irony, Lerner has built a baroquely self-reflexive, bedazzlingly complex, and
highly integrated multivolume and multigenre aesthetic apparatus to grapple
with things that have been pivotally present in his private and professional
life. No wonder that, in tune with the autofictional logic of this aesthetic
setup, his books characteristically return to those presences ever so often:
idiom, oral and written, native and not, original and translated; its public-
speaking and "interscholastic debate" varieties;[12] its poetry and prose
incarnations; writing in these and other genres; the books, texts, and other
lexical and literary objects shaped or evoked by this writing; and the private
or public reception, readings, and translations of those works. Whether it is
the author (speaker, writer, fictional alter ego) who is plying language or his

audience (listener, reader, critic, agent, publisher, translator) who is doing so in reply to what the former has spoken or penned, and whether this is happening inside or outside the imagination of Lerner's typical, first-person narrating protagonist, these all are, the author insists, instances of language use, tests of idiom "functionality" and "usefulness" where how the linguistic object self-presents ontologically, as form that *is*, and how that form is *transacted, represented,* and otherwise *used,* sometimes by speakers and writers themselves, clash inescapably and dialectically.

"Use," we will see immediately, ought to be understood broadly, and so should "language" since Lerner's novels feature reproductions of internet images of all sorts, stamps, as well as copyrighted and original drawings, photographs, paintings, installations, and other art. Besides this visual content but in close relation to it, these books burst at their narrative seams with non-linguistic objects, whose hushed chatter is a tongue of its own. Therefore, existents commonly considered "material" are not ignored in the discussion that follows. Neither are, here and elsewhere in this book, the communicational and expressive capabilities of all things or the frequently underappreciated, tangible thingness of speech and writing for that matter. That said, in this part of *Flat Aesthetics*, I deal chiefly with verbal and textual language *qua* object or form in the traditional sense of "verbal," "textual," and "language." To do so, I take my cue from Lerner's own excogitations on the dynamic of linguistic objects and their manipulations. As suggested above, this dynamic is a dialectic in Lerner's own oeuvre, where the idiom's presence in these objects, their palpable and unyielding form, on one side, and on the other, the transgression or absencing of language in further, oral or written elaborations and contentions on this form both collide and work like the two arms of a pair of scissors. Let me clarify.

The mutuality of language as form and of the use to which this form is put, Lerner maintains, is an encumbrance whenever a casual comment, public speech, poem, or other linguistic object is, once again in Harman's terminology, "literalized" or "paraphrased." Lerner takes up two kinds of literalization. Both of them have to do with form, more exactly with its *formulaic* character. What distinguishes the two classes is the identity of the literalizing agent—who or what curbs the object's ontological and semantic plays. It can be, as we will discover a bit later, form itself, the object as already formed, a concrete poem, for example. In this case, literalization is driven by an imperfection or limit baked into solidified form and showing mostly in topoi, clichés, borrowings, and other repetitive language through which the poem itself "paraphrases"—re-*uses*—previous forms. We will learn, however, that this very form, threadbare and "used" as it may be rather than brand new, "genuine," is not irredeemable, moreover, that in effect it is sometimes needed, and consequently it is neither to be brushed aside nor swapped for the meanings, contents, and functions for which language and literature have been ordinarily valued.

All the same, this is exactly what a second and more egregious type of literalizations purports. Usually carried out by readers and critics, but also by authors who claim various things about their own output, such limitations spring from the presumption that linguistic and, by extension, literary objects relay, express, allegorize, critique, and otherwise represent, thus lending themselves to translations, interpretations, allegorizations, critiques, and other discourse maneuverings that basically trade form for messages, ideas, and values extrinsic to form itself. Operating quintessentially in an exchange regime, these are object transactions that disregard, transcend, and de facto forfeit the formhood of form. They do so because they have little concern for the formal aspect of the object in their attempts to boil things down to statements about *other* things; because they tend to be couched in repetitive language, in formulas, bywords, and other *serial* tags critics have already affixed to a *variety* of linguistic objects; and because, should such literalizations result in better, more "original" paraphrases of the object, they would still replace it, stand "in lieu of" it and, for all intents and purposes, void it at the same time. Alongside the previous category, paraphrases of the descriptive-hermeneutical kind and, with them, the exchange regime at large imply, in brief, undue consumption, object *use* that *uses up*.

Because this regime is typical of most literary and non-literary implementations of language, Lerner rejects "utilization" broadly. He does so explicitly in *The Hatred of Poetry*, a manifesto whose tenets apply to his entire "project" irrespective of genre.[13] Interestingly enough, here Lerner both rebuffs "utilitarianism that is blind to everything that can't be instrumentalized" and posits that "the use of poetry is . . . entwined with its uselessness."[14] Of course, the antiutilitarian position on literary language and language in general has been de rigueur among modernist artists, writers, and critics. The point on "uselessness," though, while also calling up the art for art's sake credo, is more thought-provoking. According to Lerner, it has serious bearings on what makers of literature, *y compris* himself, do, as well as on what publics, distributors, promoters, appraisers, interpreters, translators, and historians do *with* literature—on what they trade literary works for, so to speak, and to which they ultimately reduce those works, be that a commercial value or a cognitive-affective use value such as a theme, an "impression," a political message, or even a "critique." Whether a price or an appreciation, these are all rationalizing reflexes in an exchange environment susceptible of accommodating, as capital overall does, a striking range of functions and uses that are not, however, as incompatible with one another as they may seem. For instance, treating books and art like commodites, a central problem in *10:04*, should be in principle at loggerheads with reading and perhaps also with writing this or any other books as a rebuke of lucrative gambits. But Lerner hints that, at the end of the day, *both* commodification and its critique "literalize" the literary object by paraphrasing it financially or critically and thus exchanging it for a "crass" pecuniary equivalent ("a 'strong six-figure' advance" is *10:04*'s self-ironic refrain) or for a "sophisticated" critical exposé, respectively.[15] Either way, an instrumentalization is afoot. Guilty of it is the author who redeems the manuscript for cash as is the critic for whom the published book putatively supplies knowledge, and therefore affords claims, "about" sellout writers. In the same Harmanian spirit that may rub the wrong way book-trade folks as well as academics, Lerner calls into question both uses of literature for they both jeopardize the literary object's objecthood by cashing it out in actual or cultural currency.[16]

In essence, Lerner mounts the same challenge to readers and writers, including writers like himself, who wrestle with the transactional hazards of representation, and editors, translators, and others like myself, who, one way or the other, "represent" his work and, in a dizzying feedback loop of representation and self-representation, this work's anxieties about being read and represented. At stake in Lerner—and in his critics no less—are the entwined possibility and impossibility of making literature and making claims about it, ultimately of writing and reading in the post-Cold War exchange regime. Dramatized across Lerner's books with a fervor evocative of DeLillo's 1991 novel *Mao II*, this dilemma and aesthetic impasse stem from the dominance of this regime across a cultural field where literature undergoes incongruous "calculations" as it too is expected to designate and be worth things other than the thing it already *is*, to achieve goals external to itself and be therefore describable, measurable, and valuable in terms of that "outside" (54). If poetry has value, Lerner argues, exchange culture does not recognize it in the *haecceitas* of the literary object. Instead, poetry "amounts" to anything insofar as its "thisness" can be assessed and legitimized heteronomously, that is, funneled down and subordinated to an *au-delà*, as the French would say, to a beyond and a something else. But, as *The Hatred of Poetry* expatiates on the genre's hostile reception by lay readers and "so many cultural critics" alike,

> [p]oetry is a word for a kind of value no particular poem can realize: the value of persons, the value of a human activity beyond the labor/leisure divide, a value before or beyond price. Thus hating poems can either be a way of negatively expressing poetry as an ideal—a way of expressing our desire to exercise such imaginative capacities, to reconstitute the social world—or it can be a defensive rage against the mere suggestion that another world, another measure of value, is possible. In the latter case, the hatred of poetry is a kind of reaction formation: You lash out against the symbol you are repressing, i.e., creativity, community, a desire for a measure of value that isn't "calculative." "Poetry" becomes a word for *an outside that poems cannot bring about,* but can make felt, albeit as an absence, albeit through embarrassment. The periodic denunciations of contemporary poetry should therefore be understood as part of the bitter logic of poetry, not as its repudiation. (53–4; emphasis mine)

Lerner's "logic of poetry" is "bitter" or, once more, dialectical because whatever it eventually accomplishes aesthetically or socially comes about "negatively." As "particular" poems "fail" to re-present, to serve an "outside" and thus convert into the use value they should not be required to carry in the first place, they kit themselves out for a presentation that would otherwise remain unpresentable. This is a presentation that does not presuppose use. Or, if it does, this is a new, non-consumptive use that does not extinguish, exchange, or "spend" the poem. More importantly, it also is a sort of byproduct of the "actual poem'"s "uselessness," "worthlessness," or even misuse (74). A *positive* "misuse value," as Bill Brown might put it,[17] this presentation is a surplus value that accrues *negatively*, possibly in relation but not limited to a cause, politics, social ideal, ideological claim, or other external relevance poems cannot further or decline to bear out, portray, translate into, and somehow play second fiddle to.[18] However, in "failing" to prove themselves externally and in failing *tout court* "out there" and by the standards of that out-thereness, "real" poems bounce back on themselves. Neither instrumental nor subsidiary to higher entities, they are now with a new intensity that, as Shaviro would comment, "draw[s]" us to them "for [their] own sake," "forcing us" to "acknowledge [their] integrity," their being-there as a form or *integrum*, integrated whole.[19]

As they miss, avoid, or ignore that subservient presentation, poetic objects suddenly boost their formally intransitive presence so as to open up internally, much like any other objects, "virtual space[s]" where something beyond the "phenomenal" can be "figured" (74–5). Plagued or not by patent flaws, self-begotten or, more likely, cobbling up regurgitated clichés and chunks of pirated works, an actual poem is liminal writing vulnerable to further limitations. Writing of and at the limit, this poem is a limit in and of itself, material actuality that both limits and remains exposed to "transits" and "uses." But the same form that inscribes the boundaries of the poem's presence, the extension and extent of the poem's being-there, marks out implicitly, *ex negativo*, an area of "not-yet-ness" where being is or can be. Thus, Lerner's flat aesthetic enables an entire ontological dialectic by virtue of which, in resisting *exchange* for a *preexisting* and exterior equivalent, be it another form or an end, contention, and so forth, the *existing* poem demarcates inside itself a zone of *change*, of being modes that do not exist yet. In short, the poem's "finitude" both "compromises" and promises the "infinite" formally (8). Limited by its form to what it can do, the poem also de-limits and by the same movement swings into politics. Like Walt Whitman, "himself a *place* for the genuine, an open space or textual commons where American readers of the future can forge and renew their sense of possibility and interconnectedness" (49), the poem makes room inside itself for new figurations and configurations of objects. "Great poets," Lerner avers, "confront the limits of actual poems, tactically defeat or at least suspend that actuality, sometimes quit writing altogether, becoming celebrated for their silence." In turn, "truly horrible poets unwittingly provide a glimmer of virtual possibility via the extremity of their failure," while "avant-garde poets hate poems for remaining poems instead of becoming bombs," and "nostalgists hate poems for failing to do what they wrongly, vaguely claim poetry once did" (75–6). Moreover, aside from what poets ask of themselves, we also call on them "to defeat time, to still it beautifully; to express irreducible individuality in a way that can be recognized socially or, à la Whitman, to achieve universality by being irreducibly social, less a persona than a national technology; to defeat the language and value of existing society; to propound a measure of value beyond money" (76). Poets face such exigencies and expectations like any other stakeholders of exchange culture, and "tactically" or not, they too come up short. This happens whether they make or acquiesce to demands whose fulfillment is not only unattainable but also undesirable since it would transcend and thus abrogate the objectual interiority or "flat" depth where another presence, the presence of that which is not there yet, can emerge and present itself.

Rekindled in *The Hatred of Poetry* and returning once again in the 2019 novel *The Topeka School*, a teenage memory—the primal scene of Lerner's aesthetic project and so worth reproducing at some length—spotlights this tug-of-war of limit and delimitation, impossible goal and possibility, failure and triumph. "[T]he Hypermart [that] opened in Topeka back in his high-school days," the author reminisces in *The Hatred of Poetry*, employed

young uniformed workers, uniformed both in the sense of wearing the costume of their franchise but also in the sense of uniformly following the conventions of teenage "beauty"—which was not beauty but a *sublimity of perfect exchangeability*, the roller skates themselves a gesture, albeit dated, toward capital's lubricity. Every flake or piece of puffed corn belonging to me as good as belonging to you—Warhol is the Whitman of the actual: "A Coke is a Coke and no amount of money can get you a better Coke than the one the bum on the corner is drinking. All the Cokes are the same and all the Cokes are good." The same goodness, the same sameness: The energy that coursed through me, undid me, at Hypermart—a store that was to the snot-nosed me what Mont Blanc was to Shelley—I consider that energy integral to poetry. "Poetry is a kind of money," Wallace Stevens said; like money, it mediates between the individual and the collective, dissolves the former into the latter, or lets the former reform out of the latter only to dissolve again. Do you remember that sense (or have it now) of being *a tentative node in a limitless network of goods and flows*? Because that's also poetry, albeit in a perverted form, wherein relations between people must appear as things. The affect of abstract exchange, the feeling that *everything is fungible*—what is its song? The actual song of my early youth might be eighties synthpop, but the impulse that gives rise to it, I maintain, is Poetry. (82–3; emphasis mine)

Relations may not be what they are supposed to look like, but they are certainly *made* of things. Inanimate objects participate in the Latourian making and unmaking of human relationships and of the human itself. After all, the items for sale in the uniformity emporium "undo" people. They *disarticulate* by deindividualizing the individual purchasing them. In that, they work like language twice, although they do so like a disabling one— recalling the episode in *The Topeka School*, Adam feels "spread by objects," pulled to bits and strewn about to the point of speechlessness by the opposing debate team's oratorial overkill.[20] Undoubtedly, objects are language, and vice versa, language is one of them. In an "abstract exchange" regime of equivalence, serialization, and instrumentalization, objects and language alike take the speaker apart and so ultimately betray their brief, namely, "articulation," the constitution of speech and implicitly of the speaking subject himself or herself. However, another, "non-fungible" *mode* of language if not another language altogether, a mode in which the idiom is beholden to its own objecthood, makes poetry possible, thus auguring possibility itself as an ontological and political principle and with it the hope for a new world, with its own Whitmanian "interconnectedness," "nodes," limits, and limitlessness. As Lerner observes, the energies that fuel sameness- and equivalence-driven finance, commerce, and consumption are also those setting in motion the self-consuming, singular, and intransitive discourse of poetry; the same "impulses" that disaggregate language and subjectivity and bring them to a grinding halt help Adam pull himself together as a poet—as a Lerner to be—and gear up for the truer "song" inside the "actual song."

This song is flat in the sense explored throughout *Flat Aesthetics*. This tune, this poem, *is*, proclaims its being-there. You hear it, and you may even hear things *in* it, but not through it—not *past* it, that is. Like a conch shell in which you make out the roar of hypothetical oceans, the poem is the exclusive site of such harmonies, both inside and outside, container and content. It may give the semblance of referencing this music but does not stand for it. The poem itself is this oceanic melos, both unexchangeable for something else and spacious enough to harbor and prefigure inside rather than outside itself what *it can be*, to wit, realms of the feasible, possible, and potential where objectual arrangements would not replicate those in the Topeka Hypermart and, more broadly, would not engage in replicating, resonating, and re-presenting. Thus, where store language spells out and enforces existing assemblages, languages such as poetry *presence*—anticipate and experiment with descriptions for—other, heretofore absent ensembles, as in Agamben's potentiality scenario. Back in Kansas, Lerner relives those poetic anticipations as Adam stumbles on another world, more substantial than the "abstract" big-box paradise of material goods. That other world is the world of film, drama, poetry, and art largely, a world picture whose potential temporality pushes allegorically from behind against the screen on which the movie of the actual and the "mundane" runs in "clock time" (84–5). "I felt," Lerner recounts Adam's and his various theater experiences over the years, "that other worlds were possible," a "particular alternative world" (84). This world is not quite a particular work, for the "artwork itself" remains limited even when it is "great" (84). This world *arises* in a particular work, as *Atocha* shows in painstaking detail. À la Harman and Heidegger, the "little clearing that theater makes," the scenic space Lerner "associate[s] with Poetry," opens up *in* a determinate play or poem, and into *this* world one can step provided one experiences, as Harman would also urge, that play or poem as form. Indeed, Lerner confirms, this is an "experience of form" (84), more specifically, of the linguistic object as *present* form and site as well as blueprint of *future* presentations. Because what is not already here, in and as form, cannot be without this form "as is," experiencing the object cannot use, reduce, or transcend the object either but stick to it, working with and through it until flawed form flows, "[t]he way a person's stutter can be liquefied by song" (85).

This is why Lerner not only points up the "stutter" of people, of Hypermart merchandise, and of poetry itself, but he also appreciates the stuttering, stumbling, and want of form on the bumpy road to its task, for both are crucial to "the dialectic of a vocation no less essential for being impossible" (85). The deceptively smooth "poetry" of commerce, the rhyming symmetry of barcodes, and the fraudulent cadence of Trump's "beautiful numbers" can be "de-perverted."[21] To do so, one must unyoke language from the transactional economy of the serial, the numeric, and the quantifiable and respeak it for its own the sake, aesthetically, on behalf of untransactable, beautiful form, and more generally, of beauty. And so what the writer "ask[s] the haters" is to hate more, not less. He wants them to "perfect" their disdain for poetry formally by "bringing" their contempt "to bear on poems" until the latter's impenetrable materiality "creat[es]" inside itself and in "the continuous present tense of art" a "place for possibility and present absences (like unheard melodies)" and until scorn "might come to resemble love" (85–6). This would be only fitting because, as Lerner also offers, writers themselves rage against the "merely actual" either by inspiring or by displaying "perfect contempt for it," ever in search for the "Poem they cannot write in time" (37)—the "genuine Poem that never appears" (76).

The aesthetic of contempt is then a *via negativa* for the authentic. This aesthetic does not transcend form but works on and with it, more exactly works through the form's limit—"the finite," the locus and loci communes where form takes shape *and* founders—but just to unleash the form or limit's own de-limiting "capacity" to "make a new world out of the linguistic material of this one" (37). Accordingly, the new world too is an ensemble of objects, a flat form of surfacial forms available to flat writing and to appositely flat reading. Either first-order (literary) or second-order (readerly), respectively, they both enact presentations that do not liquidate the work's objecthood, given that their writing and reading modes are neither premised on nor catering to an external causality, rationale, use, or other exchange value. Doing without any logical, ideological, or ontological crutch, flat form relies "negatively" on its own "trite" actuality *qua* form to conjure up the virtual, the possible, and therefore the political also—to *re*assemble Hypermart-like assemblages into *un*precedented ensembles.

I have italicized the two prefixes in the previous sentence to signpost a major waystation on Lerner's *via negativa* and a prima facie paradox, namely, repetition and its genetic relation to the new and the "genuine," which in Lerner's work remain self-conscientiously repetitive, a combinatorial, permutational, and quotational affair. If postmodernism was intertextual but balked at enlisting intertextuality in the production of the metaphysically sounding "real thing," Lerner's fiction is *hyperintertextual*, but its hyperintertextuality courts doggedly the new, the "profound," the authentic, the truthful, and other conspicuously non-postmodern categories. In Lerner, "actual" form instantiates an extreme form of actuality, so to say. Form does not have to be so blatantly limited, so hampered by form itself, so jam-packed with previous forms. And yet, as we will discover, Lerner's form definitely and willfully is: repetitious in an over-the-board, hackneyed, and sometimes kitschy way, bursting at the seams with commonplaces and attributed as well as unattributed quotes, and rehearsing knowingly and unknowingly, plagiaristically or less so, ironically and in earnest, graciously or awkwardly, forms already in use within the economy of literary and cultural sameness. Thus, the formal and the repetitive prove joined at the hip in the exchangeability system, with "real" form lackluster, generic, and recurrent like uniforms and "'family sized' boxes of Cap'n Crunch repeating as far as the eye could see" (82) in the Topeka superstore. At Hypermart, at its local Walmart successor, at *10:04*'s Park Slope Food Coop in Brooklyn, NY, and across the wider system of material and symbolic transactions, form is, as a rule, swapped for and recycled into forms substitutable for it, similar to it, or somehow referencing it. Limitless as it may appear, the system whose snapshot Lerner takes here and in other books is a closed circuit of sameness in which form becomes formula, that is, isomorphic to the national and world system in which this form is over and over traded, exchanged, and otherwise utilized. For such reproductive uses ultimately engender its ordinariness, render it "usual" twice in terms of what this form is and what its users do with it, and this is as true of Cap'n Crunch as is, ventures Lerner, of poems. Most poetry is *"usual"* because it is not only "used," awash with former uses of techniques, themes, tropes, and stock phrases, but because it is also unduly usable itself, liable to be used by readers, critics, translators, and occasionally by its own author as a basis for enunciations, "denunciations," and other claims about it that are themselves repetitious, paraphrases of the literary work in question as well as of criticism, "theory," and their all-too-bandied-about buzzwords. We know from Harman that such uses and paraphrases routinely deface form by exchanging it for what form is not—for the same canned language one has heard before and more broadly for the *déja-vu* language of sameness, the language or form in which the same returns, again and again, as the serial in cereal boxes.

But if form is repetitive, not all repetitions need be sameness-bound. Lerner declares in an interview that what appeals to him is the repetition in which "elements return with a difference, not pure repetition, but that notion of a return with a change to the element that's returned."[22] As Adam suspects, and as his author repeats by literally repeating Edgar Allan Poe, "linguistic repetition" may "forc[e] a confrontation with the malleability of language and the world we build with it, build upon it," to the point of "banish[ing . . .] the symbolic order" (80) of things in Hypermart aisles and beyond. In this sense, as Lerner critic Adam Colman echoes a long line of thought from David Hume to Deleuze, the reiterative is a two-edged sword. An "imperfect representation," repetition has been traditionally the telltale sign of one's inability to "invent" and thus of poietic failure as well, of failing to make one's own. This does not mean, however, that repetition "can[not also] sustain or suggest invention," the con-figuring or figuring *together* of that which has been, or has been viewed as, disjunct, separate, or unrelated.[23] Instructive in this regard is one of the many Matryoshka moments of *The Hatred of Poetry* where Lerner "repeats" and reassembles Charles Olson ("The Kingfishers"), a move that in fact entails multiple reiterations of texts and forms: Lerner already repeated Olson extensively in *10:04*, an aspect to which I will come back in part two of *Flat Aesthetics*, but "The Kingfishers" too borrowed from T. S. Eliot (*The Waste Land*) and the "assemblage" technique (73) of Ezra Pound's *Cantos*, which, according to Guy Davenport, had itself appropriated John Adams's "slash" (74). Furthermore, here Lerner also repeats himself one more time, and textually so. If the 2019 book replays the Hypermart scene three years after the latter's narration in *The Hatred of Poetry*, the 2016 essay lifts in turn from *Atocha* the sentence in which Lerner "already" summoned Olson's multilayered repetitions of theme ("change") and device (forward slash or virgule) and where, like all the "great poets" before him, he got a glimpse of the "virtual" in Olson's "actual" and actuality-tainted work (73–4). As Lerner tells us, "[Olson's] famous first line [of 'The Kingfishers']," "What does not change / is the will to change," may sound repetitive, not unlike Lerner himself in his Olson playback. Nevertheless, the verse "is," Lerner comments, "a way of announcing that [Olson's] poem is a virtual space, not yet or not just an actual poem. ('I tended to find lines of poetry beautiful only when I encountered them quoted in prose . . . so that what was communicated was less a particular poem . . .')" (74).

necklaces, novels, backpacks: A Post Is Being Formed in *Leaving the Atocha Station*

Poetry is what's there.

—John Ashbery, "The Experience of Experience"

The content of the clepsydra is a transparent medium, the content is pure form, and Ashbery's labyrinthine sentences derive their force less from their paraphrasable content than the way they measure time with their flow.

—Ben Lerner, "The Future Continuous"

Atocha practically opens with the exact words in the parenthesis above. The speaker is Adam Gordon, the narrating protagonist. Adam—whose "name was Ben or Benjamin until the last edit"—is Lerner's autofictional alter ego.[24] Like his author, who spent a year on a Fulbright in Spain roughly during the same 2003–2004 interval spanned by the plot, Adam is a Topeka, Kansas-born poet on a "research" fellowship in Madrid. The "first phase" of his "project require[s]," he quips, a matinal routine involving rolling a spliff, taking his "white pills," and walking leisurely to the Prado.[25] Here, the overmedicated flaneur would plant himself before van der Weyden's *Descent from the Cross*, a detail of which is reproduced in the book. When Adam arrives at the museum one morning—"a turning point in my project" (7), he reveals—someone has already taken "[his] place" in front of the van der Weyden. About to leave, he notices that the man by the painting is crying, "convulsively catching his breath." In a 2013 essay, Lerner would diagnose such an incident as "Stendhal's syndrome[,] also known as 'hyperculturemia' or 'Florence syndrome[,' a] psychosomatic condition in which" one is "overwhelmed by the presence of great art, resulting in a range of responses: breathlessness, panic, fainting, paranoia, disorientation."[26] Lerner's hero is not so sure. "Was [the visitor]," Adam wonders, "just facing the wall to hide his face as he dealt with whatever grief he'd brought into the museum? Or was he having a *profound experience of art*?" (8).

The questions, including their wording, not least the disjunctive "or"— the novel's stylistic trademark, as we will see—cut to the heart of *Atocha*. While hardly an answer, the paragraph that follows, and from which *The Hatred of Poetry* would excerpt the parenthetic declaration, is worth quoting in extenso:

> I had long worried that I was incapable of having a profound experience of art and I had trouble believing that anyone had, at least anyone I knew. I was intensely suspicious of people who *claimed* a poem or painting or piece of music "changed their life," especially since I had often known these people before and after their experience and could register no

change. Although I *claimed* to be a poet, although my supposed talent as a writer had earned me my fellowship in Spain, I tended to find lines of poetry beautiful only when I encountered them quoted in prose, in the essays my professors had assigned in college, where the line breaks were replaced with slashes, so that what was communicated was less a particular poem than the echo of poetic possibility. Insofar as I was interested in the arts, I was interested in the disconnect between my experience of actual artworks and the *claims* made on their behalf; the closest I'd come to having a profound experience of art was probably the experience of this distance, a profound experience of the absence of profundity." (8–9; emphasis mine)

Atocha is entirely here in a nutshell, and so is Lerner's flat art. This strategically and intricately repetitive and self-repetitive "tour-de-force vignette" is itself a link in an endless chain of repeat performances, or a knot, rather, a densely citational site of crisscrossing allusions, references, and reiterations.[27] The fragment ties together the main conceptual threads of a novel and of an aesthetic whose principal thrust pushes, via recitations, repetitions, references, and cognate symptoms of paraphrase and "aboutness," *past* such transits and transactions and ultimately beyond the jurisdiction of exchangeability, into the authentic, the genuine, and what is the genuinely "there," ontologically impeachable.[28] A *mise en abyme* of Adam's "project," and of Lerner's project as well, the passage showcases the reflective architecture of this hall-of-convex-mirrors of a novel. A twenty-first-century *Lost in the Funhouse*, *Atocha* features prominently and recurrently the 1981 videotaped interview where John Ashbery talks about the "experience of experience" apropos of his poem "Leaving the Atocha Station" (from the 1962 volume *The Tennis Court Oath*), which he reads and discusses with A. Poulin, Jr.[29] Of course, *Atocha* itself cites and recites, in more ways than one, its titular—and tutor—text, as well as Ashbery's "Clepsydra" (from the 1966 collection *Rivers and Mountains*), not to mention Lerner's own essay "The Future Continuous: Ashbery's Lyric Mediacy," which came out in *boundary 2* the year before *Atocha*'s publication and where the author dwells on "Clepsydra" and other Ashbery works.[30]

Lerner's 2010 article has drawn plenty of attention, as has the Ashbery connection in *Atocha* broadly.[31] The elder poet too gave the intertextual nexus his imprimatur, calling *Atocha* "an extraordinary novel about the intersections of art and reality in contemporary life."[32] Extolling as it is, the accolade may strike us as vague unless we read it in the context of the stress Ashbery and Lerner lay on literary and linguistic form as resistance to the exchange regime. In both writers, this form is ontologically opaque and semiologically immanent. It is something that, however it is, *is there* or, as I have said, *here*, in the hereness of the *hic et nunc*; it is not "about," nor is it self-effacing, therefore, in paraphrases and approximations vying to capture its aboutness. But to the extent that it can be said to be "about" anything—a hypothesis at which otherwise Adam balks ever so often—form is, as Ashbery, Lerner, and Lerner's hero would agree, about how art and reality "intersect" and about their intersections' defining impact on the contemporaneity about which Adam attempts, and fails, to lecture on the "literature now" panel later in the novel (161).

Literature, making it, and being a poet or a novelist are, in other words, about experiencing the world; after all, a writer's experience is where the writer and the world cross paths. However, both Ashbery in his interview and Lerner in his take on Ashbery are adamant that literature is not a *representation* of a particular experience, let alone of a particular experienced reality—poetry is not about it despite the referential breadcrumbs dropped by the poem and irrespective of what critics who follow them might claim. Instead, *literature is that experience itself*, in its very form and *as such*, *qua* form. Neither a record nor a receptacle of experience, form does not just transcribe experience but inscribes it, is *it*. Form is an energy discharge that does not merely occur during said experience, and it does not contain—it does not check or comprise—this energetic event either but crystallizes it. Concrete linguistic form is then paramount, for its own sequencing and overall configuration chart the course of poietic elaboration, delineating how the writer lived out as a writer his or her own experience, that is, how form came to be what it is. In his answer to one of Poulin, Jr.'s questions about "Leaving the Atocha Station," Ashbery declares in fact that "[m]ost of my poems are about the experience of experience . . . the particular occasion is of lesser interest to me than the way a happening or experience filters through to me."[33] And, he adds a little later, "the subject of any one of my poems [is] the poem creating itself. The process of writing poetry becomes the poem."[34] If this is true, then form—the literary object's objecthood or "pure form," as Lerner says of Ashbery's poetry—is indeed its own content.[35] On this ground, the poetic object cannot be expected to paraphrase reality, nor can it be reduced by critics to such paraphrases. There is no room left for an "about" in it, and so about-claims have no purchase on it. Thus, for one thing, the object's subject is not external to the object and, in a way, not even different from it, which brings about or reinforces the flatness of a particular poem, rendering the work intransitive, unparaphrasable, and otherwise unexchangeable for a meaning or object deeper, more "profound" than the object itself. For another thing, experience, no matter what it is, *is*, and this ontological mode is a marker of authenticity. Granted, what Ashbery, Lerner, and Adam ultimately refer to is technically a metaexperience, a term I steer clear of as the "aboutness" of the prefix might suggest that in the "experience of experience" syntagma, the former experience is somehow removed from the latter. But this is not the case. "Meta" or not, experience "becomes," as Ashbery indicates, the poiesis protocol itself. Essentially inhering in the writing flow, *being* it in the strongest ontological sense, experience is bound to *be true* to it if there is going to be an experience at all. For this reason, experience is authentic, its seemingly or effectively "inauthentic," not-so-original moments and other drawbacks of this sort notwithstanding.

This factitious authenticity characterizes Adam's experience as a museumgoer, his "style" as a poet, as well as Lerner's own modus operandi as an author in whose novel the authentic thus conceived is not just a thematic riff on the anxiety of influence but, quite the opposite, a *via negativa* formal principle predicated on deliberate and extreme derivativeness. In the same post-postmodern vein that enlists paradox, obliqueness, the *déjà vu*, as well as the *déjà lu* and a whole array of intertextual filters in the service of the immediate, the straightforward, the personal, and the bona fide, Lerner rehashes the Ashbery interview, trading on the limitations of such affiliation to de-limit himself by foregrounding the inapparent authenticity of Adam's response to the canvas and the world and in the final analysis of Adam himself as someone capable of taking them in originally, "profoundly," and creatively. Ashbery acknowledges that "listening to poetry" is to him enjoyable "because of the incompleteness of [an] experience" that basically "spreads" the poem—as *The Topeka School*'s Adam might put it—dismantling it in the listener's mind ("I wonder in and out of my thoughts while I'm listening to a poem. I wonder if I remembered to buy soap, or whether I've missed an important appointment").[36] But then, observes Ashbery, when he circles back to the poem's actual form, to "the way it looks on the page, the way the letters are shaped, the way the lines are," this form echoes "the mental, invisible image of the poem."[37] Similarly, *Atocha* and, as we saw, *The Hatred of Poetry* one more time turn to incomplete experience, to one that de-completes, renders wanting, humdrum, imitative of other experiences, and shortchanges language, literature, and art, but Lerner sets up this very experience as a stepping-stone to something else still unexperienced and yet possible, virtually there or, again, *here*. This "here" is the form of Adam's experience "as is," at the Prado or whenever he writes, lectures, and chats with friends, and it is also the form of whatever he composes and reads: unexceptional and inchoate, ad-lib and insecure, buckling under the historical burden of inauthentic, pointedly reiterated clichéd "claims" about authenticity like a Hypermart shelf under its own stock items.

An overtly Ashberian encore, the "profound experience" passage illustrates then what I determined earlier as a first category of reductions to the recognizable and what already exists. As noted, these truncations and serializations are no critical add-ons; they are built into form. Here, they are embedded in a chunk of text that, like so many in *Atocha*, induces literalizations the whole book works through to fashion itself into the novel that it is, and which, in being *that*, can be reduced neither to preexisting entities like Ashbery's writings nor to claims "about" it even if Lerner himself made them.[38] Such ulterior and external contentions and "uses" of linguistic and literary forms by others, and not infrequently by authors themselves, come, as the reader will remember, under a second category. This class is also in play in this excerpt as it is elsewhere in *Atocha* when Adam faces conjectures on and translations of his words, when he himself scrambles to figure out what his Spanish friends are saying, and even when he tries to explain himself to others, whether in Spanish or English, a sign that he is not so much lost in translation or skeptical about it as he is wary of translations and related linguistic and hermeneutical operations insofar as they entail about-claims and other language uses of the exchange kind.

Like the former type of literalizations, claims of this nature are at once invited and derailed in Adam's story, this time around diegetically. With them too we run into the tug-of-war of repetition and differentiation for these claims also deploy ossified phraseology by design. It is no happenstance that Adam references them in the museum scene *expressis verbis* repeatedly ("people who claimed . . . I claimed . . . claims made"), and he will do so throughout the novel either nominally (18, 39, 43) or in reaction to questions and assertions regarding what literature is "about" (36, 54, 127, 174). Adam feels that such pronouncements, including those he volunteers about himself, his family, and his poetry—some of them outright lies—box him in. All these formulaic and intermingling presuppositions, prescriptions, and statements "about" art, beauty, writing, poetic meaning, authenticity, value, and being a "true" poet rather than a phony faking "deep" emotional life limit him and his work. It goes without saying, it does not help that Adam puts on a pretend show for most of *Atocha*, nor that he works others' material into his own. What matters, though, and what bears reemphasizing is that these ready-to-use expression routines are the building blocks of Adam's and Lerner's "negative" poetics. Through such exercises in conventionality, form self-limits, gathers itself up to gain momentum and, reenergized, de-limit itself in another plane, where that which is not completely present in the present text can ground its presence and "actual" form can thus finally overcome its incompletion and "inauthenticity."

Ashbery's poetry itself, Lerner reminds us, made this leap, moving *across* and eventually beyond the more "conventional" mold of "Self-Portrait in a Convex Mirror." "The difference between 'Self-Portrait' and Ashbery's other great poems," Lerner proposes almost in the same language in at least two interviews, "is that the former does not make us read about our reading in the time of its unfolding, it doesn't catalyze the strange experience of presence I've been describing but rather represents a more conventional and personal retrospective mode."[39] However, most critical claims end up re-conventionalizing those "other great poems" that have sublated conventional, makeshift, and blemished form into the abode of a truer presence. Where poems of this caliber, Lerner details, open themselves up ontologically to something that for the time being is *there* but not wholly *here* yet, "about" commentary closes them back up.[40] It does so by literalizing them as a pageant of facts, actions, and other ontic minutiae prior and external to form, to the presence emerging in and through it, and to the reading experience this presence occasions. Destabilized by the poem itself, such "referents" return in critics' claims with a vengeance, Lerner asseverates, to "stabilize" the poem and thus "pin" the poet "down" even though "Ashbery has always refused to be pinned down."[41] An inertial "demand for sense pins the poet to the past . . . Most old schools of criticism are either reductive, pinning the author to what he says, arresting the flow of the poem and its capacity to measure time, or redundant, reflecting on a poem that is already the reflection of our reading." However, Lerner writes, "understanding can, happily, be dissolved into the flow of language, *enabling a kind of presence*" (emphasis mine).[42]

Significantly, conventional critical "understanding" is not reading's endgame but a hurdle to "dissolve" or, as Lerner would write in *The Hatred of Poetry*, to "liquefy," much as a true "experience of form" would Hypermart's hardened monody of sameness (85). This understanding is conventional twice: because it is convention-laden, tied down to the already said by analytical and theoretical clichés and formulas overlaying the poem's own, and also because its "referentializing" reflexes reenact the "antecedent" ontology of the already-being as they latch instinctively onto the "deictic" accoutrements of the text. "In Ashbery," Lerner expatiates, "[d]eictic language allows us to progress through long, hypotactic sentences as if antecedents and their context were assumed, as if the sentences were moving toward logical resolution." But "when we fail to identify those antecedents external to the poem"—for, as we suspect by now, fail we must—"*the poem itself becomes the most available context*," and "its processes invest its pronouns" and other deictic speech parts ("there," "then," "thus," etc.) so as to energize semantically the poem itself rather than authorize claims about an elsewhere, a before, and other literalizing circumstances (emphasis mine).[43] Galvanized by the failure of transitive deictics, the poem kicks into a presence without precedent, a hyperpresence that casts aside "overmining" ascriptions of person, number, tense, quantity, place, and related qualifiers and impels reading to follow suit. No longer "fooled," as Lerner writes, by the "vocabulary" of referential and causal claims, flat reading can now reclaim the poem, if not in terms of an indexical semiotic of exchange that trades a textual "this" for and extra- or ante-textual "that," then as an experience of the poem itself *qua* flat form.[44] The flatness at play here is semiogenetic: flat form becomes its own content and thus "thick" with possibilities. Indeed, as Lerner points out, "form becomes content as one reads[,] because the poem itself fills the vacuum left by indefinite deictics. In Ashbery's poems, meaning might not be fully present, but we have a graceful kind of non-absence: each moment feels authorized by a truth that has yet to arrive, and if it never arrives, if there is 'no luck,' we then read the poem as referring to the evanescence of reference as it evanesces."[45]

Following the lead of flat form itself, flat reading "refreshes" the poem as one would a webpage to update its content, only that there is no difference in this case between the page and the code it is made of, on one hand, and content, on the other. To press on with the computing analogy, as a "broken" internet page sometimes shows the html "underneath" it, so does misfiring deictics. What breaks down or fails to "upload" can be the poem's own deictic language and, in effect, language overall, which in *actual* communication works as one big deictic system, keyed as it is to referencing linguistic and material "antecedents." Or, it can be, post factum—post-scriptum—a critical deictics eager to exchange the presence-fostering "evanescence of reference" for precise specifications, attributions, and other evaluations of intent, scope, politics, and the like. Whatever the source of deictic malfunctions and of language's referential "dysfunctionality" largely, flat reading adds insult to poetic self-injury by pulling all remaining deictic stops, thus undoing the "closure" inbuilt or supervening about-claims have foisted on the poem. "Refusing closure"—Lerner's own phrase—is in fact the ultimate test of reading experience, as the writer hints in an interview where he also insists, once again quoting from *Atocha*, that Adam has passed the test by reading "Clepsydra" without falling for Ashbery's pronominal deictics.[46] "The best Ashbery poems, I thought, although not in these words," confesses Adam by quoting in turn from his author's *boundary 2* essay,

> describe what it's like to read an Ashbery poem; his poems refer to how their reference evanesces. And when you read about your reading in the time of your reading, mediacy is experimented immediately. It is as though the actual Ashbery poem were concealed from you, written on the other side of a mirrored surface, and you saw only the reflection of your reading. But by reflecting your reading, Ashbery's poems allow you to attend to your attention, to experience your experience, thereby enabling a *strange kind of presence.* But it is a presence that keeps the virtual possibilities of poetry intact because the true poem remains beyond you, inscribed on the far side of the mirror: "You have it but you don't have it. / You miss it, it misses you. / You miss each other." (91; emphasis mine)

Another lap around the Ashbery/Lerner reflection-cum-self-reflection Möbius strip, the three lines bringing up the rear of Adam's musings are from Ashbery's "Paradoxes and Oxymorons." They are relevant in form and content, with both rolled into one. If right before Adam's comments Lerner *transcribes* a fragment of "Clepsydra" (90–1) in its original, traditional poetry layout, with one line coming below another, the "Paradoxes and Oxymorons" bit is *reinscribed* as prose. The move is hardly innocent. As we have learned from *Atocha* and *The Hatred of Poetry*, "lines of poetry become beautiful only when" Lerner "encountered them quoted in prose, . . . where the line breaks were replaced with slashes, so that what was communicated was less a particular poem than the echo of poetic possibility" (8–9, 74). This typographical de-particularization of a "particular poem" is homologous—"structural[ly] identi[c]," Adam would say (90)—with the anti-deictic sweep of a flat reading that places little stock in "Clepsydra'"s "'but,' 'therefore,' 'so,' 'then,' 'next,' 'later,' 'it,' 'you,' 'we,' 'I,'" and other decoy indexes of "stable external referents" (90), as well as with Adam's "hackneyed" and scandalously plagiaristic flat writing itself.

What Lerner and Adam wish to accomplish eventually is open up the actual poem to the possible, to the possibility of being, more exactly. But since, one more time, "poetic possibility" is a dialectical function of the *dys*function of poetic actuality, form *as such*—this very actuality—is uncircumventable in spite of its "defects." As Lerner posits in *The Hatred of Poetry*, "[p]oems are always already failing us" (77) by tying themselves typographically, grammatically, semiotically, and intertextually to the contextual and textual already-there; or we may fail *them* by "pinning" them "down" to whatever readings, ratiocinations, and instrumentalizing uses we assume poetic deictics licenses. Either way, form presents itself, and so its presence must be reckoned with *as crafted* because, Achilles's spear-like, this presence works as a closure-and-disclosure unit. In its very staleness and improvisation, form encloses and "conceals" the virtual while making provisions for the unveiling of unsuspected virtuality. That is why, at once in keeping and at variance with postmodern tactics of originality, neither Lerner nor his hero is dismissive of literary and material, stabilizing signposts and "antecedents" (90). Instead, both work off such "referents" to bring out the unprecedented—that which has not been yet has been not so much absent as hidden, albeit imperfectly, within and *as* imperfect form, and so it can appear *in* the form's here and now. Heavily mediated intertextually, culturally, and otherwise as they are, flat writing and reading then experience themselves and prompt others to experience them "immediately."

As in postmodern poetics, this immediacy is an intermediation byproduct. But writing and reading practices of the typically contemporary, flat sort reclaim it with such a self-authenticating intensity that their presence "enables" another, "strange kind of presence," a half-present, half-absent "non-absence" ("You have it[,] but you don't have it").[47] As Agamben puts it in his marginalia to Aristotle's *Metaphysics*, this "presence of an absence" is a sign of "potentiality" or, in Adam/Lerner's words, of "virtual possibility."[48] Yet again, one should not think of this ontological domain as metaphysical; to get to it, one would not have to "transcend" the poem. Potentiality is dormant in the work, and Lerner is quite unambivalent about this. It is, he remarks over and over, form as is that, through its immanent, intransitive self-presence, sets the stage for what might be. Whatever might come would not arrive from another time and place but would be the progeny of flat form's self-flagging presence in the present. Once the linguistic object has malfunctioned deictically, its Jakobsonian poetic function does double duty ontologically, taking on, that is, an ontological role as well, and so its referential function, not harnessed to about-rationales of consumptive reading and exegesis anymore, can no longer curtail the play of potentiality either.

At that point, when both poem and reading, both "Clepsydra" and Adam's response to it have stepped beyond the descriptive claims deictic references inherently capacitate, our business as readers, far from winding down, would only rise to the next level. As Lerner postulates in an *Angle of Yaw* poem, "[w]ith what exceeds description we busy ourselves."[49] "Exceeding description," however, is not just something flat writing and objects overall perform; it also is, as I have been arguing, and as Adam underscores, the task and trial of a flat reading alive to the intransitive energies with which the poem deflects representations, exchangeability-prone measurements, and other critical adjudications as it shifts into possibility-rich hyperpresence. Lerner stresses that, for us, whether we peruse somebody else's work or listen to a translation of our own, the potential *forms*, in all senses imaginable, surfacing in the time of our experience of form as form, viz., in the fluid temporality of reading. As it "liquefies" clunky wording, stolen images, and truisms, this flow carries us the other side of limitingly descriptive about-semantics. That side—again, one *inside* form, not outside it—is the "far side of the mirror," of the mirroring, and of the mimetic more broadly. It is the other side of the screen in the Kansas movie theater and the other side of Arturo's Spanish translation of Adam's poem.

Teresa, Adam's friend, refers to this piece, Adam tells us, as "the one about seeing myself on the ground from the plane and in the plane from the ground" (36), and she also recommends Adam read it at the art gallery. Adam protests that "the poem wasn't *about* that, that poems aren't *about* anything" (36), but after Tomás recites his own, "hackneyed poem[s]'"s (38), he reads it nonetheless:

> Under the arc of the cello
> I open the Lorca at random
> I turn my head and watch
> The lights slide by, a clearing
> Among possible referents
> Among the people perusing
> The gallery walls, dull glow
> Of orange and purple, child
> Behind glass, adult retreating
> I bit hard to deepen the cut
> I imagined the passengers
> Could see me, imagined I was
> A passenger that could see me
> Looking up . . . (40)

Is Adam's poem less "hackneyed" than Tomás's? Is it stuttering and stumbling, folding back on what has been and is here worked over one more time? Or is it "flowing," opening onto what might still be? We will not know for sure until Arturo has "misused" it, to quote Bill Brown again.[50] We get the feeling, though, that the original already initiates and even advertises that opening. Alongside its reading and commentary by Adam, the poem is a "mirror-in-the-text" structure à la Lucien Dällenbach's *récit spéculaire* and one of *Atocha*'s multiply self-reflective moments.[51] Similarly to "Clepsydra" and, on another level, to Lerner's novel also, Adam's work at once makes itself and comments on its making. It does more, however, than just divulge its formula. It shows how its ars poetica doubles up as an *ars ontologica*. That is, the poem points to itself as both a meditation on and enactment of the energetic aesthetic of coming into presence. As it reverse-engineers its own actuality, the text gestures to that which, in the text itself, appears to be traceable to and exchangeable for existents prior and exterior to it such as the scraps "borrowed" from Federico García Lorca and Lorca scholars like Jack Spicer, as well as other, non-belletristic "possible referents."[52] Whether it operates intertextually or referentially, a deictics is therefore up and running, threatening to corral the poem's semantics inside an extant "about" world. This deictics does not take over the poem entirely because "Adam makes fun of his own method" while laying it bare, as Lerner himself acknowledges.[53] Deep inside the counterfeit ontology of the poem, amid all the literary *bric-à-brac*, the "willful mistranslations" (as Lerner calls them in an interview), and the playacting involved in the *Atocha* scene when Adam fakes a more serious injury than resulted from Miguel's punch (13), the poet's gaze falls on a "clearing" where something else can be experienced authentically, "profoundly."

This *Lichtung* is the horizontal projection of the vertical interval Adam "imagines" at the end of the poem between himself and himself as an other, or better yet, between himself and him experiencing himself as an other, again, over the span of the convex mirror that bestows self-speculative "depth" on experience and authenticity, genuineness, and presence on that which is experienced, be it the self or self-expression.[54] Across this vastness and within the space in which, according to the *Angle of Yaw* poem quoted earlier, the descriptive no longer holds sway, "[h]e shuts his eyes to see himself from above," as Lerner writes in the same text.[55] The novelist recycles this sentence in Adam's text so as to inscribe into the poem and into *Atocha* itself a *presencing* self-distance, a break in repetitive and superficially "numerical" routine where that which starts out as reiterative and shallow can instantiate new potential of being. As Adam himself surmises at the gallery, sometimes this break or opening is forced by "the intrinsic energies" (39) of the poem itself despite its shortfalls. Other times, however, it is a certain reading or use of the poem that loosens it up even more, "flattening" it out to unfold or expand inside it the very space in which the not-yet-present can present itself. This inscription of potential presence can be triggered, Lerner and Adam insist, by a prose reinscription of prosody, with virgules revving the poem up into a novel meaningfulness. Or, an already self-present poem such as Adam's, in which form is "sticky" enough already, can rise into hyperpresence in the aftermath of more radical reinscriptions such as Arturo's translation. These are poised to further weaken and "fluidify" deictics, unlocking them semiotically and, by the same movement, subjecting the poetic object to more complex, linguistic and cultural transformations. As Adam recollects his reactions to Arturo's reading of the Spanish version of the same poem, "[a]t first I heard only"

> so many Spanish words, but nothing I could recognize as my own; after all, there was nothing particularly original about my original poems, comprised as they were of mistranslations intermixed with repurposed fragments from deleted e-mails. But as the poem went on I slowly began to recognize something like my voice, if that's the word, a recognition made all the more strange in that I'd never recognized my voice before. Something in the arrangement of the lines, not the words themselves or what they denoted, indicated a *ghostly presence behind the Spanish, that presence was my own, or maybe it was my absence*; it was like walking into a room where I was sure I'd never been, but seeing in the furniture or roaches in the ashtray or the coffee cup on the window ledge beside the shower signs that I had only recently left. Not that I'd ever owned that particular couch or cup, but that the specific disposition of those objects, the way they had been lived with, required or implied me; not that I was suffering from amnesia or déjà vu, but that I was both in that room and outside of it, maybe in the park, and not just in the park, but also in innumerable other possible rooms and parks at once. *Any contingent object, couch or cup, "orange" or "naranja," could form the constellation that I was, could form it without me, but that's not really right; it was like seeing myself looking down at myself looking up.* (40–1; emphasis mine)

If self-recognition in Arturo's translation is difficult and rewarding, recognizing Tomás, his style or "thing" (38), and his meanings is easy but fruitless. "To my surprise," the American poet reports,

> [Tomás] poem was totally intelligible to me, an Esperanto of clichés: waves, heart, pain, moon, breasts, beach, emptiness, etc.; the delivery was so cloying the thought crossed my mind that his apparent earnestness might be parody. But then he read his second poem, "Distance": mountains, sky, heart, pain, stars, breast, river, emptiness, etc. . . . Maybe, I wondered or tried to wonder, I'm not understanding; maybe these words have a specific weight and valence I cannot appreciate in Spanish, or maybe he is performing subtle variations on a sexist tradition of which I

am not in possession. As Tomás read a third poem, "Work Dream" or "Dream Work," I forced myself to listen *as if* the poem were unpredictable and profound, as if that were given somehow, and any failure to be compelled would be exclusively my own. The intensity of my listening did at least return strangeness to each word, force me to confront it as sound and then to recapture the miracle of sound opening or almost opening onto sense, and I managed to suspend my disgust. I could not, however, keep this up; it required too much concentration to hear such familiar figurations as intensely strange, even in Spanish. (37–8)

Gumbrecht might argue that the Spaniard's poems and Adam's exemplify the divide between a "meaning culture" in which the object vanishes in attributions of meaning and a "presence culture" of "intrinsic" meaningfulness less dependent on claims submitted in or for it.[56] Claims affect Adam's poetry too but leave a larger imprint on Tomás's and other speech acts in the novel whenever, plainly put, its speakers and writers make claims, not worlds, as they trade language, in its very use, for "transcendent" justifications, rationalizations, and more generally for "meaning"—more specifically, for a meaning constructed "hermeneutically," through semantic ascriptions that annul the meaningful object itself. Such claims come to nothing repeatedly in Tomás's poetry, and Adam's response to it rehearses this failure. But because, as poets, Tomás and Adam do not fail the same way, Adam's lack of success as Tomás's translator—for a translation his response is—also differs from how Arturo "fails" to render Adam into Spanish. The "intensity" Adam's translation achieves turns out shallow and unsustainable as Tomás and Adam himself after him get bogged down in the poems' deictic morass. All this translation can do is act out the urge and inevasible failure of claim after claim—or, according to Allen Grossman in *The Long Schoolroom*, which Lerner mentions alongside Michael Clune's "Theory of Prose" essay in *Atocha*'s "Acknowledgments" (4), the impossibility of the luring possibility of poetic references, statements, contentions, and the like. The mass of conflicting about-claims ends up crashing Tomás's texts, and Adam's translation thereof follows suit, collapsing in the sterile zone where one possibility, instead of opening a window into Agambenian potentiality, into what can be and stand on its own, is instantly exchanged for another and thus canceled out, "absented" by it.

This zone is barren in a postmodern sort of way, for absence here is the final score of a semiotic and ontological zero-sum-game kind of writing and translation in which what is about to be adjudicated as true or real is already overshadowed by an other whose own alternate awaits in the offing. Claimed and disclaimed time after time, things are trapped in the limbo of "or," neither upheld nor "negated" enough, wavering on the cusp of being and never quite making it. If Adam's poetic "imposture" is brazen and cynically self-detached, Tomás's dithers "unwitting[ly]" (38) in between claims and counterclaims.

Unlike Adam, he is naïvely overcommitted to their beguiling referentiality and, despite the title of one of his poems, proves incapable of the inner distance or self-estrangement Adam's translator builds on to carve out the space in which *"that other thing"* (16) than paraphrases and references to what already is can gel. Taking hold in this Rimbaldian self-distance, Arturo's translation of Adam's poem manages to reform the original into a presencing constellation, whereas Adam's mental translation of Tomás's work does not. One co-relates, forms a presence out of bits and pieces; channeled by the de-presencing "or," the other just tracks the absencing crumbling of form and eventually of itself. As Adam's translation comes to a head, Tomás's poems do not avail themselves of the "project[ion] scree[n]" (38) Arturo supplies to Adam's work, and so they fall short of objecthood. They exist as "dead medium" (38), substitutes that never get to do their job. Awaiting indefinitely their exchange for the real thing, they are "placeholder[s] for an art" (38) postponed sine die. Their "actual[ity]" (38) remains therefore flimsy and conventional ("familiar"), ever more drained by the meaning "scenarios" (38) and related claims they successively elicit and discard.

Also stuck in the "or" gear of these warring hypotheses, Adam's translation illustrates, more than Tomás's writing itself, an entire onto-linguistic paradigm. Its traits are tentativeness, "undecidability" (39), and their "poststructuralist" derivatives: overabundance of inconsonant realities, paralyzing—rather than mobilizing—polysemy, elusiveness, uncertainty, insecurity, simulation, deceit, lying, and *Atocha* reviewers' all-time favorite, the "imposter syndrome" that makes Adam expect those around him to call his bluff at any time.[57] Expressively, psychologically, and otherwise, most of these are typical of postmodernism—of an unsparingly allusive, ironic, self-ironic, and playful poetics of ambiguity grounded in a weak ontology. A stylistic operator of the latter, Lerner's obsessional "or" is a signifier of deferred meaning and presence. Under its thumb, neither what is being said nor being itself can be self-present because it is undermined, in all senses, by the alternatives in the wings. It can only act "as if" it was present, presented as it is by a deictics that, no matter how referentially alluring it may sound, hardly makes good on the promises of its *als ob* ontology. For example, when Isabel comforts Adam after the incident his poem evokes, "[s]he began to say something either about the moon, the effects of the moon on the water, or was using the full moon to excuse Miguel or the evening's general drama ... Then she might have described swimming in the lake as a child, or said that lakes reminded her of being a child, or asked me if I'd enjoyed swimming as a child, or said that what she'd said about the moon was childish" (13–14). Just a bit later, when Isabel resumes talking, Adam "heard ... a list of things [he] thought were books or songs, hard times or hard weather, epoch, uncle, change, an analogy involving summer, something about buying and/or crashing a red car" (14). The litanies of proposed yet immediately disputed or retracted possibilities make up a toxic syntax whose self-canceling patterns pepper the novel with volleys of "or," "and/ or," "maybe," "whatever that meant" (15), "although that's not even close" (16), "but that's not really right" (41), and their disjunctive, concessive, and outright negative brethren, sabotaging sentences just formulated and communication and representation broadly, over and over (23, 24, 25, 26, 29–30, 37, 136, 49, 67, 96, 109, 134, 139, 143, 153, 157, 163, 178, etc.). Once more, Adam's wobbly Spanish is not the issue. Even his American memories become hypothetical, and he doubts their accuracy once recollection gets on the "or"'s claim-cum-disclaimer narrative teeter-totter ("Love for Topeka . . . the finger lost to snapping turtle or firework . . . Then for Providence . . . emerging from a tunnel or sleep into New York" [16]).

Arturo's translation need not be "accurate." In effect, its fidelity to the original—just another shot at referentiality—is beside the point. The point is the *form* the Spanish fashions by disengaging the English original and the American originator from the initial referents, imitated models, and collage; the point, compellingly argued by Grossman, is, in his words, the "world making" and the "person making" the American poem's stolen, deficient, and otherwise "impossible"[58] form both holds in abeyance and makes possible "negatively" in its Spanish avatar. Yet the poem's English form is not irremediably "bad" either, or, again, its badness, its second-hand effulgence and, relatedly, Adam's "imposture" are not what matters here. According to Adam himself, his poems are not so much deformed by literary flaws and thefts as they are "in an important sense unformed" (39). In the linguistic trans-formations performed by Arturo, however, their "pure potentiality, [one] awaiting articulation," gains a new ontological intensity and semantic fluidity (39). "Translation," Adam hopes, "would further keep my poems in contact with the virtual, as everyone must wonder what Arturo or Spanish was incapable of carrying over from the English, and so their failure, their negative power, was assured" (39).

But Arturo's work does more than that. Unlike Adam's, Arturo's "failure" reaches *and sustains* a presencing intensity. The translation from jejune to authentic and from poseur to presence requires just that—the labor of translation. In this regard, Adam and, in a way, Lerner as well are translated into presence, or "born translated," to quote Rebecca L. Walkowitz, with the proviso that translation is here a "matter of form," as Walkowitz also specifies in her analysis of *Atocha*.[59] More precisely, the presence founded in Arturo's translation is a function of that which begins as dysfunctional form, a precipitate of that form or a formation in the strongest sense of the term because, observes Adam, the Spanish translation and, through it, the author of the original also are effects of—and essentially are—forms "constellated" by other forms or objects. Where the transactional languages of commerce and high-school debate "spread you" as in *The Topeka School*,[60] the translational language of object constellations in Arturo's version work to gather together, to *compose* a presence.[61]

Latourian compositions and the poet- and world-making "arrangements" they produce are here the ultimate task of the translator. Whether Arturo knows it or not, he is a compositionist. His Spanish composes Adam's poem, Adam himself, and their world, taking them not only beyond the repetitive, the internet downloads, the trite, and other cheap rewards of reference but also past *via negativa* itself, into a positive negativity, if you will, where what has been "negated" and cleared out allows for a more affirming dynamic. The clearing—the *Lichtung*—requires a de-deictic travail that disarticulates the American poem, increasing its elasticity and stretching it out. Arturo softens the original's "referents," relaxing, displacing, and spacing them out to free up room where, as we saw in *The Hatred of Poetry*, readers "can forge and renew their sense of possibility and interconnectedness."[62] In a way, he further "unforms" Adam's poem but only to reshape both text and author into a form where potential meaning becomes actual and the heretofore imitative, absent meaning maker, present. Instead of going down the rabbit hole of references to the "meta" world beyond what forms and presents itself in translation, Arturo assembles that world through his own literal and metaphorical virgules. These are the assembly lines of presence; disassembling the deictics that "pins down" the original and locks it into the delusory aboutness mode in which poetic form, author, and world absent themselves, they make the poem its "most available context" and fit it out for the assembling of presence.[63] What blocks this process in Tomás's writing and consequently also in Adam's reading or translation of it is the syntactically disjunctive and ontologically disjoining play of "or." By contrast, Arturo's work operates conjunctively. Its translational thrust is not transactional, for it does not exchange words for worlds, but com-positional. Arturo juxtaposes things. He puts them side by side and together, constellating them into the intransitive presence that affords their co-presence in bigger constellations.

Arturo accomplishes all this because there is an element of translation, an incipiently compositional move back and forth across the space that, as pointed out earlier, starts opening up in Adam's writing itself. This interval separates different "postures," situations, and objects; the translator crosses it in all directions, and the result is a spiderweb of correlations. "All you are describing," Teresa, the novel's occasional *raisonneur*, tells Adam in Spanish, "is the personality of a translator. From apartment to protest, from English to Spanish'" (142). Notably, what Adam has just "described" in English with reference to her "style" and following an extensive exchange in Spanish is a self-description. He too shuttles "between media" (142), idioms, his rented place and rallies, private and political, present and past, presence and absence, and so forth. When Teresa compares him to David Locke, the impersonator Jack Nicholson plays in Michelangelo Antonioni's 1975 *The Passenger*, Adam "sa[ys] in [his] head," although he has not seen the movie, that "she was simply describing the personality of a translator" (152), and he is right. Antonioni's passenger, Adam's (*I . . . / imagined I was / A passenger that could see me / Looking up* [40]), Adam, and Lerner too ultimately are all the same, self-distant and builders of bridges across distances, com-posers of selves, things, and worlds. Adam even imagines himself "translat[ing] Teresa's poems into English" (143) and, also "in his head," does translate them along with her casual Spanish. Moreover, the translation is no different in terms of both procedure and outcomes from Arturo's. As Teresa's poetry and language overall acquire presencing form and accede to objecthood in Adam's mind, they "bec[o]me a repository for whatever meaning [Adam] assign[s] to it" (144). The "whatever" notwithstanding, this meaning is not arbitrary; it is made the same way Adam and Lerner make sense of Ashbery's poetry and Arturo of Adam's, viz., not deictically, by reference to a place, person, incident, feeling, politics, or "any particular thing,"[64] but com-positionally, by assembling these objects, sometimes individually and other times by joining them up in more complex assemblages. For, once the object is posed in translation and its opaque form, ontologically "charged," is intransitively, epideictically "there," for itself, rather than deictically transcended toward a circumstance, goal, function, meaning, or use, further compositions may occur or, to be more exact, may be revealed prismatically, as the object's surging energies wash over other objects and larger objectual conglomerates come into focus.[65] "It was," Adam himself explains,

as if she said: Think about the necklace. Think about the making of the necklace. About Isabel's brother notebook ... Imagine her brother writing. Think of the little scrap of paper Teresa tore from her novel and put into your notebook. Think of the hash transported inside one body as a solid and expelled and sold and then drawn into your body as vapor and gas. Think of the bombers purchasing the backpacks. *Always think of the objects.* Think of the necklaces and novels and bodies torn apart by the blast. Think of the making of the necklaces and the novels and the bodies and Isabel's brother in the crushed red car. But then think of a poster of Michael Jordan on the wall of Isabel's brother's room while he wrote the years down in the notebook. Where is that poster now. And think of the field opposite the telephone pole her brother wrapped the car around ... You can stay there for as long as you want ... Or you can enter the poster with the sea of cameras flashing as Michael Jordan jumps and you can leave the arena as the crowd is roaring and walk into the Chicago of the recent past where novels are being written and necklaces are being made and gases are being inhaled and dates are being memorized by brains and brains destroyed in crashes. You can see all of this from a great height and zoom out until it is no longer visible or you can zoom in on the writing hand or the face of the dead, zoom until it's no longer a face. Or you can click on something and drag it. You can adjust the color or you can make it black and white. You can view any object from any angle or multiple angles simultaneously or you can shut your eyes and listen to the crowd in the arena or the sirens slowly approaching the red car or the sound of the pen writing down the years as silver is hammered and shaped. (144–5; emphasis mine)

The specious, "click-and-drag" mimesis poised to photoshop the world instead of making it ends up taking a back seat to an objectual poetics that imbues Adam's writing with a thingness itself literally drawn to other things, so much so that the poem's language and the poet with it become the flowing movement ("without transition") to and between objects, an ability to "distribute [one]self among" them and capture their "shifting configuration" by acknowledging their being-there rather than claiming anything about them ("saying yes to everything, affirming nothing" [146]). From the paltry collage of internet junk, pilfered stories, and botched translations to this superior "configuration" of objects: fledgling in Adam, more advanced in Arturo, and brought to fruition in Lerner, this is the process that culminates in the composition of the contemporary. None of them define contemporaneity for they make no explicit claims about it; they act it out formally. They show, that is, how objects assemble it by entering into a certain combination. A material and cultural signature of our time, this historically unique arrangement is the contemporary, Adam's and ours, or at least one of its faces. Objects "form" this contemporary, as "any contingent" knickknacks "form" Adam (41) himself, and as writers, Adam and his author trace this formation.

Adam's poetry, Arturo's translation of it, and ultimately *Atocha* itself inhere in this tracing, in this "object-thinking" that leads from one object to another no matter where and what they are. The object system—the system of the contemporary—is thus reconstituted "democratically," beginning with the jewelry Adam bought for Isabel. The picture that takes shape gradually, item by item, is the contemporary world's "exploded view," to recall Bogost's term. The objects in this *mise en abyme* image are among the novel's main components, and they are spread across *Atocha*. Here, they cluster together as in the assembly diagram that comes with Bogost's IKEA coffee table. What the picture represents, however, is neither hypothetical ("as if [Teresa] said" all this [144]) nor random collage of items. We are not dealing with an inert scheme. There is a logic of sorts to it, and the configuration of things is actual too because the featured objects already have ontological standing inside and outside the book. The plot has connected all these objectual dots, breathing story life into them, but their lives are more than fictional. The necklace, Isabel, Isabel's brother, and his fatal car wreck and notebook may live exclusively "inside" Lerner's imagination, but Adam—himself within the plot's storyworld—keeps on doing the plot's connecting work and splices *Atocha*'s narrative insides (Adam's story) and the outside story (post-September 2011 history) together by practically adding 2004 to the historically memorable years jotted down in the notebook—"*1933, 1066,*

312 . . . 1936, 1492, 800, 1776" (178–9). This might look like an ahistorical "daisy chain" to Bogost, but there is more than randomness to it.[66] Year of the "Spanish 9/11," 2004 marks the transition "without transition" Adam effectuates, *in* the novel, to the Atocha bombers' backpacks. With them, object-thinking pivots from his story to history, *in* which, with yet another turn of the ontological screw, novels and their diegetic necklaces are being made but also backpacks, and brains are crushed in imaginary and documented, individual and collective disasters. This is, with a nod to Maurice Blanchot, Lerner's "writing of the disaster"—this is how Adam's diagram articulates the catastrophic nature of the contemporary or, better still, *contemporaneity itself as crisis*, as permanence, endless nowness of disaster.[67] In correlating the crashed red car, the body in it, and their "particular" (144) novelistic circumstances, on one hand, and the train cars and bodies ripped apart by the Atocha explosions, on the other, the passage also reenacts the "intersections" (178) of the private and the public and especially of the literary imagination and sociality on a planet on which there are fewer and fewer locations where one can sit out its calamities.

Linked up into material "ontographies," as "tiny ontology" might call them, objects "configure" the contemporary in *Atocha*. Part and parcel of this effort is also a stylistically ironic but thoughtful problematization of fiction's own place in the resulting "configuration." If it is to hold ontologically, to *be* and be received as such, literature would have to be relevant as literary form, historically and politically; it would have to tell, or rather *show* us, besides how our contemporary is made, how this storytelling might make a difference in the contemporary world. Literature, the "personal" (132) out of which it arises, and the contemporary as a figment of this private universe, on one side; on the other, the "historical" (132), the political, and possibly commitment to the common good: through Adam, Lerner hints that on either side, one finds oneself on the same side of the Möbius band of contemporaneity. The protagonist and his author are both there, "born between mirrors" (181) and ever "one-sided" in a contemporary funhouse where this and that side, "in here" and "out there," self and other, the individual body and the body politic, and poetry and the world reflect each other, enmesh, convert into one another, and make and remake each other more than ever. Adam becomes increasingly aware of their coming together.

Animating the beautiful chapbook eventually published by Arturo, this awareness is basically what Adam's Madrid residence yields. As to the fellowship "project," this has been a nonstarter all along; opposite to object-thinking, its positivist mode would have just added to existing poetic claims "about" the Spanish Civil War. In the "last phase of [his] research" (178), however, Adam fully takes in the interlocking of the "invironment" and the environment in the same, "outsideless" ecosystem: his body before van der Weyden's painting and "disappearing" fireflies and "confused" bats and trees ("blooming early"); the museum visitor high on "hash and caffeine" and the "warming" planet; the Prado trip and the Iraq invasion and its "unmanned drones"; the fragility of art (canvases are not to be touched) and the extinction of animal species ("[b]ees were disappearing" too); poetry writing and "rising" seas ominously "closing over future readers" (178)—a horizontal correspondent of old Spanish cities' "braided temporalities" (92), these concatenations compose the contemporary world ecosystem and, in so doing, work into an asymmetric, self-conflicted ("exacerbating contradictions" [181]), yet distinct form the "now" Adam's Spanish friends just make confident, deictically specific pronouncements about (140). Not unexpectedly, Adam declines to do the same on the "literature now" panel, another metapoietic loop in *Atocha* (161). He does not join in the "excitement of periodization" (140), in the "about" rhetoric of neat timelines, sexy catchphrases, and other "concept[ual] exaggeration[s]" (174), although he is interested in the "period" as such, in the structure of now (140). Only, he does not approach it rhetorically but poietically, as a matter of poiesis. He abhors telling people about the "new *now*" (174). Instead, once more, he "shows" it by performing it as a poet, by com-posing it. For a "post" *is* "being formed" after September 11, 2001 (140), and March 11, 2004, climate change, and Madrid's African migrants, together, do form it. But all Adam can do is dramatize this formation in a poetic praxis that unleashes the "virtual possibilities" of language (40.)

As we have seen, the actualization of the virtual is seldom entirely successful or complete in the actual poem. The realization of literature's potential, whether it is Adam's poem, Adam's diagram, or Lerner's book, is usually attempted by its users, principally critics, readers, and translators. The materialization of the "future present" potentially embedded in literature—the full, meaningful form of the contemporary as well as the more encouraging present both absent and "negatively" there, implied by its own absence from the object assemblage—largely hinges on that literature's future presentations such as Arturo's translation.[68] Literary heavyweights like Ashbery and Leo Tolstoy are no exceptions, as flat translations and readings intensify them too into a new presence, a hyperpresence that both measures a new time and occasions this time's "experience." This experience is the portal to a future-heavy present whose Janus-faced ontology weaves together fictionality and actuality, what can be and in fact comes into being in the flat mode of literary objecthood and what is not yet out there, in the world of suicide bombings and pollution. Leafing through *The Kreutzer Sonata* on the train to Granada, the city of "braided temporalities," Adam senses that "every sentence, regardless of its subject, became mimetic of the action of the train, and the train mimetic of the sentence" (89). Thus, the reader feels "suddenly coeval with its syntax," and "[b]ecause the sentences of Tolstoy, or rather Constance Garnett's translations of Tolstoy, were in perfect harmony with the motion of the Talgo [train], real time and the time of prose began to merge" (89). Reading the *Sonata*, then, *"instead of removing me from the world intensified my experience of the present"* (89; emphasis mine). "[T]his strange experience of reading," at once the experience of reading and of the clock time in which reading unfolds, gives him, Adam reflects, "a sense of harmony between the rhythms of a reproduction and the real, their structural identity, so that the subject of the sentence was," with a quote from "Clepsydra," "precisely the time of its being furthered" (90).

This "furthering" of poetry and language time into their wider contemporary ecosystem ("the real") is also what Adam "value[s]" in Ashbery. The burgeoning presence, *"the little / That was present,"* as Lerner excerpts from "Clepsydra" one more time, fills out and blooms into a more capacious present, which the text can no longer "contain," hold inside itself, once its deictics melts down and the poem itself starts "flowing" in Adam's reading (90). As a reader, Adam experiences this fluidity, "the texture of time as it passed, a shadow train, life's white machine" (90), and Arturo helps Adam's audience experience it too, simultaneously within and without the poem. This slithering, unfettered present that poetic language and language in general provide for but "can't contain," as Adam suggests here and Lerner specifies in *The Hatred of Poetry*, is the "virtual," a present pregnant with "possibility."[69] Remarkably, this possibility, what the now is not but, from inside Adam's poem and Lerner's novel, the objectual system of contemporaneity implies and calls for, is both literary and factual, current and futural. In effect, it integrates these modes ontologically.

Briming over the deictic edges of the poetic container, this present of possibility in which reading and the train pass in the same "rhythm," in the same time, and end up "braiding" fictional and empirical temporalities into one, also seeps into the "real" present, liquefying it by injecting it with the possible and a possible future different from the actual present—with the shadow of a contemporaneity to come. Elaborating on the "life's white machine" phrase, which Lerner borrows from Ashbery and uses repeatedly in *Atocha* (16, 19, 179, etc.), the novelist makes a point to reproduce a fragment from the Gertrude Stein review in which Ashbery, indirectly explaining the expression, says that literary time-making activates a temporal poiesis and, with it, possibilities beyond literature. "The poem," Lerner quotes Ashbery, "is a hymn to possibility: a celebration of the fact that the world exists, that things can happen."[70] Adam cannot imagine "poems as machines that could make things happen," yet he does not want to live in "a world without even the terrible excuses for poems that kept faith with the virtual possibilities of the medium" either (44). One more time flanked by parallel mirrors, Lerner's hero positions himself, like his author, on the middle ground of absolute, "intransitive," and non-declarative making where things themselves concatenate into a certain form to make things happen.

bees, parrot, trains: Murder by Numbers and "the Foulest of Crimes" in *The Final Solution*

Every last one of them, semaphore, lamp code, Marconi . . .

—Arthur Conan Doyle, "His Last Bow:
The War Service of Sherlock Holmes"

At last, however, he was forced to concede that there was nothing to be found. When he rose unsteadily to his feet, the throbbing of his joints was like a universal sentiment of loss, the action on his bones of certain things' implacable resistance, once lost, to ever being found . . . it was the insoluble problems that reflected the true nature of things.

—Michael Chabon, *The Final Solution*

He was, by irremediable nature, a man who looked at things . . .

—Michael Chabon, *The Final Solution*

[S]he visualized math problems [a]s a series of broken objects needing rearrangements into a more pleasing whole.

—Jonathan Lethem, *The Arrest*

Critics who have read Michael Chabon as postmodern have attended to his unabashedly demotic intertextuality at length, and for good reason. The insatiable appetite for popular material such as comics, graphic novels, fairy tales, fantasy, young-adult literature, and mystery is unmistakable throughout his oeuvre, from his 1988 debut with *The Mysteries of Pittsburgh* to the 2001 Pulitzer Prize winner *The Amazing Adventures of Kavalier & Clay* (2000) and the 2007 *als ob* hard-boiled *The Yiddish Policemen's Union*. Originally published in slightly different form in a 2003 issue of *The Paris Review*, the 2004 novella *The Final Solution: A Story of Detection* is one place in Chabon that queries, however, the postmodern reading, prompting us to ask ourselves exactly what purpose the incorporation of literary popular culture, particularly detective fiction, serves in a work viewed by many as central to the canon of twenty-first-century U.S. Holocaust literature.

To be sure, the novella's engagement with the mystery genre is quite extensive. *The Final Solution* does not simply mine this literary tradition for ploys and situations. It is, one might argue, a detective story in its own right. Moreover, to write it, the author rewrites at least two Sherlock Holmes pieces by Arthur Conan Doyle. Significantly, Doyle "was the first writer [Chabon] fell in love with," and "the first story [the American] ever wrote was" also "a Sherlock Holmes story . . . a kind of pastiche . . . inspired by the then-new example of *The Seven-Per-Cent Solution* by Nicholas Meyer."[71]

The Final Solution is not a pastiche but an elaborate rewrite replete with strategically deployed clues and narrative parallels and allusions to Meyer's 1974 pseudo-apocryphal novel *The Seven-Per-Cent Solution: Being a Reprint from the Reminiscences of John H. Watson, M.D.* and especially to Doyle's short stories "The Final Problem" (1893) and "His Last Bow: The War Service of Sherlock Holmes" (1917).

The novella would only make then for a postmodern addition to the "post-Doyle Sherlockian corpus"[72] were it not for the presencing labor of Chabon's Doylean retellings. This labor, and what renarrativization ends up accomplishing in *The Final Solution*, consists in a two-pronged narrative that acknowledges the unspeakable and unnarratable horror of the Nazi genocide but reaches beyond that which postmodern literature and theory judge impossible to recount, let alone retrieve, and *evokes* it in the spirit of the italicized verb's etymology, that is, recalls and voices into presence those murderously silenced in World War II's concentration camps. *The Final Solution* stages the by-now familiar dialectic of linguistic form that does not "deliver" and yet enables a certain presentation. As in Lerner, this form is uncommonly repetitive and quotational language that frustrates reference, communication, disclosure, and interpretation but, in its very resistance to being transcended toward a determinate meaning, reality, cause, or truth, and thus to being about something easily quantifiable and recognizable, connects readers with an entity of whose existence the characters are unaware.

This connection is Chabon's post-postmodern bid in *The Final Solution*. Admittedly, on one level of the novella, we do run into the unpresentable, into the postmodern fascination with the unrepresentable sublime, including the indescribable monstrosity of the *Endlösung*, National Socialism's "final solution" to the "Jewish problem." On another level, though, Chabon has us experience the presencing payoffs of the failure to solve, if not the problem Jews allegedly posed to Germany and other European nation-states according to one of modernity's most toxic nationalist doxas, then the case whose oddity brings a misanthropic and beekeeping detective, presumably Holmes, out of retirement, à la Doyle's "post-Reichenbach" stories.[73] This is another way of saying, at odds with most critics, that Chabon's Holmes is not completely unsuccessful. For one thing, he puzzles out a portion of the case. For another, and more importantly still, how *he* fails to handle the rest is instructive in and of itself as well as to readers, helping *them* crack the case and, more broadly, respond to the text. While his failing "style"—what his thoughts are, and what we possibly learn as the detective comes up short—does not spell out the whole solution to the uniquely complex problem at hand, it is the first step toward an understanding to which he does not seem to have actual access.[74]

The part of the case that defies his comprehension—and pretty much anybody's, although the Allies knew about Hitler's death factories as early as December 1942—has to do with the Holocaust and can be defined as the collective, historical, or "deeper" mystery of *The Final Solution*.[75] As to the "superficial" one, it is, as mentioned, positively within Holmes's grasp.[76] This mystery is the novella's individual, typically crime-fiction enigma and involves the July 1944 murder of one Richard Shane and the disappearance of Bruno, the gray parrot of Linus Steinman, a Jewish-German boy who probably arrived in Britain with a *Kindertransport* and is living with the Panicker family in a small town not far from London. Linus is, the police think, "incapable of speech" (25), but "[t]he density of his silence suggested" to Holmes "something more than unwillingness to speak" (6). It turns out, Linus was traumatized by the separation from his parents under extraordinary circumstances. His language disorder and what his self-expressive rudiments leave unspoken remain mysterious up until the story's closing scene and tie into the unspeakable mystery the reader, rather than Holmes, elucidates at that point. Bruno, on the other hand, is a credit to his species and therefore "notoriously prolix" (2). Most peculiar among his linguistic feats are, besides reciting Goethe, singing in a woman's voice and rattling off numbers, which undercover British intelligence officers such as Shane, Shane's murderer, Herman Kalb, and others assume to designate British Navy codes or Swiss bank accounts. Holmes "doubt[s] very much," however, as he confesses at the end of the novella, "if we shall ever learn what significance, if any, those numbers may hold" (129). But, adds Chabon, this was not "a familiar or comfortable admission for the old man to make" (129). We know, of course, from Doyle's Holmes corpus, and the American writer duly reminds us, that "[t]he application of creative intelligence to a problem, the finding of a solution at once dogged, elegant, and wild, ... had always seemed to [Holmes] to be the essential business of human being—the discovery of sense and causality amid the false leads, the noise, the trackless brambles of life" (129–31). At the same time, Holmes

> had always been haunted ... by the knowledge that there were men, lunatic cryptographers, mad detectives, who squandered their brilliance and sanity in decoding and interpreting the messages in cloud formations, in the letters of the Bible recombined, in the spots on butterflies' wings. One might, perhaps, conclude from the existence of such men that meaning dwelled solely in the mind of the analyst. That it was the insoluble problems—the false leads and the cold cases—that reflected *the true nature of things*. That all the apparent significance and pattern had no more intrinsic sense than the chatter of an African gray parrot. One might so conclude; really, he thought, one might. (131; emphasis mine)

One might indeed, but as the emphatic repetitions hint, that does not mean that this is necessarily Holmes's conclusion even though he will never find out what the numbers signify. In any case, he spots easily and derides what one might dub "the cryptographer's fallacy." This is an extreme variety of the hermeneutics of suspicion for which objects are stand-ins, disguises, and giveaways for something out of view and superior and external to them. In his old age, Holmes has become more skeptical about the analytical rewards of "suspicious" decoding and about interpretive reason largely. "Drained [of] meaning," "the world around him" now reads like "a page of alien text" (84). Tellingly, most references in *The Final Solution* to loss (a "universal sentiment" [84]), "uselessness" (84), lack, blank, absence, error, defeat, meaninglessness, and the overall failure to locate, identify, explain, and the like surround or are made by Holmes, ironically the story's most successful investigator. What triggers them is a cardinal feature of objecthood, namely, existential "perseverance," a "thing mood" and ontological mode akin to the Spinozian insistence by virtue of which what is tends to keep its so-being state in spite of outside pressures to change, yield to an influence, or carry out a task. For the detective, this obduracy translates into "things' implacable resistance once lost, to ever being found" (84), whether literally, such as the physical recovery of something missing, or cognitively, as in the episode where Holmes, "c[o]m[ing] into the [vicarage] garden,"

> saw a number of familiar objects and entities set about on an expanse of green as if arranged to a desired effect or inferable purpose, like counters or chessmen in some kingly recreation. Regarding them the old man experienced a moment of vertiginous horror during which he could neither reckon their number nor recall their names or purposes. He felt— with all his body, as one felt the force of gravity or inertia—the inevitability of his failure. The conquest of his mind by age was not a mere blunting or slowing down but an erasure, as of a desert capital by a drifting millennium of sand. Time had bleached away the ornate pattern of his intellect, leaving a blank white scrap. (34–5)

Passages like this have been cited as evidence that Holmes's "rational powers" are dwindling.[77] True, the former detective is no longer at the top of his game. And let us not forget that he fails to decipher the deeper mystery of *The Final Solution*. But his failure is partial, as we will see momentarily. Besides, if this mystery is "beyond comprehension," as it surely is, this has to do more with the limits of Western rationality than with Holmes's mental faculties.[78] In any event, he proves wrong the likes of Constable Quaint, who thinks Holmes is "strictly non compos [mentis]" (25). Chabon's Holmes may not be as clearheaded, as *compos* as Doyle's, but he is still the consummate compositionist who pieces things together, unriddling the whodunit puzzle, if nothing else, and thus living up to the "tales, the legends, the wild, famous leaps of induction pulled off by the old man in his heydays, assassins inferred from cigar ash, horse thieves from the absence of a watchdog's bark" (25). In com-posing surrounding objects and by the same token the solution to the Bruno–Shane case, Holmes does not quite maneuver objects into revelatory associations; rather, he follows doggedly those objects' lead. Those things are and insist on remaining there, already organized in "unlikely groupings of facts" (2) as in the garden "arrangement." He only "extrapolate[es]" (2) from those combinations. His challenge, and his skill as well, lies in riding the energy waves rolling from one item to another, in picking up on those meaning-laden outbursts and letting himself be carried by them across the object maze. Where Inspector Bellows "could not find the way to a mute German boy from a missing parrot and a corpse named Shane with a ventilated skull" (25–6), Holmes does.

For Doyle fans, this is hardly surprising. More noteworthy perhaps is Holmes's modus operandi. This is grounded in an investigating philosophy thinkers such as Jacques Derrida and Jacques Lacan, and before them writers like Poe, have variously dwelled on, and which basically postulates that the culprit, the motive, the truth, and suchlike are not transcendent signifieds taking cover behind forensic odds and ends but parts of the object web, pieces of a flat puzzle that hide in plain sight. As such, they already present themselves to the searching eye; they *are there* or, to reiterate, *here*. In this respect too, the mystery Holmes solves is superficial or, better yet, *surficial*, and as we will note, this is also key to solving the other mystery of *The Final Solution*. What he does is surf the objectual network, treading and acknowledging the opaque yet revealing surface of its hereness instead of looking through or past it in search of a depth, a beyond, and so forth. With him, investigation—flat detection, if you will—takes a gradually clarifying, sliding movement over the latticework of objects rather than their transcending. As in *Atocha*, those objects are both linguistic and non-linguistic, and they all work together to com-pose the presence of that which has been absent. The com-position is no hocus-pocus. Granted, it is evocative, and, on this account, narrative in nature. But its material protocol—the object assembly involved—should not be underestimated. The presencing evocation begins, also as in Lerner, with the surge into hyperpresence of language such as lyrics, tunes, words, and numbers, which suddenly attract attention to themselves, to their poetic and melodic form, before and as a way of conjuring up something else, an entity previously not there.

Would it be too much, then, to describe Holmes's detective flair as aesthetic, that is, as a knack for this form, for the objecthood of language? I do not think so. After all, Holmes is keen on the "elegance" of his solutions (129) or, as a character of Lethem's 2020 novel *The Arrest* intimates, on the "more pleasing whole" into which objects "need" to be "rearranged" so that we find the solution to the "problem" they pose.[79] Furthermore, it would not be farfetched to suggest that, just as the "aplomb" with which Holmes sniffs around his yard for a cardboard scrap is "canine" (83), his overall aesthetic approach to sleuth-work is bee inspired. As Doyle's readers know, the protagonist of "His Last Bow" and of some post-Doyle Holmes narratives, *The Final Solution* included, is a published expert on apiculture.[80] But beekeeping is for Chabon's Holmes first and foremost a practice of "animal pleasur[e]"; not for "profit" (74–5), this pastime is worth pursuing in and of itself, as "form," for its inherent qualities. Form is eminently apparent in the linguistic behavior of bees. They "speak" to Holmes, and he listens carefully for they clue him up on the formal being of language. "The bees," we learn in a revealing passage,

> speak to [Holmes], after a fashion. The featureless drone, the sonic blank that others heard was to him a shifting narrative, rich, inflected, variable, and distinct as the separate stones of a featureless gray shingle, and he moved along the sound, tending to his hives like a beachcomber, stooped and marveling. *It meant nothing, of course—he wasn't as batty as that— but this did not imply, not at all, that the song had no meaning.* It was the song of a city, a city as far from London as London was from heaven or Rangoon, a city in which all did precisely what they were supposed to do, in the way that had been prescribed by their most remote and venerable ancestors. A city in which gems, gold ingots, letters of credit, or secret naval plans were never stolen, in which long-lost second sons and ne'er-do-well first husbands did not turn from the Wawoora Valley or the Rand with some clever backwoods trick for scaring an old moneybags out of his wits. No stabbings, garrotings, beatings, shootings; almost no violence at all, apart from the occasional regicide. All of the death in the city of the bees had been scheduled, provided for, tens of millions of years ago; each death as it occurred was translated, efficiently and immediately, into more life for the hive. (63–4; emphasis added)

True, Holmes has been meddling, sometimes "regicidally," in the hive's affairs—"Number 4 must be re-queened" (24), he tells Bellows out of the blue—and he has done so in the name of the same unquestioned anthropocentric prerogatives at work in the exploitative-instrumental rationality of which otherwise he has grown wary.[81] Nonetheless, the detective acknowledges the formal sovereignty of insect language, the hum's self-indexing vibrancy. Hivespeak, Holmes muses, is always and solely about the hive. It is the city of the bees talking to itself and about its being a hive and what it needs to do to ensure its welfare. Whatever is said or sung in this tongue is instantly bioperformative, life-sustaining. It concomitantly conveys and does something inside and for a zoosemiotic system in which communication affords a mode of existence. In this sense, bee talk necessarily points to itself, and this pointing, this self-presentation, is its meaning. If the colony's language "means nothing," that is because it does not reference anything outside itself, in the city and world of humans. Aside from that, what bees say is hardly meaningless, though. Having built the hive and synonymous to its upkeep, their idiom has become its own context. One's attempt to understand the former by stepping outside the latter is therefore foredoomed, bringing one back to the buzz itself, which thus presents itself as both "just" buzz and meaningful *within its own frame of reference.*

This presentation—the hum itself—is a speech act as well as a live theory of "entomolinguistic" meaning. Whether Holmes gets all the theory part or not, he applies it, as the fragment shows, to the other nonhuman language spoken in *The Final Solution*, Bruno's. The bird and the bees have in common more than their "enslaved" condition, past or present.[82] Much like the hive's chat is not about London's villains and their designs, the parrot's numbers, Holmes decides, do not stand for naval code, nor do they "represent numbered Swiss Bank accounts," as Kalb himself "has been able to determine" (129). Holmes is not a batty cryptographer, and neither is his prototype, who, impersonating a spy in "His Last Bow," amuses himself by selling his German employer bogus code ("semaphore, lamp code, Marconi") as "the real goods."[83] There is a suggestion in Doyle's story that all those digits are what they are and nothing else—that *numbers are numbers,* and consequently, their reality is exclusively digital. Similarly, as I have noted, Chabon's detective appears to conclude by "doubting" (129) that the numeric "chatter of an African gray parrot . . . ha[s] . . . intrinsic sense" (131), viz., that Bruno's numbers carry any meaning *by being no more than numbers.* But then he fudges his conclusion ("One might so conclude; really, he thought, one might" [131]), which hardly encourages us to share it. Most likely, Holmes's waffling has the opposite effect on the reader who, right after Holmes all but retracts his initial position, once again witnesses Bruno's loquacity. "At that moment," Chabon writes,

> the ground rumbled faintly, and in the distance, growing nearer, there was the cry of iron wheels against iron rails. A train was passing through the station, a freight, a military transport, its cars painted dull gray-green, carrying shells and coffins to stock the busy depots of the European war. The boy looked up as it tottered past, slowing but coming to a stop. He watched the cars, his eyes flicking from left to right as if reading them go by.
>
> "*Sieben zwei eins vier drei,*" the boy whispered, with the slightest hint of a lisp. "*Sieben acht vier vier fünf.*"
>
> Then the parrot, startled perhaps by the clamor of the passing train, flew up into the rafters of the station roof, where, in flawless mockery of the voice of a woman whom none of them would ever meet or see again, it began, very sweetly, to sing. (131)

These are *The Final Solution*'s last lines, but they do not mark a closure. Instead, they open Chabon's work up onto something or somebody, rather, a presence otherwise absent or, more accurately still, forever absenced by the *Endlösung.* This presence is the fulcrum of the novella's darker mystery, which the reader unravels by using his or her "Holocaust knowledge," and which the detective would have deciphered as well had he known what the reader knows.[84]

This is the defining mystery of modernity, more precisely of modern rationality, twice: first in a broad sense, as a mystery of reason and thus as a dare to ask ourselves how European modernity, which prides itself on its rational footing, could possibly have brought on the National Socialist "solution" and thereby the Shoah itself; and second but pertaining more closely to *The Final Solution*'s plot, as a mystery of numbers *qua* numbers, which pushes us to try and wrap our mind around the unthinkable and wonder what happens—what must have happened—if the parrot's sevens, threes, and fives are merely numbers and not bank accounts or "cypher keys" (68) of interest to the Kriegsmarine. These are twin enigmas because the former is the premise of the latter and effectively segues into it. As some post-Frankfurt School thinkers insist, Western reason shows its instrumental colors in the administrative rationality that sponsored the Third Reich's bureaucracy of census, registering, cataloguing, stocktaking, and tallying as it did the equally efficient apparatuses of classification, computation, and numbers-"management" of the extermination camps. At any rate, the Nazis, one of the most radical exchange regimes on record, had no trouble "rationalizing" *das jüdische Problem*, or, with a famous title, *Die Judenfrage*, by reducing it to a question of numbers and then reducing the figures themselves in the "number-crunching" slaughterhouses of Dachau and Treblinka.[85]

In his 1995 book *Homo Sacer: Sovereign Power and Bare Life*, Agamben famously expounds on the "bare life," or *zoē*, "into which the camp[s] . . . transformed [their] inhabitants."[86] The most radical change that took place in the *Lager*, though, was not the stripping down of *bíos*—an "individual or group['s] form or way of living"—to its quasi-larval barebones, but the suppression of life altogether.[87] Biopolitically speaking, the gas chambers sanctioned, however, a situation anteceding the killings done in them. Undertaken across a range of established and emerging technologies, life's obliteration began computationally, with the infamous IBM/Dehomag punch cards, the Nazi census, and related data gathering of the Reich's "racial informatics," went on with the tagging of train cars (*"[s]ieben zwei eins vier drei"*), and was all but complete when the Jews themselves were tagged with numbers sewn to their inmate uniforms or, at Auschwitz, tattooed on their bodies.[88] The machinic "numericizing" of human beings, their ghastly "proto-digitization," was inherently annihilating. Through it, *bíos* was annihilated too, downgraded absolutely, to nil—to zero, not just to *zoē*. After all, since counting was geared to counting out, to eliminating, all assigned numerals were practically multiples of zero, and as Holocaust survivors have confessed, this is exactly how they felt behind barbed wire: "dehumanized" and "effaced," reduced to their numbers and, in them, to nothing—to nothing *but* numbers.[89] Sociopolitically disabled and precarious as it may be, *la vita nuda* is still a form of presence, whereas the Nazi numbers rescinded life. "Registering" it out of presence regardless of what else they had been intended to accomplish, the serial numbers were markers of an absence.

On one hand, Bruno acts out this de-presencing. "Men, policemen in particular," Holmes reflects in a playfully anticipatory scene, "ten[d] to discount the capacity of animals to enact, often with considerable panache, the foulest of crimes and the most daring stunts" (33). The parrot certainly disproves those men, enacting, indeed, the foulest of crimes: the Shoah as murder by numbers. Thus, he helps us imagine the *un*imaginable. This seems to be, and up to a point is, Chabon's solution to the conundrum of the unrepresentable, particularly to the Shoah as an artist's problem. The logic behind this solution—let us call this logic postmodern—goes something like this: if the numbers do not represent any of those things they may be "reasonably" linked with, then what is left for them to represent, and what they do represent, is the unrepresentable itself. In other words, what the numbers index falls outside the purview of detective reason and Western instrumental rationality largely; the digits boggle the mind—any mind, whether it is cognizant of the Holocaust or not. But the mind's inability to come to grips with those numbers does not mean that, as a cybernetically assisted and bureaucratically implemented mechanics of destruction, they did not work within that mind's boundaries. They did, with odious efficiency, which is why the bird's numbers are "just numbers" in a deontologizing sense. Despite the pressure exerted on them by the police and other British apparatuses of the modern exchange regime, the numbers convert neither to secret funds stashed away in Switzerland nor to Royal Navy communications nor to anything else for that matter because, inconceivably enough, they voided their referent altogether. This annulling, this radical discounting of the counted, is the "intrinsic" (131) meaning of Bruno's tirades. Like bee talk, his numbers point to nothing outside them; unlike it, *there is* indeed nothing to point to, outside and inside them, and so they gesture to that very nothingness: not to bare life but to nonlife, life nullified by reduction to its numeric shell.

On the other hand—and this is where Chabon leaves the postmodern unrepresentable behind—Bruno's recital re-presences. Not unlike the reverse engineering of reference in Adam's poem, the parrot's verbosity also retraces number-becoming back to the numbered and, past it, to the individual life before its numeration out of existence. Again, there is no transcendence, no meaning-rich depth to Bruno's numbers. Because there is nothing to read in them, the inspectors cannot read them, and Holmes cannot either. What Holmes can do, and does, is read the numbers with the bee buzz, approaching parrot language as he would hivespeak. Thus, he intuits, rather than comprehending rationally, the referential vacantness of the numbers and therefore moves "laterally," step by step, to the other objects in the

Bruno–Shane network: Linus, the obscure, ("atrocious[ly]" [42]) misspelled, and palindromic English writing in which he communicates with those around him, and finally Bla[c]k/Kalb, the African gray's abductor and Shane's killer. Even so, Holmes solves only some of the case, for this network—his "latticework of inferences," as he calls it (61)—turns out to be incomplete. Nor does he have the "background information" that would allow him to see why and how one of these objects (Bruno) connects another (Linus) with a much bigger network. Because of that, he may ask the right questions—"What does Bruno know? . . . Whose numbers was he taught to repeat?" (61)—but is at a loss for answers. He identifies the "vital connection[s]" [61] between, and com-poses, the bees, the bird, the boy, and the numbers, but the obtaining juxtaposition is not fully explanatory because it is not large enough. The connection between the boy and the bird is evident to the old detective as is to other characters; the narrator spares no opportunity to pinpoint it. But Holmes does not seem to notice that the parrot is a "beloved object [that] the survivor [Linus] associates with the deceased [Linus's mother]."[90] Or, if Holmes notices it—when the parrot says "Mother," for instance—he has no way of knowing what to make of the association in the greater scheme of things. Likewise, he may have even included the passing train in this vaster object conglomerate, but he would have no inkling of *how* the train relates to the numbers or to Linus, or to Linus's mother, or more importantly, to all of them *together*. The reader— the "outside detective"—does. His or her cognitive edge over Holmes and other diegetic investigators stems, as noted, from what he or she knows about the *Lager* prisoners' identification numbers and "death trains." These are objects that exist in two world sets at once: both in Chabon's fictional *histoire* and in history; in the Bruno–Shane network as well as in what might be called the Shoah network; and in the "individual" and "collective" mysteries and pertaining knowledge systems.[91] Holmes cannot travel between these worlds. But the reader can, and this enables him or her to finish Holmes's job.

To do so, he or she uses relevant Holocaust information to com-pose the trains, the numbers, and "Mother" in a more comprehensively conjectural fashion that integrates them and the rest of the Bruno–Shane objectual configuration into the Shoah constellation of objects and, correspondingly, the detective story into history and its bigger truth. The linchpin of this operation is the parrot. If he is "arguably the story's chief protagonist,"[92] that is not because he lies at the center of the most heinous crime committed in the novella—obviously, he does not—but because he acts as the object hub or copula between the two networks. In this position, he helps the reader channel his or her Holocaust knowledge in the right direction and connect the dots that for Holmes remain disconnected or, as Bogost and Harman would remark, do not connect *through* him or for his investigative benefit.[93] The parrot's crooning of the mother's song in response to Linus's enumeration ties Nazi numerics to European Jews such as Linus's mother in a clarifying, cause-and-effect sequence in the book's closing paragraphs. There, as we have seen, Linus reacts to the British train by finally breaking his silence and whispering the identification digits of cattle cars such as those that must have taken his mother to her death (nobody "would ever meet or see her again" [131]). The bird recited such numbers at the beginning of the novella (5, 9), and because he did so "with the slightest hint of a lisp" (5), one can only deduce that he had heard them from Linus back in Germany. In the old country, he must have also listened to the boy's mother sing "very sweetly" (131), because in the last scene, in "flawless" yet innocent "mockery" (131), he imitates her singing and, for good measure, identifies the original singer by reenacting a previous episode in which he both refers to her ("Mother" [20]), as the boy would have and likely did, and sings in *her* voice.

I emphasize the pronoun to drive home a point made by Chabon himself when his narrator describes Bruno's "contralto" as "disturbingly human" (20). The bird re-voices the voice of Linus's mother in a supremely ventriloquizing performance that closes the gap between original and copy and human and nonhuman. Eerily lifelike, the bird's song is "evocative" etymologically, as suggested earlier. More than just reminding Linus of his musically gifted parent, the melodic e-vocation summons her forth, out of the silence, absence, and void to which the numbers sentenced her. As the bird calls out to the mother by singing her own aria in her own voice, the call and the response splice into an ontologizing feedback loop that vocalizes her into presence, in line with a host of philosophical traditions that set up voice as a venue of being and badge of identity (distinct "personality"). In the voice—his and hers at once—the slaughtered, the absolutely silenced, step into the open, and so the voice reveals that which the numbers by themselves cannot. This melodic revelation of life is the truth behind or, better still, prior to the numbers, before people's number-becoming in the Shoah. *The Final Solution* documents this truth's self-presentation aesthetically. In recycling crime fiction, the novella assembles the genre's clues into objectual arrangements that shed light both on historical truth and on a contemporaneity that is struggling to come to terms with it in the face of renewed attempts to sweep under the rug incontrovertible realities such as the murderous "digitization" of the human in Nazi Germany or deny their enduring resonance in the present.

TWO | Display

I was thinking about the secret lives that the objects around us have led, before we see them.

— Emily St. John Mandel, quoted in Angel Lashbrook,
"A Love Letter to the Modern World"

. . . in his present state of mind, all objects were beautiful.
— Emily St. John Mandel, *Station Eleven*

Societies move forward, historian Reinhart Koselleck observed, when they shake off the burden of the "exemplary" past.[1] It goes without saying, previous ages are not inherently something to emulate. They become so. More often than not, this happens as a community's cultural and narrative apparatuses rework its events, figures, individual things, and more complex material environments into a patrimony. "Patrimonialization," as Luc Boltanski and Arnaud Esquerre have called this operation, basically ascribes value to objects, determines them as valuable.[2]

I would stress, more than the two French critics have, that this value is both pecuniary and cultural, and further, that patrimonialization is complete when the objects, commodified to various degrees, have been also set up as exempla, as models to imitate. In this sense, "patrimonialization" and the birth of modern nations and modernity generally have gone hand in hand, hence our deep-running investment in patrimonial instruments, institutions, and sites such as archives and museums. To a significant extent, collectives come together in their collections, where, in charting the genealogies of our nationality, ethnicity, racial identity, and the like, objects arrange us into defining structures as much as we arrange them in showcases. When built patrimonially, and when patrimony is thought of along these lines, collections produce stories of "us" to be reproduced and carried on beyond the moment or period in which the collection is assembled or shown, road maps for futures whose élans are largely channeled by beaten paths. In this respect, the qualms about patrimonial preservation and curating are warranted, as are "new museology" and the critical scrutiny of the decontextualized, oversimplified, conveniently whitewashed, romanticized, and imperial pasts manufactured routinely in the world's museums, galleries, exhibition halls, and private collections.

Thus understood, the patrimonial is not the only possible logic of museality, however. The last decades have witnessed a pronounced shift away from the reproductive and the nostalgic to the productive, the environmentally sustainable, and the futural—from politically conservative collecting and displaying to museal praxis and discourses informed by "future-directed frameworks" such as those art critic Terry Smith identifies in Swiss curator Hans Ulrich Obrist's endeavors.[3] Jean Baudrillard speculated that collecting is a "pastime" that may not be about the past, for collectors "can indulge in the great game of birth and death."[4] Where, according to Boris Groys, the traditional type of exhibitions "illustrates" and, I would add, shores up and extends "already established narratives," a newer, bolder category sets out to institute a presence, and a story, without precedent, exteriority, or external rationale.[5] The former is patrimonial display properly speaking. It primarily "documents," in essence recreating what has been—it is "form redux," says Smith;[6] whether it surveys a cultural movement, moment, theme, or artist's output, it tends to be re-creative, to play back what has been and has been retained and narrated in a certain fashion. By comparison, the latter class is creative, and it is so twice. It both allows the curator to "express" himself or herself more and steers his or her creativity toward an actual future. Hewing closer to the spirit of installation, this is a heterogenous, Wagnerian *Gesamtkunstwerk* of sorts that makes something new, which has not been composed in this arrangement before and which, in a way, has never been at all. But exactly because that something, that novel form, neither re-presents past forms nor carries a "meaning outside of the project" itself, it opens up to the future.[7] "The present" may well be, as a despondent Groys opines, "the only thing that we have, all of us,"[8] but the unprecedented collection on view, replies Smith, has the potential to map still uncharted temporalities, to "curat[e] the future."[9] Even if this present is no more than an "extended 'Now' full of noises, a baffling cacophony in which we attempt to find our balance,"[10] as Douglas Rushkoff, Jean-Michel Rabaté, Lionel Ruffel, and others have described it, its scattered body can be assembled—can be collected and displayed—into configurations susceptible to help visualize not just the "world picture of contemporary art"[11] and of contemporaneity broadly but also that which is amorphously present in the picture or is not there at all and yet presents its possibility.

Not unlike the absent presence assiduously tackled by Lerner, this possibility, this ghostlike future—"our resource of silence," writes Rabaté—resonates in the echo chambers of twenty-first-century actual or fictional curating activities of the installation or "constellation" kind.[12] Curators are as interested in constellations as *Atocha*'s Adam and for the same reason: juxtaposed in such impromptu, seemingly arbitrary but revealingly defamiliarizing "adjacencies,"[13] objects may connect, and their connections may tell stories that break the exemplary mold of available surveys, teleologies, and rationales. "When you put two objects together," Latin American curator Mari Carmen Ramírez contends, "you're generating a dialogue between them, which creates another type of knowledge, an innovative understanding of the works and the physical and conceptual relationship between them that does not necessarily relate to established art historical narratives."[14] Not so much retrospective as prospective, the "other" knowledge Ramírez alludes to is a constellation effect; it is conveyed obliquely, formally, not in about mode, as objects, risen into presence in museal space, start whispering to each other.

Part two brings *Flat Aesthetics* within earshot of their causerie by turning to the curating scene in post-2000 U.S. prose. Such episodes abound in twenty-first-century novels. In Foer's 2005 *Extremely Loud and Incredibly Close*, for instance, one of Oskar Schell's neighbors has an apartment "filled with the stuff he'd collected during the wars of his life," and the meticulously catalogued, library-of-Babel-like collection is something of a locus classicus.[15] The novel, and Foer's entire oeuvre for that matter, can be read in fact, on one side, as a paean to cherished "things" carried around obsessively, dug up in parks at night, tracked across New York City and, in the 2002 *Everything Is Illuminated*, Eastern Europe, and on the other side, as an attempt to survive the "cancer of never letting go" of them and the traumas nesting in them, a dilemma that also haunts Foer's latest novel, the voluminous and similarly disconsolate 2016 *Here I Am*.[16] Krauss's 2017 *Forest Dark*—an indirect response to the marital and political dramas unfolding in *Here I Am*—comes to mind next, although *The History of Love* (2005) and especially *Great House* (2010) are better known for the "usefulness" and presencing force of the "absence of things."[17] But post-2000 novels by paradigm-setting authors who established themselves in the previous century also revolve around acquiring, collecting, and laying out privately or publicly owned objects, "artistic" or not, crafted by humans as well as by other aesthetic actors. DeLillo's *Underworld* comes to mind once more in this context. The book paved the way for the museal narratives woven into the plots of *Cosmopolis*, where Packer, whose possessions comprise a solitary shark in its tank—an allusion to Damien Hirst's *Physical Impossibility of Death in the Mind of Someone Living*—wants to purchase a chapel ("walls and all"[18]), *Fallen Man* (2007), *Point Omega* (2010), and *Zero K* (2016), in which ordinary things, rocks, discarded mannequins, paintings, and slow-running movies are shown to perplexed visitors. Modernist yearnings for an uncompromised aesthetic and world impossible to put back together occasionally rub up against more future-oriented aspirations in DeLillo, as they do in younger novelists such as Arthur Phillips and Gina Ochsner, who, in *Prague* (2002) and *The Russian Dreambook of Color and Flight* (2009), respectively, share with him an archeological interest in the Cold War-era political and cultural garbage heap and an insistent preoccupation with junked Soviet statuaries, kitschy memorabilia, and the campy recycling of propaganda artifacts in flea markets and faux-retro exhibits. Below, I deal in more detail with Mandel's *Station Eleven* and Lerner's *10:04*. To my mind, they are the most poignant curatorial narratives to come out in recent memory. The catastrophic, "totaled" contemporaneity they exhibit, sometimes literally, affords, against the grain of patrimonial mourning of lost or endangered yet invariably unjust worlds, a somewhat uplifting, encouragingly futural, post-conservative, and even postcapitalist preservation politics.

freighters, snow globes, comics: Mandel's Museum of Civilization, or Survival Is Insufficient

Survival is insufficient . . . *my favorite line of text in the world.*
—Emily St. John Mandel, *Station Eleven*

[D]*ormant objects are the purest kind of object we can study . . . In principle, some objects might remain dormant forever. They might be perfectly real without ever being discovered, caressed, or capitalized upon.*
—Graham Harman, *The Quadruple Object*

Death is the mother of beauty; hence from her,
Alone, shall come fulfilment to our dreams
And our desires.
—Wallace Stevens, "Sunday Morning"

Possibly along with Ling Ma's eerily and equally premonitory 2018 *Severance, Station Eleven* became a Covid-19 classic overnight. Unenviable as it may be, the distinction does not take anything away from an accomplishment whose recognition, to which Mandel alludes somewhat self-ironically in her 2022 novel, *Sea of Tranquility*, had to wait neither for the real equivalent of the novel's Georgia Flu nor for the 2021 HBO Max miniseries.[19] On the other hand, the 2019 pandemic, especially the suddenness with which it magnified world scarcity culture and, by the same movement, impacted our relationships with the objects around us, has understandably refocused our reading of *Station Eleven* and even of Mandel's whole work. As a result, I would argue, a couple of things are clearer now than a few years ago: first, this work is a narrative system of integrated, intersecting, and recurring themes, situations, references, and characters; second, this system is centered on an object-thinking—"object considerations," writes Mandel in *Station Eleven*[20]—similar to that of *Atocha*, of Lerner in general, and of other fictional objectualists discussed in *Flat Aesthetics*; third, as we will also notice in *10:04*, this thinking modality reaches in *Station Eleven* one more time beyond the conceptual and its "about" rationalizations, bodying forth into objectual practices such as amassing, organizing, and showing in designated and undesignated, actual or makeshift storing and exhibiting sites from museums to backpacks; fourth, these practices are also practices—installations or performances— of contemporaneity in the poietic sense emphasized across this book; and fifth, the object-thinking animating them also encourages their visitors from inside and outside the novel to do some future-thinking of their own.

This futural strand is less visible in Mandel's debut novel *The Singer's Gun* (2010), where salvaging, collecting, and trafficking in counterfeit and damaged artworks—yet another theme Mandel shares with Lerner—feed principally into the thematics of fraud, debt, debt crisis, and crisis overall. At once personal and public, North American and global, the crisis got incrementally more catastrophic and world-systemic in Mandel's writing. The 2012 *Lola Quartet* echoes the 2007 subprime mortgage crisis and the recession that followed, and so does *Station Eleven*, in which the pandemic that wiped out over 99 percent of the world population struck the same "year when 12 percent of the world shipping fleet lay at anchor off the coast of Malaysia, container ships laid dormant by an economic collapse" (28). Entwined with cross-hemispheric networks of crime in *The Singer's Gun*, "international water systems,"[21] traveling over water, the planetary ocean's shipping lanes, and the financial debacle's bearings on them all come back in *Station Eleven*, where "shipping executive" (201) Miranda Carroll is dispatched to inspect the "dormant" boats, and they return again in the 2020 *Glass Hotel*,[22] along with Leon Prevant, Miranda's boss. "[E]normous, amorphous object[s] like global transport logistics," as Bogost calls them, complete with Mandel's freighters, their circumplanetary routes, and first and foremost their solemn, quasi-funereal immobility are more than a short-lived boost to the geopolitical scope of the 2010 thriller.[23] An enduring hallmark of Mandel's material imaginary, the vessels also link up, directly and indirectly, with other key elements of *Station Eleven*'s objectual repertoire. One of them is the "beautiful" (15, 66, 184) itinerant paperweight

Kirsten Raymonde, a collector herself and member of the Traveling Symphony, got as a child from another character, Tanya, who received it from Miranda, and which had been a gift from an attorney named Clark Thompson to her and Arthur Leander; comparable to the journey of *Underworld*'s famous baseball, the thing's trajectory strings together and gives meaning to characters and occurrences scattered across discrete times and places. Equally beautiful and possibly identical in kind with the "smooth lump of glass with storm clouds in it" (66) is another object in this series, namely, the snow globe Clark examines at length later on in the novel (255). Relating to the other two and also evoking *Underworld*, specifically the decommissioned B-52s Klara Sax spray-paints in the Arizona desert, are the new world's "dormant airplanes" (31), chiefly those rusting outside Concourse C of the fictional Severn City Airport, where Clark sets up his Museum of Civilization. Finally, but most significantly, worth mentioning here is Miranda's exquisitely crafted two-volume comic-book series, *Dr. Eleven*, particularly the spaceship from which the graphic novel's first installment gets its title.

Remarkably, the comics end up, like the glass globe and other "distant" relatives of the slumbering liners, among the pieces housed by the Museum. After the roving artists arrive there, their symbolic destination all along, Kirsten makes a point to always leave a volume in Clark's curatorial custody. That way, she tells Clark, "at least one book will always be safe" while she is gone touring with the Symphony (331). But if "survival is insufficient" (119), as Kristen's tattoo, the inscription on the Symphony's lead wagon, and *Star Trek: Voyager* episode 122 before them assure us, so are *Dr. Eleven*'s safekeeping and, as we will see momentarily, safekeeping and preservation in the comic itself and, on another level, in the novel as well.[24] To be sure, conservancy is not the only concern here; as Clark tips the reader, the southern Midwest, where the Symphony is headed, has become, more than a decade after the flu's outbreak, "perfectly safe" (331). Through Kirsten, Mandel ensures *Dr. Eleven* reaches the Museum and takes its place alongside the other objects, and that is paramount because the entire collection and the novel itself hinge on the comic's presence in the SkyMiles Lounge display, on the objectual "dialogue" this presence enables, and on the connections, narratives, and worldviews this silent conversation articulates. "If," as Marc Augé says, "a place can be defined as relational, historical and concerned with identity,"[25] then the lounge and entire airport are here anything but the "non-places" the French anthropologist thinks such spaces represent.[26]

Most critics who have dwelt on *Station Eleven*'s "postapocalyptic curating"[27] and "salvagepunk"[28] have read them, and the whole book with them, as a largely conservative and politically-economically decontextualized exercise in nostalgia. In their assessment, the verdict is corroborated by the Symphony's patrimonial commitment to the high-brow, "Western-centric"[29] canon instantiated by Beethoven's and Shakespeare's works, to which the artists' portfolio is heavily tilted. The comment made by one of the performers ("the clarinet") to the effect that Shakespeare's own "survival" through the plays Symphony puts up may be an "insufficient" if not "inadequate" (288) response to such a civilizational earthquake has been dismissed as tokenism, as has been Mandel's incorporation of *Star Trek* and comic books into the novel. The charges are not baseless, and the author herself did little to obviate them when she declared that she "found [her]self wanting to write a love letter to the modern world. And one way to do that, one way to write about something," she added, "is to write about its absence."[30]

But Mandel does not solely re-present the now-absent world, simply bringing it back, let alone "redeeming"[31] it, nor does she reduce it to its canonical art paragons. If she "mak[es]," as her critics themselves acknowledge, popular TV and comics "central to the plot," she does it for a reason.[32] This cultural material and especially *Dr. Eleven* do more than just "pay lip service to the multiplicity of texts that could be considered artistic."[33] As I have proposed, Miranda's book defines metonymically the other items around it in Clark's collection, but the definitional energy of this illuminating adjacency of *Dr. Eleven* in the Museum and beyond stems from the comic's colloquy with the planes right outside the terminal, with display objects such as the glass globe, and through them, with the disused boats in the novel, an interface that is modulated by the ships' connections with their real-world counterparts—the "Ghost Fleet of the Recession Anchored Just East of Singapore," as reads the title of a 2009 *Daily Mail* article Mandel also credits in *Station Eleven*'s "Acknowledgments." Moored in "old-world" history, the freighters in turn anchor the "new world" in that history's economically global troubles, and so does, according to critics otherwise displeased with the book's "nostalgic" politics, even "*Station Eleven*'s use of Shakespeare," which, as in Kevin Costner's 2013 movie *The Postman*, "helps us understand precisely what is ending with the flu, namely the capitalist 'world-system,' . . . begin[ing] to show readers how the novel's apocalyptic scenario is entangled with this system."[34]

Both the 2007 "collapse," which Miranda witnesses firsthand and reflects on during her last business trip (217–18), and Shakespeare ground, overtly and allusively, the novel in documentable history, recent and older. That does not mean, however, that Mandel holds up either as a model. The dormant vessels and the dormant, no longer performed plays, as well as other, unusable things are curated, staged, and repurposed by Miranda, Clark, the Symphony, and more comprehensively Mandel herself on behalf of an inquisitiveness whose object may be "the world we live in today"[35] but that ultimately mobilizes a farsighted imagination of "renewal" rather than a patrimonial archiving and celebratory remembering of this world. It is quite telling, in this regard, that if the pre-pandemic world ends with the bang of a *King Lear* performance, the Symphony's favorite is *A Midsummer Night's Dream*.[36] This is another hint that, on balance, this imagination is not passéist, about legacies, inheritances, patrimonies, and a world, ours, on museal life support in *Station Eleven*, but futural, scanning that world's material domains for another world, for the more promising "otherworldly" (218). Lerner's Janus-faced ontology, as I have called it, is all here, in a multiverse Borgesian reiteration where the alternative, future world "could theoretically be simultaneously present and not present, perhaps living out a shadow life in a parallel universe or two" (200). A blurry dimension of the world in which we live and whose last gasp Mandel's characters experience, that other world, or at least an inkling of it, is discernable *en filigrane* ("in filigree") in the cultural signature of the "current era" (195), that is, in the contemporary collected—etymologically, "gathered together"—in the Museum.

The collection goes beyond the vestigial and the commemorative. It has been read mostly as a pitiful index of the "absence" Mandel refers to and whose fragments Clark and Mandel allegedly shore against their fictional and not-so-fictional ruins. But that reading misses the other absence, the futural otherworld that, as in *Atocha*, the Museum's objects arrange into presence.[37] Central to *Dr. Eleven* and *Station Eleven*, the otherworldly is the display behind the display, as it were, "another world just out of sight . . . toward [which] ships mov[e] over the water" (333) and to which the novel opens out symbolically in its last line. Similar to the "non-absence" Lerner talks about apropos Ashbery, that world is not of a past all but forgotten by the new generations growing up without the internet, but of a future *in potentia*, part of the present albeit not substantially present in it. An other to and beyond our world, the otherworld is not wholly divorced from it either. This is what the cargo ships suggest, and Station Eleven, which is their comic-book equivalent, as Miranda's final "vision" implies (228), does as well, whether through its association with the inactive fleet or metaleptically, in the *Dr. Eleven* scene that reenacts the dinner party Arthur and Miranda give in California and Clark reminisces about at the end of the novel (332). The majestic freighters bring to the Museum and the novel as a whole dismal history *and* futurality, the apocalypse of *Station Eleven*'s readers as well as a "post" to it. Wrecks of an all-too-real early twenty-first-century world economy itself in shambles, the ships connect not just with Dr. Eleven's spaceship, which, badly damaged in the war against the alien invaders who took over Earth and enslaved its population, is a barely functioning "wreckage" (84) itself, but, through Station Eleven, also with the "metal Starship Enterprise" (151) August, a Symphony member, finds in one of his scavenging expeditions, and thus with *Star Trek*'s post-survivalist, post-postapocalyptic, futural message.

This is by and large the message of *Station Eleven* too—of the spacecraft and of the book. Only, like Lerner, and surely unlike Tyler, Arthur's son and the novel's end-of-days Prophet, Mandel is leery of "messages." She declines to make explicit claims about the world beyond the horizon. She neither paints that world in realistic detail nor theorizes it. Instead, and even more emphatically than Lerner in *Atocha*, she poses it com-positionally, through object arrangements. Kirsten's showdown with Tyler later in the novel, where the two trade quotes from Miranda's book and the Prophet is shot dead by one of his own disciples, is instructive in this respect. Replaying the comic's first-volume "face-off between Dr. Eleven and an adversary from Undersea" (302), the planet-like spaceship's "underwater fallout shelters" inhabited by people "clinging to the hope that the world they remembered could be restored" (213), the encounter is also a clash between two approaches to civilizational catastrophe. Both have to do with collecting as well as with collectives, with community, that is. One, the Prophet's, is radically restorative. For Tyler, the flu is the new flood, "perfect" in its "culling" capacity to weed out the impure and gather the "spared" few into a hyperbolically selective group—a "collection" of the elect (59–61). Deceptively forward-looking, his prophecy is nostalgic to a fault, which is what Kirsten implies when she throws back at him one of the comic's sentences ("We long only to go home" [302]). The mandatory nostos is reinforced by an extreme and violent patrimonialism, which "saves" humanity's exemplars for a future that will already have revealed itself outside history altogether, in an imaginary *illo tempore*. The rationale for Tyler's "new world" and, in the final analysis, this world itself are foreordained, and so salvation, in and of itself a "collecting" venture, as noted, leads inevitably to a "musealization" of human beings where the Prophet's vision disconnects people from each other and from historical reality as well.

To vastly exclusive, top-down, and passéist salvation, Mandel opposes salvaging, collecting, and displaying. These constitute museal endeavors of a different kind. More democratic and futural, these are activities in which Kirsten participates along with the rest of the traveling ensemble, which is an object assemblage in its own right—pointedly, the narrator refers to its members, and they actually call each other, by their instruments' names ("the tuba," "the contrabassoon," "the flute"), and when they do not play or rehearse, they rummage through abandoned buildings. Some of their findings wind up, alongside things donated by others, in Clark's steadily expanding Museum, where, as August explains to his fellow artists, "artifacts from the old world are preserved" (145). Granted, "[t]he entire world is a place where artifacts from the old world are preserved" (145), as another character quips, but there is nothing curatorial—no object-thinking—to the planetary junkyard. An ill-suited metaphor for the world outside the Museum, the "world-as-museum" is more of an ossuary. This sort of dismal "preservationism" has been anticipated by more realistic—and more anthropocentered—narratives of post-manufacturing decline, with focus on the former industrial regions of the United States such as in the "brass-belt" fiction of Xhenet Aliu, in whose 2018 *Brass* laid-off female workers of Waterbury, Connecticut, realize, in the same vein as the famous line of the

Horatian ode (III. xxx. 1), that they are survivors—they have been "more lasting than brass."[38] In Mandel, the desolate landscape stands out for what is not there anymore, for the "unredeemable"[39] absence around which a society genuinely different from what has been is unlikely to gather. This makes the post-flu world an inferno—"hell is the absence of the people you long for" (144) reads Mandel's recurrent paraphrase of Jean-Paul Sartre's infamous yet often misread "hell is others" from his 1944 play *Huis clos* (No Exit). The axiom is apt in *Station Eleven*, for this world has witnessed the swift degradation of the human into its murderous and asocial other, what with North America's dystopian wastelands overrun, à la Cormac McCarthy's 2006 novel *The Road*, by "feral" humans and marauders with and among whom community, a measure of human "harmony," of the Symphony sort or not, and potentially a new world are unimaginable propositions. In the vestigial vastness of the pandemic's aftermath, people wait for the jumpstart of modern history's Grand Narratives or for Tyler's prophecy to pan out. Their only concern is survival—"there is just survival out there," observes Jeevan's brother, Frank (183).

A mark of apocalyptic contemporaneity, self-preservation is both the dominant cultural mode of the post-flu years and a temporal ontology where what is cannot exceed what has been ("there is just survival . . ."), trapping survivalists in an indigent and past-beholden present the way *Dr. Eleven*'s nostalgic renegades are in their Undersea "limbo" (213, 320). No actual future can take in this abeyant temporality where what survivors wish at most is to re-presence what is now missing, so they can keep on treading the waters of the precarious yet unending now. In that, their ideal and Tyler's are not that different. The "future" they are hungry for, one from earlier history rather than from outside it, had arrived too and came to a standstill in the pandemic. It is the future anterior of "antibiotics" and "engines" (270), staples of an industrialized past that, as a character comments, sound like stuff from the future ("science fiction" [270]) to those born after the flu. "An incomplete list" of such futuristic items features "chlorinated water" for "pools," "ball games played out under floodlights," "trains running under the surface of cities," working internet and cell phones, manned state borders, and aircraft crossing the sky (31–2).

Echoed by postapocalyptic fiction that will not be late in paying homage to *Station Eleven*—"Goodbye to gasoline and bullets and to molten flourless cake," writes Lethem in *The Arrest* before actually referencing Mandel's book[40]—the language of this elegiac catalogue suggests that the desire to make the Anthropocene great again is basically one for the material world's lost instrumentality. Interestingly enough, the objects themselves are not gone; their uses—their "utilitarian" uses, to be more accurate—are. Like the planes "dormant on runaways and in hangars" (31), these entities are no longer the standing-reserve they have been. Somewhat similar to the "dormant objects" Harman talks about in *The Quadruple Object*,[41] they may be "asleep," but they are not inert, as Shaviro would correctly insist.[42] They are "autonomous unit[s]" whose autonomy, as well as "reality," stems from their having disentangled themselves from their previous relations of use, exchange, and the like.[43] The fantasy of more "proactive" nostalgics such as the Traverse City "inventor" looking for the by-now-fabled internet, "WiFi[,] and the impossible-to-imagine Cloud" (38) is to wake them up from their inoperative dormancy, bring them back to functional life, and use them as utensils, prostheses, conveniences, barter goods, and resources once more, without much thought for what this use has done to them and the planet. This fantasy is culturally and politically regressive and patrimonially so—not only does it fall back on the past and the foundational rationales incarnated in hi-tech wonders and other epitomes of "human creativity," but it also posits traditional "functional" use as ultimate value and serviceable, exploitable, and tradable things as exemplary objects.

Patrimoniality is here essentially a metaphor, not an "intentional" curatorial practice. The object-thinking in play in it comes down to object-use, to getting hold of objects that can be once again employed, traded, consumed, and so forth. By contrast, a collection entails, as Boltanski and Esquerre specify, an investment in "the useless," and this is what Clark makes in Concourse C with deliberation and dedication ("he took his role as curator seriously," Mandel writes [232]).[44] The world-as-museum is not about conserving the things in it, but quite the opposite, about preserving, *at their expense*, the human and, more broadly, the anthropocentric hardwiring of modernity. They are not collectibles but consumables, their presence drained away by the exploitatively transitive relationships humans have with them. This does not mean that objects that still work, or can be made to work again, are not beautiful, or that they cannot be collected, and an anterior future is precisely one in which "the objects [Clark]'d collected over the years, from the airport and beyond—the laptops, the iPhones, the radio from an administrative desk, the electric toaster from an airport-staff lounge, the turntable and vinyl records that some optimistic scavenger had carried back from Severn City—"(232) would be presumably freecycled, refurbished, and reintroduced into the world circuitries of instrumentality. Clark's Museum rests, however, on the suspension ("dormancy") of this instrumentality. The computers and cell phones are not in there for their use or exchange value. Clark does not cherish them for their capabilities, for the goal or place he could reach through or past them. They are there as "forms" rather than "contents." Intrinsically or potentially aesthetic, like all objects—which, to be beautiful, require neither pandemics nor curators—things are here appreciated for the aesthetic worth acquired under catastrophic circumstances, similarly to the Ur-object of the collection, *Dr. Eleven*, and in it, the hulk of Dr. Eleven's spaceship.

Mandel has been accused of "aestheticizing" things, of removing them from their economic, political, and historical context, but the abundant references to the 2007 crisis—a dry run for the much bigger Georgia Flu "collapse"—effectively *historicize* even a futurist object such as Station Eleven. The comic book and its spacecraft, the seminal presences of the Museum, are not ahistorical. To the contrary, they are entanglements of history and aesthetics, cultural sites where, appearances notwithstanding, aesthetics is historicized rather than the other way around and beauty arises, accordingly, out of a documentable historical and financial catastrophe, from which Mandel extrapolates the death of a whole object-thinking paradigm and of the world-system of material production and consumption rooted in it. Indeed, in *Station Eleven* too death is the mother of beauty, as the author echoes an entire postromantic tradition and, almost verbatim at times, Wallace Stevens's "Sunday Morning." As the novelist tells us again and again, the post-pandemic world is awash in beauty, replete with beautiful objects, from the "remnant fleet" (28) to the paperweight Kirsten carries in her bag (66, 184), and more than anything else, if on another plane of the story, "the beautiful wreckage of Station Eleven" (88). This world is beautiful not because it is dead itself, but because the world before it has died. As it did so, that world let go of objects heretofore held hostages by its use systems, and consequently ships, paperweights, and toasters acceded to the beauty of "uselessness." It is, to reemphasize, not that these objects were "ugly" before either; their handling by humans was, insofar as objects' transcendence in the acts of use, exchange, disposal, and the like made for a fundamentally unaesthetic response to their presence. Nor are they dead now that they are not operational anymore. They are just "dormant," as the beauty around Miranda and Kirsten is a corollary of objects' stillness, of their having become valuable in and of themselves for a curator like Clark as soon as they stopped serving as tools or raw material. Mandel does not beautify an oppressive and wasteful system, nor does she offer up capitalism as an aesthetics. In effect, she suggests, objects' aesthetic glow sanctions the failure of the instrumental logic of capital. Where the survivalists purport to reverse de-instrumentalization and return to "uglier," de-presencing relationships with objects, the Museum protects, celebrates, and enhances the presence of things while acknowledging in detail the global networks of manufacturing, circulation, and exploitation. As we learn in a passage whose lexicon and rhapsodic tone make it sound like a rewrite of *Atocha*'s "think about the objects" fragment, Clark

> has always been fond of beautiful objects, and in his present state of mind, all objects were beautiful. He stood by the case and found himself moved by every object he saw there, by the human enterprise each object had required. Consider the snow globe. Consider the mind that invented all those miniature storms, the factory worker who turned sheets of plastic into white flakes of snow, the hand that drew the plan for the miniature Severn City with its church steeple and city hall, the assembly-

line worker who watched the globe glide past on a conveyor belt somewhere in China. Consider the white gloves on the hands of the woman who inserted the snow globes into boxes, to be packed into larger boxes, crates, shipping containers. Consider the card games played belowdecks in the evenings on the ship carrying the container across the ocean, a hand stubbing out a cigarette in an overflowing ashtray, a haze of blue smoke in dim light, the cadences of a half dozen languages united by common profanities, the sailors' dreams of land and women, these men for whom the ocean was a gray-line horizon to be traversed in ships the size of overturned skyscrapers. Consider the signature on the shipping manifest when the ship reached port, a signature unlike any other on earth, the coffee cup in the hand of the driver delivering boxes to the distribution center, the secret hopes of the UPS man carrying boxes of snow globes to the Severn City Airport. Clark shook the globe and held it up to the light. When he looked through it, the planes were warped and caught in whirling snow. (255)

The objects are here to be "seen" and possibly unveil their "secret lives," as Mandel declares in an interview.[45] People may come to the Museum to "look at the past after their long days of work" (261), but what they actually discover in there, however, and what they *wan[t] to preserve*" (258; emphasis mine), is not objects that still do their jobs, such as instruments, tools, appliances, and other material signifiers of that past. Nor is, more generally, that past itself. In fact, as Kirsten informs François Diallo, the editor of the *New Petoskey News*, a "creative project" and sort of print version of Clark's collection,[46] there are, even outside the airport, some "towns where discussion of the past is discouraged" (115).

The display deters such retrospection by design. In the Museum, "our obsession with objects,"[47] as Mandel says in another interview, has less to do with the desire to remember, which defeats the purpose if it results in nostalgia, than it has with the need to forget. As in *Dr. Eleven*, forgetting does not mean sheer oblivion but an active, energizing un-remembering of sorts, a conscientious effort to unlearn certain cultural habitus the way Dr. Eleven "trie[s] to forget the sweetness of life on Earth" so that he and his followers can move on and build another world. A leitmotif of the novel (42, 105, 214), that "sweetness" is an emotional byproduct of a modernity that redefined human life around the ideals of convenience, comfort, ease, and luxury, all of which were derived from an unsustainable, instrumental-consumerist approach to nonhuman forms of existence. Culturally framed by its centerpiece, the entire collection endorses this tactical forgetting, urging visitors to "consider" things in and of themselves, not as objects of consumption, accumulation, trade, and similar kinds of use. This is why Clark's "object considerations" latches onto items that "had no practical use": "cell phones with delicate buttons," "impractical shoes, stilettos mostly beautiful and strange," "clean and polished car engines," a "motorcycle composed mostly of gleaming chrome," and other "objects of no real value" (258).

One more time, let Mandel's carefully minted language be our guide. What was "practical," "real," and valuable" in the pre-pandemic era—a whole world-system based on objects' accessorial status—is now gone, and Clark, a gay man who has his own memories to rely on, does not quite yearn for it, complimentary as he sounds about the "human enterprise." Instead, what shines through in his display of contemporaneity over and against a present of penury, death, and absence, is the presence of objects that finally and fully *are there*. Still "dormant," they awaken into hyperpresence or, as scholars like John Shotter might say, "real presence." That presence is real, and so the objects are more present than they have ever been, because, as in *Atocha*, it is on display epideictically, not deictically, and so it *presents itself* rather than its circumstances, attributions, meanings, price tag, and so on.[48] "Estranged" from their previous, ontologically transitive state and safe from deontologizing attempts to "restore" them, the collectibles are even more beautiful than before. They are and are treated as "art." Their aesthetic intransitivity has increased considerably; once present, they are now hyperpresent. Their new beauty is to no negligible degree the surplus value dys- and non-functionality bestow on existents extracted from the Anthropocene's relations of manufacturing and commerce, and yet, as the lengthier passage above shows, these processes are not overlooked but register as a matter of historical record. What used to be produced, priced, marketed, sold, and otherwise utilized for some human benefit now stands even more resolutely for itself and therefore *is* in the strongest sense of the verb, exists formally. Strange, other to their former functionalist, commodified, and serialized selves, or at least perceived as such, these museal hyperpresences are ontologically "contagious," presenting their being mode as a model to the world outside. A source of the SkyMiles Lounge holdings, that world is no museum, let alone Clark's Museum, as pointed out earlier, but it may become like it in an aesthetically driven future willing to submit to the beautiful, to the unique, and the irreplaceable, as the aircraft lined up on the tarmac outside the terminal accept the embrace of the glass-globe snowstorm, quietly "collect[ing,]" alongside all the world's planes, "snow on their wings" (31).

If *Station Eleven* is "utopian," as some critics assure us, then its utopia is aesthetic. In turn, the vehicle of this utopia is curatorial.[49] Clark's collection is not one of mementos. Or, its keepsakes are futural. It may collect the past, or, more precisely, from the past, but what it curates in the destitute present, and what it ultimately presents, is the future or *for* it. Vaguely sketched out as it is, the blueprint for a world to come is distinguishable in the picture Clark's object considerations paint of the post-catastrophic contemporary. As mentioned, Smith's theory of non-patrimonial curating provides for this possibility, as does Stevens's "Sunday Morning," in a language less straightforward yet particularly keen on the futural affordances ("fulfil[l] ment of our dreams") of the past, the dead, and death itself. What Clark displays—the display behind the display, as I have called it—is a dialectic of worlds, the birth of a new world from the flotsam and jetsam of the one before. It bears repeating, the demise of the old puts an end to the anthropocentered object order. Opening the door to a non-instrumental, aesthetic reset of that order, death spawns Stevensian beauty and thus an other to what has just expired, viz., to the ugly world of instrumentality. Even if the Museum were "founded to prevent the erasure of [the] history" of that world, as Fabrice Wilmann claims,[50] the body of knowledge assembled by the collection prompts rather than deters a break with the past. After all, as Diallo tells Kirsten, "[t]he more we know about the former world, the better we'll understand what happened when it fell" (114), and this understanding is important because people rarely commit to Stevensian dreams and desires before getting some sense of what is wrong with the current state of affairs. But more important than revisiting the familiar is in the Museum what Wilmann also describes as "an other-worldly appeal."[51] This is not just the tug of another world; it is also a world-othering, transformative force. The latter is the pull of the "impractical," of garments and gizmos that present themselves with greater intensity as existents that have risen to higher beauty or formhood by shedding their previous "contents"—their functions, destinations, subordinations, and rationales. The former is symbolically associated with Station Eleven.[52] In shared curatorial space, the ship bathes its ambiance in otherworldliness; conversely, the impracticality of stilettos and motorbikes missing parts becomes the logic of the otherworldly, viz., that which makes *this* world other by setting up aesthetic "uselessness" as its new rationality.

The quintessential object of the display, Station Eleven is the techno-ecosystemic trope of a potential, "other" Earth. The spacecraft is from Terra, and it has been terraformed too, built, that is, to resemble and be another world-as-we know it (42, 83) rather than an other to it. But terraforming, and with it the restaging of anthropocentric philosophies of design and technological progress, miscarries in Miranda's book, as it does in Mandel's, in T. Coraghessan Boyle's 2016 novel *The Terranauts*, and in many other post-2000 speculative fictions, another sign that contemporary U.S. authors do not contemplate a remedial-reproductive narrative of terraformation but one of more decisively innovative transformation. More beautiful than it was when it was launched—beautiful *because* all-but-un- or post-functional, not because it works sci-fi wonders but because it does not, what with the transparently allusive "damage to a number of vital systems involving Station Eleven's ocean levels" (83)—the starship is flatness itself and thereby a site of futural poiesis. Not so much a "signifie[r] of the old world,"[53] Station Eleven is the conduit of the one ahead. Its "otherworldliness"—a term Bogost uses to describe how a submarine may appear to a child—washes over the whole display and beyond, over the world outside Concourse

C also, like the snowstorm sweeping out of one of the ship's brethren, the glass globe.[54] Similarly to other symbolic objects from its family such as the freighters, the planes, by which, unsurprisingly, the Prophet feels threatened, the paperweight, which "symbolises the notion of interconnectedness that lies at the heart of the novel,"[55] and the comic book itself, whose one volume remains inside the Museum while the other travels with Kirsten (331), Station Eleven is a complex ontoaesthetic operator. Not only is it beautiful, so acutely present in its fragility and tragic inability to fulfill its assigned tasks, as Mandel accentuates so frequently, but its aesthetic energy also imparts Clark's collection and the world around it an existential thereness of sorts, a worldly "excess" evocative of the "too-much-world" haunting Czesław Miłosz in the poem Mandel uses as an epigraph to her novel. Where the virus "empties [the world] out" (190) as it contaminates everything, "connecting" the world only to break it into places isolated from one another—"[t[he world's become so local," Diallo tells Kirsten (108)— Miranda's flights of fancy, their museal display, and Mandel's imagination are poised to replenish and renew it.

photographs, instant coffee, baby octopuses: "Mere Objecthood," Messianic Readymades, and the Institute of Totaled Art in *10:04*

[W]orks . . . formally demoted from art to mere objecthood . . .
                                              —Ben Lerner, *10:04*

For me these objects—just as they were, but a little different—were ready-mades for a world to come, a future where there is some other system of value, in the art world and beyond, than the tyranny of price.
                                              —Ben Lerner, "Damage Control"

I don't think one is prepared for juxtapositions in general, is one? And yet one is constantly being faced with them.
                                  —John Ashbery, "The Experience of Experience"

The Severn City Airport Museum may look like a Duchamp exhibit, but the driver licenses and high heels are no *objets trouvés* proper although many of them have literally been found by scavengers and travelers. It is also true that most of these things are, or rather were originally, everyday objects, and not intentionally created art, a distinction the historical avant-garde sought to do away with. However, Clark collects them because, but for a few, they no longer have "real value." Of course, in *Station Eleven*, this value is, or was initially, anthropological and material, measuring objects' suitability for wearing, communicating, Web surfing, and other human activities they were *for*. An ontological mode in which things, with an apparent paradox, get to be more intensely *for themselves*, dysfunctionality, we have learned, boosts their presence and aesthetic standing. Thus, idle engines and faded IDs earn "artifact" status and a place in a curatorial project where they do not just recoup aesthetically what they have lost materially but also help envision an order of things that would not rehash past exchange regimes' value systems.

In *10:04* too, objects depreciate abruptly in the face of destruction. Likewise, as they are damaged, or so deemed, they are salvaged and curated and accrue both aesthetic value and futural-utopian potentialities. By the same token, the onto-logic of this de- and re-valuing dynamic is, as in Mandel, non-patrimonial. Lerner's novel also speaks to what the author himself describes, in a 2013 article to which I come back below, as a push to "get outside the legacy of Duchamp,"[56] and indeed, Ben, *10:04*'s first-person narrator and main hero, gives a lot of thought to what Lerner defines, in the same essay, as a "kind of conceptual reversal of the Duchampian ready-made."[57] The outcome of Lerner's effort has been questioned, however, and predictably so, "[g]iven" what has been viewed as "the Reagan-era origins of Ben's inspiration."[58] "It is no surprise," one critic concludes, "that the novel reflects literature's complicity in the very systems it disavows."[59] A variation on the theme of *Station Eleven*'s nostalgic surrender to culturally and politically dominant structures and traditions, the point is not entirely without merit, but "complicity" overstates the case. I also suspect Ben (Lerner) and some of his (their) commentators have somewhat dissonant takes on what systems are and do, in what sense a writer's fancy may challenge them, and whether it can come into play at all without availing itself of what extant setups of economy and culture have stocked, organized, and fashioned, from neoliberal mercantilism to the theo-technological sublime of Peggy Noonan's presidential speechwriting.

In this chapter, I throw my lot with readers who find *10:04*, as I have *Station Eleven* and *Atocha*, a provocative attempt to open up in the very heart of the present an authentically futural temporality, one, that is, qualitatively different from ours. What concerns me here, more than the fleeting and incoherent present, is its narrative X-ray, which, once again, makes visible a configuration of objects suggestive of both what contemporaneity is and of what it is not but has the potential of leading to, namely, a time and cultural ecology where things would be assessed, and one would interact with them, irrespective of their material worth.[60] In Mandel's book, where money went the way of the stilettos, "material" is synonymous to practical, and, we have seen, impracticality clears a path to another world (333). In Lerner's novel, which, speculative about the future as it is, is set in historical, realistically limned early twenty-first-century New York City and Marfa, Texas, material means pecuniary. In *Station Eleven*, objects automatically convert to, and are ontologically downgraded in, their objectives. Things' "exchangeability," Lerner's keyword in *The Hatred of Poetry* and elsewhere, is predicated on usability, and so is their adjunct ontology. Use—practical human use—is what they are for. In *10:04*, they are for money. Their instrumentality, their "transitivity," is monetary. What Lerner refers to as "the tyranny of price" is the particular exchange regime that underwrites this equivalence and, following from it, things' subalternity inside a system where, whatever else they are, they are handled as commodities.[61]

If cash value is the current system's defining value or "metavalue," then *10:04* imagines a systemic *Umwertung*, a Nietzschean "transmutation of values."[62] The book tells a re- or trans-valuative story in which objects regain their ontoaesthetic flatness, the fundamental dignity of intransitive beings that both *are* and are beautiful or, more accurately, accede to a new condition of beauty. Because the system in question is the market, and because the market is a world-system virtually subtending all other systems of animate and inanimate existence, being *of* this supersystem—being *for* a sum—threatens to become a requisite of being-in-the-world, in other words, to render exchangeability ontologically foundational. In brief, if capitalism commodifies, *commodification ontologizes*. Turning the tables on capitalist ontology, Lerner seeks to deontologize commodification. To that effect, *10:04*'s self-acknowledged "utopian" (134) gambit is to delink ontology from finance, that is, the provisions under which a being *is* from its being tradable. Thus, the novel envisages a scenario where the ontological modalities and stipulations warranting objects' commercialization do not apply any more. Similarly to *Station Eleven*, things in *10:04* "have 'zero value'" (129) moneywise once their formal "integrity," as Shaviro calls it, has been compromised—they have been broken up, defaced, destroyed, or so judged.[63] Moreover, demonetization does not simply "free [them] from the market," as Lerner writes in an article, but in releasing them from the subsidiary ontology of being-for, it also sets them up as possible models of future being modes and world-systems.[64]

Just as in *Station Eleven*, the venue of this dialectical seesaw is a museum, which Alena, one of Ben's romantic interests, and her friend Peter improvise in a New York apartment and baptize, in jest, the Institute for Totaled Art. The name fits, though. As Ben explains, Alena's studio houses art objects that have been "totaled" legally. These are paintings, sculptures, and other artworks that seem damaged beyond repair or whose restoration cost is higher than the insured value, and which are declared worthless after the insurer has paid out the claim amount. With Ben's assistance, Alena and Peter convince the head of a major insurance company that "totaled artworks were of both aesthetic and philosophical" import, and the firm donates a "gallery's worth of 'zero-value' art" to the "Institute" for "small-scale exhibition and critical discussion" (130).

What gets off the ground as a whim does end up having salient "implications," if not for other "artists, critics, [and] theorists" (130), then at least for the novelist himself, who is clearly enwrapped in the subject. Nor is *10:04* the first time he takes it up. "The 'Institute for Totaled Art,'" he reveals in the novel's "Acknowledgments," "is modeled on Elka Krajewska's Salvage Art Institute," whose "fictional . . . description . . . overlaps with [his] account of Krajewska's actual work," account that was part of a *Harper's Magazine* essay that came out the year before the novel's publication.[65] Where Mandel's characters scavenge for non-art objects elevated to arthood, Alena salvages canvases, photos, and other similar art objects "formally demoted from art to *mere objecthood*" (130; emphasis mine). Broken toasters and bikes, on one side; on the other, literally "broken art"—a stray Jeff Koons balloon dog, "an icon of art world commercialism and valorized stupidity[,] is shattered" (131), and, we gather, deservedly so, while other pieces have been "slashed or burnt or stained" (132) or may have just looked that way to the professionals in charge with ascertaining their marketplace worth. "Determined," in Mandel, by their practicality in the functionalist universe of the quotidian or, in Lerner, by their financially sanctioned aesthetic status in the art world of gallerists, dealers, curators, critics, publics, and their institutions, the implements and abstract drawings become "indeterminate" (130) ontologically when a violent act or sudden loss of form, components, fuel, use, or monetary value pries them and their original "determination" or evaluative framework apart. Yet not unlike *Station Eleven*'s "dormancy," in- or un-determination reenergizes in *10:04* ontologically, aesthetically, and axiologically, and so objects are not "relegated to this strange limbo" (130) forever. They do enter it as they forfeit their old, "for-" value, but Alena's place lies outside this purgatory. As Ben intimates, the Institute is rather a "transitional" space (133), a dynamic field of ontoaesthetic energies and fluctuating intensities where "supposedly worthless works" (130) accrue value, albeit in another dimension or system, to which they accede, and which they map onto to the world outside the Institute as demonetization bolsters their being-there.

An upshot of objects' "demotion" from statutory art, "mere objecthood" is thus in reality *more* objecthood. Already present in spite of cultural-economic pressures to be present-for, artifacts now rise into hyperpresence. Since they no longer are nor are thought to be for something outside themselves, even disfigured and noticeably *incomplete* items ascend to a superior completeness, to a new, self-sufficient and therefore formally appealing "integrity." In fact, Alena "considered [them] to be more compelling—aesthetically or conceptually—than they had been prior to sustaining damage" (130), a striking yet plausible reassessment whose possibility itself is just another indication that whatever an object is, that does not coincide with, nor does it depend on, its over- or undermining, anthropocentered evaluations; these differ so widely that, most likely, what "we" believe the "value," "beauty," "form," or "state" of an object to be and what it actually is are also different things.

Reinforcing this notion is Ben's own response to the Institute's holdings, which does not entirely jibe with Alena's approach to "ruined" art either. To "[his] surprise," many of the pieces did not appear "damaged at all," and Alena and Peter "were equally baffled" by "what seemed to us perfect condition" (132–3). One such item is an unframed print of an Henri Cartier-Bresson photo, on which Ben could "perceive[e] no tears, scratches, fadings, stains" (133). This prompts him to "study" it more closely and share his observations with us. The work, Ben reflects, "had transitioned from being a repository of immense financial value without undergoing what was to me any perceptible material transformation." "[I]t was the same," he concludes with one of the novel's refrains, "only totally different" (133). Reported by a human onlooker but mysteriously effectuated *by the object itself*, "[t]his was," he goes on, "a reversal of the kind of contextualization associated with Marcel Duchamp, still—unfortunately, in my opinion—the tutelary spirit of the art world; this was the opposite of the 'readymade' whereby an object of utility—a urinal, a shovel—was transformed into an object of art and an art commodity by the artist's fiat, by his signature" (133). The "decontextualization" or, as I say above, "un-determination" of the Cartier-Bresson, Ben feels, was

much more powerful than what it reversed because, like everyone else, I was familiar with material things that seemed to have taken on a kind of magical power as a result of a monetizable signature: that's how branding works in the gallery system and beyond, whether for Damien Hirst or Louis Vuitton. But it was incredibly rare—I remembered the jar of instant coffee the night of the storm—to encounter an object liberated from that logic. What was the word for that liberation? *Apocalypse? Utopia?* [italics in the original] I felt a fullness indistinguishable from being emptied as I held *a work from which the exchange value had been extracted, an object that was otherwise unchanged* [emphasis added]. It was as if I could register in my hands a subtle but momentous transfer of weight: the twenty-one grams of the market's soul had fled; it was no longer a commodity fetish; it was art before or after capital. Not the shattered or slashed works to which Alena thrilled, but those objects in the archive that both were and weren't different moved me: they had been redeemed, both in the sense that the fetish had been converted back into cash, the claim paid out, but also in the messianic sense of being saved from something, saved for something. An art commodity that had been exorcised (and survived the exorcism) of the fetishism of the market was to me a utopian readymade—an object for or from a future where there was some other regime of value than the tyranny of price. (133–4)

"Apocalypse? Utopia?" Must we choose? Why not have both? Might we not harness the former to the latter, for example? After all, this is what *Station Eleven*, Whitehead's *Zone One*, Ma's *Severance*, and so much post-2000 speculative fiction have been doing, giving the lie to the oft-misquoted (and misquoting) adage according to which "[i]t seems to be easier for us today to imagine the thoroughgoing deterioration of the earth and of nature than the breakdown of late capitalism; perhaps that is due to some weakness in our imagination."[66] But then again, to revise the same critic himself, "we can now revise that and witness the attempt to imagine [the end of] capitalism by imagining the end of the world."[67]

In a show of imaginative strength, writers such as Mandel and Lerner do just that. They view the planetary devastation of things big and small, "natural," humanmade, and "readymade" as a stepping-stone to a postcapitalist time; where a world goes bust—and because it does, they insist—another heaves in sight. Like *Station Eleven*, *10:04* encodes this dialectic of collapsing and budding worlds aesthetically, as a push and pull of two temporalities under which artworks can be. One is the present in which they are *for*—for a price, in this case—until, like entire world ecosystems around them, they get or are treated as irreversibly damaged. The ontological frailty of their being-for, Ben thinks, was only compounded by Duchamp, Andy Warhol, and other artists, vandals, and vandals posing as artists, possibly including Alena herself.[68] Whether they signed and exhibited pissoirs, smashed sculptures to pieces, as Alena does with a Koons dog fragment (132), or added moustaches to Mona Lisas, their visible and invisible "monetizable signatures" deepened the patrimonializing reach of commodification into the "gallery system and beyond" (133), into the plebeian kingdom of socks, matchboxes, and bike saddles. The other temporality is the future to which or from which art objects *return*— Robert Zemeckis's 1985 sci-fi *Back to the Future*, from whose plot the novel gets its title, is a constant reference throughout the novel. Notably, objects help picture this future by "failing" formally, in their actual or perceived deformity, and therefore commercially also, while still being art. Furthermore, in this future, they are ontologically priceless *because* they lack a price tag, and total *because* totaled, that is, present in their totality, as integra, and thus being more for themselves rather than for the sums they may fetch.

The most intriguing objects, however, are those unchanged physically. They are basically "the same, only totally different" (133), as Ben echoes, via Agamben's *Coming Community*, Walter Benjamin's Hassidic parable about "the world to come."[69] These things are effectively transformative even though they have not experienced "any perceptible material transformation" (133). The Cartier-Bresson, the "abstract diptych" (133), and other items within and, we will see below, without the Institute make up a new object order in the present. Undoubtedly, they are not the order, or in the order, we know and in which we too participate. But inside the ruling order in which we all are for the time being, they assemble, apparently outside any logic of causality, sequence, and connectivity, a cultural-material configuration—the contemporary—in which ongoing arrangements and adjudications of value, status, and meaning are altered. The same but totaled, one is tempted to riff, the objects do not just gesture to a "world to come"; they carve out a space for it, the Agambenian potentiality of *another* present, in the belly of the actual present. Nor do they leave the latter behind. They are both *in* it and *of* the future—"for or from" it, Ben observes—once they have stopped being for cash. And vice versa, they are "messianic," but their messianism is "presentist," of the hic et nunc. They have "transferred" their ontological weight onto themselves without going through "transformations" that would have carried them past the "now" signpost. It is through and in them, and therefore in the present also, that that future and its world arrive or come back, rather, both truly futural because both *after* the capitalist present, as art objects themselves return to a value and to an aesthetic recognition *prior to* monetization. Ben is right: the print and the diptych's panels have not changed at all, and yet something has, around them. Their being-there *qua* art has modified the larger system of art and being under which they exist, for now they are artworks and count as such without, on one side, the sanction of the market and, on the other, the Duchampian crutch of lucrative deformation, vandalism, and readymade iconoclasm.

The transfer-sans-transformation at work here affects or, as Ben implies, can potentially affect every and all objects. Both physically "uncompromised" (133) and no longer subject to marketplace encumbrances, the intact paintings and photos do not so much model a new kind of *art form*—the original Cartier-Bresson is no different from the one in the Institute—as they allude to a "totally different" system in which each and every object would be indeed appreciated *as form*, aesthetically, not for its value as commodity. Since all "legit" art out there probably is or is considered as unscathed as the Cartier-Bresson, the principles of the alternative system postulated by the salvaged photo print's ontology would virtually apply, one might infer, to any artwork; newly gained hyperpresence allows this and other pieces curated by Alena to reset the conditions of possibility (the "determinations") for themselves and the system at large.

The system reaches far beyond the fine arts, as we will learn before long. The art system and the world-system constantly marble in and out of each other throughout Lerner's oeuvre. The two dovetail vividly in *Atocha* on multiple levels, and they do so again in *10:04*, with Ben's visit to Alena's place a case in point. In one of the novel's theme-with-variations signature moments, Lerner's hero converts the market value of the undamaged balloon dog to "Chinese labor" ("a year or two of it" in Ben's estimation [132]) and, with a less outsourced but more personal connection, to the intrauterine insemination Alex, his female friend and eventual love interest, is hoping to have ("between one or two IUIs," he decides [131–2]). But the commercialist "icon" (131) and the Cartier-Bresson appear to belong to distinct categories. The Koons lends itself to conversion naturally, in fact presupposes it, standing as a contemporary symbol for the exchange regime that undergirds art production and trade. The regime's perfunctory, monetary interest in form is, Ben hints, allegorically built into the balloon itself, which not only is a "work of willful superficiality" but also reveals, once broken, "the hollow interior" (131). The dog embodies its brand—as well as the brand's disembodied vacuity—and the item's vandalization equals de-branding, which in this situation is terminal not just because Alena further vandalizes the balloon but because, subject to an absolute and irreversible un-determination, the piece cannot be absorbed into another rebranding cycle of Duchampian desecration. By contrast, the photo is *substantial*. This has nothing to do with its intactness, though. Less of a brand in the way in which the Koonses, the Hirsts, and the Louis Vuittons of the private collections and the biennales are, the Cartier-Bresson can unmoor itself more easily from its instrumental "for-ness." "Liberated from th[e] logic" (133) of that subservience, the Frenchman's work charges with its "liberating" energies entities well outside the Institute and the art world altogether, including meticulously branded, "outrageously priced" commodities such as the instant coffee jar for sale at the Whole Foods where Alex and Ben go shopping at the beginning of the novel in preparation for the storm about to hit New York City.

The "magical power" of the print—the pull of its aesthetic hyperpresence—is anti-Duchampian because it is just the opposite to the one resulted from "monetizable" signatures. Duchamp's branding aggression may be anti-aesthetic, but as Donald Kuspit reminds us, it is done with "commercial panache"[70] and has yielded, according to Lerner himself, an entire tradition of pseudo-"vandalism" that "*increases* dollar value,"[71] whereas the unexpected "Ashberian" juxtaposition the Cartier-Bresson provokes in Ben's mind with the coffee container both de-brands the product and renders it aesthetic. The Duchampian revolution heralded the "end of art," to quote Kuspit's title; instead, Alena's "unearthing the living dead of art" (132) may well point to a possible rebirth not only of art as art but also of art and of the aesthetic generally as an object ontology on whose model the whole world might be "saved for something" other than rampant neoliberalism, destitution, and environmental troubles. If the photo is, *as is now*, in the Institute, "incredibly rare" (133), a non-serial or de-serialized entity, so is or so can become the Whole Foods coffee jar and potentially all the coffee jars of the world and the world itself through their "horizontal" associations with the photo and other objects in its category.

As in Mandel, freeing things from the straitjacket of commodification and uncovering their one-of-a-kind-ness, their sovereignty as forms, does not "aestheticize" them if by aestheticization we mean disregarding their genetic relationships with the world economy or, worse, handling economics as a branch of aesthetics. Ben is pretty clear about this. As the big storm "estranges" peoples' "routines" (19) and dealings with ambient things in ways not unlike what occurs in the Institute, the jar—which would be called forth in the Institute episode by the Cartier-Bresson—"makes [him] viscerally aware of both the miracle and insanity of the mundane economy" (19), as he will surely be when he will link the balloon dog to Chinese workers' slave wages. "Finally . . . found[ing]" the "vitally" important if flavorless coffee Alex and he had been looking for, Ben picks up "the red plastic container, one of the last three on the shelf, held it like the marvel that it was" (19). Made, à la *Station Eleven*'s gasoline and toilet paper, all but introuvable amid the panic buying and by the same stroke an *objet trouvé* of sorts of climate-change-era emergencies, the item is another non-Duchampian "utopian readymade," a wonder rather than a fetish, for it is subject to the same aesthetic transfer as the Cartier-Bresson.

Alert as he is to the coffee can's new being mode, Ben does not lose sight of the global production and distribution mode either, evoking the toil, animate and inanimate agents, and routes that, together, had manufactured and delivered the thing to Manhattan. In a passage that reads like an echo of Clark's "considerations" about the world travels of the snow globe—and, aside from the airplane reference, the fragment does so because, as I have said, Clark's musings themselves sound like a rewrite of *Atocha*'s "object-thinking" episode—Ben pictures "the seeds inside the purple fruits of coffee plants [that] had been harvested on Andean slopes and roasted and ground and soaked and then dehydrated at a factory in Medellin and vacuum-sealed and flown to JFK and then driven upstate in bulk to Pearl River for repackaging and then transported back by truck to the store where I now stood reading the label" (19). "It was," he says,

> as if the social relations that produced the object in my hand began to glow within it as they were threatened, stirred inside their packaging, lending it a certain aura—the majesty and murderous stupidity of that organization of time and space and fuel and labor becoming visible in the commodity itself now that planes were grounded and the highways were starting to close.
>
> *Everything will be as it is now, just a little different* [emphasis in the original]—nothing in me or the store has changed, except maybe my aorta, as the eye drew near, what normally felt like the only possible world *became one among many* [emphasis added], its meaning everywhere up for grabs, however briefly—in the passing commons of the train, in a container of tasteless coffee. (19)

The coffee jar brings to mind what is perhaps the most frequently mentioned produce in American criticism, DeLillo's fruit in *White Noise*. Like the novel's equally notorious barn, the fruit is well-nigh indistinguishable from its mechanical reproduction, and so its "self-conscious quality" does not stem from its presence but from pose, from a photo-like *appearance*—it "looked," as DeLillo details, "carefully observed, like four-color fruit in a guide to photography."[72] In the 1985 postmodern classic, the thing's "radiance" is a technological afterglow, sheer optics. That is because the intensity of its being-there *qua* fruit has been stymied in advance by its photographic simulacrum. Of course, the fruit could be present in how it appears but is not or is only to a small degree, and this has to do with how and why it appears the way it does. "As is," it not so much *is* actually as it shows off its "photoshopped" version, as we might say these days, a version or copy that predates and in a certain sense precludes the original. In commercial space, the object's self-consciousness does not derive from or reflects somehow its status or history as a commodity, nor does this self-awareness originate in the object itself but in its human "observers" such as the photographer, the Gladneys, and other "families shopping at night."

Instead, the glow of the coffee container literally illuminates, *from within* the object and *for* buyers like Ben, the product's place as "a tentative node in a limitless network of goods and flows."[73] As we remember, this is how Lerner describes the Hypermart Coke in *The Hatred of Poetry*. Such "materialist" description need not be reductive—or, with Harman's term, "overmining"—for it does not presume to extinguish all possibilities concerning the thing's thingness, its being or essence.[74] "Tentative," the nodal position is not a definitive determination, as we will see right away. At the same time, turning a blind eye to such contingencies and ramifications as those clarified *by the thing itself* is liable to miss a significant portion or aspect of what has made the thing what it is. "For the udon noodle," Bogost claims in *Alien Phenomenology*, "the being of the soup bowl does not intersect with the commercial transaction through which the noodle house sells it, or the social conventions according to which the eater slurps it." "Yet," he adds, "there is no reason to believe that the entanglement in which the noodle finds itself is any less complex than the human who shapes, boils, vends, consumes, or digests it."[75] Trained to be quite curious about "entanglements" and "conventions"—and they are "complex" whether they involve people or not—the critic that I am is not persuaded by the insuperable abyss Harman, Bogost, and other Object-Oriented Ontologists and "immaterialists" open between the object's being and its being *in* various constellations alongside other objects. Again, the immaterialists are right to point out that the former "exceeds" the latter.[76] But I am reluctant to infer from this that an object's being "withdraws" behind its phenomenological manifestation. Instead, what we are witnessing is the "demystifying" revelation about to happen in Benjamin Kunkel's 2005 novel *Indecision*— "all the commodities on the shelves," narrating protagonist Dwight Wilmerding reports from an Ecuadorian grocery store, "brim and gleam with imminent disclosures," promising to "disclose their history to the touch."[77] In effect, not even the *White Noise* fruit steps behind its appearance completely although the object's self-absencing in its simulacral presentation is what gets the attention of postmodern authors like DeLillo.

Lerner, on the other hand, homes in on the object's being-there. Not only that, but Ben discovers that this being-there comes into being and, moreover, into the open—*showing* itself rather than receding—as it "intersects" with other beings and their own tangles of matter, life, and energy. They are all elements of a geoeconomic grid that, powering as it does the jar's presentation, does not render the glow solely a byproduct of the jar's being plugged into transnational networks of mass production, transportation, and exploitative labor either. In effect—and this is key—the glow is not already there, a steady lure to the consumer. The container only starts glowing when the commercial relations and relays crisscrossing in its body feel "threatened," and when, as a result, the object itself is about to extricate itself from the exchange regime and take on a life of its own. That is the life of objects under a new, aesthetic regime. The "regime change" would be another transfer without transformation, for nothing *in* the thing has changed, except that everything has, which is what the flicker signals. The "little differen[ce]" (19) is that between the jar's previous, imperiled presence in the trade networks and its impending if probably also "tentative" absence from them, a *not* being-there that in turn propels the coffee can into a fuller, ontoaesthetic being-there—into *hyper*presence. The sudden "relative scarcity" (18) deserializes, decommodifies, and "flattens" the item as the Whole Foods is on the verge of being sold out.[78] It would not be entirely amiss to see the glow as a Benjaminian aura of the quasi peerless and priceless, a visual clue that the mass-produced serial item is reverting back to an originality and beauty of sorts by bailing out of the price system and its equalizing procedures. The reader will recall that Lerner is adamant in *The Hatred of Poetry* that "albeit in a perverted form," the scansion of "things" on the Hypermart aisles is "also poetry."[79] As with the commercial sublime—and as with the Reaganite sublime too, which Ben references repeatedly in the context of another disaster, the January 28, 1986 explosion of the space shuttle *Challenger*—there are circumstances, Lerner ventures, in which the sublime, its meaning, temporality, and communal fervor can break loose from the instrumental strictures of commercialism, conservatism, and related systems of economy, culture, and power so as to embark on "little less" repetitive worldmaking projects.

Ben's project is one of those, and so is *10:04* as a whole. Both recycle at-hand cultural and material repertoires, but both are "just a little different" from postmodern recycling.[80] This is primarily because if they salvage what is, and what no longer functions or has value within current operating systems, they do so, straightforwardly and unapologetically, in the name of novel systems. Where postmodernism's recyclings are for the most part intertextual, ironic, and dystopian and tend, along the same lines, to postpone, mock, and otherwise sabotage the solidifying of clear-cut alternatives, contemporary retrofittings of textual and nontextual objects strive to presence those endlessly tabled possibilities. A postmodern such as DeLillo defers repetition; instead, a post-postmodern like Lerner repeats with a difference and therefore actualizes an ontological potential. One's post-catastrophic *Silence* absences the future, literally quietens it; *10:04* voices or, better yet, visualizes it, makes it beam out from within the bowels of the same dark present. In DeLillo's *Point Omega*, artists do experiment with futural notions and practices of time and value, but those experiments do not carry over into the clockwork-time world, which remains stuck in the instrumentalism of its for-routines. In some ways comparable to Christian Marclay's movie montage *The Clock*, which Ben views and reacts to in another important scene in *10:04*, *Point Omega*'s *24 Hour Psycho*, "a videowork" acknowledged by DeLillo at the end of his 2010 novel, slows time down without bringing its massive presencing force to bear on the installation's environs, in which nothing and nobody "count as a presence."[81] The opposite happens in *10:04*, where, we will note, the Cartier-Bresson rejoins the world, the futural phenomenology of its totaling "magic" bleeding into the "real" and making it, albeit "tentatively," provisionally, just a tad different from what it has been. "Although I knew it wouldn't last," Ben says, "as I walked back to Brooklyn from Alena's apartment across the Manhattan Bridge, everything my eye alighted on seemed *totaled in the best sense*: complete in extent or degree; absolute; unqualified; whole. It was still fully afternoon, but it felt like magic hour, when light appears immanently to the lit" (134; emphasis mine).

The world's own "glow," light is here the auratic effect of the energy release accompanying the world's self-completion. Wrecked or not, flawed or less so, the outside world too exists, needless to say, under the thumb of entrenched axiologies and codes of qualification; during the Capitalocene, the world's principal qualification and source of ontological "incompletion" has also been its commodification. This has augmented the vulnerability, weakness, and "disrepair" of the world, bringing it one step closer to being "totaled"—in the *worst* sense.[82] What the Institute models aesthetically for its neighborhood and the broader world is a re-integrating kind of totaling, one that would reinstate and respect the world as an *integrum*. This is an ontological protocol of un-determination or "un-qualification" that would "save" that world *for* a time and overall system whose possibilities already become realities in the form of the superficially or seemingly deformed items salvaged by Alena. As in *Atocha*, Lerner's formalism is realist, presentist or in play in the present reality of form, imperfect as this form may be or look, and it is also visionary, futurist. This bifold temporality turns the form's metaphysics inside out as the glow of the absolute, the noumenality of the Brooklyn neighborhood and of the

Cartier-Bresson, proves "immanent." Intrinsic to the object's phenomenality, the noumenon appears in and essentially is the object's appearance itself. Lerner's phenomenology, and flat aesthetics generally, is therefore a *phenoumenology*. It is, in other words, an aesthetic of "what you see is what is—and what you get," and we definitely get more than what we have bargained for, "appearances" notwithstanding, or precisely because they are what they are, *apparently* the same.

So are they on page 135, where two Cartier-Bresson photos credited as such by Lerner (245) show Claude Roy on the Brooklyn Bridge. Above, they are "framed" by the Institute's salvaging project; here, outside Alena's studio, they reframe the world, put a "different" twist on it. The image in them is "a bit different" from Ben on the Manhattan Bridge, which also differs from what he pictures while crossing it, namely, himself "watch[ing him]self walking" across the Brooklyn Bridge (135), à la Adam Gordon and of course, à la Claude Roy also. The Cartier-Bresson pictures too *appear* to be one and the same. There is a difference, and this is the captions underneath them: "Our world," for the photo on the left, and "The world to come," for the one on the right. As we know from *Atocha*, Lerner is fond of placing repeated and multilayered reflections of his books' tenors *en abyme*, embedding them in a variety of diegetic objects. In *10:04*, he reaches for his metafictional ploy again to foreground via the twin photos the futural and utopian propensity of the present and reality, as well as the worldly, extra-aesthetic purview of aesthetic, non-transformative but deeply altering "transfers" such as those taking place in the Institute and the Whole Foods store. As he underscores in the *Harper's Magazine* article, "much, if by no means all, of contemporary art since Warhol assumes a posture of monetary disinterestedness, one based on criticism of the market itself," and yet, he goes on, all that art "is very much for sale."[83] In Kant's *Critique of Judgment*, and also in Harman, who retains the Kantian term, disinterestedness is or should be an attribute of the art receiver's "contemplation."[84] In the article and in *10:04*, it is the Duchampian artist who claims to have no interest, financial in this case, in a work that is nonetheless for sale. Lerner's point is that one can imagine a post-Duchampian avant-garde, and with it a new art, art system, and world-system altogether, by upending the logic of Duchamp's anti-aesthetics: where Duchampians drag the "ugly" and the "banal" into the aesthetic and otherwise violate, destroy, and total the latter while de facto reinscribing it into the cycles of capital, post-Duchampians leave the art object alone, totaling, instead, the appreciation-cum-appraisal, aesthetic and non-aesthetic systems "intersecting" in and with it. Moreover, not only is the non-Duchampian readymade a latticework of relations and interlinking systems, and not only is it plugged, accordingly, into a plurality of worlds, but it is also highly "energetic"—it acts and reacts in them to other objects and object aggregates, mapping its ontology onto its surroundings and making them "a little different" from what they were before.

As pivotal to *10:04* as to *Station Eleven*, the notion of a decommodified, mundanely relevant, and ontologically "infectious" readymade informs Ben's reaction to *The Clock*. A cinematic avatar of the Cartier-Bresson print and photos, the footage *trouvé* has been "described," Ben says,

> as the ultimate collapse of fictional time into real time, a work designed to obliterate the distance between art and life, fantasy and reality. But part of why I looked at my phone was because that distance hadn't been collapsed for me at all; while the duration of a real minute and *The Clock*'s minute were mathematically indistinguishable, they were nevertheless minutes from different worlds. I watched time in *The Clock*, but wasn't in it, or I was experiencing time as such, not just having experiences through it as a medium. As I made and unmade a variety of overlapping narratives out of its found footage, I felt acutely how many different days could be built out of a day, felt *more possibility than determinism, the utopian glimmer of fiction* [emphasis added]. When I looked at my watch to see a unit of measure identical to the one displayed on the screen, I was indicating that a distance remained between art and the mundane. *Everything will be as it is now*—the room, the baby, the clothes, the minutes—*just a little different.* (54; emphasis in the original)

Some critics have adduced the paragraph as proof of the irrelevance of art-to world-making. What Ben is telling us here, though, is basically that fiction and life are locked in the ontological mechanics of Hassidic difference: fiction is like life, a story of objects ("the room, the baby . . ."), just somewhat different; the two lie side by side, separated by a narrow blank space, as the Cartier-Bressons do on page 135; indeed, there appears to be a difference between the fictional and the fictionalized, but art *ought to be* different from its milieu, singular and hard to assimilate by it, in order to be able to make *it* different, to carry the world forward by injecting it with the serum of artistic vision.

Far from obstructing the mundane bearings of art, this dissimilarity in fact predicates them insofar as it keeps both art's "determination" at bay and the "possibility" of world change alive. Therefore, moviemakers, painters, and novelists need not "collapse" the temporalities and affiliated systems of the artistic and the worldly; their job is not absolute mimesis, for they are not tasked with the impossible, but with the possible. What visionary artists do, what Ben struggles to accomplish in the book, and what Lerner himself achieves with it is, less ambitiously, ensuring that the webs of the imagination, economy, social life, and travel "intersect" synergistically, as they do in the futural architecture of the messianic object. A prerequisite of the world's aesthetic reworlding, the ontological "distance" between the readymade and reality may not be closed but shrinks as artwork reaches across the fiction-reality divide deep into life—"tentacularly," as we will learn before long—and starts tweaking it, "just a little" (54). The glow from *within* the jar, the "glimmer of fiction" Ben "feels" (54) *inside* the theater showing Marclay's film, the light "immanent" to the magically "lit" urbanscape on which Ben's gaze "alights" *outside* the Institute (134), and "the *glimmer*, however refracted, of the world to come, where everything is the same but a little different" (109), are kindred tropes by which the same optic imaginary flags both the readymade's actual entwining with global systems of material production and the "utopian" potential for these ensembles' "slightly different" reproduction through art and art-inspired modes of making and remaking.[85] No wonder Ben decides "while looking from *The Clock*," which measures art time, "to my cell phone" (which tells . . . clock time) "and back again"

> to write more fiction . . . and over the next week I began to work on a story, outlining much of it in my notebook while sitting in the theater. The story would involve a series of transpositions: I would shift my medical problem to another part of the body; replace astereognosis with another disorder, displace Alex's oral surgery. I would change names: Alex would become Liza, which she'd told me once had been her mother's second choice; Alena would become Hannah; Sharon I'd change to Mary, John to Josh; Dr. Andrews to Dr. Roberts, etc. Instead of becoming a literary executor, and so confronting the tension between biological and textual mortality through that obligation, the protagonist—a version of myself; I'd call him "the author"—would be approached by a university about selling his papers. Just like the French writer in the story Bernard had recounted the night I met his daughter, the "author" would plan to fabricate his correspondence. (54–5)

The "story," which Ben ends up composing, and which Lerner published in *The New Yorker* in 2012 under the same title, "The Golden Vanity," is "repeated" in *10:04* (61–81).[86] Subject to the aforementioned narrative "transpositions," the story-in-the-story is "just a bit" less autofictional than the frame narrative, which makes up the bulk of *10:04*. Consolidating its autobiographical position "on the very edge of fiction" (237) along the same, autointertextual lines, the 2014 novel also alludes ever so often to *Atocha*, from which it even lifts ideas, phrases, and situations such as the "self-voyeuristic" Brooklyn Bridge scene (135). The growth of the system of Lerner's oeuvre through the addition of *10:04* thus plays out, similarly to the other systems with which the textual ensemble intermingles and interacts, as a succession of revisions, reincorporations, and "versions" coming about inside and across individual entities' physical bodies and bodies of work, with novelty obtaining through marginally yet no less different repetitions and self-repetitions.

Intriguingly, the enlargement of Ben/Lerner's literary corpus—the "dilation of ["The Golden Vanity"] story" (154) into *10:04*—mirrors a development inside Ben's "pathologized corpus" (6), viz., the "dilation of [his] aorta" (129). Further, the somatic symptom itself mimics corporeal processes characteristic of the octopus Ben both has for dinner at the beginning of the novel (3–4) *and* imagines changing into ("I felt as if my limbs had multiplied" [6]) during an astereognosis examination for which he waited in a room with a "giant octopus painted on the wall" (4). As we learn from the dinner's own encore later in the novel (154), what Ben eats in the company of his literary agent in a celebration of the "'strong six-figure' advance" (4) he got to turn his story into a novel is, to be more exact, a dish of baby octopuses. "The chef," Ben details, "had literally massaged [them] to death" (3), and Ben's "ingesting" whole plates of them (3) only reinforces from the outset the animals' equivocation as both objects and agents of death and life, destruction and renewal, violent present and redemptive future. In the same vein, the cephalopod is not one but many at once, and it is many in one as well, concomitantly suggestive of self-replication and self-differentiation, of multidirectional stretching out across space, outside itself, a movement parallel to the manifold internal decentralization of its anatomy (the mollusk boasts eight "legs" and three hearts), brain (there is a central one plus a smaller one in each tentacle), and neurosensorial system.

One downside of the latter, Ben informs us, is "poor proprioception," which means that the animal is unable to "determine the position of its body in the current" (7). In Charles Olson's "Proprioception" excogitations, with which *10:04* is in conversation as much as *The Hatred of Poetry* is with "The Kingfishers," the great poet highlights the soul's corporealization. The soul, Olson offers, is "equally physical," a "corpus" and *in* the corpus; it is a bodily entity rather than external to flesh, organs, and their physiology.[87] But "the soul is proprioceptive" also, and since self-perception and perception are interlaced, its "projective" or imaginative exploits are corporeally orchestrated.[88] Our "hearts," "intestines," and the like shape our worldviews and worldmaking endeavors. In that, these too can be seen as "visceral," as critics have Olson's "ecopoetics," a term that is apt because it evokes the whole spectrum of animate and inanimate corporealities that fashion Olson's ars poetica.[89] Focusing on proprioception and on the body as driver and biological blueprint of poetic worldbuilding, Jonathan Skinner has explained how Michael McClure relies on Olson to develop his own "beast language," and I think a similar argument can be made on *10:04*.[90] Lerner too leans on Olson's proprioceptive axiomatics to get a better grasp of the incorporated nature of writing. As in McClure, this incorporation emulates nonhuman embodiment. Where the botanic poetics of Richard Powers's 2018 novel *The Overstory* helps us imagine what "writing like a tree" might be, *10:04* can be said to narrativize "octopus writing" by adopting cephalopodic physiology as a model for world poiesis.

Admittedly a handicap, the octopus's "poor proprioception" does not translate, then, as one might expect, into a poverty of the literary imagination. Quite the contrary, the lack, the deficiency, the kinesthetic "failure," if you will, give the mollusk an edge on another plane. "Octopus-like" self-perception is energizing and futurally so, catalyzing something like temporal kinesthesia. Following from Ben's "mollusk" anatomy, the impaired ability of the writer to "determine" (6) his whereabouts in one place and moment—here and now—enhances the writer's mobility in and "feel" of time, allowing him to envision himself in several "theres" and "futures." As Ben half-jokingly describes to his agent his plans to "enlarge" "The Golden Vanity" into a book, "the author changes into an octopus [and] travels back and forth in time [o]n a decommissioned train" (157)—if not in a futuristic DMC DeLorean as Marty McFly in the *Back to the Future* franchise.

Lerner's hero may not metamorphose into an actual octopus in spite of his "arm span," "thin toes," and "mild double-jointedness" (4–5) but "grows" an octopus's "soul" instead. As Sy Montgomery's 2015 bestseller assures us, the creature does have a soul, and if the novel is any indication, Ben/Lerner seems to develop an identical or equivalent cognitive-affective "organ"—to internalize the object or better yet, to be taken over by it. To paraphrase the title of Thomas Nagel's famous bat essay, Ben "feels" what it is like to be a mollusk, so much so that he identifies literally and narratively with the octopus psyche or self.[91] "*It*" [i.e., the octopus], writes Lerner, "can taste what it touches," but it cannot "determine the position of *its* body, . . . particularly *my* arms, and the privileging of flexibility over proprioceptive inputs means *it* lacks stereognosis, the capacity to form a mental image of the overall shape of what *I* touch" (6; emphasis added). Whatever its name, the psychosomatic mechanism that here is becoming "his"—if not *him* altogether—is futural in its operations given that "it" ends up un-determining "him" (Ben) in a way germane to my discussion so far.[92] Not only does this profound, organic self-identification with the nonhuman self—this octopus-becoming—enable Ben to "project [him]self into several futures simultaneously" (4), but it also hands him the post-postmodern road map of these projections to boot, that is, the literary technology and, as a bonus, even the aquatic settings of the "transpositions" by which he would develop his story into a novel ("I'll work my way from irony to sincerity in the sinking city, a would-be Whitman of the vulnerable grid" [4]). Astereognostic writing—or *re*writing rather, for it works over Ben's "found," if already published, story—juggles the re-presenting of what is, for *The New Yorker* has printed it, and the presencing of what may be. Dramatizing the futural dialectic of non-Duchampian readymade, cephalopodic expansion is, in short, an authorship algorithm, a mode of authoring.

The "repetition of the octopus imagery," Adam Colman notes, "increasingly fuses with [Ben's] meditation on himself, until he registers a sense of reality that ramifies into a reality beyond that of realistic fiction."[93]

Ultimately, the issue is not so much realism, a certain perception or stylistic treatment of reality; the issue or issues are reality itself, how Ben/Lerner's flat aesthetic handles it, and what happens in the process. Remarkably, with another keyword of the novel, reality starts "rearranging" itself (32, 38, 40, 65, 109, 182), rewriting its prose (109) with a kraken's flexibility, and "ramifications" sprouting a plethora of "transfers without" conspicuous "transformations," discreet onto-aesthetic inflections, and other similarly "differential" reiterations ford the divides between the Institute and New York City, art- and world-systems, and so forth. Object-driven, the cephalopodic-arachnid "spidering out" (216, 217, 230) of such bifurcations and excrescences is narratively multipronged and in that hard to trace, as is usually the case in network fictions by Mandel, Hamid, Haruki Murakami, Mircea Cărtărescu, Michel Houellebecq, David Mitchell, and other late-global-era writers.[94] Generally speaking, though, in *10:04*, it goes from the messianic readymade and other commercially dys- or post-functional items and spaces suddenly revigorated into auratic hyperpresence to a "world out there" over which aesthetic entities extend their haloed potentiality.

As in *Station Eleven*, that world does not change into an impromptu art museum overnight or into an Institute for Totaled Art for that matter. All the same, presencing energies ooze out of Alena's studio, as it were, enlivening the mundane in its hour of darkness, when Manhattan is about to be "totaled" in the impending "monster storm" ("its limbs moving in real time, the brain visible in its translucent skull" [233]) and the "spliced Doppler images" of its "swirling tentacular mass" (232) are further spliced with ultrasound pictures of Alex's unborn child. The sonograms of the little body inside Alex's make Ben think of "baby octopuses" (233), as do the crowds outside ("a single, sensate organism" [29]) and the whole Big Apple, which is "becoming one big organism" too, "constituting itself in relation to a threat visible from space, an aerial sea monster with a single centered eye around which tentacular rain bands swirled" (17). Individual and collective, natural and civilizational threats and their flip side, a hopefully transformative future for the endangered ecosystems of art, life, and community, twist together in the multifaceted octopus, in the octopus-like world, and in Ben's cephalopodic body and psyche (3). The latter latches onto "bad forms of collectivity" (108) and, as in *Atocha*, onto bad forms pure and simple, but with another frequent reiteration of futurality, it also helps reimagine those forms as "figures of [social] possibility" (108, 239). This "proprioceptive flicker in advance of the communal body" (28, 108) is redolent of the great American literary cephalopod, the all-embracing Whitman, and indeed, the Whitmanian vision complete with its temporal and collective buoyancy both tempts and gives Lerner pause, particularly in the Marfa residency episode (194).

A tiny desert town where Ben spends some time writing poetry and partying, Marfa lies in West Texas. However, Ben "fe[els] as though [he']d moved" there "without transition" (165)—and without "transformation" either, one is tempted to quip. At any rate, this is not the only clue that, on the map of Lerner's objectual imaginary, the place is right outside New York City if not *inside* it and even inside Ben's body, or at least isomorphic to both, on several levels; conversely, one can picture Ben's ramification-prone, octopus anatomy and habitat spreading geographically across effectively or seemingly homologous locales, cultural forms, and institutions. In any case, Marfa is an imperfect homophone of Marfan—so similar and yet different from it—and Marfan is, *10:04*'s reader will remember, the name of Ben's most plausible diagnosis, "a genetic disorder of the connective tissue that typically produces the long-limbed and flexible" (4). Likewise, Marfa's Chinati Foundation, set up by minimalist artist Donald Judd in the 1980s, reminds Ben of Alena's project. The Foundation houses "John Chamberlain's sculptures, which are largely hewn from chrome-plated and painted steel, often the mangled bodies of cars, an art of the totaled" (165), as well as some of the "specific objects" by which Judd asserted his "desire to overcome the distinction between art and life" through an "insistence on literal objects in real space" (178).[95] Before, Ben did not find that space very different from "Costco or a Home Depo or IKEA" (178) or other "Hypermarts." But the Foundation, established in a site itself "totaled"—the "ruins" of a "shed" that "once had housed prisoners from Rommel's Afrika Korps" (179–80)—strikes him as a "different" environment, pulsing with a luminous thereness paralleled by the mysterious "Marfa Lights" (192) and attuned to the cephalopodic dilations and beat of the world. Judd's "shimmering boxes," Ben reports, were situated "in the immediate, physical present, registering fluctuations of presence and light" (180). "Located in the surpassing disasters of modern times" (180), the installations appeared to him nevertheless "tuned to an inhuman, geological duration" (Ben and Roberto's dinosaur chapbook comes to mind here), to "lava flows and sills," the objects' "aluminum expanding as the planet warms" and making the observer "fe[el]," as an octopus would, "all those orders of temporality—the biological, the historical, the geological—combine and interfere and then dissolve" (180).

An aesthete that "has been observed at complicated play," the octopus is an artisan that "decorates its lair" (3). But, as with the coffee can and other components of his material imaginary, Lerner stops short of aestheticizing the object out of what Ben calls "network[s] of abstract exchange" (222). In fact, the animal's sometimes also "artisanal" origins tie into, and expose, systems of production, acquisition, and consumption at the same time that the mollusk assumes new functions that cut against their grain, and, in a similar vein, Ben pledges to give up this particular seafood. While "swallowing" one baby octopus after another early on in the novel, "the majesty and murderous stupidity of it," he senses,

was all about me, coursing through me: the rhythm of artisanal Portuguese octopus fisheries coordinated with the rhythm of laborers' migration and the rise and fall of art commodities and tradable futures in the dark galleries outside the restaurant and the mercury and radiation levels of the sashimi and the chests of the beautiful people in the restaurant—coordinated, or so it appeared, by money. One big joke cycle. One big totaled prosody . . . Never would I eat octopus again. (156–8)

We discovered in *Atocha*, and we learn once more from *10:04*, that there is a tempo in Lerner, a cadence—the meter of poetry's own potential and of potentiality largely—inherent to poetic as well as to non- or even anti-poetic forms, to superstore isles, Oval-Office oratory, markets, and anything enmeshed with exchange regimes. This syncopation, the writer observes, is flawed. The "prosody" of the eminently prosaic is "always already" totaled, and *not* in the "best sense." But this sense itself, and the overall meaning of poetry and art, can be re-totaled, if you will—it can be salvaged and can be "counted" once again for definitions and practices prior, post, or "outside the lexicon of property" (29), cash, and profit. Aesthetic object ("artisanal"), actor ("decorator"), and apparatus (model of narrative expansions), the octopus hints at interlarded micro- and macro-totalities such as art objects, the "tentacular cities" (*cités tentaculaires*) of Symbolist poetry and late twentieth-century urban "grids," weather fronts, and futures markets as it does, under the auspices of another kind of totaling, at the possibility of their differentiating repetitions.

Ben knows all this. Or, he rather "feels" it and even takes part in it the way a cephalopod might. The octopus-author is fully aware that his work is no exception, crossing money paths as his book deal does at the restaurant in the "proximity" of "investment bankers and market analysts" (156). Thus, "having monetized the future of [his] fiction" courtesy of his New York agent, *The New Yorker*, New York-headquartered publishing houses, and their cultural, mediatic, and financial operating systems, Ben decides to "turn his back" on the novel, "albeit to compose verse underwritten by a millionaire's foundation" (170) in Marfa. Only, neither genres nor places nor the objects and materials constituting them lend themselves to easy distinctions and segregations. Bridging these formal and physical gulfs are all sort of branchings and ramifications. Whitman's "impossible dream" (194), then bound up with it, dream-like, "totaled" Brooklyn, and the entire "totaled city" (240) beyond the borough, throbbing in the post-storm blackout with the bounteous presence of a readymade "escaped" from the Institute, somehow "transfer" across the distances between actuality and possibility, prose and poetry, and the urban, upper Eastern Seaboard and the rural South. Bursts of creative or, better put, re-creative synergies, and ultimately transformative, future-oriented and -inducive transfers occur over these polarities and expanses, rendering them like and unlike each other.

It is in this sense that, as Harman glosses on Latour's discussion of the Amazonian ecosystem in *Pandora's Hope*, there is no "transport without transformation."[96] Now, Lerner's "transport" or "transfer" covers the first part of the readymade onto-logic, and this segment or vector is meaningless without its non-transformative twin. Together, they suggest that in reproducing themselves onto another environment, medium, or genre, the photo, the coffee jar, the mollusk, "The Golden Vanity," and other apparently repetitive "specific objects" do *not* act repetitively in and on the systems in which they participate. As it transfers, enlarges, or replicates itself, the readymade stays basically the same *qua* form. Or, its formal changes, when they do take place, do not matter much. What matters is that far from shoring up present exchange regimes and the mundane status quo around them, this absolute or relative formal self-sameness bears on them all messianically, destabilizing them by inoculating them with its own ontoaesthetic mode. As in *Atocha*, the repetitious is ontologically intoxicating. It can unsettle the present and in that can presence, in this very present, a present to come. Also as in the 2011 novel, poetry plays an important role, for in *10:04* too poetic perception gets the world flowing, eroding and "liquifying" its values, rubrics, and divisions. Thus, Ben, who is also a poet, credits poetry with the power to flout "the distinction between fiction and nonfiction" (171) so as to afford not so much aestheticizing "conflat[ions of] fact and fiction" (170) as structural "rearrangements" of the former under impact of the latter.

We should remember, though, that Adam has his most presencing, revelatory experience in an art gallery. After a fashion, his poetry is on display there. More significantly still, the logic of his poem, especially of the poem Arturo "repeats" in Spanish, is, similarly to the systemically transformative logic of poetry in *10:04,* a reiteration of the onto-logic of totaled art, whether that art is located in Alena's Institute or in the Chinati, and whether the "real world" it positions itself to "rearrange" begins in Brooklyn or in Marfa. Judd's boxes exude, we might recall, the artist's aspiration to wipe out the "distinction between art and life" (178), as *The Clock* (54) and Alena's salvaged objects do. And so if "totaled" New York City transfers—"without transformation"—to Marfa, it should come as no surprise that the same happens in reverse, what with the "total" "dark" that, at the end of the novel, makes Ben "th[ink] of Marfa, the buildings around me like permanent installations in the desert night" (237). The "permanent installations" are the "dark towers of the Financial district" (236), whose obscurity is deepened by the "felt absence of the twin towers" (237) and even by one of the well-lit exceptions, the Goldman Sachs building. They are all one big *mise-en-scène* of the impermanence of the economic and principally monetary system under which art has been forced to exist, and they are so in a narratively performative sort of way.

What I mean is that Ben does not just imagine the allegorical phasing out of world arrangements under which artworks such as his own novel-to-be are valued as commodities, but Ben/Lerner also performs this process in front of the reader, in the form of what he or she is reading and while the protagonist/author interpellates him or her. It turns out, *10:04* itself is what Ben has written *in lieu of* the "contracted" book, which was, tellingly enough, about forgery and "fraudulence" (237), that is, "about fabricating the past" (194). *10:04* unfolds instead "on the very edge of fiction." That is not because it consists of poems, although it comprises some poetry and arrestingly poetic prose, nor is it because the symbolically titled "The Golden Vanity" and Ben's plans to expand the story in a "contracted," lucrative direction do not take up a lot of space in the resulting book, but because this book grounds itself in "an actual present alive with multiple futures" (194). Revealingly, Lerner "actualizes" one of these temporalities in Ben's faux-Reaganite future-tense "address" "to the schoolchildren of America" (239) in the novel's closing scene, where, as if on cue, "a gas lamp on Saint Mark's will flicker across genres" and even "parasitic insects will appear to me as a bad form of collectivity that can stand as a figure of its possibility" (239). Repeating the book's signature phrases one last time, Lerner offers up *10:04* as proof that "[e]verything will be as it had been" (239), with a difference.

THREE | Exit

Exit: a point between here and there, in and out.

An often subversive, only occasionally sign-posted dividing line between one thing and another. What happens when we cross over to the other side?
—Laura Waddell, *Exit*

The question of fiction is first a question regarding the distribution of places.
—Jacques Rancière, *The Politics of Aesthetics*

Democracy, Rancière reminds us, is a topo-logy, a logic of arrangements. For, as etymology tells us, one "arranges" in or across space by creating a form in and with it. At its most basic, to arrange something is to spatialize, to "bend" space—"range" stems from the Indo-European verbal root meaning "to bend," which reinforces the notion that arranging is fashioning space, shrinking, expanding, apportioning, granting, denying it, and so forth. Vastly political, such operations and attendant material and cultural practices have been subject to spatial contracts throughout the ages. In turn, these agreements' "style" and readability vary across time, traditions, and media. Redrawn in the revolutionary aftermath of the Enlightenment, the compacts sanctioning the production of space in Western modernity continue to be periodically amended. A barometer of sociopolitical and cultural change, they run a whole discursive gamut from legally specific and literal contracts to the more general and literary. The former set up detailed regulations of "space-heavy" issues such as property ownership, occupancy, eminent domain, easement, access, transit, real-estate transactions, zoning, districting, and in more turbulent times, nationalization of individual and corporate assets; the latter category may have little regulatory leverage but participates actively in the private and public construction of space.

It is refreshing to see political thinkers like Rancière rely on literature and other putatively superstructural phenomena to think this process through. As is well known, Rancière insists that the "distribution of the sensible" is an index of actual democracy in that such "apportionments"[1] of perceptible spatiality occur and can be, as he maintains in *The Lost Thread*, "community-forming" inside literature and art largely.[2] Arranging togetherness, composing it spatially, is, according to the French philosopher, what literature intrinsically does; poiesis is topopoiesis. This future-oriented and socially reconstructive political manipulation of spatial possibilities renders, in Rancière, the literary and the artistic "neo-avant-gardist."[3] For, in a fundamental way, the dispensation of power and politics generally are spatializations of togetherness; they are attributions, distributions, and redistributions of space, i.e., of sites or entire geographies where one can be with another. What grounds or undercuts politics, as the case may be, is then a certain spatial ethic or lack thereof. But the *re*grounding, the spatial reembodying of this ethic, especially when the apportionment of a society's "sensible" stock becomes politically unsustainable or undesirable, is, Rancière observes, an aesthetic prerogative in the original sense of *aísthēsis*, whether we talk about political action "per se" or aesthetic practice.[4]

In effect, "Rancière obliterates the distinction between the two," as Harman observes.[5] To paraphrase Rancière, the question of democracy and the question of art are identical.[6] This is why he leans on writers to identify progressive ("dissenting") models of "rebuilding the common"[7] spatially, that is, by means of an artistic allotment of spaces (*partage des espaces*) susceptible to eventually reinstate the democratic "possibility of another world."[8] An aesthetic undertaking twice, and in that eminently and "intensively" political, literature proves itself a primary "world-making" modality (a *manière de faire monde*) insofar as it brings to bear on extant spatial arrangements an imaginatively "rearranging" sensorium whose one-of-a-kind "reclassifying" and redistributive, "dissenting" mechanisms are geared to reassigning and redefining (*requalifier*) the world's spaces and the world itself with them.[9] Thus, new spatial contracts are written quite *stricto sensu*.

These contracts are as significant as the stylistic-linguistic, rhetorical, and deliberative ones that Nelly Wolf revisits in *Le Roman de la démocratie*. The fulcrum of Wolf's discussion of novelistic contractuality and the focus of aforementioned spatiality contracts overlap considerably. Both use an "other"'s location in a medium as a benchmark, whether that medium is linguistic (a certain language through which the other is represented by the *story*) or spatial (a place, environs, or expanse in which he or she is placed diegetically, cast inside a *plot*), and so what Wolf determines, à la Rancière, as a "distribution of language" is ethically and politically isomorphic to an apportionment of space and contractually equivalent to it.[10] For crucial to the rearrangements of language and space alike is the position assigned or reassigned to the other, a location that as far as the book's fictional universe goes, is literally an actual abode, habitat, milieu, or geographical zone. With another terminology, at issue here is whether spatial reshufflings unfold a topology and ultimately "make a world" shared by self and other. If a certain novel provides for such a world and for communality overall, then that work's spatial contract is democratic; if the novel lacks such provisions, then the contract is, concludes Wolf, "totalitarian."

The obvious point to make on Wolf's distinction is that these antithetic types are seldom present as such; ordinarily, they collide, cross, and combine into ambivalent contractualities over whose meanings critics themselves clash. The less evident point is that *all* such contracts are undemocratic unless they make explicit and equitable stipulations for nonhuman agents. In fact, most of them do. The issue, then, is not the contracts themselves but how to read them and with them, the narratives into which they are written. To my mind, they are all due for a truly democratic reading, one that would run along the lines of Bryant's "object democracy" and flat ontology broadly. Part three of *Flat Aesthetics* attempts this kind of analysis by looking into the contractual roles human and nonhuman actors play in a couple of post-2000 American novels. To that effect, what I will be perusing in this body of work is mostly the fine print of its spatial compacts. In Wolf, the large print is reserved to human entities, as is in Rancière. Because he too "insist[s] on the centrality of linguistic forms," he "endorse[s] human exceptionalism," as Shaviro has aptly commented.[11] Nevertheless, Harman finds Rancière on the whole appealing,[12] and even Jane Bennett, who has mounted a poignant critique of the French thinker in *Vibrant Matter*, allows that "opportunit[ies] for a more materialist theory of democracy" do exist in his work.[13]

If Rancière's materialism, along with his politics and aesthetics, is a humanism, tethered as it remains to human agency, expression, and benefit, then in order to make the most of such opportunities, one must decenter or, more exactly, de-anthropocenter his "sensible" by further unpacking its objectual granularity. When "asked in public whether he thought that an animal or a plant or a drug or a (nonlinguistic) sound could disrupt the police order, Rancière said no: he did not want to extend the concept of the political that far"; "nonhumans," he contended, "do not qualify as participants in the demos; the disruption effect must be accompanied by the desire to engage in reasoned discourse."[14] But "reasoned discourse," I argue throughout *Flat Aesthetics*, is neither a prerequisite of world making nor a condition of political agency more generally. "Arrangements" may be interlaced with discourse but are not exclusively discursive, and they are not solely linguistic either. On the other hand, topopoiesis, a subset and vehicle of ontopoiesis, does not just take place *in* the sensible but is also effectuated *by* it, with all manner of things participating in space making and remaking.[15] These entities are more than spatial tools, background, or symbols of human "spatial practices," as Henri Lefebvre and after him, Edward Soja and others called them.[16] These objects are spatial actors in their own right. They are world makers because they make space; they are beings that spatialize Being. In this sense, world ontology is indeed articulated, "scansioned" spatially by the order of things.[17] Not only are things distributed in space, but they also distribute it—*and they also distribute "us" in it.* These distributions enforce or "disturb," as Rancière specifies, "the clear partition of identities, activities, and spaces."[18]

Homing in on such partitions, separations, and the material entities that enable or block access, coming through, ingress or egress, this *Flat Aesthetics* segment examines how specific spatial objects get in the way or open one, to whom, and what spatial agreements are upheld or breached in the process. Thus, this part is an exploration of exits: exit as a place, threshold, mechanism, and action; exit as a passage through which one moves on and leaves behind a place, person, or community to cross into another place and join another community; and exit as the passage, passing, transformation, and narration such exiting and entering warrant or deny. The first chapter of this section deals with Joseph O'Neill's novel *The Dog* and involves an object-oriented, gender-inflected critique of the spatial sublime; the second tackles the aporias of dis- and re-location in Hamid's fiction, especially in *Exit West.* These all are, I propose, exit narratives where a "crisis" of post-Cold War Western and non-Western spatial contracts becomes legible.[19] An effect of shifting object functions and arrangements, this legibility reveals a particular structure of contemporaneity.

go, dog. go!, *scuba diving, massage chairs*: *The Dog*, *X*/It-Men, and Other Things That Go

. . . perhaps the most intelligent chaise de massage in the world.
—Joseph O'Neill, *The Dog*

Wrongfully, I withheld from her my developing interest in room theory.
—Joseph O'Neill, *The Dog*

What a home the world was!

—Joseph O'Neill, *The Dog*

In O'Neill's 2009 Pen/Faulkner Award winner *Netherland*, objects tend to assemble into a spatial world order that holds out the promise of participatory cosmopolitanism.[20] In *The Dog*, however, this order is undercut by their selective allocation across the Emirati cityscapes, where the plot is mostly set.[21] The overarching issue here is presence, human and not. It bears asking subsequently, as Rancière would, under which material circumstances humans "appear" in a certain space. Or, to rephrase, as Latour and some of his OOO fans might, which constellations of objects afford or prevent human presence there; further, when present, if people's being-thereness is accompanied by and registers with other human and nonhuman entities; and what the implications and repercussions of that visibility—or invisibility—are. This is all about the spatial politics of mobility and, deeper still, about the "thing politics" of coming, leaving, and perchance staying, of slipping in or out of object configurations. In Hamid, these operations are matters of life and death. In O'Neill, they are vitally important too. In both writers, they frustrate as much as they energize, or even more, as people learn quickly that they have removed themselves from undesirable entanglements only to step into bigger if less palpable ones.

In *The Dog*, these are, as in *Station Eleven*, part and parcel of the world-systems whose dysfunctionality the 2007 financial disaster exposed on a previously unequaled scale. By 2009, when *The Dog*'s unnamed narrating protagonist gets comfortably seated in "The Human Touch™" massage chair for his regular pedicure at Dubai's Unique hotel, the sharp downturn in world economy had been felt around the world. Unprecedentedly world-systemic, the crisis thematized its own condition of possibility and, by the same token, a defining feature of the contemporary: the planet's all-embracing networks of exchange, capital, trade, migration, labor, and communication. Equities analyst Hans van der Broeck is no doubt aware of all this in *Netherland*, but the 2008 book focuses chiefly on the years immediately following the September 11 tragedy and on the prospects of community rebuilding in the United States and beyond in the aftermath of the attacks. As so many other postmillennial fictions, *The Dog* dwells on world-systems insistently. The book's angle on such a popular theme is their relation to space. They are, O'Neill stresses repeatedly, ubiquitous: *they make up the world's physical finitude*. No matter where you are, they are there too, around you and, as in Hamid, inside you as well, your texture and context. They are in virtually everybody's face and in overdrive, constantly in runaway, catastrophe-prone mode, and threatening to normalize themselves as an absolute spatiality bereft, à la Sartre's *No Exit*, of ways out and alternatives.

This exitless spatiality is poised to be or become a totality, a spatial projection of what critics have dubbed, sometimes with overt Jamesonian riffs, "the global sublime." Keen on this aspect of the late-global era, O'Neill pictures space as a continuum rendered all of-a-piece, without an outside to it by the all-subsuming logic of the monetary, data, and consumption networks of twenty-first-century globalization. Contradiction-ridden and feebly contested, recurrently in crisis and perpetually resurgent, *The Dog*'s global sublime advertises hyperbolically if disingenuously a completed project, a reached ideal and majestically achieved, wrinkleless *totum* where the quasi omnipresence of transnational routes of travel, money, power, expertise, employment, idiom, and desire alludes to an unrepresentable *nec plus ultra*. Dismissive of local histories and oddly apprehensive of natural environments, the sublime project rounds itself off and offers itself up as a radical spatialization, a supreme sublimation of history and nature into a total space where the transformative and *outré* operations of networks have all but disabled the distinction between the world and its artificial world-systems; more advanced, more geopolitically aggressive, and more world-hungry than ever, post-Cold War world-systems are or are about to become coextensive with the world itself. This equivalence occurs in sublime space and further enhances this space's sublimity. Much as the world's temporal condition knows no timeout or interregnum, the spatial sublime is ontologically exhaustive, without topological "rest."

There appears, indeed, to be no place to step out of this networked spatiality. There is, it seems, no other to it, no barrier, interstice, or room of one's own in or beyond it. This goes a long way toward explaining why X, as his law-firm colleagues have christened him, is so obsessed with room, with his own room and more broadly with privacy, its ethics, geography, architectural form, and material ambiance, which he comments on and "theorizes" extensively. If, as we will notice, Dubai's sublime spatiality "calls forth his inner [space] theorist" (11), so does its "horizontal" opposite, the cramped New York City apartment where he feels cooped up with Jenn, his onetime girlfriend and coworker. Thus, while X's stateside theorizations speak the language of intimacy and map out the objectual arrangements of the private sphere, they also clue us in on the character's spatial behavior and expatiations in the strikingly different environment of the United Arab Emirates, where X takes a job after his breakup with Jenn. "Wrongfully," he admits in hindsight," "I withheld from her my developing interest in room theory" (71). Such "theory" reads like a contract—X is a lawyer after all—and poses questions that sound logical and widely applicable at first skim. "For example," he asks, "how many more rooms did two persons in occupation of a one-bedroom need" (71) when, he specifies with pretend pedantry, "(i) the two persons were almost never simultaneously in the one-bedroom; (ii) on the rare occasion that the two persons were simultaneously in the one-bedroom, almost always one or both of them was asleep and therefore unconscious; (iii) on the still rarer occasion that the two persons were simultaneously in the one-bedroom and simultaneously conscious, almost always one person was in the bedroom and the other was in the bathroom or the living room?" (71). The "footnote" (71) immediately following the three clauses gets very personal fast, though. "[W]hen we quarreled," says X, we would be in the same room. After a while, I'd tire of the quarrel, and I'd exit the room and go to the other room, in order to be by myself there. Jenn would follow me in, in order to continue saying things, and eventually I would leave that room and go back to the first room, and again she would follow me, and finally I'd have to go to the bathroom and lock the door, and still she would come after me, standing by the door and following me into the bathroom vocally, as it were. That happened consistently, which is interesting, because when we were not disputatious an opposite dynamic was typically in effect, namely that if I entered the same room as Jenn, she would quite soon leave that room, as if the point of an apartment was to ensure that its occupants lived apart from one another. (72)

In a way, the last sentence *is* the point, at least X's main point—and fallacy—here and for most of the novel. In response to the Jenn incident, an apartment ends up being for X an apartness, a space that sets up relationships as forms of being apart and makes those in them or getting out of them predisposed to looking for an exit and to separating themselves through space and in solitary spaces of "their own." X vaguely "hope[d] that one day we would enjoy being in the same room together" (71), but the episode made him feel that a residence was where its occupants were "alone together," as DeLillo writes in *Cosmopolis*.[22] Thus, X did not get excited about Jenn's plans to "find a bigger apartment, with more rooms" (73) and eventually "lost [his] cameral idealism" (73). His newly acquired "spatial realism" (19) got him, he assumed, "room-wise . . . on the same page as Jenn, i.e., my interest in being in the same room together had waned" (73). Recalling his final fight with Jenn, who had asked him to commit to their relationship and keep trying to have a baby together, X confesses that

> I've never felt what I felt as Jenn spoke to me in that room. I felt I was being interred from within. Each assertion she made was another shovelful . . . I couldn't take it . . .
> "No, you will never leave," Jenn said. "You will stay, darling. You will stay in this room with me until I'm finished." . . . She went on and on, irresistibly shoveling words into me, stopping every cavity of my being. I felt numb. I felt cold. I began to tremble. She was right. There were no options. *There was no going.* There was only staying. She was in the right. What I wanted put me in the wrong. I had to stay here with her. It was my duty to be in rooms I did not want to be in, to have a life I did not want to have, to have a life in which *I would not be present.* That was the effect of my duty. That was what was owed to her. I owed her an existence lacking the characteristics of being alive, a life as an apparatus of outcomes that were not mine. There was no alternative. It was my duty. I had to accept a posthumous life. (170–1; emphasis mine)

Jenn, who is never shown traveling, let alone going abroad, is both nation-bounded and a national synecdoche. No wonder X dubs the United States "Jenn-land" (235). Jenn marks in O'Neill's geoimaginary the doubly stabilizing gesture toward gendering territory and the territorialization of gender, where woman threatens to reduce the "potential" of masculinity to the meager rewards of proximity, the household, the parochial, and the national. In this sense, intimacy and country are dimensions of the same space, the gendered logic of which involves tying down and reining in male "presence" within an emasculating, static spatiality. Busting loose from the Circe-like clutches of quasi-matrimonial and national allegiance, X answers the call of a "man of the world" (6) like Edmond Batros and flies out to Dubai to join a fraternity of like-minded spirits loyal just to themselves and their pocketbooks. If the New York apartment is a space of self-demeaning and loss, Dubai is a "zone of win-win-win flows of money and ideas and humans" (107), that is, of lawyers, accountants, bankers, and other professionals making up a forward-looking "polity" of transterritorial "financial nationhood" (107). These are, as X fancies them, twenty-first-century avatars of the Djibouti *legionnaires* (6), a homosocial sodality of roving men keen on standing aside and, spatially and otherwise, above the trivia of their native environments.

If not a French legionnaire, X becomes an X-Man of sorts, an ex(it) man on the run figuratively and, we shall see, literally also, as the fellow runner in the international exit sign.[23] Does he "get out," though? Is he adequately equipped to make his escape, and if so, is his "equipment" serving him well? To be sure, his post-Jenn existence looks like one big exit act, a sequence of departures, lame hosannas to his private *Lebensraum*, unsent e-mailed disclaimers ("phantom communiques" [18]), and similarly self-exculpatory recollections whose multiparenthetic arborescence spatializes syntactically and typographically X's obsession with buffer zones, separation, and disengagement, as well as his wariness of responsibility, care (39), and other "violations" of one's space. Throughout, he fights off any prospect of co-spatiality and effective participation in other spaces and lives. Meticulously, ironically, and at times self-ironically, he struggles to justify his resistance by portraying it as a self-defensive reaction to emotional past "entrapments." The longwinded rationalizations of his fixation with Jenn, with their breakup, and with withdrawal, disaffiliation, partition, distance, privacy, and the sacrosanct right to be left alone, not to be bothered or "concerned" are as many attempts at formulating a self-exonerating ethic of personal, distant, and exclusive space. These efforts are unsuccessful because the objects confecting this space are themselves sites of failed or implausible male flights and grievances.

As in Mandel, the centerpiece of this catalog is literary. This time around, the item is an actually existing work, namely P. D. Eastman's 1961 board book *Go, Dog. Go!*, whose subtitle in later editions is *P. D. Eastman's Book of Things That Go*.[24] Eastman's volume provides important text (and illustrations too) for the contract that regulates space construction and modulates, accordingly, the being-there of objects. Notably, *Go, Dog. Go!* throws light on the novel's problematic contract of spatiality. O'Neill's title aside, *The Dog* makes a few mentions of *Go, Dog. Go!*, from which *maman* would read, in a mock-Proustian scene, to the protagonist at bedtime when he was a little boy (161). The citations, along with the novel's canine motif and allusions, build up and illuminate the larger thematics of hasty departure from an uncomfortable arrangement, place, and nearness of others, principally Jenn or her "double," Mrs. "Ted Wilson" (46). Much like *Go, Dog. Go!*'s hero, X is always running. Remarkably, he jogs "vertically," like his New York friend Don Sanchez, who runs up and down the stairs of Manhattan towers. This "vertical athletics" (23) is "asocial" for the runner seldom runs into others, and it is, we will note, also symbolic of anything vertical in the UAE. As Mrs. Wilson tells X sarcastically, "You're all runners" (49), and this is a double-edged reference to her estranged husband, who is a vertical runner in a different medium—a scuba diver.

X also took up scuba diving off the Musandam peninsula, "enjoy[ing] the feeling of privacy that being underwater offers" (52)—"[t]his was," X stresses, "fundamental to the undertaking" (52). Although Mr. Wilson and X lived in the same building, their interactions were limited to aquatic silences in the "plunging or rising" elevator (5). Having "overwatch[ed] the films of Jacques Cousteau" (3) and undergone proper training, X came to "lear[n] that the undersea world may be nearly a pure substitute for the world from which one enters it" (3). Ted Wilson—"the furtive aquanaut and standoffish elevator rider, . . . not a masked searcher for truth and justice" (122)—reached probably the same conclusion. Trading dry-land solidarity for the solitarity of the underwater *Welt* (74), his deep-sea dives got him the nickname "the Man from Atlantis" (4). X himself is such a man, having spent a night "in the Neptune Suite of the Atlantis Palm" (75) hotel, which "promises" guests "the experience of 'exploring the mysterious ruins of Atlantis'" (75). But the reference is to a 1970s TV series, *Man from Atlantis*, a sort of marine companion to *Go, Dog. Go!* The Patrick Duffy character is the drama's "thing that goes," or runs rather, for the swimmer is a runner. "From my childhood," X reminisces, "I retained only this memory of *Man from Atlantis*: its amphibious hero propelled himself through the liquid element not with his arms, which remained at his sides, but by a forceful undulation of his trunks and legs" (4). "It was not suggested by anybody," X also clarifies, "that Wilson was a superman. But it was said that Wilson spent more time below the surface of water than above, that he always went out alone," "that his preference was for dives, including night-time dives, way too risky for a solo diver," and "that he wore a wet suit the coloring of which—olive green with faint swirls of pale green, dark green, and yellow—made him all but invisible" (4). Ted Wilson not so much dove as ran, absconded.

It may have been X's fate too to be ever on a run and stand aside at the same time—he was born in a "neutral" country, Switzerland, more precisely in Zug, a toponym that means, among other things, "train" and derives from the German *ziehen* ("to pull"), which, in combinations with various prepositions, forms verbs designating movements such as leaving off and wandering. At any rate, if the Poesquely named Ted Wilson—definitely X's double—may have run away from his wife to marry her own, Dubai double, a Filipina woman also known as Mrs. Wilson, X too fled a relationship that, rehashing a narrative element of *Netherland*, makes him feel as in a "doghouse" (an "outbuilding of the phony coupledom for which both of us were responsible" [86]).[25] Not to mention that Jenn did not let him keep a dog—she was "not a dog person" by her own admission [87])—nor are, alas, the Emirati regulations more permissive. They make man's best friend into an "outlaw" (89), all the more reason for O'Neill's character to identify with Eastman's male dog and with dogs generally (86–89, 120). In the same vein, *Go, Dog. Go!* is a source of canine tropes and other "things that go" connotative of exile, ostracism, disenfranchisement, and evasion, in a markedly gendered metaphorics of wrongly denied or precipitously relinquished enclosures, areas, and choices. This rhetoric reinforces a spatial contract that binds up in *The Dog* privacy with unqualified "neutrality," room with elbowroom, and freedom with one's own space or with running for it. Under the New York contract, "there was," as we saw, "no going" (171); under the Dubai contract, and under the contemporary contracts of spatiality broadly, there is a lot of it, including a high amount of going in and out of rooms (106, 107, etc.)—or so it seems for a while.

The contract is problematic not only because it treats moral obligations to others, adjacent or remote, as inconvenient or optional despite X's declarations and "philanthropy," but also because it responds to one's putative exclusion and formalizes one's right to breathing room in terms too close to written and unwritten policies designed to keep out people who cannot afford the luxury of X's Dubai residence or access UAE public spaces the way he does. "Things that go" like them do not enjoy the mobility of X's Lebanese employers, the "high-net-worth" and Trump wannabee Batroses, and the Western lawyers, bankers, managers, cosmeticians, restaurateurs, and doctors catering to them in the UAE, including X himself. The Eastman book is not a universal Baedeker. The sex workers from the former Soviet republics, the ever-stateless *bidoons*, and the ferociously exploited Asian construction workers and landscapers gain admission to dwellings, businesses, clubs, and open spaces according to a set of segregating injunctions pertaining to gender and socio-professional visibility.[26] The Global South's multitudes are simply banned from such places unless they clean up, do work—usually the dirty work—and otherwise serve. They *appear* in the exercise of such functions, or they do not at all. The female janitors, for instance, cannot show in hotels, malls, and residential places like The Situation, the telltale name of X's majestic high-rise apartment, when they do not perform their menial duties. Prohibited from "encroaching" on the turf of the well-off other than when on the job, the migrant workforce is kept out of sight in an "alternative geography" (44) away from the glamour, glitz, and obscene consumerism of the Dubai "elites." "[W]hat really rattled me," X confesses,

> was the mysterious population of cleaning personnel. The mystery lay not only in their alternative geography—theirs was a hidden zone of basements, laundry closets, staff elevators, storage areas—but in the more basic matter expressed in Butch Cassidy's question for Sundance Kid: Who are those guys? That's not to say I viewed this tiny, timid population of women in maroon outfits as in some way hunting me down, as Butch and the Kid were, poor guys, all the way to Bolivia; but something wasn't right . . . I couldn't place those strange brown faces—somewhere in Asia? Oceania?—and I certainly had no data about the bargains that presumably underwrote my room being clean and their hands being dirty. I was confronted with something newly dishonorable about myself: I didn't want to find out about these people. I did not want to distinguish between one brown face and another. I didn't want to know whether these persons were Nepalese, Guyanese, Indians, Bangladeshis, Sri Lankans, Kenyans, Malaysians, Filipinos, or Pakistanis. For their part, these women seemed not to want to be differentiated or even seen, because they always scurried away those few times our paths crossed. Therefore it was a situation governed by mutual avoidance (44–5).

The subaltern cannot be seen because they are not allowed to be seen but also because people like X are not really interested in noticing them. It is true that the workers are obligated, sometimes *expressis verbis* by employment "contract," to keep their distance, and this physical, social, and affective interval rarely shrinks in *The Dog*. But X's attempts at reaching across it remain halfhearted. Besides, they are doomed to fail because Dubai's spatial pact suppresses, inhibits, or devalues "contact" (45). X's recurring references to the troubles into which the New York City "Subway Samaritan" got himself as a result of having stepped into an other's space and rescued a man who had fallen onto the train tracks (20, 47, etc.) are among the countless rationalizations of a topo-social setup that relegates X's "others"—much as he would Jenn—to a place external to his own spatially and affectively. His donations to the cause of the mistreated workers of the Gulf States, a philanthropic initiative that mirrors the Batroses' own, more dubious charity activities, bear witness to a guilty conscience but also to a spatial contract that forecloses direct (81) involvement. Vice versa, when he has no choice but to tolerate the nearness of an other such as Alain, Sandro Batros's son, as a "given . . . in the same room as him [X] and counting on this obligatory mutual vicinity to make [him] act in loco parentis or in loco amicus or otherwise wear some unwarranted caretaking hat," X declares that while he is "obligated to accept the son's presence," he is "not obligated to accept and will not accept any responsibility for [Alain's] greater welfare" (65).

Both regulating and baring the dark underbelly of the global sublime, the novel's spatial contract authorizes not so much infinite access, connectivity, and the affluence allegedly following from them, as their opposite: discontinuity, separation, off-limit zones, gated neighborhoods, indigence, surveillance, vulnerability before baroque bureaucracies, and an unforgiving maze of passwords, visas, checkpoints, immigration hurdles, vetting, brutal selection, and arcane but invariably discriminatory regulations. These are no-go objects shaping the spatial presence of the Gulf underclass. The "global world" of which the Emirates, in particular Dubai, and especially Dubai's skyline provide major icons and "energizing" success narrative is in reality, as Augé argues in a different context, "a world of discontinuity and the forbidden."[27] There is a system to this geography of injustice, a world-system of horizontal "hitches," disjunctions, and disparities. They are disguised as soaring flamboyance, universalist pathos, and unsurpassed urban design.

These are all attributes of the Burj Khalifa skyscraper of the Emirati "abracadabrapolis," UAE's capital city. The world-famous building allegorizes a cheerful defiance of merciless nature and of human nature's limitations as well. The Burj's triumphant silhouette is an exercise in a limitless, hi-tech-assisted sublime of the One Thousand and One Nights variety, with O'Neill's hero assuming in the Arabian desert the contemplative posture of Caspar David Friedrich's traveler in Wanderer above the Sea of Fog. "There are," X surmises,

> some who would raise an eyebrow at my favorable aesthetic assessment of the Burj. I'd invite them to come here and see the unprecedented perpendicular for themselves, but first of all to put away ideas formed in advance about this country, the brand of which, it's fair to say, places unusual reliance on the Guinness Book of World Records and in particular the sections of that book for children that are concerned with the breaking of records having to do with immensities. Unless I'm mistaken, in addition to the world's tallest artificial structure, our many Officially Amazing feats/features include the longest driverless metro, the tallest hotel, the largest gold ring, the most floors in a building, the building with the largest floor space, the biggest mall, and, I read somewhere, the most nationalities washing their hands at once. Even this last exploit (undertaken to mark Global Handwashing Day, and not, as the pre-judger might think, a mindless stunt) suggests to me that there remains intact in this small country a joyful, properly childlike sense of the lofty. Excelsior! (78)

The being-there interdictions and oddities set in train complex restrictions and displacements. Sublime infinitude's subliminal flip side is a spatial imaginary where walled-in and swanky spatial objects materialize only to make visible and police the limits of Emirati "democracy." "Awe-inspiring" as the malls and towers of Abu Dhabi and Dubai may be, there is little in the way of the Kantian "unrepresentable" about them. They are built to specific spatialization codes, but these codes are not merely "design" regulations. Or, the design of Emirati urbanscapes—buildings, roads, parks, marinas, whole artificial islands and cities—is also economic, political, and even ontological, manifestly keyed as it is to a veritable code of restrictive presence. Called "Presence Management," this is a formula concocted by a local advertising agency that employed Ted Wilson during a campaign to rebrand the UAE (121). What one is supposed to "recognize" in Wilson's "award-winning" promotional films and YouTube clips about the Gulf state is less the tired Orientalist clichés of deserts brought to life by debonair Arab hospitality and more, in Wilson's own words, a unique "'storytelling' opportunity" to limn the Emirates as a climactic instantiation of global capital's sublime teleology (150–51, 197).

Wilson's narrative leaves, however, little space for common people's stories. X's is a case in point. An appointed trustee of the Emirates-headquartered Lebanese conglomerate known as the Batros Group, X learns the hard way that *il n'y a pas de hors-système*, no "safely" systemless space to be in by himself, and simply *be*, in the strongest sense of the verb, and that some kind of "encroaching" or "sharing"—of room, responsibilities, or both—comes with the territory. He can opt out neither of social structures of concern nor of techno-communicational and economic webs and makes the mistake of treating them all as equivalent impositions. And yet, even though his job duties and location have reserved him a front-row seat to the unfolding planetary drama, the financial megafiasco is hardly the wakeup call one might expect. To the contrary, the "excess of information" volunteered by Ollie, pedicurist of the Dubai elite and X's scuba-diving buddy, works like a narcotic, conjuring up in X's mind the sedating purr of world "intellectual/moral/economic" world apparatuses (56–7). Awash in the "soothing" technicalities with which Ollie peppers the explanations of his ministrations, X

nearly fell asleep. Little wonder: I'd been lulled into a soporific feeling of all going well in the world, of clever men and women in unseen laboratories toiling and tinkering and steadily solving our most disastrous mysteries, of benign systems gaining in efficiency, of our species progressively attaining a technical dimension of consciousness, of a deep and hitherto undisclosed algorithm of optimal human endeavor coming at last within the grasp of the good-doing intelligences of corporations and universities and governments and NGOs, of mankind's most resilient intellectual/

moral/economic foes being routed forever and the blockheads and bashi-
bazouks and baboons running for the hills once and for all (57).

Entranced at the time by the cosmetician's "poetry," X reaches retrospectively
for more discerning genre metaphors (51). They hint that not all is well in
the world, a contingency to which Ollie, the "benign systems'" unsuspecting
ventriloquist, responds preemptively by humming the lullaby of false
consciousness. Embedded in the podiatric cradlesong is the favorite post-
Berlin Wall cultural bedtime story, a tale of a carefree—because presumably
admission-free—one-world pictured as a commercially and morally duty-
free zone where well-oiled networks' infallible logic envelops bodies and
minds in the anesthetic comforter of ethical insouciance and people indulge
their *dolce far niente* pipedream of unending idleness like the hero of Ollie's
anecdote about the congenial Iranian stuck in the tax-exempt shopping area
of Dubai's airport (57–9). Literally a "side effect," a consequence of
adjacency, duty to others is, X propounds, the clause of a social contract
that regulates practices and habits of "situatedness" that set us "side by
side" and alongside others, near and next to them and therefore responsible
to and for them, be they coworkers, girlfriends, spouses, neighbors, fellow
Americans, or complete strangers. When push comes to shove, X abides
begrudgingly by the proximity paragraphs of the compact. That is, he shares,
initially, various spaces, at home, at work, and so on. But he shies away from
the long-term upshots of physical co-presence. He would share spaces but
not responsibilities for those present with him at close quarters, whether in
a building, neighborhood, town, or country. "Since when," X asks, "is
residential propinquity a basis for making demands? . . . [W]hat's so special
about neighbors? . . . [C]an I ring on the doorbells of those who happen to
live in The Situation and expect special treatment? Can I burden random
door-answerers with responsibility for my well-being?"

What X is driving at is that *he* cannot be "burdened" by other "residents"
of his house, apartment building, or nation, be they lovers or "compatriots,"
at home or "in a foreign land" (42–3). As X philosophizes, part and parcel
of "Jenn-ness," of "being Jenn," is "being with *Jenn*," a co-presence mandate
(87). The major rider of the largely unformulated but active agreement
implicit, as far as Jenn is concerned, in her relationship with X is, he
intimates, precisely the "demand" that led to the "binding commitment to
Jenn the implied condition of which was to be with" her (87). This explains
why Jenn is quite adamant on the ethical enforcement of the spatial-
existential condition of being sanctioned by the Heideggerian *Mitsein*. In
other words, Jenn and all the others out there variously embodying Jenn-
ness are keen on nearness as entailing an inherent "commitment" to an
other's well-being. Whether he resides in the same one-bedroom as Jenn or
in the The Situation, X is in "The Situation" literally, living in a place and

leading a life irreversibly and tangibly circumscribed by the imperative of contiguity, vicinity, and emotional availability. Helping out financially Brett, who "approached [him] as one American [would] another" in a land not their own, X admits to an entire if ambiguously reterritorializing ritual of kinship ("kindredness"), communal bond, nationality, and affect. "I had," he acknowledges,

> misgivings about whether shared nationality was a valid reason for assisting co-national A rather than alter-national B, particularly where B's needs might be as great as, indeed greater than, those of A; yet I said yes to Brett without hesitation. It was striking how, when the shit hit the fan and people suddenly if temporarily found themselves in the same tight corner, loyalties of country were re-discovered in the matter of asking for help and giving it. Which isn't to say that there was an abrupt territorial re-organization of moral feelings; there were many who were kind without reference to kindredness, and in this sense may be said to have admirably rescued the language of goodness from its primal dirt. I might add that I feel more cleanly American than ever. Leaving the U.S.A. has resulted in a purification of nationality. By this I mean that my relationship to the U.S. Constitution is no longer subject to distortion by residence and I am more appreciative than ever of the great ideals that make the United States special. I pay my federal taxes to the last dime, and, without in any way devaluing citizenship to a business of cash registers, I can assert that I am well in the black with my country (109–10).

As one can see, ethical behavior (kindness) and the identity compass it supplies, the identity *tout court* it subtends, need not be a function of nationality ("kindredness"). This principle is, X contends, what the de-territorialization or "de-spatialization" of mutual obligation and assistance fosters. In other words, if Americanness is displaced geographically under the twenty-first-century sublime world order, the quality of being an American is, surprisingly or not, bolstered by this very displacement ethically. In X's judgment, *patria* is concurrently left behind and sublated by ex-*patriation*, somehow "purified" of the "primal dirt," of the ground, soil, or territory tainting the language of planetary human intercourse with the nationalist bias that is deeply engrained in the fabric of kin and kind. As a matter of fact, X suspects he may be a better American outside America— away from "Jenn-land"—insofar as his US residence no longer obstructs an unbiased reading of the Constitution. He is and remains, then, an American. Only, his Americanness has stopped being territorialist; it no longer operates inside the United States. To the extent that political borders, passports, custom officials, and the like enforce a jurisdictional-territorial definition of the country and its citizenry, he feels that "American nationhood is part of an outdated worldwide protection racket and that it should be possible, surely, to live without a state's say-so" (235–6).

Jenn's "say-so"? That too, of course. O'Neill maps out the personal onto the geopolitical throughout. The result is a vast array of gaps, gulfs, screens, thresholds, and other objects separating and thus giving the appearance of warranting sovereign entities, whether they are human individuals or countries. In X's assessment, this discrete world ontology solves "the terrible problem of space" (210). But does it? The problem, we gather, is twofold: distance, on one side, and on the other, promiscuity. To prevent the latter, thinks X, one must safeguard the former. In brief, this is how the world "makes room" for us: by making room *between* us. No such room, no subject—or no liberal, supposedly autarchic and "unattached" subject, at least. This subject is the spaced-out subject. One might call this X's law. The law sets up that space, both private and interstitial, as prerequisite to being because being is dwelling; being is *being in*, a function of a certain "hereness" or "thereness." Full, authentic presence, X postulates, must be able to claim this dwelling, this ground or room—or the room *as* ground—exclusively.

The Dog's objects do not uphold the law, though. They punish the spatially naïve and even "mock" them, as Hamid writes in *Exit West*.[28] Things, it appears, know better. They decline to fit the bill of the masculinist fantasies X, Ted Wilson, Don Sanchez, and other exit men invest them with. Neither the aerial nor the pelagic sublime delivers; it was never supposed to. In its own way, it too makes a mockery of X's solipsistic "dwellism." Unfinished architectural embodiments of Emirati exceptionalism are abandoned at the symbolic "mock-up" stage. Deprived of utility, they are lost objects hopelessly awaiting their capital-venture finders. They just stand there, vertical and flat at the same time, perpetually on ominous show for the benefit of their main spectator, X, whose loss and defeat are writ large on them ("I have no problem discerning the pale X of Project X—the mah-kp," X says while looking out his window [213]). Their failure—one might say refusal—to bolster the Emirati entrepreneurial sublime portends X's own, and both bear out in more ways than one the bankruptcy of Ted Wilson's deceptive rhetoric of personal and public relations, as it does Wilson's own submarine misadventures (Ollie and others assume the Man from Atlantis died during one of his dives). Granted, scuba diving and the extreme departures with which it entices the Atlantis men do not induce claustrophobia, as in Chang-rae Lee's 2021 novel *My Year Abroad*, but it does not cure X's agoraphobia either ("I must go back indoors, into a room," he tells himself once outside [107]).[29] Hired, it turns out, because he had been spotted among the "fauna" rubbing shoulders at Melania and Donald Trump's wedding—and also because the Batroses needed a fall guy for their fiscal schemes—X ultimately does get his room in the "home" of the world

(68) outside Jenn-land, but this is the room in which he is waiting for the Emirati police at the end of the novel, installed in his "Pasha Royale X400™ massage chair" (76).

Not only is the Pasha "perhaps the most 'intelligent' chaise de massage in the world," but giving in to the advances of Ollie's Human Touch™ chair makes X "feel a tiny, absurd pang of infidelity" (76). This goes to show that the Pasha is a highly complex object. Classical psychoanalysis would probably call it a fetish, but the term would be here, as it probably is elsewhere, a copout, saying more about Freudianism's anthropocentric strain than about what objects do to and independent of human rationalizations. In any event, X's chair is impossible to define if you go by how the thing looks and what it does—or it does *not* do. It is, undoubtedly, a more "docile," ever-available but conveniently unpluggable Jenn and thus an ideal sexual partner, as many an erotic scene demonstrate ("The chair and I began to tremble," X reports in one of them [77]); it is an anatomic analog to the dog X could never have nor be; it can pipe various kinds of music through its "built-in speakers" (76); and it is a miracle of mysteriously working massaging technologies. In sum, X declares,

> the Pasha remains my go-to comforter. I'm not sure how I would cope without it. Arguably this reveals something inadequate about me, but what is a private dwelling if not a redoubt against the tyranny of adequacy? And what's wrong with having a favorite chair? What difference does it make if its components include motors and rollers and air bags? Are these to be distinguished analytically, from casters and springs and cushions? Or is an uncomfortable chair better than a comfortable one? Bottom line: the Pasha hurts nobody. It's not as if it's stuffed with minuscule underlings coerced into massaging me. (76)

The chair is not only a "go-to" thing but also a kinetic "thing that goes," as its dynamic description indicates. On the move, it is also X's destination, "the place to be" and in that a space-object. By the same token, it is the ultimate aesthetic object. For it is both a site and seat of "comfort," appealing as it does to X synaesthetically and thus supplying auditory intimacy (it can play "Ambient Classics" [76]) as well as the obviously sexualized, perfect "touch." For X, it outrivals the mandated, somewhat importunate haptics of neighborly propinquity, implying that it can make up for missing social give-and-take. Sanctioning the resistance of one's dwelling to "tyranny," it is even a bulwark of freedom—until it is not, for it has never been. At the end of the novel, the ultimate thing that goes is the place-thing where X is stuck, contemplating a white wall and his imminent arrest. His "room to go," with his ultimate thing "to go" in it, proves a microcosm—a "mock-up"—of besieged, shut-off contemporaneity.

ravann, doors, cell phones: Un-Telling, "Mocking Objects," and Hamid's *Exit West*

Take back control? Make America great again? Restore the caliphate? We can do better than these. Storytellers, now is the time to try.
                    —Mohsin Hamid, "Mohsin Hamid on the Dangers of Nostalgia"

"My reporting over three decades," Robert D. Kaplan writes in his 2012 book *The Revenge of Geography*, "has convinced me that we all need to recover a sensibility about time and space that has been lost in the jet and information ages . . . Instead," Kaplan tells us, "I will introduce readers to a group of decidedly unfashionable thinkers, who push up hard against the notion that *geography no longer matters*."[30] By geography, Kaplan means basically geographical situation or location. "Location, location, location," reply, however, Hamid's "realtors" in *Exit West* (11), reassuring us that, in this sense, geography has never gone out of fashion; it still is "destiny," as "historians" promptly echo them (11). In this sense too, geography has become, if anything, even more relevant in the era of supersonic airliners, the internet, and satellite communications. After all, the scope, impact, and ambitions of contemporary world-systems of transportation, commerce, and cybernetics are quintessentially locational. As writers like O'Neill and Hamid show, twenty-first-century hi-tech webs enable one's movement while tracking it. Whether they displace us or take us where we intend to go, and whether they give or deny access to locales, goods, and information, they always *place* us—they locate us in space. X's Situation room cannot be a way out also because X's situation or "address" is known geographically, electronically, and otherwise to various agencies, bureaucracies, and data-collection apparatuses. These automatically *geoposition*; they cancel out X's "exit" by re-locating him in the very space of his "escape," in his Dubai, apartment, and chair. By virtue of their operations, he remains, irrespective of his actual whereabouts, locatable and in that forever behind Sartre's *huis clos*.

Hamid's oeuvre dramatizes largely the same "situation," and it does so also through delocalization and exit tactics brought to bear on particular spatial objects. More boldly than in O'Neill, these tactics are narrative protocols purporting to rub out of existence the usual toponymical markers of plots and characters and to open, as if by magic, literal doors into the wider world. But, not unlike in O'Neill, this objectual repertoire falls short of human expectations. People who take advantage of these inordinate suspensions of and breaks out of local spatialities and affiliations find themselves, before long, pinned down inside, and implacably "discoverable" by, national and transnational circuitries of commodities, knowledge, and control. These systems tend to re-spatialize, that is, to contain attempted de-spatializations by redrawing extant spatial contracts on bigger, regional, intercontinental, and planetary scales.

Traditionally, these compacts have pressed into service geographical mimesis, viz., descriptions of or references to topographically and culturally recognizable places. Prevalent throughout modern and postcolonial prose, mimetic spatial contracts are stylistically realist and therefore rich in the local detail that renders them legally specific. "Context-" or "position-heavy," they make their contractual actors easily locatable through an abundance of ethnographic and topological signifiers. More recent fiction has obscured, done away, and generally messed with these identifiers. Such geographical and stylistic recalibrations and ensuing contractual adjustments are germane to mutations that reflect the complex, still ongoing transition from a postcolonial world picture to one typical of a world literature and *littérature-monde* model.[31] Revolving around a "worlded" dynamic of geographical "positionality" and being, this model underwrites space agreements and affords fictional scenarios that inscribe and affiliate various localities and local actors into and with the greater world while working the latter into the cultural makeup of smaller places and communities.

Generally speaking, postcolonial literature has gone to great lengths to situate plots and human lives in geographically-historically concrete and recognizable environs bearing visible marks of the former empires, of the nation-states rising on imperial ruins in the aftermath of World War II, and of the political maps reflecting these transformations. Postcolonial authors remain committed to geoculturally and ethno-historically incontrovertible localizations of character and plot, whether these writers hail from former colonies, like Arundhati Roy and David Malouf, or imperial metropolises, like Hanif Kureishi and Zadie Smith. Their works are geographically—and contractually—strong because, to put it simply, they place identity, namely, they deploy *locational objects* as signposts to categorize, identify, and otherwise pinpoint their dramatis personae. Accordingly, these narratives teem with existing topologies and toponymies, with actual loci that are ordinarily referred to by extant, oftentimes real place names, from known neighborhoods and streets to towns, cities, regions, countries, and a whole panoply of geomarkers—designations, denominations, appellations, references, etc.—that help readers figure out where a village, town, or town district lies, what the ethnicity, citizenship, or religion of the residents is, the country in which the heroes and heroines live or happen to be at some point in the plot, and so forth. In brief, an *identifiable* place object serves as an identity conduit by providing clarifications and builds reading expectations accordingly.

A growing number of writers seem to be moving in a different direction as far as the traditional—and traditionally realistic—umbilical nexus of place and identity goes. They would appear, by contrast, geographically and, again, contractually weak. But they are not. For in their works, "weakness" or lack of topographic specificity is, as suggested, a tactic. Contemporary novelists such as J. M. Coetzee, Kazuo Ishiguro, Julian Barnes, Nadeem Aslam, Brian Chikwava, and Vesna Goldsworthy, to list but a few Anglophone authors, are increasingly keen on narratives that de-situate, re-situate, and otherwise re-locate their stories, along with those stories' settings and people, in the bigger world.[32] If other authors take pains to embed—and thus unequivocally moor *and* place—their characters geoculturally and otherwise, the likes of the later Coetzee *dis-embed* and *de-localize*, rendering the settings ambiguous or "generalizable," if you will, yet not necessarily abstract, non-realistic, implausible, science-fictional, futural, utopian, or even imaginary, made up. Geographical contextualization and the reader's capacity to determine places, historical traditions, and cultural sites do count—*pace* Kaplan—in their fictions, but they do so *otherwise*: the postcolonial-culturalist "location of culture" mantra now becomes "dis-location of culture." But it is not just that culture and people making this culture have become placeless or homeless, nomadic, "uprooted," decontextualized, or free-floating cosmopolites "from nowhere" under the sway of the late-global era's displacing forces. The writers who interest me here wield narrative technologies of displacement-cum-replacement that mix up geocultural *un-* and *re-marking*, a two-pronged operation ultimately geared to spatial reembedding. As in O'Neill, things that go do get going, but their comings and goings are traceable and, as a rule, are traced on maps that preexist their movements.

Unmarking the territory does not unmark these maps also, as Hamid's heroes and heroines learn sooner or later. This un-marking or fictional de-territorialization remains Hamid's narrative signature throughout his work, possibly with the exception of his debut novel, *Moth Smoke* (2000), which is set in Pakistan.[33] So may be his next and most famous book to date, *The Reluctant Fundamentalist* (2007), as well as *How to Get Filthy Rich in Rising Asia* (2013), but these would be educated guesses, if probably good ones.[34] In any case, we do not know for sure because oftentimes Hamid narrates either by "un-narrating," that is, by withholding information about the specific geolocations of fictional people and events, or by presenting diegetic objects such as houses, streets, community landmarks, public parks, natural scenery, and other things designating or embodying sites and environs as if they were or could also be part of faraway, sometimes unspecified yet existing and "conjecturable" countries, continents, climates, and ecologies. This possible-worlds literature is thus also a cartography of the twenty-first-century world. It is a "counter-cartography" only in that it finds itself at loggerheads with local maps, or, more exactly, it is a poor guide to actual local sites and borders of political power, territorial administration, capital, literary traditions, language, cultural prestige, and other forms and locations of institutional and symbolic authority, identity, association, polity, and expression. Otherwise, Hamid's fictional cartograms do not simply displace, isolate, and alienate characters but resettle them in broader, familiar stories, histories, territories, and communities—into a world that is wider and more turbulent, more alluring and more ominous at once. Where small maps are vulnerable to fictional redrawing and even erasing in Hamid, big maps, or maps of bigger places, hold up, suggesting that contemporary systems of cartography, location, and geolocation "fictionalize" anonymity, invisibility, privacy, and freedom itself, making them into fictions, dangerous delusions. Hamid is mindful of this risk. To a certain extent, one might say that his work thematizes it.

To clarify, let me note first that more than any other literary genre, the novel and in particular the realist novel of still fairly young postcolonial literatures are or set out to be "geo-centered." This geo-centering, this identifying description or referencing of place, is both a literary and political project, given that geo-centering here refocuses the novel on *recovered localities* such as land, idiom, community, and their suppressed histories. Ethno-geographically strong or "thick," this geo-centering works because the novel itself works like a GPS: the narrative geopositions the character, and so the story is a story of geolocation. But what about recent novels that delocalize by unplugging or rewiring our GPSs? In other words, what happens when the gizmos break down, lack in expected accuracy, fail or refuse to orient the reader, and so on? How are we supposed to react when the geopositioning "equipment" "mocks" its user? What about fictions that set in train multiple, varied, competing, ambiguous, or "macro" kinds of localizations that place the action on more than one plausible stage, perhaps wider than cities, regions, and even countries? What about those narrative devices that operate on several, larger scales and so, instead of finding or observing their humanity in a precisely identified or determined village X or city Y, lead the person sitting in the driver's seat of the novel—the reader— to consider a range of locations, a plurality of broader possible worlds concomitantly? What "model" of narrative GPS do these stories turn on as we work our way through them?

One would probably love this kind of GPS in one's car no more than I do my Garmin at a French roundabout. Nevertheless, this sort of disorientation or competing orientations is, as the founder of "geocriticism," Bertrand Westphal, would probably say, "spatiologically" *isotropic*, inducing the "systemic indecision" that generally defines, as the critic also contends, postmodern fiction in contrast to the prevailingly *isotopic* treatment of space in more traditional, realist literature.[35] Where the latter's predominantly "coherent" approach to space situates, the former tends to de-situate by substituting hints and references to a range of possible locations for the systematic or consistent focus on the same place or on the same, unambiguously identified places. There is, I suppose, an autobiographical motivation behind Hamid's isotropism—behind his "defective" geopositioning device: a self-described "Lahore-born nomad," the author has "not lived . . . since leaving [his] birth city . . . at the age of eighteen . . . in any one place for more than four years," as he discloses in "A Home for Water Lilies," a piece from his book of essays *Discontent and Its*

Civilizations.[36] Whether the writer's nomadic life has any bearings on his art or not, the bottom line is that the latter's hallmark is a narration that does its job, as Rebecca Walkowitz contends, "reluctantly."[37]

What does this mean? It means that these books tell stories by un-telling them. This negative narrative poetics is fairly complex and even controversial with some critics. Here, I single out three of its major procedures. They all work through specific spatial operators or objects. I call the first procedure or technique *inclusive*; the second, *exclusive*; and the third, for lack of a better word, *transclusive*. Let me begin with the second. I label it exclusive because it functions by excluding information. That is, it omits or declines to release data and thus specify the geopolitical signposts that ordinarily assist the reader to determine locations and thereby identify, for example, in which city or country—and even at what moments in history such as years, decades, and so on—the plot unfolds, what the ethnicity, citizenship, or the faith of the characters is, etc. *How to Get Filthy Rich* is famous for the extreme scarcity or sheer inexistence of such signifiers of place and identity as proper names, place names, street names, and historical and cultural occurrences that would help with narrative geopositioning. There are plenty of material objects to work with, though. But, here as elsewhere in Hamid, all this stuff is non-locational or non-situational, which makes reading Hamid exciting conjectural work, a reading game whose rules are laid down in the book's spatial contract. If the village where the novel's main hero is born is less important, for it is left behind by his family early on in the story, and so it can arguably remain unnamed, the city where they all move, apparently one of the planet's megalopolises, is home to the also unnamed protagonist's business and provides the settings for the whole novel. Such lengthy and measuredly poetic passages comprise the bulk of the fine print of the book's spatial contract:

> Your city is not laid out as a single-celled organism, with a wealthy nucleus surrounded by an ooze of slums. It lacks sufficient mass transit to move all its workers twice daily in the fashion this would require. It also lacks, since the end of colonization generations ago, governance powerful enough to dispossess individuals of their property in sufficient numbers. Accordingly, the poor live near the rich. Wealthy neighborhoods are often divided by a single boulevard from factories and markets and graveyards, and those in turn may be separated from the homes of the impoverished only by an open sewer, railroad track, or narrow alley. Your own triangle-shaped community, not atypically, is bounded by all three . . .
>
> Your city is enormous, home to more people than half the countries in the world, to whom every few weeks is added a population equivalent to that of a small, sandy-beached, tropical island republic, a population that arrives, however, not by outrigger canoe or lateen-sailed dhow but by foot and bicycle and scooter and bus. A limited-access ring road is under construction around the place, forming a belt past which its urban belly is

already beginning to bulge, and from which ramps soar and arc off in every direction. Your bus barrels along in the shadow of these monuments, dusty new arteries feeding this city, which despite its immensity is only one among many such organs quivering in the torso of rising Asia. (20, 82).

"Rising Asia" is here the sole mark of geographical specificity. The reference is tongue-in-cheek too, undercut as it is by the cliché's reiterations across the novel, which not only are locationally generic and stylistically ironic but also convey a non-Asian perspective—no doubt, it is the Bloomberg TV experts who have been trading in the "rising Asia" stock phrase rather than the poor residents of Asian villages and slums. Regardless, the city is an "objective" reality. A horizontal antithesis of the Emirati vertical sublime of glass, steel, and clean, efficient technology, Hamid's megalopolis is a messy, throbbing biological thing. An organ in Asia's "torso" and also a multiple-cell organism itself complete with "dust arteries" and other organ-things of its own, the city is structurally comparable to Lerner's octopus. It has risen, it seems, independent of human perspectives, expertise, and developmental rationalizations, growing exponentially into a spatial macroobject inside which smaller, human and nonhuman objects carom around like pinballs knocked by forces beyond their control. This is the ambiance of the male hero's entrepreneurship, which the novelist sketches out on the same tone and with the same studied imprecision. "Your office," Hamid writes,

is adjacent to your factory and storage depot, in the city's outskirts, on one of a thousand and one rutted streets where a few years ago were only fields but now little green can be seen, unplanned development having yielded instead a ribbon of convenience stores, auto garages, scrap-metal dealers, unregistered educational institutes, fly-by-night dental clinics, and mobile-phone top-up and repair points, all fronting warrens of housing perilously unresistant to earthquakes, or even, for that matter, torrential rain.

Here along its spreading rim live many of the recent additions to your city's vast population, some of them born centrally and pressed out by the urban crush, others tossed up from regional towns and villages to seek their fortune, and still others arriving as castaways, fleeing homelands to which in all likelihood they will never return. Here, as well, resides the physical hub of your enterprise. You have thrived to the sound of the city's great whooshing thirst, unsated and growing, water incessantly being pulled out of the ground and pushed into pipes and containers. Bottled hydration has proved lucrative. (120–1).

Such "metro-realist" surveys abound in the novel, and there is, of course, no reason not to call them representational. Quite the contrary. Yet it is obvious that the author paints the place with a brush that is as poignantly descriptive as it deliberately stops short of naming and, by the same token, identifying any specific locale. But why does Hamid leave his dramatis personae and places *de facto* stateless, placeless, and even nameless? Why does he "un-qualifiy" them so systematically throughout, here as in his other books? One answer is that he wants to "world" the plot, its characters, and place, to "open up" the story and its "Asian"—possibly Pakistani—environs to the bigger world. The novel is, very simply speaking, about the downside of the narrative of social mobility, which *How to Get Fithy Rich* represents and critiques by masquerading as a self-help book. Both the genre and the social Darwinism saga are international or, more precisely, have internationalized American cultural stories. Hamid uses them, as he does his "un-narrating" ploy to make the presumably or most likely Pakistani "Dream" story appeal to Anglophone audiences in North America and beyond. But vice versa, he also wants to help such readers *relate*—in Nicolas Bourriaud's sense—to the novel, to draw this public, primarily those of us familiar with the American Dream genre, into a diegetic environment in which the difference from "our" world is still marked (hence the listing of objects signifying colonial history, poverty, chaotic urban sprawl, and the like) yet no longer explicated or explicitly reinforced—disambiguated—by Urdu onomastics and toponymy. These are then exclusionary narrative decisions ultimately meant to *include* by setting up the text as a "relational sphere" susceptible to accommodate a more "worlded" readership community.[38] The ploy works hand in glove with the other, properly *inclusive* technique mentioned earlier, namely the second-person narrative or "narrative address." While testing the "limits of realism," as narratologist Monika Fludernik has shown,[39] you-narration—another staple of Hamid's style—produces here both "vagueness" and a kind of "excess" or multiplication of addressees and their worlds.[40] Consequently, the "you" whom the first-person extradiegetic narrator speaks to in the 2013 novel can be, for example, the main hero, the Asian man determined to get "filthy rich," or the reader himself or herself. And so the story unfolding under our eyes can be both geoculturally specific, limited to the diegetic universe of "Asia" (or only "India," "Pakistan," or "Bangladesh"), *and* "ours," Western or (North) American readers.' Either way, the storyworld is not confined to any Asian country and imaginary ecology.

In *The Reluctant Fundamentalist*, a number of countries, with the United States, Chile, and Pakistan among them, are indeed named and provide geoculturally specific settings at various junctures. But this "specificity" of locale does not translate into an equally clarifying pronominal rhetoric, which remains beholden to the same "negative" communicational logic that undergirds *How to Get Filthy Rich*. Once again, this logic does depend on information. So important in *The Reluctant Fundamentalist*, the second-person character and addressee are acknowledged directly—metafictionally, one might say—*to be* information actually, much like other human entities referenced by pronominal signifiers of all sorts:

We're all information, all of us, whether readers or writers, you and I. The DNA in our cells, the bioelectric currents in our nerves, the chemical emotions in our brains, the configurations of atoms within us and of subatomic particles within them, the galaxies and whirling constellations we perceive not only when looking outward but also when looking in, it's all, every last bit and byte of it, information.

Now, whether all this information seeks to comprehend itself, whether that is the ultimate goal to which our universe trends, we obviously don't yet know for certain, though the fact that we humans have evolved, we forms of information capable of ever-increasing understandings of information, suggests it might be the case . . . all of us learning to combine this information, to find patterns in it, inevitably to look for ourselves in it, to reassemble out of the present-time stories of numerous others the lifelong story of a plausible unitary self. (159–60)

The fighter-jet pilot, the decision-making top brass on the ground, and the equity trader, like the rest of us, Hamid offers, process information to find where they are and so ultimately themselves, who they are. In embarking on this topo-existential adventure, we watch our inner radars and screen the outer world for a narrative pattern that geolocates one way or the other, placing something—a desire's object, an objective, target, occurrence, or goal—somewhere in the world so we can relate to that place and whatever is placed in it and by the same token constitute ourselves, be. Resulting from this search, however, is not a "unitary" or stable self for this entity is itself unremittingly constituted and reconstituted by and across information grids and monitoring systems themselves evolving and shifting. Put together, taken apart, and shuffled around, located and relocated like the city dwellers of *How to Get Filthy Rich*, it is an object *to* bigger objects and object systems. "From the perspective of the world's national security apparatuses," Hamid's narrator observes in *The Reluctant Fundamentalist*, "you exist in several locations" (161), physical and digital, and oftentimes simultaneously so. Wherever you are or arrive, you are a geolocatable spot, an intersection and effect of organic and inorganic circuits of energy, data, and labor, with the nameless entrepreneur's failing body reenacting the multifaceted intersectionality of Mandel's glass globe and Lerner's coffee jar. "To be a man whose life requires being plugged into machines, multiple machines, in your case interfaces electrical, gaseous, and liquid," writes Hamid in *How to Get Filthy Rich*, "is to experience the shock of an unseen network suddenly made physical, as a fly experiences a cobweb." "The inanimate strands that cling to your precariously still-animate form themselves connect," he explains,

to other strands, to the hospital's power system, its backup generator, its information technology infrastructure, the unit that produces oxygen, the people who refill and circulate the tanks, the department that replenishes medications, the trucks that deliver them, the factories at which they are manufactured, the mines where requisite raw materials emerge, and on and on, from your body, into your room, across the building, and out the doors to the world beyond, mirroring in stark exterior reality preexisting and mercifully unconsidered systems within, the veins and nerves and sinews and lymph nodes without which there is no you. (183–4)

"As a fly experiences a cobweb": the comparison summarizes the space contract written into Hamid's fiction. "Unseen" world networks of capital, toil, knowledge, and travel suddenly light up in nonhuman (Lerner) and human (Hamid) objects and show them on various maps. These objects remain traceable for, whether inclusive or exclusive, narration winds up situating them in wider cobwebs.

So does *transclusive* storytelling, which operates somewhere in between the other two types. If inclusive narrative adduces information that squeezes the elsewhere, the bigger world, and its actors into smaller places, and if its opposite, exclusive narrative, suppresses data so as to de-specify local events and report them as if they could take place elsewhere or even anywhere in the wider world, transclusive narrative lays emphasis on the transiting process and its material conduits, viz., on getting out of one location and into another and on passages, pathways, windows, portals, doors, and other places and things of this sort.

Yet again, the "trans" in "transclusive" is not the "trans" in "transgressive"; one de-locates only to re-locate. Witness Nadeem Aslam's tellingly titled 2004 novel *Maps for Lost Lovers*. If Hamid "worlds" Pakistan or Southeast Asia, Aslam "Pakistanizes" Great Britain, so to speak. *Maps* centers on the Southeast Asian diaspora, in particular on the Pakistani immigrants to Britain who live in the fictitious British town Dasht-e-Tanhaii ("Desert of Loneliness").[41] This is the title of a famous poem written in Urdu by Pakistani poet Faiz Ahmad Faiz, but the name of the poem is also given to the entire planet (377). Furthermore, there is hardly any reference in the book to recognizable and identifiable British toponymy and topography, place names, names of streets, neighboring towns, etc. Aslam too withholds information of this nature, except for scant references to London and its department stores and universities. Instead, the streets, landmarks, lakes, and roads bear names given by the Pakistani as well as Bangladeshi, Sikh, Punjabi, Hindu, and other Southeast Asian immigrants "[r]oaming the planet looking for solace" (9). We do know, of course, that the story is set in the UK. But the author's description of his characters' environment is deliberately focused away from signs of "Britishness" and other similar locators. "Natives" and their culture are portrayed mostly through the immigrants' eyes and thus "de-Britishized," which renders the kingdoms of plants, birds, insects, and elements abundantly and "disorientingly" present. Compounding the disorientation is the absence or paucity of detailed references to advanced technology and to British material culture generally, at least compared to the extensively described natural world of a surprisingly elemental, lush, almost subtropical—"Southeast Asia"-like—Britain. Indeed, this is not the ever-rainy, cloudy UK or not only that UK but a whole world, with its continents, cultures, and dramas telescoped into a dramatically "defamiliarized," fresh Britain.

The main source of this freshness is a cartographic perception whose prime meridian no longer runs through the Greenwich Royal Observatory but bends around a geopositioning "sensibility" more closely attuned to a world-system in which the sensuous materiality of objects—people, plants, birds, insects, elements, weather phenomena, clothes, foodstuffs, and so forth—supplies the major reference points. There are, accordingly, historically drawn up and politically sanctioned world maps, on which the UK and countries like Pakistan, along with their peoples and traditions, are oceans and cultures apart, but then there are also object maps, especially the *biomaps* the UK-residing Pakistanis live by. The sites, toponyms, intervals, and divides on these maps look strikingly different from what one sees on extant maps, and this difference, this remapping of a world asunder as one world by radically redistributing the planet's elemental and organic material, is as corporeal and immanent as it is transcendent, divinely authorized. Unhappy as she is in her new country, Kaukab, one of the novel's heroines,

> knows her dissatisfaction with England is a slight to Allah because He is the creator and ruler of the entire earth—as the stone carving on Islamabad airport reminds and reassures the heartbroken people who are having to leave Pakistan—but she cannot contain her homesickness and constantly asks for courage to face this lonely ordeal that He has chosen for her in His wisdom.
>
> She often reminds herself that Allah had given Adam his name after the Arabic word *adim*, which means "the surface of the earth"; he—and therefore the whole of mankind, his descendants—was created from earth taken from different parts of the world. His head was made from the soil of the East, his breast from the soil of Mecca, his feet from the West. (31)

In this "theo-ecological" or perhaps "eco-Islamic" sense, humankind is *ab ovo* multiply and inherently ecumenical. True, people *are* earth, of it. But they are so planetarily also, to wit, in a way that makes the earth a shared home, a commons. While nation-states, religions, ethnicities, languages, and cultures can be mapped out and managed territorially, they take a back seat to humanity's pre-civilizational, "Adamic," or "trans-territorial" identity. This has survived millennia of post-Adamic "Babelization" and can be mapped out as well, but the obtaining map paints a picture of a planet hard to find on available world maps. Absent from any atlas and jarringly at odds with political reality, this image is primarily one of transits, bridges, passageways, continuities, and at-distance kinship, juxtapositions, and proximities. "Look what I found," Kaukab tells her husband when, in her kitchen, she comes across a seed of *ravann*. "In the palm of her hand," the narrator informs us, "is a shiny blue bead, the outer skin flaking away to reveal the ivory within." "'The packet [Kaukab points out] said *Product of Italy*. That probably means they grow *ravann* in Italy. Is Italy somewhere quite close to Pakistan'"? (57).

Needless to say, Italy, or Britain for that matter, is not anywhere near Pakistan geographically. But the *ravann* resets nearness and, more generally, placeness. For there is also a geography whose coordinates, locations, and distances are measured by the grain and other plants, animals, foods, and products that shape people's concrete experiences of space. In this spellbinding geography of the senses, of unforgettable and identity-shaping tastes, flavors, and related daily-life rites, Italy and Pakistan draw near to each other. They may share a border and even territory much like British and Lahore soils would in Kaukab's ideal garden (98). Akin to the rechristening of British places and roads by the Southeast Asian inhabitants of the Desert of Loneliness, the "re-territorialization" of Pakistani plants and soil in Italian crop fields and Kaukab's garden plot—she "contemplated" having whole sacks of topsoil shipped in from Lahore [98])—betrays a topo-centered attempt at a "semblance of belonging" (159) away from the original roots and through an intimate relation with the UK that repositions Britain on an a "post-autochthonous," "Adamic" world map of common earth and soil, ground and grounds.

"Semblance" is key in the sentence above. Not only are Aslam's maps aspirational, but the gap between them and actual world territories has also been widening in the twenty-first century, rescinding spatial and political agreements of the 1990s such as those worked out under the auspices of the EU. Aslam's Britain is an unwelcoming and selfish country poised for Brexit, as is even more violently Hamid's in *Exit West*. Objects like Pakistan's *ravann* and fertile dirt may be transclusive, that is, allegorizing various transplants and transports, but they do not undo the policies, reflexes, and practices of exclusion, nor do they check the state apparatuses and technologies of surveillance, geopositioning, and control. As *Exit West* suggests, if the "contemporary age," or "our" present, were mapped out, and its history and politics reencoded spatially, the resulting picture would be one of discontinuities, fissures, and rebuilt walls, giving the lie to the neoliberal rhetoric of universal access, freedom of movement, and "porous" borders and redistributing horizontally the cracks in O'Neill's perpendicularly defiant sublime. Still, Hamid's novel also implies, the picture would be incomplete without the powerful lure of bridges across chasms and of holes in hastily erected fences, of ways out and in enticing and at the same time "mocking" not so much O'Neill's exit men and other adventurous globetrotters but the migrants, the asylum seekers, the refugees, and others for whom exiting is not a choice. The lure *and* failure and the spatial allotments these permit and subsequently void make up the "legend" one needs in order to orient oneself on such maps especially when the territory seems the stuff of fairy tales.

The "fairy-tale" reference is not a critical metaphor. It does not point solely to storytelling either although the narrative sound of *Exit West* and of Hamid's work in general pastiches discreetly romance, including Greek romances such as Longus's second-century AD *Daphnis and Chloe*, the Milesian tale (*fabula milesiaca*), narrative accounts of travel and miraculous exploits, fantasy, Märchen, and other popular genres of this category. Beyond stylistic resonances, there are also similarly deliberate, thematic echoes of the fantastic and the wondrous, and they are lowbrow (children's literature) rather than highbrow (magical realism). Whether or not the *ravann* is world literature's reprise of Jack's beanstalk, Hamid responds indirectly to Aslam's quasi-supernatural botanic passageway into another universe and directly to Brexit's catastrophic "exit into fantasyland"[42] with extraordinary exits of his own—*Exit West*'s mysterious and extensively debated "doors."[43] Aslam sets up the *ravann* as a British portal into Pakistan but is careful to hedge his anti-"georealism." Kaukab still wonders if "Italy [is] somewhere quite close to Pakistan," which is the author's way of signaling that the narrative "pact" of his text is realist rather than magical realist. Instead, Hamid's doors open, under more dramatic circumstances, mostly in the opposite direction, allowing for movements out of the former colonies, which are now ravaged by poverty, armed strife, and autocracies of various stripes, and into richer, Western countries (notably, the title of *Exit West*'s Spanish translation is *Bienvenido a Occidente*). Furthermore, as Hamid narrates these movements, he simply forsakes any concerns with "credibility"[44] or with what the Russian Formalists and their followers would have termed "realistic motivation." The doors—*Exit West*'s Ur-object—violate, accordingly, the overall realistic poetics of the novel, and they do so because their source is not the social, political, and geopolitical "observation" that engendered the text as a whole. The latter is a narrative cartogram of our immediate, surrounding world, while the lead cartographic actor's provenance is, similarly to *Station Eleven*, otherworldly.

There are, of course, ordinarily working, real and realistically describable doors, but they do not fascinate Hamid. In an article published a few months after the June 23, 2016 Brexit referendum and only days before the UK release of *Exit West*, he reveals that "he turned to fantasy" when he was nine years old and just back from California, where he had been born. "I read," he tells *The Guardian*'s readers, "*The Chronicles of Narnia* by C. S. Lewis. The idea of children passing through a wardrobe into a strange and magical land seemed entirely plausible to me." He also "read the Middle-earth novels of J. R. R. Tolkien. The importance (and intricate navigation) of clan, family, history, honour and formality, even as practised by hobbits or elves, must have been a useful education to this until recently California boy now finding his way in Pakistan."[45] Wardrobes and similar "exit objects" open gateways to new albeit actual lands in *Exit West* too, where an African man, apparently, gets out of a closet in a home in Sydney, Australia (8). The novel's own protagonists, Nadia and Saeed, step through the "supply cabinet" (103) of a dentist's office to flee their unnamed, war-torn homeland, ending up in the bathroom of a beach club on the Greek island of Mykonos (104), and this episode is replayed all over the world by their migrant brethren, who wind up in Tokyo, Dubai, Vienna, London, Rio de Janeiro, Amsterdam, Namibia, and Californian places such as La Jolla, Palo Alto, and Marin, where the couple ultimately settle.

The most significant feature of *Exit West*'s closets, wardrobes, lavatories, sheds, rooms, buildings, and enclosures of all kinds is a door, but interestingly enough, this is not or does not quite work like the well-known physical object with a panel, screen, or partition swinging back and forth on its hinges and outfitted with a handle, a lock, and the rest of the hardware. Hamid's door is, one might say, a "soft" structure—not even a structure per se but the hollow the door concurrently limits and delimits, as well as what that space performs or facilitates once de-limited by its own shape, once made available, that is, to people eager to take advantage of it. The door boils down, then, to an opening or what looks like one, a gap inside the doorframe and the passing that aperture enables. At once an exit (out of a place) and entrance (exit into a place), the boundary (sometimes a real threshold) *and* its crossing rolled into one, the door is a dynamic entity throbbing with the "kinetic energy of what pushes and pulls us."[46] "Made" out of motility, it is therefore neither a place nor a place's limit but a flow, a point of exit and moment in an exiting–entering process, an energetic form affording travel between nonadjacent places. Not just a "dividing line between one thing and another," as exits are supposed to be,[47] the door is a thing itself, a *moving* thing twice, swinging open and always forth. Carrying people along in its slipstream, it is not only a thing of space, but, like so many other objects in whose "streams of time" we "splash and intersect with each other" (81), it is also a "thing of time"—"[w]e are all migrants through time," Hamid writes memorably (209).[48]

The thing is also everywhere, a planetary thing if not the planet itself. "[I]t seemed to Nadia and Saeed," Hamid writes in *Exit West*, "that the whole planet was on the move" (169). Thus, Hamid's doors instantiate a modality of navigating the geocultural world-system and enabling transits and transitions back and forth between the United States, Pakistan, and other countries and locations in the world in ways absent both from realist fiction and non-fictional systems of transportation, geography, and cartographic representation. As Hamid confesses in the same article, "I had always been a daydreamer, and I whiled away long hot summers in Lahore playing make-believe, by myself, or with my cousins." He "became," Hamid explains, "fascinated by atlases, with their gorgeous multicoloured maps, their different icons for settlements of different population sizes, their snaking, undulating contour lines," and "by almanacs, with their brief descriptions of countries: a snapshot of history, demographics, chief exports, climatic conditions." But geographical make-believe is creative or re-creative, rather, for the boy "began to make countries of [his] own" by redrawing the maps. He would start by "mark[ing] out their borders in pencil on my maps, sometimes claiming this peninsula and that island for my new nation state, sometimes that mountain range or valley," and then he "would write out their histories in a few paragraphs, what goods originated there, what languages people spoke." "At first," he details, "these countries were scattered archipelagoes of discontinuous territory, part of the San Francisco Bay Area, for example, joined in nationhood with Lahore and its surrounding districts." "Later, though"—and this is where the nine-year-old's cartographic game gets serious, ontologically speaking—he "began to create countries on non-existent islands that [he] would conjure up from the sea. These places were geographically unified but demographically varied. Lahoris and San Franciscans were often among the inhabitants, but equally often there were people from other places, from China, Kenya, Brazil or France. These islands sat in the middle of the Indian Ocean, or in the Pacific, but if one could travel to them and see their people, they might well look like the people of New York or London today."[49]

Fast-forward several decades to *Exit West*, Lahoris or residents of Syria, Lebanon, and other Middle Eastern countries critics have identified as Nadia and Saeed's are journeying to far-flung, prosperous, and presumably less violent lands through "special" doors (72) only with clothes on their backs and cell phones in their backpacks. As noted, such doors are egress–ingress units consisting in the space or energy field coterminous with their surface. The book repeatedly limns that "rectangle" (8) as "black" (103), dark, a "darkness" (103), "of complete darkness" (8), or, more allusively still, "the heart of darkness" (8). In an interview, Hamid links this blackness to the similarly colored "rectangles" of the electronic devices he used in Lahore during the Syrian crisis to "teleport" regularly by videocalls and watching movies.[50] But deep blackness strikes Nadia as both foreboding and aesthetic. In that, doors are like windows. They both change attributes in her besieged city, and because of that, "one's relationship" to them shifts also (71). A "window was the border through which death was possibly most likely to come" with stray bullets and "flying shards of glass" (71). But a window's blackness is not just ominous. "Glanc[ing] at her windows," Nadia "think[s] that they looked a bit like amorphous black works of contemporary art" (72). There is little about Nadia's windows that is "artistic," nor does civil war make them into "art." But they spring into fresh presence, acquiring an aesthetic quality as they no longer fulfill their domestic tasks; they are utterly "dysfunctional" if not counter-functional, making the residents vulnerable. In fact, their job is now "defensive," keeping the outside out. A giveaway of both that outside's own darkness and of the non- or less instrumental "thing" they have turned into, the windows' blackness indexes aesthetically the ontological intensification of being-there that, as we have seen throughout, accompanies an object's flattening *out of* its "normal" operations and assuming "special" ones. The immediate "effect" of this flattening on Nadia, as on characters of other novels discussed in *Flat Aesthetics*, is attention—attention to something that suddenly looks like "art." The windows force her to consider them for the first time, or at least to consider them *sub specie aestheticae*, and so do the doors. "The effect doors had on people," Hamid writes,

> altered as well. Rumors had begun to circulate of doors that could take you elsewhere, often to places far away, well removed from this death trap of a country. Some people claimed to know people who knew people who had been through such doors. A *normal* door, they said, could become a *special* door, and it could happen without warning, to any door at all. Most people thought these rumors to be non-sense, the superstitions of the feeble-minded. But most people began to gaze at their own doors a little differently, nonetheless.
>
> Nadia and Saeed, too, discussed these rumors and dismissed them. But every morning, when she awoke, Nadia looked over at her front door, and at the doors to her bathroom, her closet, her terrace. Every morning, in his room, Saeed did much the same. All their doors remained simple doors, on/off switches in the flow between two adjacent places, binarily either open or closed, but each of their doors, regarded thus with a twinge of irrational possibility, became *partially animate as well, an object with a subtle power to mock*, to mock the desires of those who desired to go far away, whispering silently from its door frame that such dreams were dreams of fools. (72–3; italics mine)

The window is a border without a redemptive beyond and therefore without a crossing either. It is, one might say, an honest limit, for there are no two ways about it, as it were; it is a limit that in *Exit West* conspicuously limits ("traps") one inside, *au-deçà* of the boundary, thus questioning its own ascriptions of propensity to openness and to a truly open *au-delà*, of a genuine, "outside" projection and cognate symbolism, which suggestions abound in classical socio-aesthetic analyses such as Georg Simmel's "Bridge and Door" essay.[51] The door, on the other hand, is a border actually bordering on a beyond to it and "illustrat[ing]," as Simmel would also have it, "the possibility at any moment of stepping out of this limitation into freedom."[52]

The question is whether this ambiguous border-cum-its-breaking delivers. More to the point, the question is not if Nadia, Saeed, and thousands of others like them step across real and imaginary thresholds in their home countries, for they positively if magically do, but what they are stepping into. At the end of the day, *Exit West*'s answer is less encouraging than both Simmel's and Hamid's own in *The Guardian* prelude to the 2017 book launch. The novel's doors vaunt access to faraway places, and, granted, they do make travel dreams come true. When asked about the teleporting ploy, Hamid insists that it helped him shift the focus away from the trip to arrival, from the onerous getting there to *having got there*, which somehow appears to him more "relatable," more equalizingly human. "Take away the journey," he says, "and you have a person who was in one place, and now is in a different place, something that happens to all of us—when we leave our parents' homes, for example. I don't intend to minimize the dangers and difficulties of migration with the doors. I intend to minimize the strength of our instinct to treat our fellow humans as 'other.'"[53]

Hamid's magic portals are then both the journey and its narrative ellipsis.[54] To Nadia, the door's darkness "felt," accordingly, "equally like a beginning and an end" (103), "like dying and like being born" (104) and hardly anything in between, but the sleight-of-hand elision of the trek as duration and life process still begs the question of destination—of whether or not the newcomers bask on the other side in the Simmelian "freedom" of Hamid's multiethnic utopia. They surely do not in *The Dog*, be they latter-day "legionnaires" of X's ilk, undocumented *bidoons*, or indentured Asian laborers. Nor do they in *Exit West*, and for the same reason: as we will also notice in the next part, every now and then, things insist on teaching us a thing or two. To do so, they exert "subtle," quasi-"animate" volitions and strengths of their own, through which they act like us and on us, moving us physically, in space, but sometimes deceiving us as well, disentangling us from our little cobwebs of community and history only to release us into bigger ones, at the same time spurring and "mocking" our flights. "Normal" objects do that too, but we do not feel the bite of their irony because we are too caught up in their everyday use, in making them "transparent" as *we* open a door, for example. Instead, "special" objects just are there, present, and "do what they do," *act*. Thus, Hamid's teleporting doors simply *open*, stepping out of their traditional usefulness to and handling by "us," into a hyperpresence that suspends their instrumental transparency—their "opacity" shocks Nadia (103)—and affects us in fashions that are unexpected and even ironic. We may not sense the derision right away either, but eventually we do for it "rearranges," as Lerner would say, the sensible world around us.

Critics have been quick to pick up on the Rancièrian politics of such rearrangements in *Exit West*.[55] It bears underscoring, however, that, first, this politics is spatial, and second, Hamid's Ur-objects rearrange not so much space *for* people as people *in* it. No matter where Nadia and Saeed land, this space always has a certain technopolitical texture to it, in that they never occupy "free" space—not even when, in Marin, they get places of their own. For, ironically, they cross time and again into territories already "taken," controlled and canvassed, that is, by national and international systems of communication, data collection, security, and defense. On this account, what the doors open out into up until the end is not an openness, and in my view, this queries the book's spatial politics. "Magical" trans-territorializations such as Nadia and Saeed's draw automatically techno-informational re-territorializations, geopositionings, and other re-limitations of this kind. It is worth remembering, along these lines, that in the *Guardian* piece, Hamid himself likens the doors' blackness to cell phone screens, and more importantly, that the novel's phones participate in the irony of dis-location-with-re-location, alongside doors, satellites, drones, and other exit objects.

Ever-ambiguous "weapons" (17), phones too are things of wonder. "Sniff[ing] out an invisible world, as if by magic," their "wands"-like "antennas" (39) help Saeed reach Nadia in their hometown. The devices provide privacy and even protect Nadia from the sexual aggression of male gazes and bodies, her social-media "opaque usernames and avatars . . . the online equivalent of her black robes" (41). Phones supply covers, lifesaving buffer zones, and bridges, but they "teleport" and render invisible because they belong to broader systems dealing in distance and its shrinking, in invisibility and in making visible. The systems are, one might say, "ironic" for they watch the phone watchers. The twenty-first century's ultimate tool, they seem to have lives and designs of their own, doing either less or more than asked, with effects ranging from the hilarious, as in Daniel Kehlmann's *Fame*, to the worrisome.[56] *Exit West*'s skies are always crowded with "networked machines for the most part invisible" (86), the "flying robots high above . . . [making] Saeed wal[k] with a slight hunch" (88). In London, "a small quadcopter drone" (92) hovers above a Tamil family about to be apprehended by the police, and Nadia has the weird feeling that she is the very news she is reading on her phone (157). Significantly," it is "under the drone-crossed sky and in the invisible network of surveillance that radiated from their phones, recording and capturing everything, that" Nadia "suggested [to Saeed] . . . that they abandon" the UK and "pass through a nearby door she had heard of, to the new city of Marin, on the Pacific Ocean, close to San Francisco" (188). After they drift apart, "Nadia move[s] . . . into a room" at the cooperative where she is working, and the "change" "struck [her] with a shock of recognition, as though a door was opening up, a door in this case shaped like a room" (216). It is the first time Hamid's doors open into a room that "came to feel to her like home" (217), and yet the tiny home is both hers and not, shared not only with the coop's members but also with the "tiny drones" "kee[ping] a watch on their district" (205). Tellingly, the book closes, during Nadia and Saeed's "reunion" fifty years *après*, with another surveillance scene, where Saeed mentions the Chilean desert's starlit sky while high above the old city "bright satellites" (230) track them. The "transiting" (230) machines and the phones talking to the machines as the two talk into the phones annul and create distance and information, and from the very beginning, over the phone, Saeed "became" to her "present without presence." "[S]he did much the same to him" (40), and so they would "touch" and "penetrate" each other "without bodily adjacency" (41). The devices would draw them to one another by "distancing [them] from [their] physical surroundings" (185), but Nadia and Saeed would also "distance themselves from each other on social networks" more and more (223), ultimately absencing themselves from each other's presence. Technologies compete and conspire to reposition them in a space and in a present in which Saeed's and Nadia's locations become separate but not unknown. Hamid does make a last-minute gesture toward a "plausible desirable future," inklings of which "began to emerge" in a Marin bursting with innovations in music, cuisine, and even politics (217). But whether or not the local "regional-assembly" project (220–1) will come to pass and, if so, whether or not it will revisit the spatial and political contracts in vigor are questions the novel does not answer. This is one more reason to stick with them, also apropos of things, material assemblages, and political assemblies, in the next part.

FOUR | Revenant

There were plenty of things in the world that deserved to stay dead, yet they walked.

—Colson Whitehead, *Zone One*

Let the cracks between things widen until they are no longer cracks but the new places for things.

—Colson Whitehead, *Zone One*

A book "about things" cannot ignore "the thing" itself, and so *Flat Aesthetics* turns to it now. Here, " 'the thing' itself" is neither the Kantian *noumenon* nor John Carpenter's 1982 movie, although *The Thing* would be worth discussing in this context. "The thing" is the zombie.[1] I find the appellation remarkably apt. The undead are *the* things insofar as they flaunt their thing-being more poignantly than most other things. Whether they truly are inanimate, non-sapient, purely corporeal, and hopelessly mechanical in demeanor or not—matters far more complex than they seem, as we will discover below—zombies enact these attributes more emphatically than most other objects. Zombies are, one might argue, uniquely forthright about their thingness; at any rate, American zombies are. "*English* zombies!" blurts out Denis in Thomas Pynchon's 2009 novel *Inherent Vice*. "Look at them, man," the hero carries on, "American zombies are at least out front about it, tend to stagger when they try to walk anywhere, usually in third ballet position, and they go, like 'Uunnhh . . . uunnhh,' with that rising and falling tone, whereas English zombies are for the most part quite well spoken, they use long words and they glide everywhere, like, sometimes you don't even see them take steps, it's like they're on ice skates. . ."[2]

In Denis's view, the American monsters are closer to thingness, to being "it." They look the part too for, in the majority of movies, TV series, and literature in the genre, they have ruined or lost the material appendages, socio-professional capabilities and appearances, and overall emotional and cognitive *functionality* of an "American person."[3] I propose in this segment of *Flat Aesthetics*, as I have throughout the book, that such dysfunctionality or, as I put it elsewhere, intransitivity—destructively, violently, and even murderously as it oftentimes manifests itself—is culturally instructive and may well be, under certain circumstances, culturally constructive. By "instructive" I mean instruction literally. In fact, I ask in this part's first chapter if American zombies have something to teach "us," those still fitting and, we think, "functioning" in the culture, accepting its constraints and reflexes, going through its motions and to MAGA rallies ("usually in third ballet position"), and so forth. Is there a zombie pedagogy, in other words? And, if there is, what are its political implications? Is the zombie's "Uunnhh . . . uunnhh" some sort of statement on the American polity? I raise the same questions—and the answers, I believe, are a bit more precise—in the second chapter, which revisits the most important text in the highbrow U.S. zombie canon, Whitehead's novel *Zone One*.[4] Commentators have paid cursory attention to the book's objectual imaginary—no surprise the best they can do is rehash "postcritique" axioms in a spectacle of critical *laissez-faire* that strikes me as ironically neoliberal.[5] My takeaway from *Zone One* is, as it was in the sections devoted to Mandel and Lerner, somewhat more "criticist," in the sense clarified by this part's opening half and borne out, I suggest, by *Zone One*, more specifically by the "things" in it. Similarly to other books by Whitehead in which the zombie "inhabit[s] the imaginations of their protagonists,"[6] as well as to *The Intuitionist* (1999), *The Underground Railroad* (2016), and Whitehead's fiction generally, there is in *Zone One* an untold eloquence to things, a loquacity beyond logos. What I do not mean to suggest, however, is that things, zombies or not, are in the novel merely rhetorical effects, carnivorous "flowers of rhetoric," to recall Lacan or, more exactly, Bryant's objection to Lacan and his followers.[7] Quite the opposite, they are rhetorical sources, mute—yet not speechless—things that tell us things.

As elsewhere in *Flat Aesthetics*, what they tell us, the "instruction" they provide, as I say above, is no anthropomorphic construction although, as I acknowledge in the introduction, it is multiply speculative and therefore on some level at least residually anthropomorphic. Commanding not a language of words but of energetic transfers impacting other things nearby or remote, things "speak" in that their actions or sheer being-there affects other things. Either way, their idiom is one of deeds, and what they do in *Zone One* is eminently if ambivalently political, bearing extensively on the U.S. body politic, particularly on the official project to revivify some of its prejudicial and even racist elements in the postapocalyptic aftermath. Insofar as that project itself is hegemonic—for it purports to reinstate a certain hegemony— zombies' thing-language, what they effectuate or convey, can be said to be anti-hegemonic or have anti-hegemonic ramifications, to engage in a "critique," after a fashion. Nothing prevents us from thinking of the things in terms of "*entanglements* of objects," as Barad, Bryant, and others encourage us, from paying heed, at the same time, to the politically tilted, hegemonic setup of objectual com-positions and webs, and from assessing what the zombie rampage does to it.[8] Even if there is "no one agency entirely responsible for the patterns" of entanglements, it does not follow from this that "within an entanglement . . . pattern there can be no hegemon."[9] The ontological and aesthetic flatness of things is indeed . . . one thing; political flatness, quite another, as *Flat Aesthetics* shows repeatedly.

copula, ding, assembly: Zombies and the Body Politic

[T]hings metaphorically connote the soulless body . . .
—Barbara M. Benedict, "The Spirit of Things"

Their mouths could no longer manage speech[,] yet they spoke nonetheless[.]
—Colson Whitehead, *Zone One*

While the flesh-eating ghouls have been popping up all over America for almost a century now, their numbers have dramatically swollen of late. A major symptom of contemporaneity, literary and otherwise, the zombie industry is booming. No longer an unwonted revenant from Hollywood's restless netherworld, the loathsome creatures have become a cultural epidemic that makes you wonder: which is more contagious, the zombie bite or theme? Sporting their hallmark rags or still reasonably groomed, the walking dead keep stumbling out of America's obsessional closet to take over neighborhoods, malls, campuses,[10] and freeways in popular and experimental, cult and mainstream art forms alike, and sometimes in all at once, as in Kathy Acker's *Empire of the Senseless* (1988), Joyce Carol Oates's *Zombie* (1995), Don DeLillo's *Underworld* (1997), E. L. Doctorow's *The Waterworks* (1997), and closer to us in postapocalyptic narratives such as Ling Ma's *Severance*, in "ethnofictions" such as Aleksandar Hemon's 2015 *The Making of Zombie Wars* (2015), and in African American zombie novels of which *Zone One* is just the most prominent example.[11] This is an all-out invasion. No genres, media, and fields are safe. It has been happening in literature commonly understood as postmodern but also in its poorer relative, pulp, and in the

Stephen Kings and Brian Keenes feverishly mining the subject in between; in movies such as Ruben Fleischer's 2009 comedy *Zombieland* and in TV cartoons, with *The Simpsons* and *South Park* leading the pack; in run-of-the-mill commercials and in the anti-commercial Ronald McDonald Internet "exposés"; in cultural-political satire à la George Saunders and in creepy mashups like Seth Grahame-Smith's 2009 *Pride and Prejudice and the Zombies*; in music videos and computer games from Michael Jackson's 1982 *Thriller* and the *Resident Evil* multimedia series to comics such as the 2008 *Zombie Broadway*; in masterpieces that have already undergone "zombification" as well as in zombified classics to be,[12] no less culturally blasphemous than the "Schwarzeneggerized" rewrites of Mark Leyner's avant-pop *Et Tu, Babe*;[13] in mock-scientific zombie vade mecums and manuals, a cottage industry whose output ranges from Max Brooks's "traditionalist" 2003 *Zombie Survival Guide* (billed as "Complete Protection from the Living Dead") to Mac Montandon's "revisionist" 2010 "Completely Scientific Guide to the Lives of the Undead" (titled *The Proper Care and Feeding of Zombies*); and last but not least, in reputable venues from newspapers and magazines to academic journals and university presses, where philosophers of consciousness debate "physicalism" and economists quarrel over the "zombie economy" and the "zombie companies" thriving in it.[14]

This fast-growing body of work has time after time reembodied figures, scenes, plot lines, and sociocultural allusions from George A. Romero's 1960s trend-setting films. However, in getting "new life," the Romero hits and, with them, the entire "ghoulish genre" only emulate the obstinacy of their staple character.[15] "This thing just won't die!" the handful of humans left standing in zombie flicks invariably scream—amusingly enough, an outburst itself haunted by Hamlet's undying "Rest, rest perturbed spirit!" (1. 5. 181). Alas, both in Shakespeare's Denmark and in Romero's America, the "thing" refuses to oblige. The dead have died and not quite. They may have drawn their last breath, but they are not dead; they are "deadish," as a (still) human hero quips in the 2004 remake of Romero's 1978 *Dawn of the Dead*. Literalizing an afterlife that for many of "us" remains a vaguely religious metaphor, zombies, rather than Max Brooks's readers, may be the consummate survivalists after all—*Survival of the Dead* is the title of Romero's 2009 movie. Anything but "completely and thoroughly dead,"[16] they return to take up residency in the limbo of U.S. culture and, from there, to gross out, horrify, and confound, but I contend, also to "enlighten" us, to tell us something about ourselves. For, when read with the grain, "the thing" may not actually speak to us, or we may not hear it. It remains or appears to remain "mute." At most, it "tells" us what we expect or want to hear, namely, of its fundamentally nonhuman essence, of that which is so unlike us, rational beings, that it cannot tell us anything at all, let alone about the limits, the mechanical routines of our own rationality. But when read against its grain, the zombie starts speaking to us despite or, better yet, by means of its unspeakably "irrational," "thingified" look, thus engaging us through the very radical difference it stages so willfully. How is this possible?

An epitome of nonhumanity, zombies are, it seems, more than simply "different" from people. The dissimilarity is total, allayed by no residual overlap, affinity, or commerce across the existential-intellectual gap between "us" and "them." This radical contrast explains why we are drawn so hypnotically to the catatonic hordes and also why they have supplanted vampires as our unmitigated Other in the collective imaginary.[17] Some critics argue, in effect, that zombies fascinate Americans to a degree Dracula's progeny never have. Their demonism ever part-time, dampened by the "soft" alterity built into it, bloodsucking monsters retain a modicum of humanness because they are endowed with sentience and, more importantly, with consciousness, "twisted" as it may be. Not so zombies, even though, as in *Zombie One*, one still has to shoot them in the head to put them out of their putative misery. There are, of course, exceptions such as that confounding Laurell K. Hamilton's zombie "animator" Anita Blake.[18] As a rule, however, they have every semblance of lacking consciousness. Consequently, they do not possess the individuality most vampires boast. True, a vampire's bite may dehumanize its human victim, but because vampiric contact is not automatically infectious, it is not instantly metamorphic either. As Elizabeth Kostova reiterates Bram Stoker's observation in her Vlad Țepeș thriller *The Historian*, several bites are required for the transformation to occur.[19] Even so, this vampirizing dehumanization is "mushy." Not unlike the Borg's "assimilation" of *Star Trek*'s Captain Picard, it is usually neither perfect nor irreversible given that it does not de-individualize. Again, zombification does. Accordingly, the zombie, being one or turning into one, performs the unadulterated, "thing-ifying" difference between the nonhuman in its serial, mindless, soulless, and inanimate form, on one side, and the human and its equivalents, the sentient, individual, and the rational, on the other.

Zombies are, then, our absolute opposite. Not only that, but they are keen on *looking* absolutely opposed to how we see ourselves as living entities in general and *homo sapiens* in particular. Preserving just the material veneer of humanness, the zombie is, and insists on appearing to the spectator or reader, as the human in its most de-spiritualized or a-spiritual, a-cognitional, reified embodiment: the human as mere embodiment, the human *qua* body, the body as exclusively physical body, and, as a number of writers and moviemakers hint, critically or not, the zombified body as racialized, Black body.[20] Except that, trading on the anatomy of "corpus" and "corpse" simultaneously, the zombie body does not have the proper structure of a human body either. The tautological regime of zombie phenomenality, in which how the "thing" appears to us is no more than that, an appearance, an epidermal phenomenon or "show" of deceptive layers, surfaces, and looks, holds sway over the zombified body too; the latter stages, quasi theatrically, the mere façade of human physicality. This corpus no longer incorporates. In other words, it is not an organic apparatus, an anatomic-physiological system that contains and thus depends on organs with functions vital to the unifying, coherence-building workings of the mind, but something like a depthless, decentered, and socially decentering "body without organs."[21] If in David Lynch's corporeal "universe ... bodily depth constantly invades the surface and threatens to swallow it,"[22] zombification flattens the body into a one-dimensional "surfacial" assemblage with no insides and no inside. Rendering thingness not anorganic but organless, this vertical surfaciality of sorts marks a major step in the zombie body's "thing-becoming."[23]

Anima demoted to animality and its abominable Kabuki theater of bodily postures and cognitive impostures, the Cartesian subject here totters before us only to cancel itself out effusively in its dejected hypostasis of object or "thing" groping around for our flesh. The "thing" will never eat its fill, though. Its hunger for us is bottomless because, as a venerable philosophical tradition reassures us, so is the gap between the human as cogitative subject and the nonhuman other as subject solely *to* our cogitations and thereby object or thing. Which is to say, not only are we, humans, the sole and absolute subject, entitled to our epistemological absolutism, but the object on the other side of the human–nonhuman divide is absolute too and so irredeemably hostage to the stultifying immanence of its gruesome materiality. In brief, we, humans, are a *res cogitans*; we are a, or better still, *the* "thinking thing," in which the heavily emphasized first term tones down the "thing" (*res*) in us. For, as the Cartesian dictum has it, if we think, and if we therefore are subjects—if we are, *tout court*—this happens at the expense of the thing, of the object.[24] At the same time, the only reality granted to the object of our cogitations is opaque re(s)ality, the self-imploding black hole of unthinking "thingness" or, as Lacan underscores, the twice "dumb" reality that does not speak and hence remains silent because it cannot think to begin with.[25]

Disseminating this tradition across the high- and lowbrow cultures of contemporary America, the zombie plays up the object's hopelessly objectual condition by putting an "abjectual" spin on it through a tactical overdramatization of the somatic object as *abject object* or cadaver. The underlying assumption here is that, in the "dead body," the object's destitution or, as Baudrillard says, "prostitution,"[26] its ab-jection or re-jection to the otherworld's non-subjective otherness and to its inert, a-rational thingness, is categorical and definitive *and* will be registered as such by "us."[27] Thus, the object's "obscene,"[28] ignominious objectuality, the cadaveric "abjectuality" on which zombie cinema dwells so obstinately, flags the subject's rational downgrading to object, to a thing that, Sartre claims, while it can be said to "exist," is not as *we* are.[29] It is, bluntly put, so *we* can fully be. Sanctioned by the "accursed" ontology of subaltern beings, it is as tool, prosthesis, and transitive medium—it is *as* human substitute, rational ersatz, and extension of or "detour on the royal road" to the [human] subject.[30]

This fall from the rational grace of subjectivity, now a condition safely earmarked for us, humans, alone, is further compounded rather than alleviated by the former subject's "atypical" survival as zombified body: a fraudulent survival, un-whole and in that unholy, "diabolically" partial.[31] Metaphysically speaking—speaking, namely, from the standpoint of a simultaneously rationalist and theological tradition of adjudicating what makes the true subject human and under which circumstances it is "operational"—this "subject" would be better off if, once clinically dead, it vanished from our world without a trace and "stayed," as one of Kostova's characters opines, "respectably dead" than if it stuck around and appeared, in the aforementioned sense of "appearance," as thing-like body.[32] Following its "half-death"—*demi-mort*, in Lacan—and "disrespectful" of this interstitial state, the body may and does appear. But, the same tradition has it, this appearance represents, as earlier, just that, an appearance, smoke and mirrors without substance precisely because all there seems to be to its reality is corporeality, to wit, flesh.[33] On the face of it—the inhumanly defaced face the zombie's body turns to us—there is no subject in or with the pseudo-resurrected body that puts in an appearance. Therefore, we are tempted to conjecture, the body is now merely a "thing" or, as Hamlet tells Rosencranz and Guildenstern, "The body is with the King, but the King is not with the body." "The King," Hamlet adds, "is a thing . . . [o]f nothing" (4. 3. 23–6). But is the anthropological subject, the subject "as we know it," the only heading under which knowledge can find an agent and thus give itself a vehicle and a form, in short, a body? To ask the question differently: Is the thing necessarily a-subjectual, utterly unable to exert cogitative and articulatory functions equivalent or comparable to a living person's? And, if it is not, how exactly do zombies help us warm up to the notion of a thing's "personhood," as Barbara Johnson might say.[34]

One of Shakespeare's notoriously cryptic places, the passage above has been interpreted in a disconcerting number of ways. Most critics agree, though, that the body in question is more than meets the eye. The body, they maintain, is not, or not only, Polonius. More remarkably, we are not dealing exclusively with empirical bodies either. Along these lines, two distinct bodily formations come into play here: the King's "natural" body and the monarch's body politic.[35] One is private, physical, hence mortal. It dies and does not tarry. Or, if it does, it does not do so as such but as its metaphorically disembodied double or "spirit"—as the body's "other body." Bodying forth the law, authority, and kingship, the "somatic" body's alternate is more of a transcendent, collective-juridical concept, a signifier of political desire, of monarchic will and legitimacy. These bodily attributes of the ruler are sui generis "things" that do not fade away upon the death of his perishable body. They outlive his mundane exit, pass into the rightful heir's corporeal aggregate, or steer clear of dubious pretenders and usurpers. In this sense, Claudius *is* a King/thing of no(-)thing. "Thingified,"[36] he looks the part but is hardly (with) "it," the real King/thing. This is why the law, which he violated when he poisoned Hamlet's father, cannot possibly be with Hamlet's uncle; it is the murdered King who retains authority even after death has degraded his physicality to no-thing, to nothing physical—to the ghostly revenant. Urged by his son to "rest," the King cannot take a break because the law is still "restless," active. In or with him, power, *imperium* in Latin, remains imperative, and the first action it demands regards Claudius because his crime has reduced the law and its embodiment to a no-body, to spirit, immaterial specter.

The King's appearance is thus a "phallophany," a *phallophanie*, as Lacan writes in his seminar on desire (Book VI).[37] For, what appears (cf. Gk. *phaínesthai*) or reappears, rather, in the King's phallic apparition—what comes to light in the Heideggerian enlightening *Lichtung* tragically opened up by *Hamlet*'s revenant and makes itself known to the Danish prince, to his spectators, and to human consciousness more broadly—is the luminous essence of the phallus as Ur-index of relation, as "with" marker. An arch-signifier, the phallus is a signifying thing. If it means any-thing, then that thing is signification and significance—it does not "mean" them actually but *is* them, performs them. It points to how things relate to one another, come about, signify, and overall get done in our world, to who is running them, that is, *with* whom "it," the law or moral-political authority, lies or should lie. The copulative phenomenology of the "with" is here paramount. What this "with" articulates (formulates, lays down) here is articulation itself as key world principle since the link and the aptly named "signifying chain" in which we are all enmeshed, our sociopolitical and affective-phantasmatic ties, the logical-grammatical copula and the very act of copulation are the building blocks of the world's languages and codes, both encoding this world and helping to decode it ontologically, semiotically, and politically by revealing the relatedness of being—how bodies of people, culture, institutions, and non-sentient things are "with" one another.[38] Thus, on one hand, the phallus sets up the world as existential, sexual, cultural, political, and cultural juxtaposition—tradition, transmitted culture, is quintessentially phallic too—and, on the other hand, it assists us in parsing the world syntax accordingly. The premier phallic function, Lacan submits, is to "lift the veil"[39] from the libidinal underpinnings of cultural-political codifications and hierarchies. "With" the King, the phallus-thing returns from the dead to unveil to the living the makeup of the symbolic, "how things are." The King shows itself so as to show that which must be shown to "us," humans, because we cannot discern it on our own. The unveiling presupposes the veiled—verbalized, symbolized, disguised—status of things human, but the apparition, "the thing," appears so that *those* things do not remain forever unapparent to "us." It follows, then, that the "truth" the ghost conveys is both hermeneutic and critical. Otherwise put: this truth has to do with our world as much as with our capacity to "get" it and implicitly with the human itself, more specifically, with the critical shortcomings of human consciousness.

As Lacan insists elsewhere, this is the profound and disturbing revelation the subject experiences "in the place of the Other."[40] More basically, it is in the place taken up by the King's reappearance as apparition, as "other" to Hamlet and us all, that we get a glimpse of some("other")thing we ordinarily do not make out from our station in the world of the living, namely, of how limited our capacity for knowledge can be. For, if it "knows its place" in the hardened order of things mortal and immortal, human and nonhuman, animate and inanimate, as it usually does, the human risks not knowing itself, and more often than not ignorance and its corollary, self-ignorance, are the price we, humans, pay for the entrenched cultural-metaphysical sedentariness that locks us inside our *Weltanschauungen* and frameworks. So, against an entire Cartesian line of thought this time around, we may conclude that one is and one owns up to what one is as a cognitive subject *where one normally is not*; that, perforce "beyond us"—and generally beyond, *au-delà*—learning is an away game; that knowledge reveals itself to the knowing subjects in the realm of otherness, in Michel de Montaigne's *ailleurs*.[41] Canvassed ad nauseam in our daily routines, the social remains, unfortunately, a site of blindness: being-in-the-social, and by extension being overall, is a blind spot, a topo-epistemological handicap. Instead, the place where the phallus appears marks the scene where the workings of human desire and power can be queried and made apparent. Returning from the otherworld in an appearance *of necessity* other to us, the King's ghost shows up, Lacan asserts, "to bring to the subject's mind" [*pour ... porter à la connaissance du sujet*][42] what in the subject's abode gets in the way of his or her knowledge: the political underlays of the social terrain itself and, deeply engrained in our consciousness, the self-sufficient rationalism that blinds us to power's "veiled" grip over our lives.

But, if zombies are not vampires, they are not ghosts either. They are less than spectral, or perhaps more, higher up the nonhuman scale. Arguably, ghosts are not ghastly enough, at least compared to zombies, whose "over-the-top," thingified bodily appearances look stranger than disembodied apparitions and so carry superior "heterological" value. Does this matter? It does because, if we entertain the notion that the Other rises to raise human consciousness—if the King must come back *as* an Other to orient us in the symbolic and, within it, in the nuts and bolts of the ideological—then, the more hair-raising the Other, the more consciousness-raising its rise: the more "other" to us the revenant's form, the more unfamiliar to us its resurgence, and the more cognitively defamiliarizing its presence *among* us and *to* our human "condition." No doubt, the hero of the 2006 comedy *Fido* constitutes an exception, for, as a rule, zombies are neither well behaved nor "trainable," likely to remember or relearn our cultural rites, walk our dogs, manicure our lawns, become the caring fathers we have never had, and so on. Their dehumanization or, more accurately, their incapacitation as functioning human subjects is and must be acted out in the symbolic world of the living as absolute, in the absolute of thing phenomenology because, unlike specters, they can *embody* the Other absolutely, that is, they can "lend" otherness their body *and no more than that*. "A true ZOMBIE['s] ... eyes," fancies Q_P_, the serial-killer protagonist of Oates's 1995 novel, "would be open & clear but there would be nothing inside them *seeing*. & nothing behind them *thinking*. Nothing *passing judgment* ... Nor *memory*."[43] And vice versa: since the zombified body entails a thoroughgoing dehumanizing of the human, the "veritable" Other, the Other as the "real thing," necessarily appears to us as a zombie (kind of) thing.

To most commentators, the thingness of the thing—the human as zombie body—allegorizes the "human reductionism" striving to "reduce a person to body, to reduce behavior to basic motor functions, and to reduce social utility to raw labor," hence the usual references to earlier films such as *White Zombie* (1932), *Revolt of the Zombies* (1936), *Revenge of the Zombies* (1943), and even *Modern Times* (1936).[44] Instead, what I would foreground in the "thing" no matter how this appears and speaks (or does not speak) to us at first blush is not principally a feature we lose as mindless zombies, but to the contrary, something we gain intellectually from the thing, some-thing we get to see in ourselves once we have seen it in or as thing: not a cognitively regressive narrative allegorizing the old chestnut of modernist "alienation," but a progression in knowledge and even in self-knowledge, odd as it may— and does—"appear." For it is in such extreme thing-incorporation that the Other plays its "unveiling," analytically othering role best, naming for us that which otherwise would remain "unknown," "unimaginable" to us, humans;[45] it is, specifically, as bodily thing that the Other "calls the subject into question,"[46] puts up the twofold high drama of "our" social reification and false consciousness most effectively. The zombie "critical method" and its focus—our sociocultural positioning—are, then, isomorphic: as a "thing of flesh," "fleshed out" as thing rather than airy spirit, the Other stands ideally poised to awaken us to our material embodiment and related conditioning, viz., to how much the loftiest of our representations and values, and our ability to "see through" them all no less, are conditioned by material arrangements geared not only to holding our world together but also to screening its makeup from our gaze.

Therefore, what Derrida refers to as the "spirit of Marxist critique"— Marxism's critical *Geist*—may well prove less pugnacious in ghosts than in zombies.[47] In fact, ever since Georg Wilhelm Friedrich Hegel, the *Geist*, both "spirit" and "ghost" in German, has been coopted by the metaphysical methodology and vocabulary of Western humanism. Its critical thrust repeatedly exorcised, the *Geist* has been harnessed to the teleological project of the human, and on this account too, *somatology*, the "a-spiritual" logic of the body-thing, poses a more serious threat to the metaphysics of the human than Derrida's post-Marxist "spectrology."[48] First and foremost, this threat and, potentially following from it, the re-visitation of some of our basic "grand narratives" stem from the zombie's bodily performance—from that which makes zombie somatology a radical heterology. Granted, werewolves, vampires, ogres, mummies, poltergeists, and phantoms are heterologies too, but zombies are a heterology with teeth in more ways than one.[49] These teeth have a uniquely eloquent bite to them in the sense that if indeed, as Derrida claims, the "love[r]s of justice" stand to learn a lot from a "ghost"[50] in which they nevertheless recognize themselves as much as they do in vampires—*Our Vampires, Ourselves*, reads the title of Nina Auerbach's book on the subject[51]—then the same "scholars" and "intellectuals," along with the rest of us, "should learn"[52] even more from zombies.

Learn what, one might retort. And again, what can we learn from a thing that has come "to represent an absence of spirit" and "soul"?[53] Suppose we are, at long last, prepared to accept that "[t]he human body is an instrument of knowledge," as Paul Auster writes in his 2010 novel *Sunset Park*.[54] Can we say the same about the zombie body? To answer, let me offer first that startling in the spectral *Unheimliche* is a Freudian recognition, an almost necromantic resuscitation of what has been, a reenactment or comforting mimesis of the human subject; what comes back from the *ultra-monde*[55] in and "with" the specter and its phallic paraphernalia of authority, control, and privilege is thus the reiteration of a cognition originated in, and referencing, our *hic and nunc* and so fraught with all the philosophical and anthropocentric concessions consciousness has been making in the name of our "reasonable" humanity. By contrast, unsettling in zombie *Unheimlichkeit* are the "body beyond recognition"—bodily otherness—and its own phallic flipside, namely, a deeper, more difficult, and troubling realization analogously surging from beyond human consciousness and cutting through that which customarily confines our thought processes to preset intellectual grids and status quos.[56] It is the zombie uncanny that truly "goes against one's waking" and, more broadly, rational, human "wishes or beliefs."[57] What pulls us toward vampires, and what, in them, "teaches" us, is a psycho-cultural matrix of self-identification, the vampiric *in* the human, for at the end of the day, "[v]ampires [are] [l]ike [u]s."[58] Admittedly, they are monsters, but in their monstrosity—in their botched metamorphosis—we view ourselves. Like the specter, the vampire is a *speculum*, a "mirror" of and for the human. To that extent, what the vampiric or ghostly mirror image of ourselves uncovers and reflects back to us is, critically and politically, a mixed bag: not just the phallic as heretofore unavailable insight into the logic of our world— the phallus as "embodied . . . *nous* and . . . *logos*," according to Lacan[59]—but also the world's "phallogocentrism," as Derrida contends, against Lacan, in "Le facteur de vérité."[60] In such monstrous vehicles, the phallic tenor at once enables and disables "learning" and the critique grounded in it. What accounts for this ambivalence is that which, in vampires, ghosts, and other Others of this kind, reminds us of what has created them in the first place: human rationality and its apparatus, consciousness. Living on in vampires and, with heightened pathos, in disembodied revenants like spirits, consciousness, complete with its all-too-human reflexes and compromises, bears out Hamlet's suspicion that "conscience does make cowards of us all." "[T]he native hue of resolution," the Prince goes on in the famous Act III monologue, "is sicklied o'er with the pale cast of thought" (3. 1. 85). Put another way, while we may learn something from the specter, we "lose the name of action" in the bargain—learning is one thing; acting on what we have learned is quite another. "Cast" as they have always been in consciousness and its representation systems, the thought or thoughts in question are not only liable to accommodate the represented epsitemologically, but they are also "weak" politically.

Beholden to a "weak thought" redolent of Gianni Vattimo's *pensiero debole*, the thinking subject may end up "neutraliz[ing]," Derrida worries, "[the specter] through naturalization,"[61] that is, by explaining away the specter's nature. And so, premised on the spirit's bodilessly "logocentric" pantomime, the naturalizing and rationalizing constructions we put on the world are predictably "despiriting," as it were, bound to do ideology's bidding. By the same token, they translate into correspondingly insubstantial "actions"—into, some say, "decaffeinated revolution, a revolution which doesn't smell of revolution."[62] On occasion, we may "catch" somebody's consciousness promisingly unawares "in the open," in another place, in the place of the Other as "thing" —"The play's the thing / Wherein I'll catch the conscience of the King," announces Hamlet in Act II (2. 2. 605–6)—and yet consciousness, moral conscience included, cannot solve actual problems as long as it does not have the strength to pose itself as a problem to the world-as-world, to the world's concrete body of bodies, of smells, noises, contacts, and views. In this light, what *Inherent Vice*'s FBI agents say of unscrupulous real estate mogul Michael Wolfmann should be taken literally. "We'd always assumed," they admit, "that Michael's conscience would never be a problem. After all his years of never appearing to have one. Suddenly he decides to *change his life* and give away millions to an assortment of degenerates— Negroes, longhairs, drifters. Do you know what he said? We have it on tape. 'I feel as if I awakened from a dream of a crime for which I can never atone, an act I can never go back and choose not to commit.'"[63] After his "crisis of conscience"—once his conscience "appears"—Wolfmann disappears but only to reappear later in "the clutches of the [same] System," "back to them old greedy-ass ways."[64] Following his institutionalization, he lumbers around all doped up, at the same time cured and sicker than ever. Is Wolfmann Freud's Wolfsmann? A Lazarus *à rebours* perhaps? In any event, he turns up fully, *obtrusively* zombified. But he must be so in order to draw attention to himself, and more notably still, he must draw attention to himself because this is the only way *we* may pick up, in his pre-crisis demeanor and in everyday America generally, on what Doc, Pynchon's private-eye hero, refers to as "all telltale zombie symptoms."[65]

As one can see, not only does the zombie dissimulate and disclose concurrently, but it cannot accomplish either without attempting both at once. It ramps up its corporeal spectacle of difference to the point where the horrified spectator is no longer afforded any identification with Wolfmann whatsoever. If initially Pynchon's reader may have "related" to Wolfmann and more broadly to entrepreneurial America, that becomes fairly impossible after the realtor resurfaces in all his otherworldly inhumanity as bodily thing plodding along like a speechless automaton. But, again, this shocking reemergence is of the essence; this is how the "Other as [Freudian] *Ding*" (thing), *must* "present itself to us," given that, as Lacan accentuates, "the Thing only presents itself to the extent that it becomes word, hits the bull's eye, as they say"[66] [*pour autant qu'elle fait mot, comme on dit* faire mouche].[67] More plainly, Wolfmann would not have assumed a form so discrepant from ours, i.e., he would not have presented himself before us as a thing, as a no-thing by human standards, had he not had some "other," more important thing—Lacan's *Chose*—to present or communicate *to* us; Wolfmann's ghoulishly astonishing, theatrical-discursive rhetoric of self-presentation conveys his "message" by virtue of the same negative dialectic of phallic presentation according to which the stranger the messenger and his delivery the stronger the message and its impact on the receiving subject.[68] Thus, he presents *us* with something to "think about" in *our* world of symbolic deployments insofar as *his* "comeback" boggles our mind, representing for us as it does an "encounter" with a thing that resists symbolization since its meaning lies, Lacan states it plainly, somewhere "beyond the *automaton*, the return, the coming-back."[69] Wolfmann addresses us, has "things" to say to us, *because* he looks so *un*like us, so inhuman, "thingly." He makes *us* reflect *because* reflection, consciousness, and so on do not seem available *to* him. He speaks to us *because* he is, or *sounds*, rather, speechless—as Lacan also glosses on the Other's "mute" recital, the thing becomes *mot* ("word," in French) by way of its very silence. It is in this aporetic wordlessness pregnant with meaning, dialectically "telling," that the Other is "on target" (*fait mouche*) *and* targets us; through its unlikely presentation, "the Other as *Ding*" "tells it *like* it is," to us.[70] This observation too should be taken literally. Not only must the telling (the phallic signifier) be a thing *and* thing-like, must be carried out in a *dingliche* fashion or appearance, but the "it," "*[l]es choses don't il s'agit*"—the "things" the *muet* (silent) Other talks about if not in so many words (*mots*),[71] that which is told us and concerns us in zombie "phallophany" (the signified)—must also be some(-)thing germane to the form the telling and the "mute" interpellation of the human take up.

The bestselling *Walking Dead* multivolume graphic novel forefronts this thought-provoking interpellation insistently. This should come as no surprise. In the introduction, Robert Kirkman, the series creator, likens his work to "[g]ood zombie movies[, which] show us how messed up we are[,] . . . make us question our station in society . . . and our society's station in the world. They show us gore and violence and all that cool stuff too . . . but there's always an undercurrent of social commentary and thoughtfulness."[72] Kirkman's protagonist, former Kentucky policeman Rick Grimes, his family, and friends are "addressed" by the undead into a "thoughtfulness" that, inchoate as it looks, was unavailable to humans prior to the zombie outbreak. In a way, interpellation is here metaphorical. Except for the occasional grunts, the interpellating things remain silent, inarticulate. At the same time, it is literal in that it does articulate a demand, a challenge to human consciousness to recognize and possibly overcome its "station." In the makeshift camp outside Atlanta from volume 1 and especially in the former prison where volume 4 is mostly set, the zombies surround the survivors and provide an omnipresent audience under whose scopic pressure Rick and others take steps to rescind their compliance with "every retarded little rule we ever invented to make us feel like we weren't animals" and come up with "new rules" instead.[73] The old rules held together the human world Rick's group has been trying unsuccessfully to salvage, a social model fundamentally compliant, in effect rooted in allegiance to law and in which daily interaction of the group members and sociality largely are dramatized as "congenial" law enforcement.

This is particularly obvious in volume 1, where Shane, Rick's one-time partner and a big believer in "rules," equates their survival with the government's ability to take charge, a suggestion of which, we will discover, *Zone One* is equally dismissive. For somebody like Shane, the current situation is a deviation from the norm, a wrinkle in an otherwise dependable, rational sociopolitical narrative. The state of exception brought about by the crisis, he believes, is both illegitimate and temporary. On this ground, as far as he is concerned, it makes no sense either to question pre-zombie legal setups and social affordances or to adjust to the present. By contrast, Rick, while acknowledging the present's abnormality, senses in it, albeit still vaguely, an opportunity if not a necessity to query the norm itself. To Shane, what they are going through is a "mess" the government and its agencies will somehow sort out, rationalize, and the army will "clean up" sooner or later, as it valiantly attempts in Whitehead. Rick, however, feels that the mess is here to stay, marking as it does a profoundly messy, fast-changing world whose shifting practices and boundaries of gender, sexuality, religion, class, property, community, and humanity, emphatically thematized across the volumes, make him take another look at the world left behind.

What "it" all comes down to is this: in keeping with the logic of phallophanic self-articulation, the thing the zombie body *as* thing conveys to "us" also is—or is of the nature of—the thing itself. The Freudian–Lacanian *rebus* is, self-reflexively—and with the kind of self-reflexiveness absent in "us"—about *res* itself.[74] More enigmatic, more indirect, and nonetheless more urgent than a spectral communiqué, this ultimately if unintentionally carries or can be decoded as a message about the re(s)ality of human consciousness, about how reified, how thing- and automaton-like, and ultimately how mindless the human mind and the human broadly stand in the signifying system and in the clasp of socio-systemic relations built on it. Only consciousness cannot and does not appear so to itself. It does, however, to its "selfless" Other, the zombie. Unaware of the situation, of the "System" and its grip on us, human consciousness acts, or rather merely reacts, as false consciousness, playing along docilely. Busy to fulfill its social "mandate," as Lacan dubs it, the subject's consciousness fails to question the subject's world.[75]

By contrast, the thing is a brazen provocateur: as Heidegger proposes in *Being and Time*, the "thingliness [of things can be or] becom[e] a problem"[76] that may end up problematizing the world. "As in *W[hat Is a] T[hing]*," the book the German philosopher devotes exclusively to the thing, "the question 'What is a thing?' brings," Michael Inwood comments, "the whole world into play."[77] Asking about the world's *choses* (derived from Lat. *causae*) is an etymologically and philosophically apposite way of "bringing into play" the world's *causes*, its reasons—its "thing rationalities"—for being the way it is.[78] The play at hand is the material play (cf. the French *jeu*) of thinking, of thinking and its high stakes (*enjeux*). A chief ingredient of the genre from the first Romero movies to Amelia Beamer's 2009 Alcatraz "romance" *The Loving Dead*, the zombie uprising gestures, quite overtly, to the social disobedience for which humans have become unfit, but more significant, and hence less transparent, is the allusion to what lays the groundwork for any questioning and dissent in a world of dematerialized values, namely, to the requisite retrofitting of thinking as thing-thinking, as "thinging." For the thing/*Ding* does no more (and no less) than that—"its thing"—by helping us see how things connect to one another in their bigger "confederacy," as Bennett calls it. Here, in Heidegger's political "assembly" (*Ding*, in the Old High German),[79] things (*Dingen*) are "thinged out" (*gedungen*)—discussed, sorted out, legislated on, and otherwise "assembled" into symbolic configurations. It is to these spaced-out things, to these configurations of desire, meaning, and authority that, as we will see in *Zone One*, the zombie's thing-appearance alerts us on closer inspection. Revelatory and "instigative," its thingness jars "us" into "thinging" critically, into critical thinking "about things." In that, "it" is neither quiet nor stupid, regardless of how ungainly, taciturn, and overall mindless its bodily performance seems—or precisely because this performance looks so. Supremely and necessarily amphibological, the thing's dumb show is just (for) show, a half-camouflaging, half-revelatory self-performance where performing bodies set out to "catch" *our* "conscience" by acting out—by presenting rather than explicitly engaging—*our* re(s)ality and its corollaries: objectification, instrumentalization, and serialization.

Does this mean that "we all *are* zombies who are not aware of it, who are self-deceived into perceiving themselves as self-aware?"[80] Is "the zombie monster ultimately terrifying because in it one sees one's self"?[81] Whitehead's answers below are intriguing also because, to anticipate, they account for the complexity of "the thing." The thing is no(one)thing if one looks in it for some(stable)thing, hence its association in *Zone One* with water, flowing, and fluidity imagery overall. Furthermore, there are various kinds of zombies or, better yet, degrees of zombification in the novel, and the writer's main point is neither that, as members of a particular culture, "our" behavior is conditioned and therefore already somewhat mechanical, zombified nor that "we" fail to grasp our zombification. Instead, Whitehead stresses that what the zombies "tell" us and how they act are culturally and politically positive, and therefore fighting the things, resisting them, is not necessarily the thing to do. In any case, if we were actual zombies rather than subject to an array of zombifying pressures, then "the things" would stop making a difference, metaphorically or otherwise. Although those pressures are not without consequences, and although we employ the zombie as an unflattering human simile in movies, casual conversation, political analysis, and economics, we are not *it*.[82] Of course, we may *imagine* ourselves as being it as much as anything else. But even that would take a serious stretch of the imagination, let alone that it would rub against our own cultural unconscious, which intimates that, properly speaking, "we" cannot be (like) them if we cannot be where they are or where they are from. On this score too Lacan is unequivocal: to that place—the "world of the Other"—we have no access.[83] Unthinkable and unspeakable, beyond the symbolic and thus uncompromisingly alien, the zombie-thing world remains inaccessible to us.

But not the other way around. While we, humans, "stay put," unwittingly cooped up inside symbolic arrangements and, yes, sometimes zombie-like, the abject thing designates, as Julia Kristeva argues, a "limit-object," an object equally limited (confined) and limitless, intrinsically transgressive.[84] So we may not go over to the "other" side—or we may, but with a one-way ticket. A "threshold" type of bodily unit, as Deleuze and Guattari might describe it,[85] the zombie, however, does cross over to us, and, to repeat, it is this dramatic asymmetry between us and "it," the irreconcilable disjunction enacted as body thingness, that in prompting the crossing, implicitly sets in train what I have labeled zombie pedagogy. This seemingly non-negotiable difference from the resurgent thing that defies symbolization is instrumental— and a prerequisite—to the rediscovery of the symbolic as problematic and ultimately to the resurgence of "our" self-awareness. To be "for real" and thereby help us make sense of the world, the return of the Lacanian Real must be mind-blowing and thus "make no sense" on first blush, and it achieves this absolutely, as that-which-we-are-absolutely-not, in the form of the zombie body or thing to which, try as we may, we find no way to "relate." But the impossibility of a rational-emotional connection with that which, in its "impossible," unhinging appearance, shocks us out of our analytically and socially inoffensive habits supplies the steppingstone to ascertaining, albeit tentatively, our own condition of possibility. If, in order for "us" to be and cope with the world as is, we must be oblivious to the intolerable truths nesting at its core, then, writes Slavoj Žižek, the thing also must burst forth in all its unbearable materiality, as "the ultimate horrible Thing," so that we "put things together" and render this core's content somewhat visible.[86] We may still have a hard time picturing what lies within it. For all intents and purposes, it may still mark a no-thing, a hiatus in the Lacanian socio-semiotic continuum analogous to the irruption of the apocalyptic creatures of Pieter Brueghel's *Triumph of Death* and Sergei Eisenstein's "lost" film *Unterwelt* into the leisure landscape of DeLillo's *Americana*.[87] Nevertheless, not unlike a potter's vase, which is shaped by the emptiness inside it, the ordinary "plenum," along with its underpinning ties, associations, and allegiances, comes together around this reordering crack in the symbolic order,[88] and for that, the illegible void opened up by the thing's rise is also where this meaningful togetherness, this copulative condition and conditioning of the human, presents itself and calls for "our" consideration.

It is in this inevitably circumventing sense that all zombies are "cultural zombies," and, in their extreme "thingness," American zombies are culture-specific or specifically "about" America.[89] Bearing critical witness to the culture they have left behind, their afterworld is not postcultural but *meta*cultural. In that regard, once more, their posthumousness is nonhuman but not posthuman. Their hereafter is given over to our present, which *they* revisit so that *we* might revise it. Attuned to phallophany's contrastive dialectic, then, this revision should not focus on the vacuum of the "thing," which remains inescapably unreadable, but on the surrounding vacuity, the glamorous thoughtlessness of the culture around it. The body liminal shines light, accordingly, on the body politic's limitations, constraints, and elaborately induced knee-jerk reactions—in *Dawn of the Dead*, zombies converge on the mall "instinctively" because that is where "the lobotomized masses of middle-class laborers and consumers that comprise late capitalist society"[90] flock "rationally" in their "free" time, not just during the zombie pandemic. Thus, the thing's thingness itself, its muteness or incoherent mumbling, pinpoints, with unmatched if unsuspected eloquence, the incoherence of human wishes and justifications; revenance and the entire spectacle of monstrous hauntology are a critique of human ontology. Zombie hypermateriality unearths the material constitution of our desire along with the sociocultural apparatus designed to hide the desire's content in plain sight. As in Romero's 2004 film *Day of the Dead*, "we" fail to "domesticate" *them* because "we" are already domesticated, sold on said justifications; similarly, they bite us so as to punish us for this domestication, i.e., for how they themselves led their own lives when *they* indeed were (like) us, but also to "tell" us what they are doing *by doing (the) it (thing)*, namely, by unleashing an orality in which the distinction between "biting" (devouring, mastication, etc.) and enunciation no longer operates.[91]

Embodying phallophanic dialectic with a "clarifying" vengeance, the zombie bite is phallic communication *par excellence*. As such, the bite is the thing-talk—language as pure, "speechless" orality—that stands outside "the chain of language [*parole*]," tracing language's outside, the unspeakable and the violent impasse or interruption in communication within language itself. But this bloodcurdling static, this intolerable break in discourse, is also the vociferous emptiness around and from which the speaking subject's position and the plenitude of linguistic exchanges get their contour.[92] This is how rigor mortis—sign, as common wisdom has it, of lack of consciousness, judgment, speech, in sum, of humanness—bespeaks, in the same circumvolutory way, our lack of rigor and passes judgment on human consciousness and its vulnerability to the affluent-consumerist mythology of freedom, free will, and agency; this is how "evil" shows off an "intelligence" of its own, capable of debunking what Baudrillard identifies as "Integral Reality: the irreversible movement towards the totalization of the world . . . the growing hegemony of the powers of good"[93]; this is, after all, death that might do the living some good insofar as only in or "with" it, in and through the thanatological re(s)alism of the half-dead thing, the nuts and bolts of Baudrillardian hegemony come into view; this is how, in its zombie context, Hamlet's dilemma might just start making sense again—how the "not to be" part and the "wisdom" and "eloquence" of not-being might just get us thinking, once more. Successively coupling and decoupling the cognitive and the conscious, the conscious and the cerebral, the cerebral and the rational, the rational and the subject, the subject and the human, the human and the living, the living and the organic, and the organic and the body, the zombie raises the time-honored question with renewed urgency.

corsica, dust, skels: The Insistence of Things and the Object of Race in Whitehead's *Zone One*

These things remained.

—Colson Whitehead, *Zone One*

[T]he impossible return to things before.

—Colson Whitehead, *Zone One*

As in Mandel's *Station Eleven*, Lethem's *Arrest*, Ma's *Severance*, Chang-rae Lee's 2014 *On Such a Full Sea*, and other recent fictions of global collapse, things get suddenly dys- or post-functional in *Zone One*. They malfunction or give up the ghost altogether as they break down, lose power, and so on.

Implements in working order are rare. People mourn "cable TV, basketball," and "local organic greens cold-washed three times" (115), while an army lieutenant delivers an impromptu eulogy for the Cloud (116). Some foodstuffs are once again made available, especially to the military, it appears, by corporate "sponsors" cozying up to the new government in Buffalo, but most household staples, gadgets, and consumer goods no longer exist.

Those still around *insist*, though—with a vengeance. The insistence of "the things" (19, 20, 96) themselves is overpowering. Unstoppable, the revenants keep returning en masse, eventually flooding New York and presumably other cities in the United States and around the world. The zombies' prodigiously Walkyrian homecoming marks the novel's grand finale, to which I will attend a bit later. For now, let me note that the more ordinary, less ambulatory, and less murderous *things* are equally insistent, although what they pester us about differs starkly from what *the things* "convey." Shabby, discarded, and useless as they may be, the everyday odds and ends are no less adamant about presenting themselves, and they do present themselves everywhere. The "flavored gums," the "lip balms that would never again be manufactured," the "despised driver's license photos that were the only proof" that the people in the pictures once "[ha]d had faces," the "just-in-case tampons," and "[a]ll those keys to those apartments now painted in blood" (63) persist in a "pure," partially or entirely de-instrumentalized state that seems to charge them with a superior eloquence. Whitehead's mysterious pandemic has flattened objects into a ponderous presence bursting at the seams with an insistent rhetoric.

Their clamorous being-there is not lost on Mark Spitz, the novel's protagonist. Spitz is a member of the "Omega Unit," an armed team tasked with "sweeping" "Zone One," viz., with flushing out and eliminating physically any zombies left in lower Manhattan. Bereft of their living tenants, the island's high-rises are now a "collection of figments and notions of things" (9), but figments, notions, and profound cultural and political implications are also writ large *on* things—on the occasional undead the Omegas promptly "put out of its misery," as well as on the quotidian bits and pieces the soldiers bump into in bachelors' lofts, pizza parlors, and corporate headquarters. In the fifteenth-floor offices of a law firm mopped up by Spitz's unit, for example, "the . . . furniture"

> was hypermodern and toylike, fit for an app garage or a graphic-design firm keen on *sketching the future*. The surfaces of the desks were thick and transparent, hacked out of plastic and elevating the curvilinear monitors and keyboards in dioramas of productivity. The empty ergonomic chairs posed like amiable spiders, whispering a multiplicity of comfort and lumbar massage. [Spitz] saw himself aloft on the webbing of the seat, wearing the suspenders and cuff links of his tribe, releasing wisps of unctuous cologne whenever he moved his body. Bring me the file, please.

He goosed the leprechaun bobblehead with his assault rifle and sent it
wiggling on its spring. Per his custom, he avoided looking at family pictures.
   He interpreted: We are studied in the old ways, and acolytes of what's
to come. For all that has transpired outside this building in the great
unraveling, *the pure industry of this place still persisted. Insisting on
itself.* He felt it in his skin even though the people were gone and all the
soft stuff was dead. Moldering lumps shot out tendrils in the common-
area fridges, and the vicinities of the dry watercoolers were devoid of
shit-shooting idlers, but the ferns and yuccas were still green because they
were plastic, the awards and citations remained secured on the walls, and
the portraits of the bigwigs preserved one afternoon's calculated poses.
These things remained. (13–4; emphasis added)

The place is a locus of "tradition" (13) not only because it is a law practice—
it *was* a law practice actually, for nobody reports for work anymore—and
not just because "tradition" is what the pictures of the "founding fathers
keeping watch from the great beyond" (13) whisper at the passing soldiers
either, but also because what the firm has been set up to effectuate, and more
importantly yet, what its material remainders continue to do, is *transmit* the
"old ways," pass them on to, and *as*, the future. In the fluttering heart of the
violently and globally tested now, *Zone One*'s objects compose a structure—
the contemporary itself—that showcases a contest of tomorrows. The
sweepers move across this structure, which has, as in other postmillennial
narratives discussed in *Flat Aesthetics*, a "catastrophic" shape. Echoing
the worldwide disaster, the objects forming this configuration are
characteristically broken, when, as in *Station Eleven*, they have not become
obsolete or their users have not died, along with all the "soft stuff." But
"broken," "obsolete," and "dead" do not equal inactive. Indeed, Whitehead
hints that the law offices are one big thing-machine still humming and
"industrious" in a way that winks not just at zombie survival past its natural
life course but also at an ontological resilience, a stubbornness to perpetuate
itself, the cultural and professional routines it has so far afforded, and a
whole tradition into and, again, *qua* future.
   Void of their original substance and purpose, computers, watercoolers,
artwork, and plasticky trimmings are reduced to "pure" form. In fact, they
point to it, even "insist" on it, and their tenacity grants it a certain thickness,
a self-expressive density. This form, then, is not an empty husk exactly.
Hollowed-out instrumentally, it is, *as form*, rhetorically substantial or vibrant,
as Bennett might say. In other words, the forms and arrangements of office
equipment "talk" about something by allegorizing its configuration. Spitz's
"interpretation," which Whitehead highlights *as such*, is right on target: that
some-thing, which things "sketch" formally, is the future, a particular kind of
future. "Useless" and steeped in "the old ways," and thus lifeless twice, the
zombified things of the past, including attorneys and other "law professionals,"

are present accomplices ("acolytes") of things to come. The existing, prescriptive form of futuristic furniture and other objectual allegories of "crushing" (13) efficiency and Ivy League brainpower provide a "master form" or "stencil" (59) that, laid over the chaos, maps the catastrophic now into a future—into *its* future, that is, into *this* now as future. "Buffalo" is the "exalted foundry of th[is] future" (43), and to "hone" (98) it, its founders need this master form or cast of America as preserved, presumably, by its "normative" microcosm, Manhattan. The government eggheads, the author writes, "wanted the sweeper data to superimpose it on their map of the smithereens and generate" their computer models and other think-tank "prophecies" (59). To ensure things "remain" and thereby the thing-map too remains readable, the military command has printed on "No-No Cards" (15) strict orders against "brutalizing, vandalizing, or even extending the odd negative vibe toward the properties whenever possible" (14–15).

As in *Station Eleven*, the "prophecies" are not prospective but retrospective, and the names under which they go betray their pseudofuturality. Some of the designations are less declaratively political and more technically descriptive ("reboot" [43]); others piggyback on one-sidedly cheerful views of American history ("reconstruction" [9, 43, 56, 75, 111, etc.]); and still others are outright propagandistic in an unimaginative, corny kind of way ("American Phoenix" [148, passim]). But they all allude to a repetitive reset, picturing as they do the future as a "return to normalcy," where "normal meant 'the past,' . . . the unbroken idyll of life before" (81). This fiction endures in the forms of things and the zombie-like sociocultural, vocational, and political practices, rituals, and proclivities those forms have been enabling and carry forward. In private and public, indoor and outdoor spaces, the Omegas stumble, over and over again, on the freeze-frames of a movie that seems just about to resume, "almost as if" its main character, "[American] culture, was picking up where it left off" (99). Silent as it is, the film "sp[eaks] of a vanished order that might reassert itself" (56), and whether that past order was "normal" or not, Kaitlyn, the sweeper unit's commander, deems the persisting forms of the "extinguished, . . . weathered but still legible [world]" "pristine artifacts of normalcy" and, tellingly enough, salvages some of them (58). Unlike Clark's curating in *Station Eleven*, hers is a deeply conservative, repetitive gesture that plays back the procedures, reiterations, and cycles of "prelapsarian days" (258). Once again, Spitz "interprets" things for us and gets it right. As the Omegas "stan[d] before a line of hair dryers in a tony hair salon, nigh shod in jellyfish clumps of brain," and Kaitlyn reminisces about "summers [spent] at her grandparents' cabin" and "doing the usual stuff" (57), he "saw it clearly":

Kaitlyn's implacable march through a series of imaginative and considered birthday parties—her parents were so thoughtful, here was a blessing bestowed from one generation to the next—each birthday party transcending the last and approaching a kind of birthday-party perfection that once accomplished would usher in an exquisite new age of bourgeois utopia. They strove, they plotted, they got the e-mail of that new magician in town, with his nouveau prestidigitations. Maybe, [Spitz] thought one night, it wasn't utopia that they had worked toward after all, and it was Kaitlyn herself who had summoned the plague: as she cut into the first slice of cake at her final, perfect birthday party, history has come to an end. She had blown out the candles on the old era, blotted out the dinosaurs' heavens, sent the great ice sheet scraping forth, the blood counts zooming up into madness. (56)

Flipping thoughtfulness into thoughtlessness, routine turns the bourgeois into an automaton and suburbanite utopia on its head. As Whitehead suggests, the cakes, the candles, the illusionists' e-mail addresses, the birthday and Halloween parties' costumes and "plastic accoutrements" (63) along with the myriad of "artifacts" (63) orchestrating life's mundane patterns and "special occasions" alike make up one big zombifying machine. This machine—the very system of American culture, arguably—has been barely functioning after "Last Night" (47), but since it had been in operation long before, the zombies are not something entirely new. Like any crisis, they amplify and throw into bolder relief preexisting realities.

Not a zombie per se, Kaitlyn is and has been zombie-like, as has been the world around her. "New York City in death was very much like New York City in life," the author half-jokes (80). "[B]ewitched by the past," city businesses cater inertially, block after block, to a clientele as "discontinued" as the "zero-utility" contraptions in the display windows quietly "colonized" by dust (278), a highly symbolic substance in Whitehead, as we will see shortly. Spitz feels that the metropolis "refuse[s]" to let go of "the typewriter-repair shop, the shoe-repair joint with its antiquated neon calligraphy, . . . the family deli with its germ-herding griddle" (278). The city, he "th[inks,] . . . protect[s]" its old-things emporium no less than the stores that "sold the new things, the chromium gizmos that people needed" (278), or than places such as the law firm, where space-age fixtures, materials, and design make similarly high-pitched references to the contemporary. They all interpellate the passerby in the "dying vernacular of nostalgia" (278) for, technologically outmoded or dernier cri, they all yearn for a perfunctorily futural future, for what will have been. Outlets of "desires" a priorily "exterminated" (178), objects old, new, and again, even "futuristic" point behind them to the pre-plague world, as do "Kaitlyn and her stories of the past" (58). "Persist[ing] in her" (58), Spitz comments, the stories and their storyteller with them "[are,]" together, "another stencil to lay over the disaster, to remind [his team] of the former shape of the world" (59). The bric-à-brac in Kaitlyn's recollections thus participates in the crafting of the same "future" as the one over which the government experts are "toiling" (59) by mapping, Spitz realizes, the "sweeper data" onto their dissimulated nostalgias—"Why else were the [Omegas] in Manhattan," Spitz asks himself, "but to transport the old ways across the violent passage of the calamity to the safety of the other side? If you don't believe that . . .why are you here?" (58–9).

Spitz is not a believer, though. He is definitely pessimistic, if not a literary embodiment of Afro-pessimism.[94] Nor is the "other side" truly other to the past. Of that, Spitz is quite certain. If he "banished thoughts of the future" (31–2), that was not just for self-preservation purposes (32) at a time when sentimental "reveries" and other "distractions" of the sort could get you killed; after all, as Gary, another Omega, observes (32), Spitz does get "distracted," almost fatally if ironically, while considering that "[i]f you weren't concentrating on how to survive the next five minutes, you won't survive them" (32). In effect, Spitz is annoyed by the "pheenie bullshit" (32), specifically by the phony futurality packed into the "American Phoenix" hoopla's fantasies of cultural and political reanimation. Indeed, reanimate what? As he wonders later in the novel, "Would the old bigotries be reborn as well, when they cleared out this Zone, and the next, and so on, and they were packed together again, tight and suffocating on top of each other? Or was that particular bramble of animosities, fears, and envies impossible to re-create?" His conclusion is disheartening: "If they could bring back paperwork . . . [then] they could certainly reanimate prejudice, parking tickets, and reruns," and so the whole zombified America of Kaitlyn's birthday accessories and of the law firm's interior color scheme, complete with all the other schemes they evoke and feed into, could reawaken (288). Needless to say, there is a difference between birthday fun and prejudice. At the same time, they are all repetitions, reenactments. In a way, parking tickets and reruns are all reruns, automatisms, "sociomechanical" formations engendered by the same cultural system of reiteration, and Spitz is right to worry that once the more benign routines ("paperwork") have resumed, the less innocent can easily follow suit—as he observes, many "things in the world that deserved to stay dead . . . walked" (288).

Those "things" comprise social reflexes, affects, and other repetitive practices and dispositions swirling around race and racism, which, for the most part, *Zone One* designates generally and obliquely as "animosities," "fears," "prejudice," and "old bigotries." Such euphemisms belong to a litotic lexicon that is part and parcel of a tactic of racial under- and un-naming. Echoing this stylistic maneuver narratively is a cunning strategy of omission by dint of which Whitehead discloses Spitz's racial identity allusively, and jocularly so (147), fully reveals and addresses it late in the novel (287), and more broadly deploys signifiers of Blackness, Black community, African American history, slavery, and racial injustice figuratively and sparingly.

Far from Whitehead to imply, however, that the "postlapsarian" is also "post-racial."[95] To the contrary, *Zone One*'s post-plague America is as colorblind as the post-recession United States, which served as the 2011 book's inspiration. So did, as the author has acknowledged, the 9/11 tragedy and the Manhattan "cleanup" under mayors Rudolph Giuliani and Michael Bloomberg, a model of urban "revitalization" whose racial undertones resonate in the devastation wreaked on the downtown by the marines and even in the Omegas' actions.[96] Both the sweepers' work in the Zone and Buffalo's national designs attest not only to the hyperbolic revival of the exchange regime—all consumption and pleasure are now "incorporated," "sponsor"-controlled to a quasi-dystopic degree—but also to germane, classist, anti-immigrant, repressive, and outright racist ploys and policies of gentrification, exclusion, and "purification," for which the anti-zombie campaign and rhetoric provide new vehicles and disguises. These are anything but deracialized. Inside and outside them, the "object of race," particularly Blackness, undoubtedly "remains" too. Furthermore, its remainders are not in one place but "all over the place." They insist and pervasively so—their insistence is a dimension of the "system."

To capture this systemic endurance in the face of unprecedented ruin, Whitehead does not approach, however, the "race thing" as a some-thing to expatiate on apart from the rest but as one thing amid the "remaining" others. He refrains, accordingly, from singling it out and even from naming it directly, nor does he treat it individually, as a discrete entity. In this sense, the writer is right to stress in a 2012 interview that *Zone One* is not "about" race—or, I might introject, not about race the same way *Sag Harbor*, whose "cast" is "95 percent African-American," "isn't to [him] that much about race" either.[97] Put differently, the diegetic ubiquity of race and the homologous organic saturation of the narrative with Black characters and issues in *Sag Harbor* and, we will note, in *Zone One* as well render a separate thematization of the racial object a superfluous if not counterproductive paraphrase à la Harman. Not unlike Lerner and other writers of interest to *Flat Aesthetics*, Whitehead is largely weary of "aboutness." In *Zone One*, he rejects the thematic-explicative tack because, first, the object presents itself forcefully in the postapocalyptic United States—as it does, he underscores on various occasions, in Barack Obama's America—and second, this self-presentation is com-positional, taking place in relation to other objects, their forms, and the vaster form or ensemble their spatial dispensation configures. This presence may not be conspicuous but is there, encoded in the object arrangements surviving in paralegals' cubicles, fast-food joints, and antique shops, and on another level, in Kaitlyn's remembrance of things past, Buffalo's retro "prophecies," the traumatized survivors' somnambulant behavior, and a small fraction of "the things" themselves, the "stragglers."

The distinction between the latter and the bloodthirsty zombies—the "skels"—is pivotal in *Zone One*. They are all things, but the skels are the real thing, "the things per se." If skels are hardcore zombies, stragglers are the "soft" version. The straggler is the ultimate embodiment of what another character, the Lieutenant, describes as "our robotic routine" (270). A byproduct of cultural zombification, "straggler thinking" marks, as the same hero points out (271), both people who have survived the plague basically untouched by it epidemiologically, such as Kaitlyn, for example, and those who have been turned by it into harmless zombies, even though Gary would be bitten, ironically enough, by a straggler "fortune teller." The incident aside, stragglers are human "mannequins" forever stuck in a "succession of imponderable tableaux" whose objectual repertoires, on the fritz now as much as their former users, recapitulate the whole array of pre-disaster cultural and professional postures and survey the entire socioscape of clockwork inertia. The things are frozen in the movie frames of Americana, and all they do is "ke[ep] watching th[e] movies" (61) of their former lives, with themselves in those films as ever-serviceable extras, "their limbs adjusted" by the "inscrutable hand" of an invisible yet heavy-handed director. Whitehead's gallery of living and not-so-living statues features "us" all: "the former shrink," the "patient [who] failed to arrive," the "pock-faced assistant manager of the shoe store," the "vitamin-store clerk," the man forever attempting to make a xerox (61). These—we—are things thingified by the "old routines" (261), human machines "powered down by the plague" (261). The question Whitehead raises through Spitz, if rather indirectly, is, can the machines be "reinitialized for an alternative purpose"? (261). Can they be made to work again, in a less machinic, pre-programmed mode? If so, what would it take to "void" (261) the previous cultural software?

The shrink, the store manager, the salesguy hawking big-ticket wares, their entire professions, as well as the "way of life" built on them are either gone or out of order, so to speak, but the order of things that has put them all in place and in the specific places they occupy with respect to one another inside the American entanglement of things remains. The therapist's "requisite lounge chair," the shoe salesman's "foot-measuring instrument," the health store "clerk's ... tiny bottles containing gel-capped ancient remedies and placebos," the plant shop owner's pot of soil "earmarked for a city plant" ("for wasn't every citizen on the grand island a sort of sturdy indoor variety that didn't need much sunlight"?), the "wedding dress ... cradled" by the woman in the dressing room, the copy machine's hood (60–1), and countless such not-so-vivant tableaux are as many links of the pre-catastrophe thing chain in which America's operating system—the system behind our cultural system—lives on.

The operating system is barely operational, though. Still there, it is unable to set things in motion as before; the hardware it used to activate has gone bust. The things are now broken *as things*, as members of their formerly functional "crowds," and all the implements, knickknacks, and tools can com-pose is dioramas of American melancholy. The chain or entangled chains of things have come apart, and links are strewn all over the place. They are spaced out because the plague and its offshoots, the "other" things—the zombies—have cut the connections among them, hence the quasi-general deadlock. But national paralysis is also blocking or dampening, for now, explicit displays of racial hatred and concerns, which is why neither racism nor the broader racialization of culture is overtly present in the plot. Instead, their presence is diffused; nowhere in one place and not one single thing either, it is everywhere and in every-thing. This presence is "soft" and more difficult to make out than before because it is either removed from the present by fiction and wistfulness, as in Kaitlyn's stories, or scattered across a present that has been sliced up by the plague into "a series of intervals differentiated from each other only by the degree of dread they contained" (81). There is nothing post-racial about this ruptured, slackened, and grisly object network; it is just that its lax, malfunctioning, or utterly unserviceable relays of materiality and meaning only warrant a less straightforward and less consistent presentation of the "race thing." The Buffalo prophets are dead set on piecing the network back together. If successful, they would reestablish the larger sociomaterial arrangements within which "strong" American practices and discourses of race and racism have been and will likely be possible once more. Is their project keyed deliberately or primarily to rebuilding the concrete conditions of this possibility? Is the actual goal here to "re-create" the *thing-structure* of temporarily suppressed or deflected anxieties and idiosyncrasies (288)? The answers are not terribly important. What matters is that this re-thinging of America, this reassembling of the nation—to fall back on the Heideggerian lingo one more time—would also reconstitute and resurrect a certain body politic. That body, that "thing" or *Ding,* however, is one of those "things in the world that deserv[e] to stay dead" (288).

This is where the things themselves, the real zombies, come in. They are the "other" undead, like and unlike all the other things that in *Zone One,* refusing to die and remain dead, persist instead in the modality of a mechanical, "clinical" life, road maps to a dreadful past rather than portals to an authentic future. Human or not, organic or inorganic, the non-skel things, whether a zombie-like straggler or a computer chair, are all stragglers in the fundamental sense of rambling spatially, spreading, and getting away from each other so that the ensemble inside which they functioned disintegrates and loses its operationality, as do they themselves, individually. This is how every-thing, small or big, simple or deceptively simple, and the vaster complexes of things they com-pose crumble, begin to shift, come unstuck, and wind up floating around jostled by inertial reflexes and residual dynamics from one "interval" to another. In post-collapse America, things come apart and then to dust or its variety, the ashes that never stop falling down on the Omegas. In the ashes, things break up into particles and also acquire a watery quality. Liquefied, they start flowing, whether vertically, as rain, or horizontally, as "the things" themselves in their majestic oceanic tide at the end of the novel (302–4). Alive with dispersing energies that, intriguingly enough, bode well for a veritably "vital" and futural "enterprise"

(270), this fluidity makes for a destabilizing and dissolving, quasi-aquatic medium symbolically germane to life and change and at odds with the government's struggle to reassemble the expired structures of the past.[98]

If any-thing, such structures are firm and stable things, or, more accurately, people ascribe them a "political" physicality marked by fixity, immobility, and the terra firma of tradition. These connotations cluster around a whole range of solid objects antithetical or somehow semantically contrasting to a more politically progressive, kinetic imaginary featuring or alluding to running, flowing, swimming (hence Mark Spitz's nickname), flooding, water, and the like. Gary's "island" is one of those objects. A place presumed to be above the stormy waters of history, the island is in fact a picture advertising Corsican tourism. Zombie-looking Gary thought, it seems, that Corsica was a Spanish territory and, in an ironic show of misplaced hopes and geographical naïveté, even tried to learn Spanish in preparation for an escape to the island. He dies holding the photo in his hand, and after "pr[ying] the fingers," Spitz takes the glossy illustration and puts it in his own back pocket. The fortune teller's victim, Whitehead writes, "had been carrying it for a long time, from the creases and chewed edges, pocket to pocket to pocket . . . It had been carefully ripped from a magazine, a level fur of fibers describing the inside edge" (316). The painstakingly detailed description of the ad is quite telling. "On one side," we learn, "the island bulged from the blue waters of the Mediterranean, a knuckled lump of rock. It looked like a grenade, [Spitz] thought" (316). On the opposite side, "a street scene unraveled," which Whitehead scans for us with cinematic flair. Zooming in, he pursues the links in the thing chain one after another, checking them off as they step in front of the camera eye: "[a] slim alley pullulated with men and women mid-errand, perhaps around noon"; "[a] trinket store hawked postcards on long wire racks, azure rectangles featuring more pictures of the island"; "[a] young couple enmeshed fingers at a small table outside a café, the red and white and brown logo of the espresso distributor half shadowed on a sign over the entrance"; "[t]he table, aslant, jabbed its legs into cracks between cobblestones"; and bringing up the rear, "[a] matchbox and a wad of napkin, the discarded shims, lay next to the woman's red sandals" (316–17).

As elsewhere in *Zone One*, attention to the material minutiae of such Latourian chains is unrivaled. Strings, tangles, and piles of things already crowd "Corsica." There are so many, *too many* of them, including, *en abyme*, more commercial images of Corsica itself, that they already threaten to sink it, as it were. Is the place really safe, then? Is the grenade about to blow up? We will never know. But things do not look good. At any rate, the novelist frequently debunks "islandism" and other etymologically and politically cognate fantasies of isolationism, survival, and salvation of pre- and postapocalyptic America. Besides, the description of the Corsican scene is no different from Whitehead's survey of episode after episode of domestic and public life on the novel's main island, Manhattan. What is more, Manhattan itself ends up drowning in a *World War Z*-like climactic zombie deluge.[99] "The ocean," Whitehead reports,

> had overtaken the streets, as if the news programs' global warming simulations had finally come to pass and the computer-generated swells mounted to drown the great metropolis. Except it was not water that flooded the grid but the dead. It was the most mammoth convocation of their kind Mark Spitz had ever had the misfortune to see. The things were shoulder to shoulder across the entire with of the avenue, squeezed up against the buildings, an abhorrent parade that writhed and palsied up Broadway until the light failed. The damned bubbled and frothed on the most famous street in the world, the dead things still proudly indicating, despite their grime and wounds and panoply of leaking orifices, the tribes to which they had belonged, in gray pinstriped suites, classic rock T-shirts, cowboy boots, dashikis, striped cashmere cardings, fringed suede vests, plush jogging suits. What they had died in. All the misery of the world channeled through this concrete canyon, the lament into which the human race was being transformed person by person. Every race, color, and creed was represented in this congregation that funneled down the avenue. As it had been before, per the myth of this melting-pot city . . . The dead leaked in massive piles on the other side of the wall, mounting between the barrier and the buildings on the north side of Canal . . . The barrier was a dam now, suppressing the roiling torrent of the wasteland. It would not hold. (303–4; emphasis mine)

In the wake of the plague, the fabled melting pot itself is melting down. Along with its dreadful content, the container of all things American—the structure of all structures—is gushing down Broadway, flooding, dislodging, and further softening all that is solid, brimming over barriers, knocking down any-thing left standing, and dissolving whatever Buffalo deems "worth bringing back" (270). The government people seek to firm up the fluid world, put up levees and barriers, close the "intervals" making up the fragmented and pulverized "present," and mold the dust of things—the "clay in their hands" (81)—into a reassuring future anterior; they just want the machinery of American thingness jumpstarted, not "reinitialized for an alternative purpose" (261). The skels push "innovatively" in the other direction. The things are not into repairing things, restoring their shape, and putting them back together. They would definitely approve of the epigraph to the novel's first part: "The gray layer of dust covering things has become their best part" (1). It is noteworthy that the motto is not an exact and complete excerpt from Benjamin's short essay "Traumkitsch"[100] ("Dream Kitsch"), which in translation reads as follows: "No longer does the dream reveal a blue horizon. The dream has gone gray. The gray coating of dust on things is its best part."[101] In Whitehead's version, the emphasis is no longer on the post-Romantic state of the dream but on the "dusty" state of things, on their ruin and disrepair. Things' cinders make up things' "best part," in Whitehead at least, because, the skels "suggest," something good may come out from disuse, erosion, and obliteration—from things' complete destruction, that is.[102] Thus, to "reconstruction"—re-creation of what will have been—the skels oppose an aquatic, genuinely futural "rhetoric of creative destruction."[103]

Somewhere in between, Quiet Storm, a wrecker truck driver nicknamed after "the title song of a 1975 album of Smokey Robinson,"[104] "engage[s] in [her] own reconstructio[n]," "carv[ing]" a vision out of the same "weak clay" of nowness by assembling abandoned highway vehicles into indecipherable thing-arrangements ("mosaics") likely to "outlas[t] all of Buffalo's schemes" (290). These purport to heal the wounds of and between things, to "tighten" the loose network of Americana. "Wr[iting] her way into the future" (290), Quiet Storm is still a "structuralist," unfathomable as her thing-writing is. Instead, the monsters no longer write; they erase writing. They surge over remaining boundaries and over any cultural remainders, enlarging the network's holes and ultimately wipe it out altogether to make room for some-thing effectively new—for a new American ensemble of people, things, and values. "Why they'd tried to fix this island in the first place" Spitz no longer "see[s]" after the skels flood the city. Repeatedly described by Whitehead as the regular American, "typical," culturally wired for playing along, and prepared to survive by its own self-assumed, "tactical" mediocrity—with another irony, "Spitz" means "top" and "peak" in German—the protagonist reaches a revealing conclusion before symbolically jumping into the skel tsunami: "Best to let the broken glass be broken glass, let it splinter into smaller pieces and dust and scatter. Let the cracks between things widen until they are no longer cracks but the new places for things" (321). This is still Spitz talking, to himself, but this is also zombie rhetoric, what they "tell" Spitz during their Broadway pageant, in the thing-language of sheer annihilation. While "[t]heir mouths could no longer manage speech," Spitz realizes, "they spoke nonetheless" (304), of bloodshed and destruction, of course, but also of the possibility of a world in which, once again "packed together" (288) as we would be, we would not fall back on "old bigotries."

FIVE | Kinship

"There is no dead matter," he taught us, "lifelessness is only a disguise behind which hide unknown forms of life. The range of these forms is infinite and their shades and nuances limitless."

—Bruno Schulz, *The Street of Crocodiles*

There is no dead matter," he taught us, lifelessness is only a disguise
—Jonathan Safran Foer, *Tree of Codes*

. . . a vitality obscured by our conceptual habit of dividing the world into organic and inorganic matter.

—Jane Bennett, *Vibrant Matter*

In his foreword to the Penguin edition of Bruno Schulz's *The Street of Crocodiles* and *Sanatorium under the Sign of the Hourglass*, Jonathan Safran Foer tarries with a metaphor central to Schulz's poetics and to a time-honored tradition of world making in the arts, philosophy, religion, and related cultural practices. The trope is "rubbing," and it encapsulates an entire technology of form.[1] This technology, it turns out, is a dialectic: on one hand, rubbing covers a surface with a script, drawing, or other graphic shape by moving a marking device or finger across paper, canvas, walls, and, of late, keyboards, mousepads, and touchscreens; on the other, rubbing uncovers existing form or handles it in such a way that the form's meaning itself is "unveiled." To rub, then, is to im-press and ex-press, oftentimes both at once. One rubs to write and read, to enclose through and in form as much as to disclose—also by resealing into a form—something to oneself and others according to a set of inscribing, describing, and reinscribing protocols such as making, retrieving, revisiting, remaking, and unmaking.

While these operations flesh out the logic of tradition broadly, they echo, in Schulz, the historical mechanics of Jewish culture, particularly the Kabbalistic "passing on" of a body of knowledge. In this context, the dialectic of form is also one of being, an ontology of what has been and what can still be, anew or, under certain circumstances, new. Literary and life forms go therefore hand in hand. The generation and regeneration of forms, their trans-formations over time and space, whether in philology or in phylogeny, abide by the same rules. Conversely, these principles are as literary as they are ontological; they apply to texts inside literature as they do to things outside it—*and to texts* as *things*. It is in this complex, literary, and mundane sense that Schulz took up rubbing and thus participated in the "transmission" of vitality and in the reenergizing re-forming of forms across whole networks of human, humanmade, and nonhuman objects. He performed his rubbing on all manner of material and cultural things, including "influences" such as Kafka. Of course, Kafka had done it too, most famously and consequentially, resetting arguably the modern paradigm of rubbing, transmission, and transmutation—he "rubbed" really hard on Hassidic tales, for instance. Later on, others would treat Schulz the way he did Kafka. In fact, Foer himself rubbed out or, more accurately, cut, *un*wrote words and passages out of the English version of *The Street of Crocodiles*, and what was left untouched he published as his 2010 novel *Tree of Codes*.[2]

Foer's un/writing technique is a literal, highly intrusive, and textually "interventionist" rubbing. There is even a name for it: "die cutting." Obviously not a Yiddish phrase, "die cutting," Foer offers in an interview, is "almost like a Yiddish word" because it is "onomatopoetic." It sounds, he elaborates, like that which it designates; the phrase is a shadow of its meaning.[3] Foer does want, indeed, to rub our noses, as it were, in the concrete and oftentimes brutal physicality of intertextual workings, into all the "dying," killing, cutting, and Oedipal aggression built into the homage, appropriation, and sheer love that make up the amphibological symptomatology of the anxiety of influence. As Foer acknowledges in the afterword to *Tree of Codes*, composing his "see-through" book by de-composing its Schulzian matrix and dislodging its textual units was, to him, a narrative recovery comparable to pulling a scrap of paper out of the Wailing Wall. And, he also confesses, "[a]t times I felt that I was making a gravestone rubbing of *The Street of Crocodiles*."[4]

Rubbing has, then, its equivocations and shortcomings, its dangers and caveats. Foer is hardly unaware of them. As he acknowledges, this de-composition is serious business. Interfering with what is there, with what exists in and as a complete structure, and de-completing the "thereness" of this form are matters of life and death. The risks are worth taking, however. In "un-finishing" what Schulz has finished and published as such, in cutting those holes or absences into *The Street of Crocodiles*, Foer opened up a space, a circuitry of fertile interstices in which the seeds of new things can be sown. Hollowed-out form, form that lacks something, is formative, germinative. As in Lerner and others studied in *Flat Aesthetics*, the de-completion, the "breaking" of form, and broken forms in general are no semiotic dead ends. To the contrary, they carry extraordinary potential, much like broken hearts can shelter infinity, as Krauss's rabbis reassure us in *Forest Dark*.[5] "The breaking of form" can "produce meaning," Harold Bloom posits in his "Breaking of Form"[6] essay, and he is right at least insofar as, "repaired" or left in disrepair—as we will see in the closing chapter of this part—broken form asserts an opaqueness, a for-itself presence that can lead to or morph into another form and thus expand the extant mesh of forms on and off paper the way one "expands" a written Hebrew word by filling in the "gaps" between its consonants or Talmudists "expand" on the "Written Torah."

The particular mesh on which the final section of *Flat Aesthetics* focuses is the one inside which Schulz's rubbings play out in concert with an entire phenomenology of cutting, abbreviating, amplifying, interpolating, changing, and other transformations affecting textual and non-textual objects alike. Schulz did not make this lattice of relations and imbrications; he only worked himself into it in more ways than one. Nor did it originate with Kafka. But because Kafka is at its center, or he is its most recognizable center and reference point, I would name it the Kafka network or, better yet, the Kafka family. Of course, Kafka had a regular family as most of us do, one of blood, and his work made the members of this family famous and even infamous. It is not this family that concerns me here, but one understood much more broadly, although this family can also be said to be "biological." This family is a site of onto-semiotic kindredness, a knot of relations among kin of two kinds—a family of two families, if you will. I would describe it as an aggregation of two different and not-so-different object clusters that intersect, interact with, spring from, and in turn boost Kafka's oeuvre. Spread out across and even outside cultural spaces and biological species, all "relatives," regardless of family, are what I have called "agents of the Kafkaesque";[7] they have been making and remaking Kafka, his themes, reputation, legacy, and even texts for a century now.

Human and literary, one family consists of "Kafkian" or "Kafka-like" writers who have formed, over the past one hundred years, a literary world-system, a vast network that throws a "crisscrossing set of pathways" over "deep" space and time, as Wai Chee Dimock might put it.[8] This network is built in the proximity of the master and less so, in direct and indirect, explicit and implicit contact. It has come about as a multifaceted relation of kin, kind, location, community, and tradition, as well in the absence of the relative, out of the *correlative* pathos of influence and being influenced, of telling and retelling, of transforming and being transformed by the already formed. This is, as Dimock might also note, a cultural and intertextual network born in and outside "nonadjacency" and "nearness of blood," an "alchemical overcoming of distance" that *spatializes*, projects topologically, in space, the creative and re-creative alchemy of rubbing, the con-tagious aesthetic of haptics, of the writer's magical touch.[9] This distance, we shall notice later on, does have a geocultural core but ends up bringing together that which can be viewed as a truly spaced-out and strikingly heterogeneous Kafka family of kindred if distanced spirits. It encompasses Kafka himself, his "precursors"—in the strong sense of the term but also in the T. S. Eliotian sense rehearsed by Jorge Luis Borges in his 1951 essay "Kafka and His Precursors"—and it comprises Kafka's heirs as well.[10] These are authors who rehearse Kafkaesque themes or make references to Kafka and his works but also writers who, more obliquely, force us to consider, à la Borges, Kafka as their precursor. Besides the Jewish-Polish Schulz, Jewish-American Foer, and Blecher, the "[Jewish]-Romanian Kafka," the trio that concerns me in this part's first chapter,[11] they are legion, from Philip Roth, Cynthia Ozick, and Hamid to Coetzee, Murakami, Borges himself, his Argentine compatriot Ricardo Piglia, Latin America's magical realists, and Romania's greatest Kafkian, Cărtărescu.

Yet again, the network is not one but at least two, and these two are both closely related and interlaced.[12] They are joined at the hip of the Kafka corpus and spread out at different angles or along different axes, with "Kafka" the hub or hinge on which pivot two ontological charts of the living or two genealogical trees of being—and of being Kafka, a Kafkian author, and a Kafkaesque "thing" or theme. One is, as mentioned, Kafka's human family of literary forerunners and followers. The other is Kafka's nonhuman, animal family, as Foer and before him Benjamin suggest, one in which, also under Benjamin's tutelage, I would include the most "forgotten" among the family members: the humbler branch of "inanimate" yet far from "dead" things. The human family is by and large known to us. The other is, as Foer echoes Benjamin, Kafka's "unknown family."[13] As this part's opening chapter shows, the former is a vehicle of the latter, which features representatives of what Henry Sussman has called, apropos of Schulz, the "continuum" of human and nonhuman life,[14] from fish, vermin, birds, and dogs to book pages, rubber tubes, Odradek-like spools, trash, and mannequins.[15] The second chapter deals with Krauss, one of the most prominent Kafkian figures in American literature since Roth. What intrigues me in *Forest Dark*, her latest novel, is a sui generis, twin principle of de- and re-composition. This is a modus operandi that recycles the absencing–presencing logic of Jewish tradition, enabling both commoners and celebrated writers such as Krauss's diegetic alter ego, Nicole, to disentangle themselves from what has been passed on and exists while adding, as they are expected, another chapter to the "Jewish story." As they do so, they enlarge their family both literarily, or intertextually, and ontologically, or "inter-objectually."

fish, peacock, ram: Schulz, Blecher, Foer, and Kafka's Unknown Family

*Kafka always felt familiar to me . . . like a kind of crazy uncle in
the family.*
> —Nicole Krauss, "Nicole Krauss on *Forest Dark*"

*The line between water and sky was lost: the line between himself and the world.
He watched the waves, and felt himself to be also endless, repeating, filled with
unseen life. The lines from the books on his table swam up from the pages before
his eyes.*
> —Nicole Krauss, *Forest Dark*

Inside Kafka's human circle, Schulz occupies a singular place, close to the center. True, he may not have been extensively involved in the Polish translation of *The Trial* that came out under his name in 1936, but he was a dedicated reader of Kafka in the original. Furthermore, some of the discrepancies uncovered by Jerzy Ficowski between the two writers in his Schulz biography make more sense than others, while still others are trumped by undeniable kinship of form and ontological imagination, immediate ethno-religious and cultural context, and historical tradition.[16] The differences, in brief, do exist, and it is understandable why all the talk about the "Polish" and "Romanian Kafka" rubs some Polish and Romanian critics the wrong way. But this resistance takes little away from the productive and reproductive "rubbing" in which Schulz and Blecher pointedly engaged and to which they have been in turn subject inside the Kafka network. I hope the reader will indulge my abuse of the verb in scare quotes a few more times because Schulz, for instance, was a gifted draftsman too and turned to rubbing, if unsuccessfully, not only to write and thus make, side by side with Witold Gombrowicz, a major contribution to Polish and world modernism, but also to stay alive—Scheherazade-like, glosses Foer—by painting murals in the house of Felix Landau, the Gestapo officer supervising Jewish labor in the Polish (now Ukrainian) town of Drohobycz.

The kinds of rubbing involved here—not of but *off* Kafka in Schulz's fiction, then *on* Kafka in the Polish translation of *The Trial*, as it was, and once more *on* Landau's walls—are intertwined, for they all occur under the Kafkaesque sign of the ontological flux across the boundaries separating life forms in the post-Cartesian imaginary underpinning modernity, as we shall see momentarily. In Schulz, rubbing is, Foer observes, what the narrator's father, before morphing into a crab, does to the pages of his ledger to "reveal plumes of color" at one point in Schulz's short story, "The Book," the opening fragment of *Sanatorium*.[17] As a Kabbalist hunched over the Torah, Joseph N.'s father patiently rubbed with a wet fingertip ... until the blank pages grew opaque and ghostly with a delightful foreboding and, suddenly, flaking off in bits of tissue, disclosed a peacock-eyed fragment; blurred with emotions, one's eyes turned toward a virgin dawn of divine colors, toward a miraculous moistness of purest azure ... Sometimes my father would wander off and leave me alone with the Book; the wind would rustle through its pages and the pictures would rise. And as the windswept pages were turned, merging the colors and shapes, a shiver ran through the columns of the text, freeing from among the letters flocks of swallows and larks. Page after page floated in the air and gently saturated the landscape with brightness. At other times, The Book lay still and the wind opened it softly like a huge cabbage rose; the petals, one by one, eyelid under eyelid, all blind, velvety, and dreamy, slowly disclosed a blue pupil, a colored peacock's heart, or a chattering nest of hummingbirds.[18]

Of course, the tradition of transmutating rubbing—the "tradition" (Kabbalah) *tout court*, perhaps, ever a matter of doing and undoing, completing and de-completing, rubbing in and scratching off palimpsests, of peeling away the textual onion's layers in rabbinic reading to unearth deeper and deeper containers of meaning—goes on. For what the father does inside Schulzian form, what the son does on the walls in Landau's house, and what later owners of the place will do to the shapes and hues on those walls as they repaint them white will be done—or undone, done in an opposite direction and before Foer himself will take on the narrative walls of Schulz's book—by somebody else, who took it to the actual walls in Landau's place. Sixty years after Schulz was shot dead by another Gestapo officer, Karl Günther, "whose Jew" Landau had murdered, documentary moviemaker Benjamin Geissler "rubbed," as Foer reminds us, "at one of the walls with the butt of his palm, and colors surfaced. He rubbed more, and forms were released. He rubbed more, like doing the rubbing of a grave, and could make out figures: fairies and nymphs, mushrooms, animals, and royalty ..."[19]

Kafka, Schulz, Blecher, and storytellers like them rub at the walls, pages, and paper-thin walls around things, at the rationality that leaves its imprint on our habits and worldviews, "at the facts of our lives," writes Foer, to "give us access ... to what's beneath," fantastic, magical, strange, absurd, surreal and yet so real as this new and hidden world logic might seem.[20] But because of the magnitude of the earth-shattering impact of this onto-logic, of this unrevealed "big magnificence," rubbing is, thinks the American author, "too gentle a word for Schulz's writing."[21] This gentleness leads in Foer, though, a bit contradictorily, to an incomplete digging—hence *Tree of Codes* and its digging and cutting into the very body of Schulz's book— while it also supplies an instrument for further digging, cutting, or slicing open by others, as well as a provocation to do so and change in the process. "His books," Foer tells us, "still have that effect on me. Good writers are pleasing, very good writers make you feel and think, great writers make you change. 'A book must be an ice-axe to break the seas frozen inside of us,' Kafka"—Foer's self-acknowledged foremost role model—"famously wrote. Schulz's two slim books are the sharpest axes I've ever come across. I encourage you to split the chopping block using them."[22] In *Tree of Codes*, Foer himself wields the axe, or its robotic and computerized versions, along with the cognate techniques of cutting, amending, and emending on the very block of Schulz's text; he does so also on his own, in the 2002 novel *Everything Is Illuminated*, which features a prolonged journey through Ukraine, as well as in the 2005 masterpiece *Extremely Loud and Incredibly Close*, in which father, son, and narrator, like in Schulz, edit and report fragmented pages and pieces of the *New York Times*, World War II survivors' memories, and overheard conversations.

But rubbing, digging, peeling off, or whatever you might call the Schulzian insight cutting through the surface of books and reality to the quick of another, seemingly illogic onto-logic does work like an axe or, more exactly, scalpel, carrying out a "gentle," perhaps stylistically deceptive exfoliation of the father's folio and of the world as we know it or think we do, a *lecture-écorché*, as French critics might say. This "flaying reading" applies itself to the Talmud-like Book—the Book with capital "B"—that haunts *Sanatorium* and to the world, two isomorphic entities between which Schulz's narrator makes no distinction. Akin to the father's ledger, the stamp album is a Book-in-the-Book, a *mise-en-abyme* instantiation of Schulz's own world-opening project and, by the same token, of the Talmudic book, as David A. Goldfarb has underscored.[23] The "nature" of the contingent spring morning becomes "legible," notes the storyteller in the album while the latter turns into a seasonal Midrash, the "great commentary on the times, the grammar of [spring] days and nights" that parses the provincial syntax of Schultz's hometown to bring to light the planet to which even a boredom emporium such as Drohobycz belongs.[24] For "[s]tamps," writes Schulz, "introduce" one to more "complex" games of the imagination and to its world of worlds. Thus, "[f]rom the reddish mists of the ninth hour, the motley and spot-red Mexico with a serpent wriggling in a condor's beak is trying to emerge, hot and parched by a bright rash, while in a gap of azure amid the greenery of tall trees a parrot is stubbornly repeating 'Guatemala, Guatemala' at even intervals." Then, "[i]n May," with its days "pink like Egyptian stamps," "[t]here sailed across the sky the great Corvette of Guyana . . . amid storms of gulls," with Haiti, Jamaica, and other faraway places following suit and pushing the boundaries of the Galician market square farther and farther so as to signal that "no Mexico is final" and every-thing, every finite object and "final" point is in reality a way station, a "point of passage which the world will cross, that beyond each Mexico there opens another . . ."[25]

In the hands of the "narrow-minded," however, the album is worthless, illegible. For it is, as Schulz maintains, "a universal book, a compendium of knowledge about everything human" and beyond.[26] A key aspect of Schulz's literary project is here in a nutshell. Most fundamentally, this undertaking works like the two arms of a scissors as it envisions a twin onto-topological reconstruction of existence, of the human, geographical and cultural place *and* of the place of the human alongside all other things, inside the latticework of all that exists, human or not. For one thing, this repositioning is at loggerheads with the tunnel vision of isolated and self-sufficient parochialism, exceptional nationalism, and ethnocentrism. For another, this relocation destabilizes anthropocentrism and the similar isolationism and exceptionalism modernity's imagination has often deployed to center the human ontological hegemon and unplug it from the horizontal grid of the same life energy that, at various junctures across this "vitalist" playground, looks like a bird, an aging father, or any other equally existing object only to become something else, which may or may not exist or behave according to the available descriptions, definitions, or habits of humans, animals, plants, rocks, and their bodies.[27] This is because, Schulz remarks, "[m]ost things are interconnected, most threads lead to the same reel. Have you ever noticed swallows rising in flocks from between the lines of certain books, whole stanzas of quivering pointed swallows?" "One should read the flight of these birds," he concludes.[28]

Weaving together echoes of Neoplatonism, *Sefer Yezirah*, later Kabbalah, and Hassidic tales of animals and transformations, this reading follows in the footsteps of Kafka's rubbing off and flaying of the habitus both ingrained in and rendered invisible by human sociality, a condition or conditioning protocol that Kafka *makes* visible in his "becoming-other" or behaving-like-an-other, "minor" literature to which Deleuze and Guattari have attended so revealingly. This writing or rewriting of the human into vaster worlds geoculturally and ontologically is a top priority of early-mid-twentieth-century experimentalism and lies at the core of a modernist, revolutionarily non- and authentically post-humanist agenda keen on extending "an invitation to us humans to enter into a different relation with the world, . . . to rethink the human globally" at the Darwinian cost of "toppling it" from its "central and fixed position."[29] The lynchpin of this reading is Schulz's many-sided "interconnectedness." This is the operator that opens up locations, the location of the human, and the meaning of life to bigger worlds, assemblages, and understandings where one is ontologically equal to and lies alongside others and therefore must live up to the exigencies of this *co-presence*. This operator does its job, and its operations are both "fantastic" and precisely "historicized," much like in *The Trial*, "The Metamorphosis," "In the Penal Colony," "Report to an Academy," "Investigations of a Dog," "The Cares of a Family Man," and elsewhere because it is activated at a precise historical and geographical point of modern Europe, to which Kafka, Schulz, and Blecher belong, an intersection to which they bear witness and in which they discern both the death of sociocultural forms and potential for their rebirth. Franz Joseph I, the ruler of the Austrian-Hungarian Empire, who died in 1916, twenty-one years prior to the publication of *Sanatorium*, passed through Drohobycz in 1880, twelve years before Schulz's birth, and was indirectly present in the writer's life in many ways, marks this moment and place according to a logic that Schulz's jocular-associative style hides and lays bare simultaneously. As Schulz writes in his 1937 book, when the emperor "appeared on the world stage,"

> the world reached a happy point in its development. All the forms, having exhausted their content in endless metamorphoses, hung loosely upon things, half-wilted, ready to flake off. The world was a chrysalis about to change violently, to disclose young, new, unheard-of colors and to stretch happily all its sinews and joints. It was touch and go, and the map of the world, that patchwork blanket, might float in the air swelling like a sail. Franz Joseph took this as a personal insult. His element was a world held by the rules of prose, by the pragmatism of boredom. The atmosphere of chanceries and police stations was the air he breathed. And, a strange thing, this dried-up dull man, with nothing attractive in person, succeeded in pulling a great part of creation to his side. All the loyal and provident fathers of families felt threatened along with him and breathed with relief when this powerful demon laid his weight upon everything and checked the world's aspirations. Franz Joseph squared the world like paper, regulated its course with the help of patents, held it within procedural bounds, and insured it against derailment into things unforeseen, adventurous, or simply unpredictable . . . He standardized the servants of heaven, dressed them in symbolic blue uniforms, and let them loose upon the world, divided into ranks and divisions—angelic hordes in the shape of postmen, conductors, and tax collectors.[30]

We are here in Robert Musil's Kakania—Kafkania?—an overbearingly paternalist imperial bureaucracy of uniforms, overall uniformity, and prosaicism. Kafka, his world, his "inoperative" community, his human and nonhuman ancestors, and his critique of the nipped-in-the-bud blooming of sons, young talents, and fresh forms are all here. The Talmudic album "unreads" the Empire's cloistral apprehensions and, through the aviary world imaginary, reinscribes the godforsaken market town into bigger worlds, reiterating a transposing routine, a transport and a transmutation in which humans, animals, plants, and other things—natural or manufactured—morph continuously into one another and erect in the process portals to another reality. Where stasis and status quo, complete with their panoply of sociopolitical and cultural practices, freeze matter, forcing it to gel unduly into the late-imperial prosaics of ossified forms, the narrator's father, we learn in *The Street of Crocodiles*—and we relearn *ad litteram* in the Tree of Life-like biomechanics of *Tree of Codes*—is, unlike Franz Joseph, a true Demiurge and poet who believes that "[t]here is no dead matter," and "lifelessness is only a disguise behind which hide unknown form of life."[31] Matter is an energetic life continuum that can be mapped out as God—or, more likely, its self-appointed uniformed deputies—did. But the father insists that matter can also be redistributed into a new, planetary ecology of togetherness in which energy, thought, affect, value, resources, and rights can be allotted according to a less anthropocentric dispensation system. With an eye to the latter, the father lectures us about the "priority" trash deserves, about tailors' dummies within which a vital force is held hostage, and about "races of wood" and their "suffering" in the forms humans imposed on them such as wardrobes. But he also talks about trans-formations that can be either reparatory or damning, and he puts his mouth where his money is by undergoing several metamorphoses himself, into a bird, a cockroach, and a many-legged, crab-looking *Kreatur*, alongside countless other instances of quasi-fantastic yet realistically described transmogrification, cross-species transgression, personification, animalization, humanization, and objectualization or thing-becoming with which Schulz's fiction crawls—all puns intended.

But, much as the metamorphic imaginary at play in the stamp album episode and in Kabbalistic textual maneuverings more broadly leans on the very imperial apparatus of the postal service to render Drohobycz a gateway to the planet and thus appoint the local and local humanity as knots in and passageways to much broader and diverse geographies and life schemes, Kakania too is more than it meets the eye. For there is an ethno-cultural and existential flipside to the bureaucratic-militaristic Empire's forlorn Galician corner, to this place plagued by chronic *ennui*, monotonous, insecure in its provincialism, apologetic about its rural fabric, and visited by fantasies of metropolitan sophistication. This reverse is an unprecedented multi- and cross-ethnocultural dynamic. This dynamic, this sociocultural modality of being with an other and of experimenting with life and culture, of "rubbing" at surfaces, habits, and boundaries, some would argue, still has a lesson to teach the struggling EU. Imperial nostalgia or not, wishful thinking or less so, this lesson falls back on an existing and extraordinarily fertile geocultural region in the agonizing Empire's northeast. Spanning an area historically claimed or currently administered by a number of nation-states born on the ruins of Austro-Hungary—Poland, Ukraine, Romania, and their mass-murdering invaders, Germany, the former USSR, and today's Russia—this zone roughly extends from Central-Southern Galicia to northeastern Romania's region of Moldova, whose eastern half, Bessarabia, once re-annexed by Stalin before the end of World War II, became a Soviet Republic and, after 1991, the independent country that goes by the name of the Republic of Moldova.

Lying in the middle of an expanse that a century ago functioned as a loose cultural entity that gives to this very day literary historians wedded to the "methodological nationalism" model—as Ulrich Beck named it—big headaches is Bukovina. The region is nowadays split between Ukraine and Romania, with Czernowitz (Cernăuți in Romanian) its urban center.[32] Inside and outside Bukovina, to the south all the way to Southern Moldova and to the east hundreds of miles into the Pale of Settlement, the throbbing heart of this unique geocultural system is what one might define, by Western standards, as a half-urban, half-rural small town, a thriving and expanding village of the shtetl type feeding its human and cultural energies into bigger cities such as Czernowitz and Lvyv (in Ukraine), Iași (in Romania), Chișinău (in the Republic of Moldova), and further into Europe and the world beyond. Indeed, the modestly urbanized enclave for which Drohobycz is typical has been seminal to the earth-shattering changes across the European and world arts at the beginning of the twentieth century. Bringing together a plethora of coexisting ethnic, religious, and linguistic communities and their longstanding, multicontinental traditions, the Drohobycz microcosm, again and again reinstantiated throughout this region of the crumbling Empire, yielded stunning syntheses that would alter the course of modern literature and art history.

It is well known that the birth of the avant-garde and some of its "isms"— or, at the very least, one of its births—took place around here. There would be no Dadaism without Tristan Tzara, who was born Samuel Rosenstock in the northern Moldavian town of Moinești in 1896. And, incidentally, there would be no Tzara without his Romanian precursors Urmuz (Demetru Dem. Demetrescu-Buzău), without whom, I might add, there would be no Eugène Ionesco either. For Tzara and Urmuz—the Ur-model of all Romanian avant-gardists—were, alongside Marcel Iancu, Victor Brauner, Ilarie Voronca, Gherasim Luca, and other Jewish-Romanian "geniuses," as Andrei Codrescu calls them, deeply instrumental to the rise and dissemination of absurdist-Surrealist arts in Romania and beyond during and after World War I.[33]

Blecher was one of these geniuses. Like them, and as with Kafka, Schulz, and Foer, as with Ionescu/Ionesco and Czernowitz-born Paul Celan, Blecher compels us to rethink—also in a context marked by personal and collective tragedy—the machinery of tradition and innovation, place, language, belonging, and affiliation, minority and majority status, and thus also to reconsider what makes one a Romanian, Czech, Polish, Ukrainian, German, Jewish, or American writer and anything in between all these classifications and designations in such urgent need of scrutiny in the era of World Literature. The world and the literature projecting it are important here not only because the default unit of modern literary-historical analysis, the nation-state in its ethno-linguistic and territorial embodiment, proves reductive in the face of the region's sub-, cross-, a-national, and programmatically cosmopolitan, transnational and transhuman deployments and exchanges of creative energies. Also to be taken into account is that if few Romanians are aware that Blecher was born in 1909 in Botoșani, a Romanian Drohobycz just east of Romania's Bukovina (he died only twenty-nine years later in another Moldavian Drohobycz, Roman), they do learn in school that the country's "national poet" and foremost claim to "universality," the anti-Semitic and xenophobic poet Mihai Eminescu, was born in Botoşani in 1850. So different in many ways, the two are both plugged into transnational networks of texts and beings, at the crossroads of empires and ontological kingdoms, and equally remarkable, they both peel back imaginatively the veneer of reality and nowness. In so doing, the belated Romantic Eminescu harks back nostalgically to a fictional past and passé style, whereas Blecher, decades later and under the sign of Kafka, Salvator Dali, Urmuz, rising Existentialism, and burgeoning Jewish-Romanian avant-gardism, is a harbinger of a new world.

As in Kafka and Schulz, this world is not entirely revealed. It is not completely hidden either. This is why Schulz describes it as a "semireality" that exists and beckons the visionary writer through the cracks in the visible everyday.[34] It is the writer's perception that forces this reality's whole body to surface. The *empirical* world is *all* surface, but it is the world Schulz and Blecher are after. "Reality," writes Schulz in *The Street of Crocodiles*—and repeats Foer in *Tree of Codes*—"is as thin as paper,"[35] a cover to rub off. A half-reality in Schulz, the *papier-mâché* surroundings that camouflage something else, another logic and flow of life, are deemed a "surreality" in most of Blecher's critics, a "hyperreality" in commentators like Codrescu,[36] and "irreality" by Blecher himself. Published in 1936, his most important book forefronts the "irreality" concept in the title, *Adventures in Immediate Irreality* (*Întâmplări în irealitatea imediată*), one followed, the next year, by *Scarred Hearts* (*Inimi cicatrizate*). Both books, as well as *The Lighted-up Burrow* (*Vizuina luminată*)—which Blecher's own Max Brod, Jewish-Romanian avant-garde poet and archivist Saşa Pană, published in a volume in 1971—are relentless and "authentic" explorations of this "irreality," but I should probably say *authenticist*, for two reasons. First, because the term, intensely used by Romanian critics, implies a reference to André Gide and his uncompromised analysis and self-analysis; and second, because it is in relation to this brutally "sincere" and "immoralist" art that Blecher develops a presentation modality allowing him access to an invisible world via a *realistic* canvas of the immediate and the visible.

As in Kafka and Schulz, the fantastic, the absurd, things' "new existence," as Blecher writes in *Adventures*," nest in the plain sight of "normal" reality or right underneath it; it is "only the flimsiest of membranes" that "separate[s]" the "certitudes" the book's narrating protagonist "live[s] by" from the "world of incertitudes" beneath.[37] In an important sense, then, Blecher's is an amphibious existence, partaking as it does, like Schulz's, in multiple ontological registers at once, in worlds that do not register socially but exist and in a world that does register socially but harbors others that do not. As Blecher rubs at surfaces and conventions clothing and shaping the most banal things, as he "flays" the material repertoire of the familiar, these objects spring into a life outside their habitual ontological regimen, modify their state or behavior, and transform to awe and unsettle. Like "leather-bound" books, "these true-to-life details, perceived from the distance of my swoon, stupefied and stunned me like a last gulp of chloroform. It was what was most humdrum and familiar in the objects that disturbed me most. The habit of being seen so many times must have worn out their skins, and they sometimes look flayed and bloody to me—and alive, ineffably alive."[38] Once the "transparent paper they had been wrapped in till then" was "removed," things did not only seem ready to be "put to new, superior uses," but they were

> seized by a veritable frenzy of freedom, and the independence they declared of one another went far beyond simple isolation to exultation, ecstasy. Their enthusiasm for living in a new light encompassed me as well: I felt powerful bonds linking me to them, invisible networks making me every bit as much of an object, a part of the room, as they were, the way an organ grafted onto a living organism goes through subtle physical metamorphoses until it becomes one with the body once foreign to it.[39]

The keywords here are "they" (the "objects"), "network," "body," and "metamorphoses," and it is important to point out that, in Michael Henry Heim's superb translation, the original *anastomoze*—anastomoses or connections occurring between originally separate body parts such as blood vessels—become "networks." Thus, Heim bolsters the connection idea while losing the organicist connotation that is, however, reinforced right thereafter to suggest the human's equal-footing integration into the animal-objectual, "flat," non-hierarchical, and more humane co-dependence of organic and inorganic life. This is, indeed, *hyper*realism, an intensification rather than evasion of reality, much like the Blecherian absurd is an exacerbation of a logic animating life in the ever-reenacted pantomime of the little Polish, Ukrainian, and Romanian towns Jews left for Dachau, for Romania's Transnistria death factories, or for Israel later on.

These are "humble towns," as Foer characterizes them in *Everything Is Illuminated*. So is Foer's shtetl of Trachimbrod, scene of unspeakable horrors during the Nazi invasion, and so is Drohobycz or Roman. Before being decimated in the Holocaust, during the decades between the two World Wars, throughout the half-century of Soviet rule, and in the post-Cold War era as well, they had been and have remained places of unbearable boredom, monotony, and unremarkable, wilting life showcasing its automatisms to the fullest, but also sites of unparalleled creativity, of a visionarism capable of plumbing reality's irreality. To this day, these are drab worlds of damnation and revolt, of blindness and illumination. Here, to paraphrase Foer, nothing is illuminated yet everything can be. Here, people, animals, and inorganic objects live out their pedestrian lives or take flight over rooftops as in

Chagall or like the narrator's father in Schulz, only to come down, sometimes tragically, like most things that go up in modernism, with Foer's September 11, 2001 postmodern Kaddish, *Extremely Loud and Incredibly Close*. Little happens in this thing-world, or so it seems. For a lot in fact happens, but only the highly observant few pick up on it. In other words, the nonsensical, the fantastic, the surreal, the absurd, and the illogical are not a matter of invention but of discovery, of paying attention. The dog-becoming men, the shape-changing buildings, the machine (rubber tube)-becoming in Schulz and the cockroach- and tree-becoming of narrator, the human-becoming of police dogs and their uprise *Planet of the Apes*-like, the shops made out of and like what they sell (such as sausages) in Blecher, as well as the mannequins whose bodies without organs are more "real" than reality because, in both, they do not hide their artificiality—all this need not be "invented" or sowed into reality.[40] It only has to be harvested. The things are there, and they present themselves. More than in Kafka, tuberculosis—Pott's disease, in Blecher's case—heightens the senses to alert the narrating patient in his own, French sanatorium to other dimensions or worlds of the material world, whether it is the surrounding "lava of matter"[41] in *Adventures* or the self sealed inside the carapace of its plaster cast, as in *Scarred Hearts*.[42] For, as a character of the 1937 book contends, if the healthy are "monotonous animal[s],"[43] then the ill may lean on the body in pain to get a new purchase on the living continuum, with illness accruing the kind of "oblique animal perspective" for which the protagonist of *Adventures* envies a dog.[44]

On this flattened-out *Zauberberg*, suffering is an eye-opener physically and metaphysically or, more precisely, ontologically. In one sense, *my* suffering is irreducible to somebody else's. In another, though, it equalizes. It teaches me about the horizontal ontology in which, as we suffer, we share in the world's common physicality and, as we are threaded by the same vitality in crisis, we find ourselves anthropologically dethroned and repositioned within the spectrum of an animality stretching beyond the human and the animate. This space is a pedagogical ecology because inside it we stand to learn fundamental things about ourselves. Across the Kafka family, animals oftentimes teach humans what it means to suffer, the meaning of suffering, and with it the very meaning of being human. "Animals!" exclaims Schulz in *The Street of Crocodiles*, "the object of insatiable interest, examples of the riddle of life, created, as it were, to reveal the human being to man himself . . ."[45] In crucial moments of somatic, mental, and emotional distress, individual or collective, animals just *present* themselves so as to embody exemplarily both presence and its loss, the importance of being present for another, human or nonhuman, the Levinasian duty of ethical *Mitsein*, the strictures of being-with and of co-presence in the flat ontology of *ta ónto*, of things that are—period.

Foer's novelistic tour de force *Here I Am* captures, already in its title, both this ethical presence and its animal derivation, and here I can only begin to untie the thick knot that this landmark accomplishment of twenty-first-century American and world fiction constitutes in the Kafkian web of material imagination and literary-cultural intertextuality. To be sure, Foer goes back to Kafka in all sorts of ways. Directly, he does so in *Eating Animals*, which is very much in dialogue with Kafka's vegetarianism and quotes, for the purpose of this conversation, the famous passage in Brod's book where the biographer reproduces the words his friend reportedly spoke to a fish from the Berlin aquarium: "Now at last I can look at you in peace, I don't eat you any more." It is noteworthy, as Foer observes, that Kafka is no longer ashamed to look at the fish because he can now sustain the animal's gaze, and so he does not look away, ashamed of his meat-eating habits;[46] once more, the animal looks at us, and intent, or its anthropomorphic projection, is a moot point here because, whether intentionally or not, that look de-fines us, humans, for ourselves, carries us over our limits and shortcomings, and ultimately empowers.

Indirectly, Foer answers Kafka's call through Schulz. *Extremely Loud* takes up the same indirectness via Günter Grass, with Oskar Schell, his tambourine, his invention of Surrealist objects such as airbag-fitted skyscrapers in response to a traumatic post-9/11 world, and the key meant to unlock a door *not* meant, however, for Oskar's access to the solution of his problem, for healing the void left by the death of the father in one of the Twin Towers, and more broadly for "the cancer of never letting go."[47] *Extremely Loud* is thus about post-traumatic "letting go," about mourning and survival, and so is *Here I Am*. Both reference, more than Philip Roth's 1962 novel and the marital troubles of its plot, the letting go *Ur-szene*, if you will—the Akedah story of Genesis 22.1–18. "Here I am," Abraham answers God's call: I am present and ready to let go of Isaac in the name of my duty to you, which trumps everything, including my basic obligations to the human world and even to my family.

The comments Kafka made on the Mt. Moriah episode in response to Søren Kierkegaard's Abrahamic glosses from *Fear and Trembling* are well known, but it is here helpful to remember that Kafka dwells on Abraham's "worldliness," on what, in human society, holds Abraham up and back, preventing him from hearing the divine call at all, deferring or even deterring his "here I am," his unconditioned submission to God, and Isaac's sacrifice.[48] In *The Gift of Death* and *Literature in Secret*, Derrida is keen on the same worldly context and case against the sacrifice, but he also alludes to the sacrifice that *is* being performed in Genesis 22.13. Displaced onto the ram caught in the thicket of the same world in which familial obligations entangle Abraham, the sacrifice does occur on Mt. Moriah and is perpetuated throughout the history of the world. Both "human and . . . nonhuman," Derrida stresses, this sacrifice makes this history possible in its true, worldly, cross-faith, Abrahamic, and powerfully trans-ecumenic, cultural and ontological sense.[49] And yet we humans so easily forget this or choose not to remember the presence and the gaze of animal actors in this scenario, ignoring their central role in the very making of the human. The voiceless ram *is present*, and thus humans build a world, a structure, and an ethics of co-presence. The fish *was there*, looked and was looked at, and thus Kafka relearned his humanity and, in the process, another, more ethical way of looking the other—the animal—in the eye. The family dog in *Here I Am*, Argus—the "all-seeing" Panoptes—is there also, in the vet's office, about to be euthanized if not sacrificed, and thus Jacob and his family learn the lesson of letting go while being present for one another in a world that must go on.

hilton, suitcase, ein-sof: *Forest Dark* and the Machine of Jewish Literature

[M]y father, a scholar of history, taught me that the absence of things is more useful than their presence.

—Nicole Krauss, *Great House*

"This is why the rabbis tell us that a broken heart is more full than one that is content: because a broken heart has a vacancy, and the vacancy has the potential to be filled with the infinite."

—Nicole Krauss, *Forest Dark*

[L]iterature resides in the sphere of the endless[.]

—Nicole Krauss, *Forest Dark*

How does one "create an absence"? I have always steered clear of this phrase, but *Tree of Codes* has forced me to consider its inapparent logic. Rubbing, digging, making room, cutting holes and breaking open, making an opening, perchance a *clearing*: I can see now how this absencing technology, as I have called it, can be creative or at least part of a creative dialectic where making, in the poietic tradition and "transmission" history of the Kafka family, takes the no-less-arduous labor of unmaking. For one can create *in* an absence; one can put things there. But to do that, one may have to *create* that absence thing in the first place. This means, as we will see immediately, that absencing, making or preserving an absence, has a positive aspect to it, and that absence does not amount to a wholly clean slate either, to sheer nothingness. Foer answers Schulz's call, and Kafka's through it, by in-scribing, as we have noticed, a potentially bountiful absence into *The Street of Crocodiles*. He did not "complete" or rewrite Schulz's text, nor did he imagine it "otherwise," as numerous Kafkians have done so memorably; he cleared, in it, pockets of Agambenian potentiality. In *Forest Dark*, Krauss responds to the "crazy uncle" of her family in a largely similar fashion.[50]

To do so, she, or perhaps just Nicole, her main heroine in the 2017 novel, goes to Israel. In a way, the country is a reiteration and transgeographical extension of the Drohobycz "microcosm," a Pale of Resettlement that "even if on the outside [it] is obsessed with borders, on the inside it lives without boundaries" (234). A space of fluid rather than absent boundaries, Israel is organically *animated* by a ceaselessly transforming "hunger for life" and "existential crisis" (234). These reverberate into a vitalist and metamorphic ontology where, literally *in* their very drabness, brokenness, and incompleteness, objects grow the strength to remake and sustain themselves, in their forms or in new ones, across divides that, according to more orthodox views of things, separate them into alive and inert, organic and inorganic, human and not, old and new. Such things surge into presence and gesture at other presences, again, *not* for "our" benefit. Notably, what makes the spectacle of this hyperpresence possible, and what in lacking, flawed, or lost objects *creates* untold possibilities—things not there yet and therefore unnarrated also—is an absence, some-thing missing or amiss.

Forest Dark crawls with things that, accidentally or purposefully rubbed out of existence, are no longer there, and it does so from the first paragraph, across which marches the cockroach that may have been the last *Kreatur* to see former New York City attorney and millionaire Jules Epstein, one of the novel's main characters (3). A very brief list of such things includes: the unfinished ending of the apocryphal Kafka play Nicole is badgered by rumored Mossad operative and bona fide University of Tel Aviv literature professor Eliezer Friedman to complete (166–7); Friedman's dog, which keeps Nicole company in the house where Kafka may or may not have spent his final years, as Friedman alleges; presumably full of Kafka's unpublished manuscripts, a suitcase, which Nicole leaves behind in the Israeli desert; Kafka himself, who disappears, also according to Friedman's conjectures, from Europe, managing somehow to make *Aliyah* and relocate to a kibbutz where he took up gardening and lived as Anshel Peleg in quasi-complete secret—after all, Friedman offers, there is a reason *Amerika*'s intended title was *Der Verschollene*, "*The Man Who Disappeared*," or, adds the professor, "even *The One Who Went Missing*" (195); the valuable "things" Epstein starts "giv[ing] away" (9) after his "transformation" (10) so as to "clea[r] a space to think," as he tells his son Jonah (10); the long-gone forests of Israel and of former powers clashing on Jewish lands through the ages, empires whose "downfall [was] caused [by] deforestation" and ensuing "erosion, . . . floods[,] and desertification" (241); Epstein's intertextually tailored, Gogolian "overcoat"—Krauss too has come out of it, it seems—as well as Epstein's phone and precious fifteenth-century Italian altar panel, a "small annunciation" whose "flatness," he suspects, is "suffused with the infinite" (36);[51] and with them all, the world itself, not a vessel for these things but these very things, what they com-pose together as they themselves decline to be containers, receptacles, and vehicles for alien contents and ends.

Before he himself became an "inscrutable absence" (6) by vanishing into the desert while subbing for another absent entity, an actor who had been hired to play David in a small-budget movie, Epstein gets from Rabbi Menachem Klausner a crash course in Isaac Luria's mystic theory of the finite world. Epstein met Klausner, the "founder of Gilgul, a program that brings Americans to Safed [in Israel] to study Jewish mysticism" (19), at a New York City dinner for Palestinian leader Mahmoud Abbas. At the event, the rabbi filled in for Epstein as a speaker and lectured on *menucha*, the divine absence or "pause from work," a form of "rest" only apparently opposed to creation and calling in fact, as Klausner told his audience, for creation and recreation (20–1). In a similar vein, the rabbi lectures Epstein in Safed on the "withdrawal of God" "to make space for the finite world, for time can only exist in the absence of the eternal." "How does the infinite—the *Ein[-]Sof*, the being without end, as God is called—create something finite *within* what is already infinity?" asks Klausner rhetorically. "And furthermore," "how can we explain the paradox of God's simultaneous presence and absence in the world," the *immanent* presence of the "transcendent"? Summarizing the Lurianic theory of the divine "total absence"–"total presence" unit,[52] Klausner explains to Epstein that God "first withdrew Himself, and in the void that was left, He created the world." But not only was *Tzimtzum*, "divine contraction" or "withdrawal," a "necessary precursor of creation"; this "primordial event was [also] seen [by Luria] as ongoing, constantly echoed" both "in the Torah and in our own lives" (106). "For example," Klausner says,

> from the withdrawal of God's divine light, the rabbi, blue eyes sparkling with local candlelight, leaped to the empty space, whose spot of darkness held the potential for the world. And from the empty space that held the potential for the world, he leaped to the creation of the world, with its days and measures.
>
> Like so, the tall, limber rabbi born in Cleveland, transplanted to the ancient land of the Bible, leaped like Jackie Joyner from the infinite to the finite . . .
>
> "But the finite remembers the infinite," Klausner said, holding up a long finger. It still contains the will of infinity!"
>
> *The will of infinity*, Epstein repeated to himself, weighing the phrase in his mind as one weighs a hammer to see if it is enough to drive the nail . . .
>
> "And so everything in the world longs to return there. To *repair* itself to infinity. This process of repair, this most beautiful of processes which we call *tikkun*, is the operating system of this world. *Tikkun olam*, the transformation of the world, which cannot happen without *tikkun ha'nefesh*, our own internal transformation. The moment we enter into Jewish thought, Jewish questioning, we enter into this process. Because what is a question but a voided space? A space that asks to be filled again with its portion of infinity?" (144–5)

Tikkun ties conspicuously into *Gilgul*, "transmigration" or "reincarnation" in Hebrew and a foundational concept in Lurianic Kabbalah. It is also, as Friedman reminds Nicole, "nearly the same" as the titles of the Hebrew and Yiddish translations of "The Metamorphosis" (*Ha Gilgul* and *Der Gilgul*, respectively). In Krauss, *Gilgul* is not just the name of the Safed "program." One of *Forest Dark*'s chapters is titled "Gilgul" and reports on Kafka's own multiple "transmogrifications" in his work, name (kavka ["jackdaw" Czech]/Amshel/Amsel ["blackbird"]), physical appearance (*kavka*-esque), and "posthumous" (181–2) Palestinian life in the metamorphic paradises of his flower and vegetable patches (269). Moreover, as Krauss reveals in an interview, *Gilgul* would have been the title of the book itself had she had her way.[53]

"*The Metamorphosis*," the Israeli scholar elaborates, "has always been a story not about the change from one form to another, but about the continuity of the soul through different material realities" (194). And so is *Forest Dark*, a twofold narrative that tells the sequential and mundane story of one space- and time-bound thing after another while hinting at the Neoplatonic–Kabbalistic multiplicity *and* kinship of all things. Running through them all and intersecting conceptually with Judaic theosophy, recent astrophysics, string theory, and Nicole/Krauss's own view of things, is a life force that, as it renews itself steadily in the material, discrete, and temporary objects of our world, does so concurrently in an infinite array of other objects and worlds, all of them offspring of the same seminal energy, visibly and invisibly related, and portals to one another. As Nicole ruminates, life "appears" (48) to take place in separate objects and in their places such as "long hallways," "waiting rooms," "foreign cities," "terraces," "gardens," "hospitals," "rented rooms," "crowded trains," and so forth. But what if this universe is a "multiverse" (45)? What if it occurs only in one place, from which one dreams, however, the Borgesian dream of all the other places and worlds? What if the "finite beings" (48), spread around as they seem to be in the physical space of the world-as-background or -vessel ("holding tank" [48]), make up only one string of entities, visible, touchable, limited in space, time, and number, impressive as their size, quantity, and variety may be? What if this chain of actants and acts is just one story to tell, and what if we—me, you, a certain human subject and the human generally—are not its subject, its narrative center and rational protagonist? What if the story is essentially subjectless, with people, bugs, suitcases, and everything else equal-footing characters in it? What if, Nicole finally asks herself, it is not the finite existents, including ourselves, "who move through space, but space that moves through us, spun on the loom of our minds? And if all of that is so, then where is this place from which we lie and dream? A holding tank in nonspace? Some dimension we're unconscious of?" (48). Or "is it," she hypothesizes, "somewhere in the one finite world from which billions of worlds have been, and will be, born, a single location different for each of us, equally banal as any other?" (48)

In Nicole's multiverse, life may be in one place or thing but is not cooped up in it. Whole worlds spring forth from that place-thing, whatever it is, and the spring, the rush, and the flow of being carry the memory of the source from one bend to another, each turn and twist of the stream firming up into a temporal, finite "place" or object, and each of these bearing the potential to unreel its own string of realities and narratives thereof into infinity. One can make a world—and other worlds alongside them—out of any of these things, God-like, or less ambitiously, like Nicole/Krauss, one can "lie" about that world, dream it up, narrate or "storyworld" it, as we will discover below. Either way, one has first to locate or "create" in them a space for creation itself, whether one blows or finds a hole or holes in them, an absence simmering with presence in potentia. As we have seen, there are so many such opportunities in *Forest Dark*. They are all objects that present themselves to Nicole/Krauss. She does not make them; they are not her instruments; nor is she trading them for more valuable, meaningful, or beautiful things. In a manner of speaking, they make *her*, for it is in their poietic midst that she overcomes what is unmaking her as a writer and woman in a failing marriage. They help fill the void tormenting her, the absence of her novel and children; indeed, objects help her deal with her professional "absence syndrome," her writer's block. It is not that she actually "does things" to or with them. At most, she does things, as suggested above, *out* of them, in that she builds on the incompleteness or lack with which they present her as they accede to their hyperpresence, and she mines that space of absence for possible worlds.

The absence in question reinstantiates, as Klausner would argue, the *ayin* or "nothingness" on which "what is" is predicated, the "empty space [God] needed [in Adam]" to make room for Chava (Eve) and before that in himself to make the world of all things human and nonhuman. "To create man," Klausner tells Epstein,

> "God had to remove Himself, and one could say that the defining feature of humanity is that lack. It's a lack that haunts us because, being God's creation, we contain a memory of the infinite, which fills us with longing. But the same lack is also what allows for free will. The act of breaking God's command not to eat from the Tree of Knowledge can be interpreted as a rejection of obedience in favor of free choice and the pursuit of autonomous knowledge. But of course it's God who suggests the idea of eating from the Tree of Knowledge in the first place. God who plants the idea in Eve. And so it can also be read as God's way of leading Adam and Eve to confront the vacated space within themselves—the space where God seems to be absent. In this way it is Eve, whose creation required a physical void in Adam, who also leads Adam to the discovery of the metaphysical void in him which he will forever mourn, even as he floods it with his freedom and will."

It was in the story of Moses, too, Klausner went on. The one chosen to speak for his people must first have speech removed from him. He put a coal in his mouth as a child and burned his tongue and so was unable to speak, and it was this absence of speech that created the possibility of his being filled with God's speech.

"This is why the rabbis tell us that a broken heart is more full than one that is content: because a broken heart has a vacancy and the vacancy has the potential to be filled with the infinite." (106–7)

Have "[I] made myself susceptible"?, Epstein asks Klausner. The rabbi does not answer. It is pretty clear, however, that the former lawyer's "radical charity" (11)—the frenzy with which he has cleared out "all the things around him" (10) in the wake of his parents' death—has indeed made him "susceptible." Nicole has "created," and is flailing painfully, in the same "vacancy." She is already mourning her marriage, and so her heart is broken, not in "working order" emotionally because unfulfilled, insufficiently filled with its self-sustaining intensities. Also inside her, an "absence of speech" is deferring discourse and her novel with it. But deferral does not foreclose; it is not a closure or displacement. Instead, it affords conception ("dreaming") in a "vacated" place-thing, no matter how trivial and lacking the thing may be.

For Nicole, that thing is the hotel whose black-and-white pictures are reproduced in the novel (54, 55, 56) along, remarkably, with an image of the exterior of the house (174) in which Eva Hoffe, Brod's heiress, is allegedly still keeping Kafka's manuscripts at the time of Nicole's visit to Israel.[54] "In that moment," when Nicole, after listening to a radio program on the "multiverse," gives us her own thoughts on the subject (45–8), she "knew unequivocally that if [she] was dreaming [her] life from anywhere, it was the Tel Aviv Hilton" (48). This is the place where she "repairs" not to fix things, to repair them, but to repair *to* them and get her bearings as a woman and author. The *repaire*—the "place," "abode," "lair," or even "hole," at its French source—is solid and yet somehow hollow at once, not necessarily in disrepair but fitting the bluntness, grit, and dusty shabbiness of its surroundings. The "Brutalist" building is at worst a "monstrosity" (53) and at best a paragon of the anodyne. The concrete rectangle is not exactly an architectural allegory of Paradise unless Paradise is the one imagined by Kafka in the *Parables and Paradoxes* fragment excerpted in *Forest Dark*'s epigraph: the world in which we "currently" (*dauernd*) are.

It is interesting that Krauss prefers a motto translation that foregrounds our "now," our "current" life as we are leading it, surrounded by time-bound, decaying, and not necessarily well-maintained, complete, and beautiful things.[55] No wonder the "monstrosity" is wrapped in "a kind of mystical aura" for Nicole (49), and this aura, here as in other works discussed in *Flat Aesthetics*, has to do with inapparent beauty and novelty, as well as with their counterintuitive potential in "finite" things. Like those things, the hotel is a paradoxical yet genuine locus of creativity. On one side, it is a quintessential absence domain, as things go missing in it; along the same lines, it even gets increasingly lifeless as people keep jumping to their death off its balconies. Aesthetically dysfunctional in its extreme-modernist, content-oriented functionality, lacking in "personality," and nondescript, the place is, on the other side, a hotbed of life and its description, of life making and literature. "Life," Nicole informs us, "began for me there" (she was conceived in the Tel Aviv Hilton). This is also where she had a defining "experience" of loss and finding, absence and presence, early on as a child, when her brother found a diamond earring in the swimming pool, and she felt that an "opening—a small tear in the fabric of reality" (49)—was there possible, the way "a foot was put in the way of a door closing" (51). The more Nicole thinks about the building, the more she "sense[s] that it serve[s] some larger purpose . . . something to do not with us but with far larger entities" (53).

Stuck in her "mind like a kind of blockage," the ugly monolith "encodes" in its repetitive design ("unrelenting grid") a "message nearly as mysterious as the one we've yet to unlock at Stonehenge" (53). There is, of course, the actual message, "the Kafka assignment," which Nicole gets from Friedman at a nearby restaurant "a few minutes' walk from the Hilton" (71). And then there is the other message, the more important one, which Nicole eventually does get at the Hilton, or "from it," and which largely helps her, and certainly helps Krauss, gain "the power of narrative" (52), "the instinct to give things shape" (167). It is not a message proper, an information of some sort, a "content," but a form. That form eventually helps Nicole handle—rather than simply eliminate—the "formlessness" (67) with which she has been wrestling as a writer, woman, and mother, for, as we shall see, that form does not "contain" (67) that fluidity of content and matter and therefore does not supply the closure or completion Friedman has been hoping for. Vibrating with forming energies, its barren appearances notwithstanding, the hotel itself is that "presencing," lacking yet world-making form, "house of the mind that conjures the world," as Nicole/Krauss phrases it so aptly (68). The house or the *Heim*, the Germanic and Yiddish word for "home" on which Nicole glosses by dint of a few references to the Freudian *Unheimliche* (68–71), is familiar and even familial, given its role in Nicole's family throughout the years, but also unfamiliar, uncanny. It is the return destination, a place to repair to not in order to fix and complete what has been but to revisit so as to move on and make something new. In that regard, the novel Nicole is trying to write, and definitely the one Krauss is writing, is "modeled on the Hilton" (64), on the unsightly, deformed form that contains possibilities without inhibiting them. "[M]aybe I was turning to the wrong language," Nicole mulls over the Freudian lexicon. "In Hebrew, the world is *olam*, and now I remembered that my father had once told me that the world comes from the root *alam*, which means 'to hide,' or 'to conceal'" (71). "In Freud's examination of where *heimlich* and *unheimlich* dissolve into another and illuminate an anxiety (something that ought to have been concealed, but that has nevertheless come to light)," Nicole concludes, "he nearly touched the wisdom of his Jewish ancestors." In her view, Freud "fell short of their radicalism," failing to fully grasp the world's concomitant hiding and revealing (71).

Forest Dark illustrates a literary praxis that extends innovatively into the twenty-first century the wisdom Nicole is talking about. Shaping the novel is a poetics of repair and homecoming whose intertextual, cultural-historical, and ontological returns—in all senses—are not repetitive and nostalgic but creative and futural, much like Nicole's going back to the Hilton, to her family in the end, as well as to Kafka and his own family. The dull, the lackluster, the well-known, the lacking, the incomplete, the broken hearts, families, texts, and all the other place-things to which Nicole repairs without repairing them are potential windows into *Ein-Sof*. In Krauss's imaginary of lack and loss—we could call it a "negative" imaginary, but it would be misleading—there are things patently and famously endowed with this potential: Kafka's unfinished books, the Temple, Paradise, or Eden's various terrestrial brethren in the book such as the lush gardens of Kafka's Palestinian post-life (196), the non-Cartesian, neo-Dantesque forest of fertile "pausing" ("for rest" is Epstein's pun [211]) and "multiversal," enlightening unknown (47) to which *Forest Dark* alludes in the title and Nicole expatiates on recurrently, or the trees Epstein's money helps replant on Israel's hills. "[T]he gray whale who'd lost his way and ended up off the shore of Tel Aviv" (130) would belong in this transparently symbolic object set also. But Krauss is equally drawn to the master's biography and the Israeli legend, to the actual Kafka corpus and the rumored archive, to the Kafka "play" and its twice apocryphal version, to the "Jewish story" and what Nicole "adds" to it (thinks Friedman [74]), to the Text and its scholarly afterlife, to the Written and Oral Torah, to the sacred and the mundane. In fact, for a novelist, the Ladurée tin box holding Epstein's baby teeth or the green book Maya, Epstein's daughter, gave his father—objects of absence or gone missing—are even more alluring, as some object ontologists would say. These things are the "real" (really "finite") dreamworld and storyworld nurseries, "verified" sites of what can be again and otherwise, endlessly, because they are palpably embodied, incorporations that have already occurred. More tangibly than others, such things are, as both Luria's and Kafka's descendants would emphasize, as Nicole herself ventures in her multiverse comments, and as I have noticed apropos of Schulz, way stations on the road of life running through objects and through the worlds in them and using them as disguises and allotropes of myriad other objects and universes, all of them visibly or invisibly related.

The feeling of this ontological kinship and "diffusion" overwhelms Epstein in Jaffa in a scene that reads like a page out of Schulz or Blecher.

"His days," Krauss writes, "became diffuse," and he no longer makes out the "the line between water and sky." In effect, "the line between himself and the world" has become barely traceable. He spends his time "watch[ing] the waves, and felt himself to be also endless, repeating, filled with unseen life." As in *The Street of Crocodiles,* "[t]he lines from the books on his table swam up from the pages before his eyes." Before nightfall, "he would go out and walk, agitated, waiting, lost among the narrow streets, until turning a corner and coming upon the sea all over again, he was unskinned" (236). On his homestretch, Epstein keeps circling back to his repair of endlessness, himself "endless," at once filled with life and open to life's repetitions, both one of them and their conduit, self-present and yet preserving a vital and vitally presencing reserve of absence. This repetitive rite, this flaying friction against the world, rubs him the right way, as it were, erasing the "lines" between him and not-him, between his finite body and the *Ein-Sof* in a fashion redolent of the Schulzian *écorché* of textual and existential lines, layers, and denotations. Rubbing and skinning de-form Epstein in that they open him up to his potential being, like Abraham, whom God urged "to go out of himself so that he might make space for what God intended him to be" (264–5). De-formed, Epstein becomes "new to everything" (233) and ready to participate in the life of other forms, living and not, or living in forms we still need to learn to recognize. Thus, de-formation or its extreme form, formlessness, is productive. "Unmaking" in a poietic, expansive, and "diffusive" way, it is a "return" of Epstein's magnanimity. He gave his dearest objects away, and, tellingly, most of them evaporated into the in-finite *silva oscura* of the "unfathomable" (46) instead of founding new locations and owners. He de-completed his thing-world, peeling off and divesting himself of layer after layer, and eventually he himself would de-complete, reversing a child's growing and transformation process of "slowly recomposing oneself out of the borrowed materials of the world" until "he is all and only the world ... [w]hich is to say: alone in himself" (130). "[I]ncompleteness," on the other hand, "our still yet unfinishedness," ensures a "potential for change," "even [a] transformation" (47) that runs in the opposite direction, where one does not make oneself as children do, according to Nicole, but de-composes instead into the same "atoms" so one can disperse into the same "surroundings" out of whose particles one pieced oneself together as a finite being, separate from the world (130).

Nicole's writing, or lack thereof, is also a de-composition exercise and comes about in similar circumstances. It is, more accurately, an unmaking effort for she does no writing in Israel, failing or, more likely, unwilling to acquit herself of the task to "complete" Kafka. Yet this unmaking has similarly positive reverberations. The *possibility* of this writing, including the possibilities nesting in the premeditated in-completion of the play Friedman would want to see made into a film, is present or presented, rather, in another mysterious shell-thing, another dubious, perhaps empty container of *Forest Dark*. This is the suitcase in which Hoffe may or may not hold the legally contested manuscripts, with the unfinished text among them. After waiting a while outside Hoffe's house, Nicole "heard something being dragged down the stairs, as heavy as a body, and when I hurried back around the corner to the front," Friedman, the improbable "Mossad" operative, "emerged, pulling behind him a black suitcase. The stitching had come loose along the seams, and the handle was bound in duct tape" (173). The suitcase looked to Nicole more like one "a door-to-door kiddush-cup salesman" would carry "than a Mossad man, or even former Mossad, or even former Mossad from the broom-closet department of Jewish literature. Not that this stopped me from believing, with a surge in the heart, that something of the lost Kafka was contained inside it" (173).

The container's odd looks and the theatricality and implausibility of the entire scene are textbook markers of the *Unheimliche*, and indeed, right below the picture of Hoffe's own Brutalist building, Nicole confirms that the suitcase is both uncanny and about to make things even more so for her. "If things were not strange already," Nicole declares,

> from the moment the suitcase was in our possession, things became far stranger. Now it seems to me that before the suitcase I was operating in a world of familiar laws but unusual circumstances, but afterward the familiar laws began to shiver and bend a little. More than that, it seems to me that I had been moving toward that bend for a long time without knowing it, which is to say, moving toward the suitcase, a suitcase that in some sense I'd been aware of since I was seven, having been given it in a story. But I'd had to wait all these years for it to finally open into my life. (174)

The suitcase has been there Nicole's entire life. Nicole has been "moving" toward it even though it comes from the childhood story of another suitcase shrouded in mystery and, without ever opening, opens into another story, which may not exist (the "play"), and more importantly, into Nicole's life story, opening this story up. And so, what Nicole does in the desert while reliving Kafka's Palestine life in Kafka's former "house" and wearing Kafka's "coat" no longer translates the views of others (Friedman, the "Mossad," the "Jewish state") into her personal action. "Awake in Kafka's bed," she "falls out" of the chronology of mechanically repetitive, mimetic behavior into a more propitious, future-oriented temporality in which "things spring out, ... break[ing] through and unfurl[ing] themselves in the light" (258). This is "kairotic" (259) time, a temporal projection of a sovereign order of things reeling out its endless metamorphic chain. Nicole realizes now that she has "failed to fulfill the promise of [a] vision [she] once had" before she started "emulating" others' "thoughts and actions" (262). She is "certain" that "a period had existed in which I looked at the things of the world without needing to make them subordinate to order. I simply saw, with whatever originality I was born with, the whole of things, without needing to give them a human translation" (262). What she "saw" was a visualization of *kairos* or "right moment" of things, a "kairotics" or "timely" self-presentation of objects that dispensed with human ordering and by the same movement afforded her "originality," freeing her too from that ordering and its conventions.

In the clarifying aftermath of Nicole's delirious bout with fever, Friedman's dog too "sensed that time was returning to us" (270), as Nicole says. This is kairotic time, and it is a time to act too (270). It measures an "opening" (260) through the human order, a dis-ordering of conventions, expectations, and forms that opens them up and keeps them so, susceptible to reformations and reincarnations without end, to the *Ein-Sof*. If indeed "literature resides in the sphere of the endless, and those who write have no hope of an end" (270), as Nicole wanted to tell Friedman, then not ending Kafka's play and losing the suitcase to boot are kairotic actions. They are inactions only on the face of it. For they are creative forms of doing comparable to the for-resting *menucha*, to unknowing and unmaking that forego the closure and fight off the ordering that stunts the infinite in finite forms. In this vein, "unfinishing" the play extends the text's life in its current *and* future reincarnations, literary and otherwise, while protecting Nicole's dignified stature as an author and enabling her to channel her efforts in effectively creative—rather than re-creative, ancillary—directions. It does "keep the great machine of Jewish literature rolling forward" (125) too, if not the way Friedman would have wanted it done, that is, by buying into the "claims" (270) individuals like Hoffe, the community, tradition, and even the state stake to its writers ("You think your writing belongs to you?" Friedman asks Nicole [125]) and whose presumptuousness aggravates Krauss as it does Lerner. It keeps the "transmission of national literature" (165) open-ended and adds a chapter to the "Jewish story" but not by humbly serving as an amanuensis to the master and the literary and cultural-political order he has posthumously been forced to incorporate. In-completing the play is Nicole's "Kaddish for Kafka" (271), mourning that keeps his literary "soul . . . bundled in the bundle of life" (271).

CONCLUSION | Composing the Contemporary

Some of the most spirited twenty-first-century critical debates are riffs on the question raised by Latour in the title of his 2004 article "Why Has Critique Run out of Steam? From Matters of Fact to Matters of Concern."[1] A much-discussed about-face, the piece has been billed as Latour's coming to his realist senses. A "post-epistemological" change of tune or not, Latour's recent work speaks to a growing concern with "facts," "truth," "authenticity," "materialism," "material aesthetics," "reality," "the real thing," "things," and other elements of the new "presence paradigm" that has been receiving more and more attention in the wake of the ontological turn sweeping across the humanities in the new millennium.

Such issues have brought together an army of philosophers and critics. A short list would include Meillassoux and the new "realist metaphysicians" of *choses en soi* in France;[2] former Derrideans like Gianni Vattimo and Maurizio Ferraris in Italy; post-hermeneutics, neo-avant-garde, "present-tense poetics," and *Präsenztheorie* scholars such as Gumbrecht, Robert Hermann, Armen Avanessian, and Anke Hennig in Germany;[3] historians and presence theorists like Eelco Runia[4] and "metamodernists" such as Timotheus Vermeulen and Robin van den Akker in the Netherlands;[5] students of "post-aesthetics," "presence-effect," and post-Marxist materialism such as Alexandru Matei, Daniel Clinci, Vasile Mihalache, Laura Mesina, and Sorin Alexandrescu in Romania;[6] "new materialists," "immaterialists," and material-aesthetics proponents such as Bill Brown, Bryant, Bogost, Harman, Shaviro, Bennett, Barad, and Mark Foster Gage in the United States; critics of the "politics of presence" like Diana Taylor[7] and, led by Rita Felski, the recent cohort of post-critique advocates on both sides of the Atlantic.

To reiterate one last time, I talk about presence in this context because to me, presence is not an ontotheological fantasy but to the contrary, a thing that presents itself materially, affirms its being-there, and impacts, refers to, and otherwise engages with other things through its presentation. I avail myself of presence because I am interested in things' self-presentation, and this preoccupies me because, unlike some of those named above, I believe this is what things—objects, beings, existents, "what is"—have been doing with unprecedented, sometimes devastating, and culturally definitional force over the last decades. To paraphrase the title of Marina Abramović's famous performances, *things are present*. Their presentation sets this interval apart historically and aesthetically, and as I have tried to show, postmillennial American fiction provides a stage and a script for this presentation. I have argued in fact that, since 9/11, novels by Whitehead, Mandel, Lerner, and others have brought about a new aesthetics.

Hierarchy to flatness. I have called this aesthetics flat because it is an ontoaesthetics, that is, an ontology-grounded or, better yet, ontology-driven aesthetics where all things are aesthetic objects for, ontologically speaking, all objects *are* on the same plane. Flat ontology's levelness of being carries over into this aesthetics' "democracy," accounting for the aesthetic potential of energy discharges and intensities with which all objects present themselves no matter what they are. Therefore, flat aesthetics is *nonhierarchical*. As is well known, this is not the first attempt to expand the aesthetic realm. It is, however, one of the more recent and systematic efforts, in literary criticism and theory at least, to enlarge this domain beyond the anthroposphere and, "tactical"—or sine qua non—anthropomorphism aside, to approach object-oriented aesthetics on its own terms, without humanizing its actors. One could say actually that in reading *10:04*, the risk would be "animalizing" Ben. Remarkably, that is impossible because Ben is already a mollusk or mollusk-like, and his book, as well as Lerner's, is written proof of this animalization.

Exchange regime and intransitivity. This aesthetics is intransitive because, as objects act aesthetically, and in order to do so, they ward off transitive treatment. *Station Eleven* tells us in no equivocal terms that existents prefer to be destinations instead of transits. This is why things either decline to discharge their "duties" or resist attempts to transcend, rationalize, and otherwise subject objects to uses, swaps, or translations that do not appreciate them for what they are in and of themselves, for the ontological singularity they insist on retaining, but for what they can be applied to or converted into. These operations are underwritten by an entire exchange regime. The core value of this regime is exchange value. Colliding with the semantics of fungibility, "flat" is also antonymous to "lackluster" or "thin." It does not denote sameness, monotony, scarcity, superficiality, and transparency, but their opposites. As I deploy it in the previous chapters, flatness is a rich, variegated, and dense domain of ontoaesthetic vibrancy extending far beyond human life and artifacts as well as beyond life traditionally conceived. It is not primarily a geometrical attribute, an immaterial or one-dimensional extensity in space, but an *intensity in being*. Flatness marks the high degree to which an object sets itself forth, asserting its being-there, its objecthood, or form as something unignorable and impossible to paraphrase, bypass, and otherwise maneuver or leave behind in the name of a task, goal, god, place, price, equivalent, meaning, and so on. American postmillennial writers take on the neoliberal exchange regime head-on. To rephrase: this "critique" may or may not be their intentional project, but things do it anyway, inside and outside these authors' works.

Hyperpresence and thing-energy.   Inherently, things are never just transits, accessories, and ontological Cinderellas. They are not "transparencies" but "obstacles," to recall the title of Jean Starobinski's famous book on Jean-Jacques Rousseau.[8] In any exchange regime, they are, however, transited, traversed, and transparentized as a matter of course. These are deontologizing routines that sometimes affect existents and sometimes do not, "getting" to them to various degrees and with a range of repercussions. In their uses, abuses, and subservience, and despite such sub-states of being, objects-qua-equipment are nevertheless present. The furniture in the law office checked out by the Omegas in *Zone One* was there, present, before the plague, when the firm's high-powered attorneys were still coming into work. Instrumentality does not foreclose presence. But post-instrumental objects can and, as Mandel and others report, do rise into hyperpresence. These objects become present with new intensities, with an energy that, first, draws attention to objects themselves, to objects-as-objects, to their objecthood, form, or aesthetic dimension rather than some meaning, content, or external purpose. This is opaque form that, second, after pointing to itself, to its materiality and opaqueness, attracts, holds, and ultimately reroutes its thing-vibrations toward other things, marshalling its own vibes and reorienting other objects' so as to illuminate not so much a beyond, a causality, prototype, political baseline, or code, but laterally, something more significant and more revelatory: the rest of the objectual ensemble.

Prismatic discharges.   In this sense, evocative of a "voluminous" surface that does not mirror but refracts, "flat" signifies "prismatic" or, more accurately, *acts* accordingly, prismatically. The aesthetics of flatness—the aesthetic of objects both flat and on the same ontological plane—mobilizes a particular optics of presentation, of an indirect and incremental appearance that steers energies, "concerns," and "gazes" obliquely across the object, toward and across the entire object system so that the latter itself heaves into view eventually. Ontologically speaking, objects do not mirror—explain, legitimate, serve—anything other than themselves. They are not inherently specular even though "we" cannot help but speculate *about* them, as I have too, and even though such speculations need not be arbitrary. A specular medium reflects and, in so doing, replaces an object with its image and other reflections and contents, so much so that whatever appears in the mirror forces the mirrored object to withdraw. But there is nothing self-protective, esoteric, or cognitively rewarding about this withdrawal. Specular aesthetics is a metaphorics that, far from accessing the object's "essence," as some object-oriented ontologists assume, displaces both object and essence altogether. Thus, the specular is overly speculative, a vehicle for the metaphysical. The prismatic—the prism-object—on the other hand, is not a self-substituting mirror, a gateway to transcendence. By the same token, prismatic or flat aesthetics both makes provisions for the object's presentation and enables further presentations; it deflects an object's replications, replacements, and exchanges and prompts further appearances of objects and other revelatory self-presentations horizontally. This aesthetic dynamic is compositional. As we have seen, it arranges a wide array of objects into configurations of contemporaneity. These arrangements are the workings of flat aesthetics and the ultimate affordances of strong ontology.

Things, realism, and literary form. Today's world is a test of our philosophical realism, of our capacity to rise up to things' objective reality. This realness is not only what objects embody; it is also what they display. They all make such presentations, these days more poignantly and more significantly than ever, and the show of being they put on does not require "our" cognitive, emotional, and political presence even though, as I say, they test it. In the twenty-first century, they present themselves with a strong ontological vengeance and thereby deliver a set of powerful and undeniable facts. These facts are things. Such ecologically, economically, politically, militarily, and otherwise factual things exceed and "resent" any interpretive, rhetorical, or discursive handling of their reality in a form that *would take any-thing away from the blunt being-there of their materially uncircumventable thingness.* This does not mean that this actuality is untainted culturally, in no way shaped or "constructed" by language, culture, and history—in other words, not constituted in friction and association with . . . "things of this nature." In this sense, realism, mine at least, tolerates a certain amount of constructionism. This realism is not *naïve* realism or pre- (/a-)cultural empiricism, and in that it is not entirely incompatible with postmodernism—but then, again, cultural forms and the minutiae of cultural and linguistic formation, as well as words themselves can be viewed as things, as part two of this book does.

Postmodernism and weak ontology. The dominant aesthetic, cultural, and epistemological paradigm of the second half of the past century, postmodernism rose by dint of sophisticated language games played with this reality and its representation history. To some, these games are a willful and extreme variety of literary correlationism. They comprise jocular-ironic, intertextual-quotational renditions of reality in the Derrida–Umberto Eco–John Barth line, assorted "constructionisms," "relativisms," "fictionalizations," and other tactics bent on "deconstructing" *what is* and thereby revealing it as ideology, simulacrum, rhetorical effect, trace, infinite semiosis, meaning deferral, lack, absence, and so on.

There is definitely more to postmodernism, poststructuralism, and cultural and identity studies than this cultural-epistemological police sketch. In a fundamental book published three decades and a half ago and in spectacular anticipation of a mutation on which thinkers like Bryant dwell these days at great length, Brian McHale defined the transition to postmodernism as an *ontological* turn away from the epistemological primacy of modernism even though, let me add quickly, that was a shift to a rather "weak," plural, ambiguous, "unstable," and ever-intertextually and culturally prepackaged ontology.[9] In any case, I would also point to recent attempts to reconsider the "realist fiction" of postmodernism[10] or to Matt Mullins's groundbreaking 2016 book *Postmodernism in Pieces: Materializing the Social in U.S. Fiction*, which sets out to "flatten" postmodernism and its grasp in a way germane to my approach to *post*-postmodern fiction.[11]

The postmodern baroque. Regardless of the material it worked with, a "constructionist," "ludic," and ontologically weak literary and cultural form did not seem at the end of the day best suited to account for the stronger and stronger ontology of things marking the post-Berlin and especially the post-9/11 world, sometimes in the catastrophically salient mode of one major financial, political, natural-ecological, or pandemic disaster after another. This fast-growing discrepancy between form, on one hand, and on the other, context and presumed content or reference rendered the tapering off of the postmodern the most significant cultural development of the 1990s and reinforced postmodernism's identity and understanding as a Cold War phenomenon.

But the eventual waning of the postmodern aesthetic in the twenty-first century was also the doing of postmodernism itself, of a postmodernism in overdrive or in its baroque phase. What I call the postmodern baroque inheres in an agonal mode of literary and cultural production that is quintessentially and compulsorily reproductive. Under its auspices, novels, short stories, movies, architecture, fashion, and a whole culture in the United States and elsewhere started in the early 1990s self-repeating over and over and faster and faster, thus repeating repetition itself, reworking, that is, "classically" postmodern poetics of literary-cultural reprise.[12] Important works continued to build up the postmodern canon during this time, but they could not reverse the movement's agony. During the last decade of the past century, postmodernism became one big aesthetic encore unable to rejuvenate itself by opening itself up to other things and to things generally. Its closed-system self-repetitiveness wound up exhausting it and all but severing the umbilical cord linking the postmodern to the surrounding world and this world's urgencies—to contemporary relevance, one might say, and to contemporaneity at large.

After 1990, postmodern fiction found itself in the throes of an excessively self-reiterative narrative routine. The 1990s postmodern generation rehashed with gusto the big names of the 1970s, producing, as McHale, Cowart, and others have shown, a whole series of Freudian pairs of love–hate symbiosis—Pynchon, DeLillo, Robert Coover, Roth, and Barth on one side, and David Foster Wallace, Leyner, Powers, William Gibson, Dave Eggers, Bret Easton Ellis, Jonathan Franzen, Jennifer Egan, and Mark Danielewski, on the other. Even household figures such as Pynchon self-rewrote freely and disappointingly, with his 2013 *Bleeding Edge* a rather uninspiring *Crying of Lot 49* remake. Leyner, the quintessential avant-pop writer and cult figure on U.S. campuses in the late 1990s—an American Jasper Fforde on steroids—kept wondering about how Arnold Schwarzenegger might look playing the protagonists of *My Fair Lady* and *The Diary of Anne Frank*. In a 1992 essay, Wallace called this kind of stuff "the metastasis of originality."[13] Was he immune to it, though? What is the 1996 meganovel *Infinite Jest*'s infinite bulk if not the remaking—the remaking and the unmaking—of *The Making of Americans*, the repeating of the hyperrepetive Gertrude Stein with an addictively recursive twist quite literally?[14] Wallace repeated the repetitive modernist and postmodern, the irony wrapped up in the irony he said he was so sick of, and yet he could not get enough of until nothing worked anymore.

In full swing, this metastasis, this paroxysm of "coming after" and the blasé déjà-vu chronicles of the postmodern baroque became an old chestnut, out of sync with the new world, and so the young writers of the 1990s, some of them mentioned above, along with those coming after them, started turning away from the reiterative poetics and to "new authenticism," "realism," "docufiction," "autofiction," "sincerity," and "postirony," controversial as these designations and practices may be. All of a sudden, postmodern ontology appeared old, inadequate, and sterile, especially over and against the backdrop of the world's brutal newness, and looked both powerless *and* powerfully symptomatic of what was going on. This helps understand the survival and, in fact, the expansion of cultural discourse that aggravates, Wallace-style, the repetitive drive of the typical 1990s TV show, *The Simpsons*, in a whole host of rip-offs all the way to *Family Guy*, the cultural syndrome of the new millennium. *Family Guy* is to *The Simpsons* what Wallace is to Pynchon. Where *The Simpsons* usually alludes to, or fully retells, one classic or so per episode (Mark Twain, Shakespeare, etc.), *Family Guy* is one big string of postmodern allusions and references, to the point that plot becomes parasitic on intertextuality. The latter invokes both real and made-up things or people, including the Simpsons, in a *repetitive-citational frenzy* that ends up *un-referencing* and disembodying the world.

Exhaustion 2.0. Geared as they were self-reflectively toward literary endogeny itself, postmodern baroque's intertextually inbreeding protocols looked like a sign of both paradigm exhaustion and poor receptiveness to the world's woes, to what really *was* and mattered in it. Postmodernism had marked an ontological turn, as McHale argued, but postmodern ontology began to seem weak and out of touch with a painfully present, *urgent* world. Shopworn aesthetically, the postmodern did not strike authors and audiences as either interesting or suitable anymore. There were, of course, exceptions. But, by and large, ever-accelerating, mandatorily ironic, self-reflexively ingrown, and repetitious intertextuality was unsustainable, nor did it appear to resonate to the world's troubles, and so it wound up making postmodernism look like a style of self-serving disconnect, an artsy site of disjunction between literary craftsmanship and the world. While some of the postmodern classics were, and are, still active and command attention in the United States and elsewhere, postmodernism is no longer the cultural dominant.

Compounding the crisis of the postmodern is the revival of populism as well as the rise of TV reality and news media overall as "show," "production," and ultimately *unreality*. I have argued repeatedly for a historical and political postmodernism, and the notion that postmodernism and poststructuralism have paved the way to Holocaust deniers, Brexitarians, Trumpists, Berlusconians, *i tutti quanti* is such a stretch that I will not bother to refute it here. Still, the ebb of "reality," of what counts as "real" and scientific "fact" in culture and social discourse, and of the very significance of matters such as truth, fact, and evidence has often been blamed on the spread of postmodern and poststructuralist buzzwords and on the deepening of lay audiences' distrust of specialists on the heel of the "deconstruction" of grand narratives such as Marxist teleology, the talking cure, archaic notions of class, gender, and sexuality, an operation the larger critical culture of suspicion is deemed to have carried out or sponsored. No wonder in his preface to the English translation of Ferraris's *Manifesto del nuovo realismo*, Harman concurs with Ferraris, who opines that "postmodern relativism has reached its logical outcome in right-wing populism."[15] Only, "relativism" itself is an unexamined platitude for which the postmoderns are not responsible, nor are they for the populist-rhetoric pandemic devastating polities and public discourse the world over, from the United States to India and Hungary to Brazil.

The cosmodern transition and the onset of the contemporary. In *Cosmodernism* and partially in *Reading for the Planet*, I attended to postmodernism's late-global expansion and "protracted" twilight after the

Cold War.[16] By 2000, the "cosmodern" transition out of the postmodern had basically been over. This is clearer now than it was a decade and a half ago, when I was working on my 2011 book. The year 2000, or 9/11 for that matter, is obviously not the "origin" of the contemporary given the latter's historical genealogy. It may not be the *année charnière*, the "hinge year,"[17] 1989 was or felt like for a while either, but it is definitely a plausible point of what Jérôme David has called, after Michel Foucault, historical "crystallization."[18]

Postmodernism is not "dead," though. Few movements of such magnitude fade away completely. More importantly, as I have pointed out repeatedly, postmillennial writing mines it for techniques and even extends it in some respects. At any rate, the postmodern has meanwhile become, first, a technology and second, a historically fixed category, bookended in the United States by the late 1960s and mid-late 1990s. Postmodern scholarship may even get a boost from this historical stabilization, which may lead to fresh perspectives and new questions altogether. In all likelihood, these would be shaped by the novel cultural paradigm that took hold firmly around the dawn of the new millennium: the contemporary. As this gets better and better individualized, which is happening under our own eyes, the 1990s may turn out to have been not only the passage out of the postmodern but also part of a broader transition, the postmodern itself as a wholly transitional phenomenon. To French critics like Lionel Ruffel, this postmodern is the name of the world cultural entr'acte between the modern and the contemporary;[19] to American scholars such as Mark McGurl and Amy Hungerford, the postmodern has all but lost its distinctiveness, "transitory" as this may have been, and got gobbled up by the "long modernism" designated by the bulging suitcase term "post-45" era.[20]

Where is the discipline of literary history going after postmodernism? It is headed, I think, where the world itself is. Literary-cultural history and our profession generally are doing their best to catch up epistemologically with an increasingly strong planetary ontology, that is, with how the world most known to us—the finite planet—is and presents itself in the twenty-first century. More and more frequented will be, I predict, the lexicon, methodology, and thematics pertaining to material "presentation" or *presencing*, to the coming into presence of the planetary thingness that we have been exploiting, overusing, polluting, discarding, or disregarding during the Anthropocene.

Com-posing "our" contemporary.   Some refer to the past few decades as post-postmodern. The term is ugly but reasonably serviceable even though, to my mind, it overplays the contemporary's dependency on the postmodern; contemporaneity is more than U.S. literary culture's adverse reaction to postmodernity, although it is that too, principally in ontological matters. Other critics talk about the contemporary in terms of genre.[21] To still others, it boils down to hyperglobalization, generalized interconnectivity and "suspension" of the art object in its relational effects,[22] market hegemony, and commodification of aesthetic production. A good many commentators view it as permanence of the transient and as a reign of the chaotic, an aggregate of disjunct and culturally asymmetric temporalities.[23] And a minority thinks that "as far as really important things go, contemporaneity does not exist at all."[24]

In a sense, this is not far from the truth. Much like the "environment," historical "context," or the "present," with which it is related, the contemporary does not *pre*exist as a given background to "action figures," including those who in Tim O'Brien's 1990 novel *The Things They Carried* move things around. In postmillennial U.S. fiction, things themselves do the carrying—they are carriers of contemporaneity. They deliver, give us a contemporary, *our* contemporary, through their acts. Objects con-figure contemporaneity, make it. In this sense also, one is not a contemporary already,[25] but one becomes so as one is finding its, his, or her place in such configurations or is being somehow affected by them. It is in these com-positions, in these ontological collations and juxtapositions, that one becomes con-temporary, both co-temporal or coeval to and meaningfully, culturally-materially associated with other entities nearby or remote by virtue of logics and causalities of various kinds and visibility levels. All these objects are "surfacial"—things are there, do not hide from "us"—and yet, as Ashbery says, we may not be "prepared" for their "juxtapositions."[26] This material "thereness" is object writing, objects themselves writing, hence the prospect, half intriguing, half anxiety-ridden, of both a literature and a criticism without "us," fiction writers and critics.

Contemporaneity and the present.   The contemporary becoming of a flat panoply of actors obviously takes place in time, in the helter-skelter of the present, from which it is nonetheless different. Thus, the contemporary is both untimely and never anachronistic. Very simply speaking, if present, unfolding history is contemporaneity's raw material, contemporaneity is— gives—this present's form. Without relinquishing their dynamic state, objects arrange themselves into com-positions of contemporaneity—into what I have defined as the present's material-culture profile or signature. The aesthetics of this signature, of this object writing, is objectual and derived from flat ontology, from an ontology of democratic and strong presence—from the ontology of a radical "is." The new aesthetics is a dramatization of this ontology, of a world thingness that may be in fact quite weak physically, not to mention politically, but asserts both its strength and fragility powerfully, with a great show of presence. In this respect, the contemporary is also an aesthetic of presence.

I have approached postmillennial American fiction as a venue for object arrangements underpinned by this aesthetics. As a compositionist, I have both reported and speculated on their coming together, shape, and occasionally—inevitably—meaning, even though the distinction between what objects perform and what they mean in these and other compositions is awfully blurry. In *The Dog*, for instance, what scubas are, what they do or fail to do for X and the entire ensemble X participates in, *is* their meaning, and that also applies to the ensemble itself. At the same time, speculations on scuba diving, massage chairs, male pedicure, Emirati skyscrapers, and their associations are not unwarranted, and such marginalia to object compositions are not in short supply in *Flat Aesthetics*.

Futurality and the contemporary as contretemps. "The future," writes Derrida in his "Exergue" to *Of Grammatology*, "can only be presented in the form of an absolute danger." The future, he goes on, "is that which breaks absolutely with constituted normalcy and can only be proclaimed, *presented*, as a sort of monstrosity. For that future world and for that within it which will have put into question the values of sign, word, and writing, for that which guides our future anterior, there is as yet no exergue," he concludes.[27] The post-2000 era is no longer Ulrich Beck's "world risk society," a runaway but manageable modernity ultimately capable of getting a "handle on things." *The future as pure and collective danger* is, as ecocritics have insisted for decades now, the danger of the future itself. This is a futureless future or just another installment of a present—ours—in which, stuck in the second gear of instrumental rationality, "we" are failing, again and again, to make provisions, philosophically, politically, and otherwise, for a time to come other than under the modality of planetarily destructive monstrosity.

This seems to be one conclusion the postmillennial, ongoing proliferation of dystopian, catastrophic, and postapocalyptic genres in American fiction is forcing us to draw. Is flat aesthetics then also calamitous, an aesthetics of the disaster and end of times? The answer would have to take into account that objectual compositions inside this body of work often comprise future-oriented structures of potentiality that challenge various exchange regimes and political-economic and cultural systems. While *Exit West* and *The Dog* paint less hopeful pictures, the darkest scenes in *Zone One* and *Station Eleven* afford visions of futurality by insistently deflecting cultural and political nostalgias. In these novels, or in a novella such as *The Final Solution*, the only narrative treated in *Flat Aesthetics* that is not set in the immediate present or future, the past is critically revisited with an eye to transforming present material setups and mentalities. If the contemporary can be said to be the photo that obtains in the novels' camera obscura as writers develop the negative of the present, then the photo could also be viewed as an object scheme in which sometimes a dim future shows itself as the mysterious object in Michelangelo Antonioni's *Blowup*. Thus, the contemporary is or can be not only "anachronistic" in regard to the present, but also "uchronic" to it, a present-time *contretemps*—in all senses—with the present, as in *10:04*. Contemporary aesthetics' uchronism may help us understand the pronounced speculative dimension of postmillennial fiction.

A Material Aesthetics of Repurposed Techniques. In its thingness, flat aesthetics may lay claim to neo-avant-garde status, although somebody like Lerner may reject the Duchampian connection, as he does in *10:04* and elsewhere. Similitudes do exist, though, with Dadaists' fixation on the trivial and everyday objects and, for the same reason, even with pre-modernist movements such as Parnassianism. Closer to us, while the postmodern is no longer an active paradigm, postmodernism's techniques, formal dominants, and appetite for the lowbrow and popular are also aggressively and characteristically repurposed by postmillennial American writers. In line with the overall materialism of the contemporary, this may explain the robust genre infusion of their output. Detective and science fiction, dystopia, the cross-genre zombie tradition, horror, erotica, the fast-expanding jargons and styles of social media and digital communications such as e-mail and texting inform landmark works by Lerner, Mandel, O'Neill, Foer, Percival Everett, and many others. On the other hand, and also in dialogue with postmodernism, this prose is heavily and sometimes multiply metafictional and autofictional. Flat aesthetics is eminently material, but in such authors, the omnipresent and insistently accentuated thingness of storyworlds does not foreclose metalepsis, self-reflexiveness, essayism, and more generally a material presencing and concretization of form and issues of textuality, a treatment of literariness in its thing-literality that in somebody like Whitehead, Mandel, or Foer is oftentimes superior as effect to the most self-referential moments in the likes of Raymond Federman and Ronald Sukenick.

Things, fiction, politics. Postmillennial fiction intervenes in the disputes around the vexed issues of the "factual," "true," "real," and "significant." At times, it does so directly, in authors such as Eggers and Franzen. More interesting and more widespread is its indirect intervention. Numerous post-2000 fictional narratives respond *qua* fiction to the populist rhetoric of "fake news," "alternative facts," reality TV, and to politics conducted as "show," "production," and scripted pathos. Concomitantly, this corpus reacts to the oftentimes catastrophic realities and truths we are facing today. As mentioned earlier, the assault on what makes an event, data set, or scientific evidence incontrovertibly true, a premise of public reasoning, and by the same token a basic social glue predates recent political deployments of this rhetoric. The latter's cognitive and ontological toxicity, its ability to chip away at our intellectual resistance to the onslaught of simulated and fabricated realities, its capacity to erode our sense of what counts as actual, of what *is*, have been a commonplace of media critique and a charge routinely brought against postmodern art and culture since the 1970s.

Whether they are inevitable or not in a hypermediated spectacle society whose most visible cultural logic was arguably postmodern up until the 1990s, the depletion of reality and, bound up with it, the weakening of our collective will to try and sort the real wheat from the rhetorical chaff, pay attention, and respond rationally have been developments with which American authors have been increasingly wrestling, particularly after the birth of the internet and especially in the twenty-first century. And here is the apparent paradox: in the fiction business, these writers use the very tools of their trade to grapple with the deleterious effects of fictionalization and the related crisis of reality in various *non*fictional, social arenas.

Object assemblages constitute and illuminate political networks, as do Lerner's Hypermart uniforms, octopus, and coffee can. Apparently politically neutral objects both constitute and reveal webs and outcomes of exploitation, pollution, excessive commodification, and injustice. Things are political objects, or, if you will—and given their centrality in things-systems—political *sobjects*. Realistic philosophically, contemporary fictions ply a make-believe flat aesthetics that *de*-fictionalizes the world around us, rendering it palpably and incontestably there—or "here"—and thus urgent, overwhelmingly present. This is why I determine this aesthetic an aesthetic of presence. Quite revealingly in the "post-truth" era of manipulatory relativism and populist demagoguery, this aesthetics rests on things that present themselves, are incontrovertibly "in our face," true and undeniable in their raw existence, be they a historical reality still bearing on our lives today such as slavery or the Holocaust, a scientifically proven fact, an environmental disaster, an everyday occurrence of minuscule proportions, a rock, an artifact, or any other thing we touch, move, think, or somehow handle. Flat aesthetics reawakens us to the imperative reality of things human and nonhuman, sentient and non-sentient.

Notes

Preface and Acknowledgments

1 This is my translation of Alexandru Macedonski's poem, whose original Romanian title is "Rondelul lucrurilor." The work is included in Macedonski's 1927 posthumous book, *Poema rondelurilor*.

2 See Thomas Friedman's book, *The World Is Flat: A Brief History of the Twenty-First Century* (New York: Farrar, Strauss and Giroux, 2006). Friedman uses the flat world as a trope of leveling globalization.

3 Ian Bogost, *Alien Phenomenology, or What It's Like to Be a Thing* (Minneapolis, MN: University of Minnesota Press, 2012), 10, where the author insists that "[t]he philosophical subject . . . must become *everything*, full stop."

4 Bogost, *Alien Phenomenology*, 11.

5 Samuel Alexander differentiates between the "footing" and "eminence" of "existences" in volume 1 of *Space, Time, and Deity*. Levi R. Bryant quotes Alexander's distinction in the epigraph to the introduction to *The Democracy of Objects* (Ann Arbor, MI: Open Humanities Press, 2011), xiii.

6 On objects' famous (or infamous) "withdrawal," see Graham Harman, *Object-Oriented Ontology: A New Theory of Everything* (London, UK: Penguin, 2018). I come back—inevitably if briefly—to this notion in the introduction.

7 Christian Moraru, *Cosmodernism: American Narrative, Late Globalization, and the New Cultural Imaginary* (Ann Arbor, MI: University of Michigan Press, 2011); *Reading for the Planet: Toward a Geomethodology* (Ann Arbor, MI: University of Michigan Press, 2015); Jeffrey R. Di Leo and Christian Moraru, eds. *The Bloomsbury Handbook of World Theory* (New York: Bloomsbury, 2022).

8 Lionel Ruffel, *Brouhaha: Worlds of the Contemporary*, trans. Raymond M. MacKenzie (Minneapolis, MN: University of Minnesota Press, 2018).

9 The phrase in quotation marks alludes to Mark Blackwell's remarkable essay collection *The Secret Life of Things: Animals, Objects, and It-Narratives in Eighteenth-Century England* (Lewisburg, PA: Bucknell University Press).

10 See Karen Barad, *Meeting the Universe Halfway: Quantum Physics and the Entanglements of Matter and Meaning* (Durham, NC: Duke University Press, 2007).

11 "[C]ontemporary philosophers have lost the *great outdoors*, the absolute outside of pre-critical thinkers: that outside which was not relative to us, and which was given as indifferent to its own givenness to be what it is, existing in

itself regardless of whether we are thinking of it or not; that outside which thought could explore with the legitimate feeling of being on foreign territory—of being entirely elsewhere" (Quentin Meillassoux, *After Finitude: An Essay on the Necessity of Contingency*, trans. Ray Brassier, with a preface by Alain Badiou [London, UK: Bloomsbury, 2016], 7).

12 Bogost, *Alien Phenomenology*, 38.

13 See the important essay collection edited by Kiene Brillenburg Wurth, Kári Driscoll, and Jessica Pressman, *Book Presence in a Digital Age* (New York: Bloomsbury, 2019). Worth mentioning here is also Luciana Gattas's chapter "Of Presence and Electronic Literature" from *The Bloomsbury Handbook of Electronic Literature*, ed. Joseph Tabbi, 323–34 (London, UK: Bloomsbury, 2018), and Casey Michael Henry's *New Media and the Transformation of Postmodern American Literature: From Cage to Connection* (London, UK: Bloomsbury, 2019).

14 On "somatism," see Iain Hamilton Grant, *Philosophies of Nature after Schelling* (London, UK: Continuum, 2008), 7, passim.

15 See Timothy Morton, *Hyperobjects: Philosophy and Ecology after the End of the World* (Minneapolis, MN: University of Minnesota Press, 2013).

16 On the aesthetics of the quotidian, see Yuriko Saiko, *Everyday Aesthetics* (Oxford, UK: Oxford University Press, 2007).

INTRODUCTION | The New Aesthetic, the Contemporary, and Compositional Criticism

1 Graham Harman, *Immaterialism: Objects and Social Theory* (Cambridge, UK: Polity, 2017), 7.

2 Harman, *Immaterialism*, 6.

3 Graham Harman, *Art and Objects* (Cambridge, UK: Polity, 2020), 44.

4 "Correlationism," explains Meillasoux, the philosopher the term is associated with, "consists in disqualifying the claim that it is possible to consider the realms of subjectivity and objectivity independently of one another." Correlationism contends, the philosopher quotes from French phenomenologists Philippe Huneman and Estelle Kulich's 1997 *Introduction à la phénoménologie*, that "'the world is only insofar as it appears to me as world, and the self is only self insofar as it is face to face with the world, that for whom the world discloses itself'" (*After Finitude*, 5).

5 The "flat aesthetics" phrase has been in use occasionally and especially in OOO-influenced art theory. For example, in her article "An Aesthetic of Everything Else: Craft and Flat Ontologies," Barbara Wisnoski works off Harman and "flat ontology" to "show how flattened aesthetic frameworks, what I call *flat aesthetics*, recognize the ordinary experience of making [i.e., craft] in relational terms, as part of a dynamic network of agential forces" (*The Modern Journal of Craft* 12, no. 3 [November 2019]: 205). Rhett Russo also uses the

expression in the essay "Architecture, Deep and Cryptic," in *Aesthetics Equals Politics: New Discourses across Art, Architecture, and Philosophy*, ed. Mark Foster Gage (Cambridge, MA: The MIT Press, 2019), 277.

6   Bryant, *The Democracy of Objects*, 19, passim.

7   See, for example, Robert Hermann's tellingly titled book *Präsenztheorie: Möglichkeiten eines neuen Paradigmas anhand dreier Texte der deutschen Gegenwartliteratur (Goetz, Krausser, Herrndorf)* (Baden-Baden, Germany: Egon, 2019).

8   Bryant, *The Democracy of Objects*, 32.

9   Bryant, *The Democracy of Objects*, 86.

10   Bryant, *The Democracy of Objects*, 86.

11   Graham Harman, *Object-Oriented Ontology: A New Theory of Everything* (London, UK: Penguin, 2018), 9, passim.

12   Steven Shaviro, *The Universe of Things: On Speculative Realism* (Minneapolis, MN: University of Minnesota Press, 2014), 55.

13   Harman, *Object-Oriented Ontology*, 72, 83, 85.

14   Bruno Latour, *An Inquiry into Modes of Existence: An Anthropology of the Moderns*, trans. Catherine Porter (Cambridge, MA: Harvard University Press, 2013), 327.

15   Bruno Latour, *Reassembling the Social: An Introduction to Actor-Network-Theory* (Oxford, UK: Oxford University Press), 165.

16   David Cowart, *The Tribe of Pyn: Literary Generations in the Postmodern Period* (Ann Arbor, MI: University of Michigan Press, 2015), 1.

17   Harman, *Art and Objects*, 9. "[B]eholders," Harman asserts confidently, "are needed for art just as carbon is required to form an organic chemical" (*Art and Objects*, 174).

18   Gilles Deleuze and Félix Guattari, *A Thousand Plateaus: Capitalism and Schizophrenia*, trans. and forward by Brian Massumi (Minneapolis, MN: University of Minnesota Press, 1993), 31–2. Intensity is, of course, a pivotal concept in the two thinkers, particularly in Deleuze and especially in Chapter 5, "Asymmetrical Synthesis and the Sensible," of his 1968 *Difference and Repetition* (trans. Paul Patton [London, UK: Bloomsbury, 2014), 293–343.

19   Shaviro, *The Universe of Things*, 67, passim.

20   Harman, *Art and Objects*, 75.

21   On the formal nature of the artistic event, see Alain Badiou, in Alain Badiou with Fabien Tarby, *Philosophy and the Event*, trans. Louise Burchill (Cambridge, UK: Polity, 2013), 68.

22   On the compatibility of "construction" and the recalibration of the critique project, see Mihai Iovănel's essay "Neocritique: Sherlock Holmes Investigates Literature," in *Theory in the "Post" Era: A Vocabulary for the Twenty-First-Century Conceptual Commons*, ed. Alexandru Matei, Christian Moraru, and Andrei Terian (New York: Bloomsbury, 2021), 251–66.

23   Harman, *Art and Objects*, 69.

24 Harman, *Object-Oriented Ontology*, 38. For a convincing critique of
    "withdrawal," see Shaviro, *The Universe of Things*, 30–43.

25 Martin Heidegger, *Sein und Zeit*, Neunzehnte Auflage (Tübingen: Max
    Niemeyer, 2006), 73–5. For one English version of the terms, see Martin
    Heidegger, *Being and Time. A Translation of Sein und Zeit*, trans. Joan
    Stambaugh (Albany, NY: SUNY Press, 1996), 69. Other versions, including
    "ready-to-hand" for *Zuhandenheit* and "present-at-hand" for *Vorhandenheit*,
    are available.

26 Harman, *Art and Objects*, 128.

27 Shaviro, *The Universe of Things*, 50.

28 Shaviro, *The Universe of Things*, 50.

29 Harman, *Object-Oriented Ontology*, 86.

30 Harman, *Object-Oriented Ontology*, 86.

31 Harman, *Art and Objects*, 98.

32 Timothy Morton, "Use the Force," in Gage, *Aesthetics Equals Politics*, 77.

33 Morton, "Use the Force," 77.

34 Here and elsewhere, I use the term "democracy" as Bryant does in *The
    Democracy of Objects*.

35 Bill Brown, "Thing Theory," *Critical Inquiry* 20, no. 1 (Autumn 2001): 4. The
    article became chapter one in Brown's *A Sense of Things: The Object Matter of
    American Literature* (Chicago, IL: The University of Chicago Press, 2003),
    21–50. Also see Stephen R. Yarbrough, *The Levels of Ambience: An
    Introduction to Integrative Rhetoric* (Intermezzo. E-book: http://intermezzo.
    enculturation.net/09-yarbrough.htm, 2018), 29.

36 Bryant, *The Democracy of Objects*, ix.

37 On network as a concept and "tool to help describe something," see Latour,
    Reassembling the Social, 131.

38 Steven Shaviro, *Connected, or What It Means to Live in the Network Society*
    (Minneapolis, MN: University of Minnesota Press, 2003), 5.

39 Shaviro, *The Universe of Things*, 54. "Allure" has been theorized first by
    Graham Harman in *Guerilla Metaphysics: Phenomenology and the Carpentry
    of Things* (Chicago, IL: Open Court, 2005), 142–4.

40 Adam Fure, "Aesthetics Postdigital," in Gage, *Aesthetics Equals Politics*,
    110.

41 Karen Barad, *Meeting the Universe Halfway: Quantum Physics and the
    Entanglements of Matter and Meaning* (Durham, NC: Duke University Press,
    2007), 81, passim.

42 On parataxis, see Harman, *Art and Objects*, 66.

43 Patrick Jagoda's *Network Aesthetics* (Chicago, IL: The University of Chicago
    Press, 2006) is also characteristic of this moment and approach in network
    scholarship.

44 Latour, *Reassembling the Social*, 46.

45 Graham Harman, *Speculative Realism: An Introduction* (Cambridge, UK: Polity, 2018), 43.

46 Harman, *Speculative Realism*, 43.

47 Harman, *Immaterialism*, 8.

48 Harman, *Art and Objects*, 30.

49 Rita Felski, "Context Stinks!" *New Literary History* 42, no. 4 (Autumn 2011): 573.

50 Jane Bennett, "Systems and Things: A Response to Graham Harman and Timothy Morton," *New Literary History* 43, no. 2 (Spring 2012): 232.

51 Harman, *Art and Objects*, 30.

52 Harman, *Immaterialism*, 8.

53 Harman, *Immaterialism*, 8–11.

54 Harman, *Immaterialism*, 7–12.

55 Bruno Latour, "An Attempt at a 'Compositionist Manifesto,'" *New Literary History* 41, no. 3 (Summer 2010): 471–90, especially 475–85.

56 Hans Ulrich Gumbrecht, *Production of Presence: What Meaning Cannot Convey* (Stanford, CA: Stanford University Press, 2004), 79–80.

57 Bill Ashcroft, "Transcultural Presence," in *Presence: Philosophy, History, and Cultural Theory for the Twenty-First Century*, ed. Ranjan Ghosh and Ethan Kleinberg (Ithaca, NY: Cornell University Press, 2013), 122.

58 Ranjan Ghosh, "Epilogue: Presence Continuous," in Gosh and Kleinberg, *Presence: Philosophy, History, and Cultural Theory for the Twenty-First Century*, 194.

59 On the critic as curator, if in a sense different from mine, also see Fredric Jameson, "New Literary History after the End of the New," *New Literary History* 39, no. 3 (Summer 2008), especially 385–7.

60 Bogost, *Alien Phenomenology*, 35, passim.

61 On the "non-coincidence of the present with itself" and a largely poststructuralist take on the present, see Michael North, *What Is the Present?* (Princeton, NJ: Princeton University Press, 2018), 11, passim.

62 Giorgio Agamben, *Potentialities: Collected Essays in Philosophy*, ed. and trans., with an introduction by Daniel Heller-Roazen (Stanford, CA: Stanford University Press, 1999), 179.

63 Manuel DeLanda, *Intensive Science and Virtual Philosophy* (London, UK: Bloomsbury, 2011), 66–7.

64 Morton, "Use the Force," 70. The critic has developed this point previously in the 2012 article "An Object-Oriented Defense of Poetry" published in *New Literary History* 43, no. 2 (Spring 2012): 205–24.

65 A notable intervention in the discussion of such dyads as fleshed out by recent U.S. fiction and film is Josh Toth's *Truth and Metafiction: Plasticity and Renewal in American Narrative* (New York: Bloomsbury, 2021).

66 As Hannah Arendt writes in *The Origins of Totalitarianism*, "the ideal subject of totalitarian rule is not the convinced Nazi or the convinced Communist, but people for whom the distinction between fact and fiction (*i.e.*, the reality of experience) and the distinction between true and false (*i.e.*, the standards of thought) no longer exist" ([New York: Harcourt, 1985], 475).

67 Giorgio Agamben, *The Coming Community*, trans. Michael Hardt (Minneapolis, MN: University of Minnesota Press, 2009), 103.

68 Christian Moraru, *Reading for the Planet*, 88.

69 Emily Apter, "Rethinking Periodization for the 'Now-Time,'" in *Being Contemporary: French Literature, Culture and Politics Today*, ed. Lia Brozgal and Sara Kippur (Liverpool, UK: Liverpool University Press, 2016), 30.

70 Theodore Martin, *Contemporary Drift: Genre, Historicism, and the Problem of the Present* (New York: Columbia University Press, 2017), 2.

71 Cowart, *The Tribe of Pyn*, 1. On the contemporary as historical "moving target," also see Emily Hyde and Sarah Wasserman, "The Contemporary," *Literature Compass* 14, no. 9 (September 2017): 1. Jeffrey J. Williams and Robert Kilpatrick provide a similar survey in "Fiction: The 1980s to the Present," *American Literary Scholarship* (2018): 297–316.

72 Martin Rueff, "La concordance des temps," in *Qu'est-ce que le contemporain? Texts réunis par Lionel Ruffel*, ed. Lionel Ruffel (Nantes, France: Cécile Defaut, 2010), 94.

73 Sebastian M. Hermann, Katja Kanzler, and Stefan Schubert, "Historicization without Periodization: Post-Postmodernism and the Poetics of Politics," 6. https://www.academia.edu/27364209/-Historicization_without_Periodization_Post-Postmodernism_and_the_Poetics_of_Politics [2016] (accessed May 12, 2020).

74 Brian McHale, *The Cambridge Introduction to Postmodernism* (Cambridge, UK: Cambridge University Press, 2016), 62–122.

75 David Blackburn, "'The Horologe of Time': Periodization in History," *PMLA* 127, no. 2 (March 2012): 305.

76 See Wai Chee Dimock, "Historicism, Presentism, Futurism," *PMLA* 132, no. 2 (March 2018): 257–263.

77 Apter, "Rethinking Periodization for the 'Now-Time,'" 32.

78 Eric Hayot, "Against Periodization; or, On Institutional Time," *New Literary History* 42, no. 4 (Autumn 2011): 740.

79 François Hartog, *Regimes of Historicity: Presentism and Experiences of Time*, trans. Saskia Brown (New York: Columbia University Press, 2017), 115.

80 Hartog, *Regimes of Historicity*, 17–18.

81 Hayot, "Against Periodization," 745.

82 Hayot, "Against Periodization," 746, 754.

83 Hayot, "Against Periodization," 746.

84 Hayot, "Against Periodization," 746.

85 Susan Stanford Friedman, *Planetary Modernisms: Provocations on Modernity across Time* (New York, NY: Columbia University Press, 2015), 72.

86 See Jeremy Green, *Late Postmodernism: American Fiction at the Millennium* (New York: Palgrave Macmillan, 2005).

87 Paul K. Saint-Amour, "Perpetual Interwar," in *Postmodern | Postwar—and After: Rethinking American Literature*, ed. Jason Gladstone, Andrew Hoberek, and Daniel Worden (Iowa City, IA: University of Iowa Press, 2016), 166.

88 Hayot, "Against Periodization" 747.

89 Susan Stanford Friedman, "Alternatives to Periodization: Literary History, Modernism, and the 'New' Temporalities," *MLQ* 80, no. 4 (December 2019): 387.

90 Katie Trumpener, "In the Grid: Period and Experience," *PMLA* 127, no. 2 (March 2012): 354.

91 Fredric Jameson, *A Singular Modernity* (London, UK: Verso, 2012), 29.

92 Timothy Morton, *Realist Magic Objects, Ontology, Causality* (Ann Arbor, MI: Open Humanities Press, 2013), 15.

93 Don DeLillo, *Cosmopolis* (New York: Scribner, 2003), 90.

94 Andrei Codrescu, *The Disappearance of the Outside: A Manifesto for Escape*, with a New Preface (St. Paul, MN: Ruminator Books, 2001), 193–207.

95 Timothy Morton, *Humankind: Solidarity with Nonhuman People* (London, UK: Verso, 2019), 37.

96 Shaviro, *The Universe of Things*, 43.

ONE | Language

1 Ben Lerner, *10:04* (New York: Picador, 2014), 4, passim. All references to this novel are to this edition.

2 On words as "toys" and their non-correlationist, non-constructionist "autonomy," see Brian Kim Stefans's excellent book *Word Toys: Poetry and Technics* (Tuscaloosa, AL: University of Alabama Press, 2017).

3 DeLillo, *Cosmopolis*, 5.

4 Don DeLillo, *Point Omega* (New York: Scribner, 2010), 116.

5 Don DeLillo, *The Silence* (New York: Scribner, 2020), 51.

6 Don DeLillo, *Underworld* (New York: Scribner, 1997), 538, 542.

7 Barbara Kingsolver, *The Poisonwood Bible* (New York: HarperCollins, 1998), 487.

8 Joseph Broker, "Involutions of the Word: Lorrie Moore and Jonathan Lethem," in *The Contemporaneity of Modernism: Literature, Media, Culture*, ed. Michael D'Arcy and Mathias Nilges, 113–14 (New York: Routledge, 2016). Broker pursues similar linguistic "involutions" in Lethem's 1999 novel *Motherless Brooklyn* (114–17).

9 Jonathan Lethem, *Girl in Landscape* (New York: Random House, 1998), 31, 62, 64, 67, etc.

10 Jean Kwok, *Girl in Translation* (New York: Riverhead, 2010), 39.

11 David Teh has dealt with "inexchangeable" objects in Jean Baudrillard in "What Is a Sovereign Object? Baudrillard and the Inexchangeable," an article published in *International Journal of Baudrillard Studies* 5, no. 1 (January 2008), https://baudrillardstudies.ubishops.ca/what-is-a-sovereign-object-baudrillard-and-the-inexchangeable/ (accessed December 5, 2020). Focusing primarily on the French thinker's 1983 *Fatal Strategies: Revenge of the Crystal*, Teh discusses how Baudrillard's objects defend their "opaque" sovereignty by defying dematerialization through measurements, appraisals, uses, and exchanges. In Teh's account, Baudrillard's crystal is "an object that refuses to surrender to commensurability, that resists overcoding by the commodity. It spells immobility—physical, economic, social and semiotic. It is a model of refraction and reference leading nowhere, just a play of signification where nothing (no value) remains to be signified other than the subject himself, disappearing in his fascination." By contrast, Lerner's objects and the objectual world of contemporary American fiction generally are neither "indifferent" nor "immobile." They do "resist" explanation, calculation, and commodification, but they do so actively and "energetically" via refractions leading, most meaningfully, to other objects.

12 Ben Lerner, *The Topeka School* (New York: Farrar, Straus and Giroux, 2019), 23. Such debates, in which Adam Gordon excels, are central to the novel.

13 In one of the best readings of Lerner's work, Daniel Katz even writes that "it would be more true to say that the novels themselves are no more than extensions and prostheses of a poetic project which remains, by far, the dominant element, and that these novels very much act in the service of the poetry of Ben Lerner[,] which 'occurs both within and without them" ("'I did not walk here all the way from prose': Ben Lerner's Virtual Poetics," *Textual Practice* 31, no. 2 [2017]: 321).

14 Ben Lerner, *The Hatred of Poetry* (New York: Farrar, Straus and Giroux, 2016), 52. Hereafter, references in the text are to this edition.

15 Ben Lerner, *10:04*, 4, passim.

16 Graham Harman, *Art and Objects*, 123.

17 Bill Brown, "Thing Theory," in *The Bloomsbury Handbook of Literary and Cultural Theory*, Jeffrey R. Di Leo, ed. (New York: Bloomsbury, 2022), 720–1.

18 Focusing primarily on *10:04*, Adam Colman has argued for the "new uses" to which Lerner puts failure. Colman makes his case in *New Uses for Failure: Ben Lerner's 10:04* (New York: Fiction Advocate, 2018). On this subject, also see Alexandra Smith's PhD dissertation "Writing Against the Image: Teju Cole, Ben Lerner, and Aesthetics of Failure" (University of Sydney, 2015).

19 Shaviro, *The Universe of Things*, 53.

20 Lerner, *The Topeka School*, 133.

21 Ben Lerner, "Letter from America: Trump's measures," *Critical Quarterly* 62, no. 2 (July 2020): 7–8. https://onlinelibrary-wiley-com.libproxy.uncg.edu/doi/full/10.1111/criq.12550?sid=worldcat.org (accessed October 19, 2020).

22 Ben Lerner, "A Conversation with Ben Lerner," interview by Catherine Bush, *Brick: A Literary Journal* 91 (Summer 2013): 38.

23 Colman, *New Uses for Failure*, xxvi.

24 Ben Lerner, in "Ben Lerner & Ariana Reines," *Bomb*, October 1, 2014, https://bombmagazine.org/articles/ben-lerner-ariana-reines/ (accessed August 29, 2021).

25 Ben Lerner, *Leaving the Atocha Station* (Minneapolis, MN: Coffee House Press, 2011), 7. Further references in text are to this edition.

26 Ben Lerner, "Damage Control: The Modern Art World's Tyranny of Price," *Harper's Magazine* 327, no. 1963, December 2013, https://harpers.org/archive/2013/12/damage-control/ (accessed December 28, 2021).

27 Katz refers to Lerner's "vignette" in "'I did not walk here all the way from prose'" (321).

28 Katz too tackles *Atocha*'s "about" moments and logic of "aboutness," relating them to Ashbery also ("'I did not walk here all the way from prose,'" [320–1]) and to the use of positive reference and negation thereof in Ashbery and Lerner.

29 Ashbery, "The Experience of Experience: A Conversation with John Ashbery," with A. Poulin, Jr. *Michigan Quarterly Review* 20, no. 3 (Summer 1981), 242–55.

30 Ben Lerner, "The Future Continuous: Ashbery's Lyric Mediacy," *boundary 2* 37, no. 1 (2010): 201–13.

31 Besides Katz's article, other pieces like it, and interviews in which Lerner himself talks about Ashbery, worth mentioning here is scholarship such as Lucy Eleanor Alston's "'Always think of the objects': Ekphrasis as Aesthetics in the Contemporary Novel" (MA thesis, Victoria University of Wellington, New Zealand, 2014, http://researcharchive.vuw. ac.nz/bitstream/handle-/10063/3570/thesis.pdf?sequence=2) [accessed August 3, 2021]) and especially Damiano Schina's "'A Place for the Genuine': Ben Lerner's Poetics of Liminality" (MA thesis, University Ca' Foscari, Venice, Italy, 2018, http://dspace.unive.it/handle/10579/13257 [accessed August 4, 2021]). The latter is a very thorough discussion of Lerner's first two novels, major themes, and relationship to Ashbery and other authors. Schina makes insightful observations on liminality and other issues I raise in this chapter.

32 Ashbery's words are included in "Praise for *Leaving the Atocha Station*" (Lerner, *Leaving the Atocha Station*, 1).

33 Ashbery, "The Experience of Experience," 245.

34 Ashbery, "The Experience of Experience," 251.

35 Lerner, "The Future Continuous," 204, 206.

36 Ashbery, "The Experience of Experience," 248.

37 Ashbery, "The Experience of Experience," 248.

38 "I don't feel like I have any more authority over how to read that line than anyone else," says Lerner about the ending words of his novel ("A Conversation with Ben Lerner," interview by Catherine Bush, 38).

39 Lerner, "The Future Continuous," 210. Lerner repeats the statement in another interview, quoted by Katz in "'I did not walk here all the way from prose'" (329).

40 Lerner, "The Future Continuous," 206.

41 Lerner, "The Future Continuous," 206, 201.

42 Lerner, "The Future Continuous," 202, 210.

43 Lerner, "The Future Continuous," 205–6.

44 Lerner, "The Future Continuous," 206.

45 Lerner, "The Future Continuous," 206.

46 Ben Lerner, "An Interview with Ben Lerner Conducted by Gayle Rogers," *Contemporary Literature* 54, no. 2 (Summer 2013): 226.

47 Lerner, "The Future Continuous," 206.

48 Agamben, *Potentialities*, 179.

49 Ben Lerner, *Angle of Yaw* (Port Townsend, WA: Copper Canyon Press, 2006), 87.

50 Bill Brown, "Thing Theory," 720–1.

51 See Lucien Dällenbach, *The Mirror in the Text*, trans. Jeremy Whiteley with Emma Hughes (Chicago, IL: University of Chicago Press, 1989).

52 Lerner, "An Interview with Ben Lerner Conducted by Gayle Rogers," 230.

53 Lerner, "An Interview with Ben Lerner Conducted by Gayle Rogers," 230.

54 Lerner, "An Interview with Ben Lerner Conducted by Gayle Rogers," 230.

55 Lerner, *Angle of Yaw*, 149.

56 Gumbrecht, *Production of Presence*, 79–80.

57 On poststructuralism, postmodernism, and post-postmodernism in Lerner, see Katz, "'I did not walk here all the way from prose,'" 335.

58 See Allen Grossman, *The Long Schoolroom: Lessons in the Bitter Logic of the Poetic Principle* (Ann Arbor, MI: The University of Michigan Press, 2000), a major source for Lerner's poetry theory.

59 Rebecca L. Walkowitz, *Born Translated: The Contemporary Novel in an Age of World Literature* (New York: Columbia University Press, 2015), 41.

60 On high-school debate and the language issues derived from this cultural and linguistic practice, also see Ben Lerner's essay, "Contest of Words: High School Debate and the Demise of Public Speech," *Harper's Magazine*, October 2012, 60–6.

61 Bogost also insists in *Alien Phenomenology* (52) that language consists of objects, as one of the epigraphs to this part suggests.

62 Lerner, *The Hatred of Poetry*, 49.

63 Lerner, "The Future Continuous," 206.

64 Lerner in "Ben Lerner & Ariana Reines."

65 John Shotter discusses epideixis with reference to Aristotle and L.W. Rosenfield's glosses on the etymology of the term and rhetorical tradition. See Shotter's essay "Creating Real Presences: Displays in Liminal Worlds," in *Rhetorics of Display*, Lawrence J. Prelli, ed. (Columbia, SC: University of South Carolina Press, 2006), 272.

66 Bogost, *Alien Phenomenology*, 81.

67 See Maurice Blanchot, *The Writing of the Disaster*, trans. Ann Smock, new ed. (Lincoln, NE: University of Nebraska Press, 1995).

68 On the "future present of every reading," see Lerner, "The Future Continuous," 213.

69 Lerner, *The Hatred of Poetry*, 72.

70 Lerner, "An Interview with Ben Lerner Conducted by Gayle Rogers," 233.

71 Michael Chabon, "A Conversation with Michael Chabon," in Michael Chabon, *The Final Solution: A Story of Detection*, with Steven Inskeep (New York: HarperCollins, 2005), 5. All references in the text to *The Final Solution* are to the HarperCollins 2005 edition.

72 Mihai Iovănel, "Neocritique: Sherlock Holmes Investigates Literature," 251–66.

73 *The Final Solution*'s indebtedness to Doyle has been analyzed in detail, usually in relation to the Holocaust. I mention here only Robert A. Moss, "Michael Chabon's *Final Solution*: An Appreciation," *The Baker Street Journal* 60, no. 1 (Spring 2010): 54–9, Stef Craps and Gert Buelens, "Traumatic Mirrorings: Holocaust and Colonial Trauma in Michael Chabon's *The Final Solution*," *Criticism* 53 no. 4 (Fall 2011): 569–86, and Anna Richardson, "In Search of the Final Solution: Crime narrative as a paradigm for exploring responses to the Holocaust," *European Journal of English Studies* 14, no. 2 (2010): 159–71.

74 On the meaning-making role played by knowledge about the Holocaust in the reading of *The Final Solution*, see Anna Richardson, "In Search of the Final Solution," especially 161–4.

75 Andrew Buncombe, "Allied forces knew about Holocaust two years before discovery of concentration camps, secret documents reveal. Archive shows Adolf Hitler was indicted for war crimes in 1944," *Independent* April 18, 2017, https://www.independent.co.uk/news/world/world-history/holocaust-allied-forces-knew-before-concentration-camp-discovery-us-uk-soviets-secret-documents-a7688036.html (accessed November 21, 2021).

76 On the "superficial mystery narrative" in *The Final Solution*, see Richardson, "In Search of the Final Solution," 165.

77 Craps and Buelens, "Traumatic Mirrorings," 572.

78 On the instrumentality of rationality and its imperialist expression in *The Final Solution*, also see Craps and Buelens, "Traumatic Mirrorings," mainly 579–81. As the critics point out, "[t]he fact that the Holmes character solves the mystery of the murder and of the missing parrot but does not come even close to unraveling the unspeakable secret shared by the parrot and the boy indicates the impotence of reason in the face of the genocidal mystery of the Holocaust, whose truth eludes even the greatest of detectives" (572). Craps and Buelens's broader objective is a reading of *The Final Solution* that breaks with the "pietist" view of the Holocaust by reinscribing the Nazi genocide into the history of European colonialism.

79 Jonathan Lethem, *The Arrest* (New York: HarperCollins, 2020), 38.

80 On Holmes and beekeeping in Doyle's and post-Doyle Holmes, see, among others, Iovănel, "Neocritique," 258–59.

81 Craps and Buelens, "Traumatic Mirrorings," 579.

82 Craps and Buelens, "Traumatic Mirrorings," 579–80.

83 Arthur Conan Doyle, "His Last Bow," in *His Last Bow: A Reminiscence of Sherlock Holmes* (Mineola, NY: Dover, 2016), 158.

84 What Chabon's readership knows about the Holocaust, as opposed to what *The Final Solution*'s characters, including Holmes, do not know, and some of them will never learn, plays an important role in the novella. On this issue, see Anna Hunter, "Tales from Over There: The Uses and Meanings of Fairy-Tales in Contemporary Holocaust Narrative," *MODERNISM / modernity* 20, no. 1 (2013), primarily 61–4.

85 See, in particular, Bruno Bauer's 1843 famous book *Die Judenfrage*, to which Karl Marx immediately responded in the highly controversial 1844 essay "Zur Judenfrage," which was translated as "On the Jewish Question" and reprinted, either in the original or translated, by itself or alongside other Marx texts, on numerous occasions.

86 Giorgio Agamben, *Homo Sacer: Sovereign Power and Bare Life*, trans. Daniel Heller-Roazen (Stanford, CA: Stanford University Press, 1998), 171.

87 Agamben, *Homo Sacer*, 1.

88 On racial data collections and rising computer technology in Nazi Germany, see Luke Munn, "Machine Readable Race: Constructing Racial Information in the Third Reich," *Open Information Science* 4 (2020): 143–55. https://doi.org/10.1515/opis-2020–0011 (accessed December 2, 2021).

89 On number-assignment and -tattooing, their "dehumanizing" and identity-effacing effect at Auschwitz, and relevant testimonies by Aharon Appelfeld and Primo Levi, see Canales Gustavo Sánchez, "Holocaust Imagery in Michael Chabon's *The Final Solution,*" *Americana: E-journal of American Studies in Hungary* 9, no. 1 (Spring 2013), http://americanaejournal.hu/vol9no1/sanchez-canales (accessed November 4, 2021).

90 Sánchez, "Holocaust Imagery in Michael Chabon's *The Final Solution*."

91 For parallels between the Holocaust and the detective plot revolving around Bruno's disappearance, see Richardson, "In Search of the Final Solution," especially 159–64.

92 Craps and Buelens, "Traumatic Mirrorings," 578.

93 See, for instance, Bogost, *Alien Phenomenology*, 6.

TWO | Display

1 Reinhart Koselleck, *Futures Past: On the Semantics of Historical Time*, trans. and with an introduction by Keith Tribe (New York: Columbia University Press, 2004), 36.

2 Luc Boltanski and Arnaud Esquerre, *Enrichissement: Un critique de la merchandise* (Paris: Gallimard, 2017).

3 Terry Smith in Hans Ulrich Obrist, "Curating as Medium," 118, which is included in Terry Smith, *Talking Contemporary Curating* (New York: Independent Curators International, 2015), 114–38.

4 Jean Baudrillard, "The System of Collection," in *The Cultures of Collecting*, ed. John Elsner, John Roger Cardinal (Cambridge, MA: Harvard University Press, 1994), 7–24.

5 Smith, *Talking Contemporary Curating*, 61–3. On collecting, stories, and storytelling, see Mieke Bal, "Telling Objects: A Narrative Perspective on Collecting," in Elsner and Cardinal, *The Cultures of Collecting*, 97–115.

6 Smith, *Talking Contemporary Curating*, 78.

7 Boris Groys's contention in his interview with Smith in *Talking Contemporary Curating*, 61–3.

8 Groys in Smith, *Talking Contemporary Curating*, 84.

9 Smith, *Talking Contemporary Curating*, 119.

10 In *Crimes of the Future: Theory and Its Global Reproduction* (New York: Bloomsbury, 2014, 37), Jean-Michel Rabaté quotes Douglas Rushkoff on the chaotic "Now," which Rushkoff has tackled in his 2013 book *Present Shock: When Everything Happens Now*. Ruffel's *Brouhaha* is a variation on the "present-as-chaos" theme.

11 Smith, *Talking Contemporary Curating*, 103.

12 Rabaté, *Crimes of the Future*, 37.

13 Smith, *Talking Contemporary Curating*, 103.

14 Smith, *Talking Contemporary Curating*, 241.

15 Jonathan Safran Foer, *Extremely Loud and Incredibly Close* (Boston: Houghton Mifflin, 2005), 154–6.

16 Foer, *Extremely Loud and Incredibly Close*, 17.

17 Nicole Krauss, *Great House* (New York: W. W. Norton, 2010), 287.

18 DeLillo, *Cosmopolis*, 30.

19 Created by Patrick Somerville, the ten-episode HBO Max miniseries *Station Eleven* began to air on December 16, 2021.

20 Emily St. John Mandel, *Station Eleven* (New York: Knopf, 2015), 255. All references to this book are to this edition.

21 Emily St. John Mandel, *The Singer's Gun* (New York: Vintage, 2015), 18.

22 Emily St. John Mandel, *The Glass Hotel* (New York: Knopf, 2020), 47–9, passim.

23 Bogost, *Alien Phenomenology*, 23.

24 Mandel credits the *Star Trek: Voyager* episode and the author of its script, Ronald D. Moore, in the "Acknowledgments" note to *Station Eleven* (335).

25 Marc Augé, *Non-Places: Introduction to an Anthropology of Supermodernity*, trans. John Howe (New York: Verso, 1995), 77.

26 Augé, *Non-Places*, 94, 96.

27 Carmen M. Méndez-García, "Postapocalyptic Curating: Cultural Crises and the Permanence of Art in Emily St. John Mandel's *Station Eleven*," *Studies in the Literary Imagination* 50, no. 1 (Spring 2017): 121, 127, passim.

28 Mark West, "Apocalypse Without Revelation? Shakespeare, Salvagepunk, and Station Eleven," *Open Library of Humanities*, 4, no. 1 (2018): 1–26, https://doi.org/10.16995/olh.235. (accessed September 10, 2021): 1–3.

29 Méndez-García, "Postapocalyptic Curating," 125.

30 Emily St. John Mandel quoted by Angela Lashbrook in "A Love Letter to the Modern World: On Emily St. John Mandel's *Station Eleven*," *Flavorwire*, 18 November 2014, www.flavorwire.com/489116/a-love-letter-to-themodern-world-on-emily-st-john-mandels-station-eleven (accessed September 2, 2021).

31 West, "Apocalypse Without Revelation?" 21.

32 Méndez-García, "Postapocalyptic Curating," 115.

33 Méndez-García, "Postapocalyptic Curating," 115.

34 West, "Apocalypse Without Revelation?" 1.

35 Lashbrook, "A Love Letter to the Modern World."

36 On Shakespeare and the "renewal" imagination in *Station Eleven*, see Matthew Leggatt, "'Another World Just out of Sight': Remembering or Imagining Utopia in Emily St. John Mandel's *Station Eleven*," *Open Library of Humanities*, 4, no. 2 (2018): 11. https://doi.org/10.16995/olh.256 (accessed September 2, 2021).

37 In "Reading Very Well for Our Age: Hyperobject Metadata and Global Warming in Emily St. John Mandel's *Station Eleven*" (*Open Library of Humanities* 4, no. 1 [2018]: 1–27), Martin Paul Eve looks primarily at the novel's "metadata hyperobjects" and how they permit "access to worlds that are out of sight" (5).

38 Xhenet Aliu, *Brass* (New York: Random House, 2018), 157–8. In *Domesticated Wild Things* (Lincoln, NE: University of Nebraska Press, 2013), Aliu's short stories offer a preview of the 2018 novel's material universe.

39 West, "Apocalypse Without Revelation?" 21.

40 Lethem, *The Arrest*, 15. The novel mentions *Station Eleven* (*The Arrest*, 176).

41 Graham Harman, *The Quadruple Object* (Alresford, UK: Zero Books, 2011), 123.

42 Shaviro, *The Universe of Things*, 147.

43 Harman, *The Quadruple Object*, 123.

44 Boltanski and Esquerre, *Enrichissement*, 290.

45 Lashbrook, "A Love Letter to the Modern World."

46 Fabrice Wilmann, *Emily St. John Mandel's* Station Eleven (Cheltenham, Australia: Insight, 2018), 28.

47 Emily St. John Mandel quoted by Lesley Wheeler in "'How to Make a Living without Losing Your Mind': An Interview with Emily St. John Mandel," *Contemporary Women's Writing* 14, no. 1 (March 2020): 1.

48 John Shotter, "Creating Real Presences: Displays in Liminal Worlds," in Prelli, *Rhetorics of Display*," 273–4.

49 On Mandel's utopianism, see Leggatt, "'Another World Just out of Sight,'" and Diletta De Cristofaro, "Critical Temporalities: *Station Eleven* and the Contemporary Post-Apocalyptic Novel," *Open Library of Humanities* 4. 2 (2018): 1–26, https://doi.org/10.16995/olh.206 (accessed September 12, 2021).

50 Wilmann, *Emily St. John Mandel's* Station Eleven, 53.

51 Wilmann, *Emily St. John Mandel's* Station Eleven, 53.

52 "Beauty," writes Pieter Vermeulen in an essay on *Station Eleven*, "emerges when things are weaned from the forms of life that used to organize their production, circulation, and consumption" ("Beauty That Must Die: *Station Eleven*, Climate Change, and the Life of Form," in *Studies in the Novel* 50, no. 1 [Spring 2018]: 18). Chronicling precisely the aftermath of this "weaning" process, the novel bears witness to the rise of beauty rather than to its Keatsian death, as the critic seems to suggest.

53 Wilmann, *Emily St. John Mandel's* Station Eleven, 31.

54 Bogost, Alien Phenomenology, 52.

55 Wilmann, *Emily St. John Mandel's* Station Eleven, 25.

56 Ben Lerner, "Damage Control: The Modern Art World's Tyranny of Price," *Harper's Magazine* vol. 327, no. 1963, December 2013, 17. https://harpers.org/archive/2013/12/damage-control/ (accessed December 28, 2021).

57 Lerner, "Damage Control," 19.

58 Jacqueline O'Dell, "One More Time with Feeling: Repetition, Contingency, and Sincerity in Ben Lerner's *10:04*," *Critique: Studies in Contemporary Fiction*, 60, no. 4 (2019): 448.

59 O'Dell, "One More Time with Feeling," 448.

60 Critics who have been intrigued if not entirely persuaded by *10:04*'s picture of a world potentially outside the sway of monetization include Leonid Blimes ("'An actual present alive with multiple futures': Narrative, Memory and Time in Ben Lerner's *10:04*," *Textual Practice* 34, no. 7 [2020]: 1081–1102), Ben Davies ("The Darkness-within-the-light of Contemporary Fiction: Agamben's Missing Reader and Ben Lerner's *10:04*," *Textual Practice* 34, no. 10 [2020]: 1729–49), and Alison Gibbons ("Metamodernism, the Anthropocene, and the Resurgence of Historicity: Ben Lerner's *10:04* and 'The Utopian Glimmer of Fiction,'" *Critique: Studies in Contemporary Fiction* 62, no. 2 [2021]: 137–51).

61 Lerner, "Damage Control," 22.

62 Revaluation or "transvaluation of all values" (*Umwertung aller Werte*) is a nihilist concept Nietzsche develops throughout his work, beginning with *The Antichrist* and all the way to the posthumous *The Will to Power*.

63 Shaviro, *The Universe of Things*, 53.

64 Lerner, "Damage Control," 21.

65 Lerner, "Damage Control." On Krajewska's Institute, see, among other similar places, Elka Krajewska, "Salvage Art Institute," http://salvageartinstitute.org

(accessed January 20, 2022), and Columbia University Graduate School of Architecture, Planning, and Preservation, "No Longer Art. https://www.arch.columbia.edu/exhibitions/14-no-longer-art-salvage-art-institute (accessed January 22, 2020).

66 Fredric Jameson, *The Seeds of Time* (New York: Columbia University Press, 1994), xii. As several critics have pointed out, Jameson misquotes here, as he will again in his 2003 "Future City" article (*New Left Review* 21 [May 2003]: 65–79), a comment made by cultural historian and radical activist H. Bruce Franklin on J. G. Ballard.

67 In "Future City," Jameson writes: "Someone once said that it is easier to imagine the end of the world than to imagine the end of capitalism. We can now revise that and witness the attempt to imagine capitalism by way of imagining the end of the world" (76).

68 See Lerner's considerations in "Damage Control," 15.

69 Agamben, *The Coming Community*, 52. Lerner refers to the Hassidic parable in the novel's epigraph and then credits Agamben in "Acknowledgments" (*10:04*, [244]). In turn, Agamben reproduces the story from Benjamin, who heard it from Gershom Scholem.

70 Donald, Kuspit. *The End of Art* (Cambridge, UK: Cambridge University Press, 2004), 29.

71 Lerner, "Damage Control," 15.

72 Don DeLillo, *White Noise* (New York: Penguin, 1986), 170.

73 Ben Lerner, *The Hatred of Poetry* (New York: Farrar, Straus and Giroux, 2016), 83.

74 Harman, *Immaterialism*, 13.

75 Bogost, *Alien Phenomenology*, 30.

76 Bogost, *Alien Phenomenology*, 30.

77 Benjamin Kunkel, *Indecision* (New York: Random House, 2005), 216, 236, 38.

78 "The generic item that is instant coffee," writes Ben De Bruyn in his excellent essay on climate change and global commodities in *10:04*, "is made newly individual by weather-induced scarcity, and its resultant glow—an unreality effect, if you will—illuminates the many lines of industry converging in this commodity." See De Bruyn's "Realism 4°: Objects, Weather and Infrastructure in Ben Lerner's *10:04*," *Textual Practice* 31, no. 5 (2017): 951–71. In my interpretation, the glow only intensifies the presence—the "reality"—of the object.

79 Lerner, *The Hatred of Poetry*, 83.

80 On postmodern literary and cultural recycling, see my book *Rewriting: Postmodern Narrative and Cultural Critique in the Age of Cloning* (Albany, NY: SUNY Press, 2001).

81 DeLillo, *Point Omega*, 7.

82 On the literature and theory of the planet viewed as a system of vulnerable networks and actors, see especially Wai Chee Dimock, *Weak Planet: Literature*

and Assisted Survival (Chicago, IL: The University of Chicago Press, 2020), 2, passim.

83 Lerner, "Damage Control," 14.

84 Harman, *Art and Objects*, 35.

85 As Schina points out, "The halo and the aura are" in Agamben's *The Coming Community* "Halos" chapter, from which Lerner borrows the Hassidic story, "connected to the realm of possibility, of the possible worlds which function as an alternative to the world we live in now" ("'A Place for the Genuine,'" 105).

86 Ben Lerner, "The Golden Vanity," *The New Yorker* 88, no. 16 (June 11, 2012), https://www.newyorker.com/magazine/2012/06/18/the-golden-vanity (accessed December 23, 2021). Lerner acknowledges this publication also (243).

87 Charles Olson, *Collected Prose*, ed. Donald Allen and Benjamin Friedlander, with an Introduction by Robert Creeley (Berkeley, CA: University of California Press, 1997), 182.

88 Olson, *Collected Prose*, 182.

89 See Jonathan Skinner, "Visceral Ecopoetics in Charles Olson and Michael McClure: Proprioception, Biology, and the Writing Body," in *Ecopoetics: Essays in the Field*, ed. Angela Hume and Gillian Osborne, 65–83 (Iowa City: University of Iowa Press, 2018), especially 65–75.

90 Skinner, "Visceral Ecopoetics in Charles Olson and Michael McClure," 75.

91 Thomas Nagel, "What It Is Like to Be a Bat," *The Philosophical Review* 88, no. 4 (October 1974): 435–50.

92 On this mechanism as a "soul," see Sy Montgomery's marvelous book *The Soul of an Octopus: A Surprising Exploration into the Wonder of Consciousness* (New York: Simon & Schuster, 2016.)

93 Adam Colman, *New Uses for Failure: Ben Lerner's* 10:04 (New York: Fiction Advocate, 2018), 45.

94 I define "network fiction" narratively, basically as systemic complication of classical linearity resulting in spatiotemporally heterogeneous, multilayered, and intersecting subplots. For a cybernetic definition, see David Ciccoricco's *Reading Network Fiction* (Tuscaloosa, AL: The University of Alabama Press, 2007).

95 Rosalind Krauss, "'Specific' Objects," *RES: Anthropology and Aesthetics* 46 (Autumn 2004): 221–4.

96 Graham Harman, *Prince of Networks: Bruno Latour and Metaphysics* (Melbourne, Australia: re.press, 2009), 76.

THREE | Exit

1 Jacques Rancière, *The Politics of Aesthetics: The Distribution of the Sensible*, trans. with an Introduction by Gabriel Rockhill, with an Afterword by Slavoj Žižek (London, UK: Continuum, 2011), 12.

2   Jacques Rancière, *The Lost Thread: The Democracy of Modern Fiction*, trans. Steven Corcoran (London, UK: Bloomsbury, 2017), 74.

3   John Roberts, "Revolutionary Pathos, Negation, and the Suspensive Avant[-] Garde," in *The Idea of the Avant Garde and What It Means Today*, ed. Marc James Léger, 138 (Manchester, UK: Manchester University Press, 2014). Roberts refers to Rancière's books *The Future of the Image* and *The Emancipated Spectator*.

4   Jacques Rancière, *En quel temps vivons-nous? Conversation avec Eric Hazan* (Paris: La Fabrique, 2017), 50.

5   Harman, *Art and Objects*, 130.

6   Rancière, *The Politics of Aesthetics*, 13.

7   Rancière, *En quel temps vivons-nous?*, 51.

8   Rancière, *En quel temps vivons-nous?*, 72–3.

9   Jacques Rancière, "La pensée de la politique aujourd'hui," in *La modernité après le post-moderne*, ed. Henri Meschonnic and Shiguehiko Hasumi (Paris: Maisonneuve and Larose, 2002), 49, 46.

10 Nelly Wolf, *Le Roman de la démocratie* (Saint-Denis, France: Presses Universitaires de Vincennes, 2003), 47.

11 Shaviro, *The Universe of Things*, 87.

12 See, for example, Harman's review of Rancière's work in *Art and Objects*, 130–7.

13 Jane Bennett, *Vibrant Matter: A Political Ecology of Things* (Durham, NC: Duke University Press, 2010), 106.

14 Bennett, *Vibrant Matter*, 106. Bennett posed this question to Rancière at Goldsmith College in 2003. See *Vibrant Matter*, 151 (note 32 of chapter 7).

15 On ontology, topology, and world making, see my book *Reading for the Planet*, especially 91, 102, 105, 114–15.

16 See Henri Lefebvre, *The Production of Space*, trans. Donald Nicholson-Smith (Oxford, UK: Blackwell, 2009), 8.

17 Michael Inwood, *A Heidegger Dictionary* (Malden, MA: Blackwell, 1999), 215.

18 Rancière, *The Politics of Aesthetics*, 13.

19 On the crisis of literary contracts, see Wolf, *Le Roman de la démocratie*, 96.

20 For a discussion of cosmopolitanism and related issues in *Netherland*, see my book *Reading for the Planet*, 168–76.

21 Joseph O'Neill, *The Dog* (New York: Pantheon Books, 2014). All references to O'Neill's novel are to this edition.

22 DeLillo, *Cosmopolis*, 185.

23 On the history and even future of exit signs, see Laura Waddell, *Exit* (New York: Bloomsbury, 2020), especially 31–66.

24 P. D. Eastman, *Go Dog. Go!: P. D. Eastman's Book of Things That Go* (New York: Random House, 1989).

25 Several stories included in O'Neill's 2018 collection *Good Trouble* (New York: Pantheon Books) rehearse *The Dog*'s marital subplots as well as spatial issues such as vicinity.

26 Marc Augé, *La Communauté illusoire* (Paris: Payot and Rivages, 2010), 8.

27 Augé, *La Communauté illusoire*, 7.

28 Mohsin Hamid, *Exit West* (New York: Riverhead, 2017), 73. All references to Hamid's novel are to this edition.

29 Chang-rae Lee, *My Year Abroad* (New York: Riverhead, 2021), 261.

30 Robert D. Kaplan, *The Revenge of Geography: What the Map Tells Us about Coming Conflicts and the Battle Against Fate* (New York: Random House, 2012), xix.

31 I usually capitalize "World Literature" to designate the scholarly discipline and subject matter. Here and elsewhere in my work, the phrase is lowercase when it refers to the world's literature or to literature as a world phenomenon, whether "world" has a special meaning or not. On World Literature, world literature, and related issues, see my essay "Worlding Comparative Literature," in *The Bloomsbury Handbook of World Theory*, ed. Jeffrey R. Di Leo and Christian Moraru, 101–18. On *littérature-monde*, see Michel Le Bris and Jean Rouaud, eds., *Pour une littérature-monde* (Paris: Gallimard, 2007). The book was followed by *Je est un autre. Pour une identité-monde* (Paris: Gallimard, 2010), also edited by Le Bris and Rouaud.

32 Just a few examples of authors and novels illustrating the "re-situating" model: Kazuo Ishiguro, *The Unconsoled* (New York: Knopf, 1995); Brian Chikwava, *Harare North* (London, UK: Random House UK, 2010); Vesna Goldsworthy, *Gorsky* (New York: The Overlook Press, 2015); Salman Rushdie, *Two Years Eight Months and Twenty-Eight Nights* (New York: Random House, 2015); Zadie Smith, *NW* (New York: Penguin, 2012); J. M. Coetzee's "Jesus" trilogy— *The Childhood of Jesus* (New York: Viking, 2013); *The Schooldays of Jesus* (London, UK: Harvill Secker, 2016); and *The Death of Jesus* (London, UK: Harvill Secker, 2019).

33 Mohsin Hamid, *Moth Smoke* (New York: Riverhead 2012).

34 Mohsin Hamid, *The Reluctant Fundamentalist* (New York: Mariner Books, 2008); *How to Get Filthy Rich in Rising Asia* (New York: Riverhead, 2013). All references to the two novels are to these editions.

35 Bertrand Westphal, *La Géocritique. Réel, fiction, espace* (Paris: Minuit, 2007), 65.

36 Mohsin Hamid, *Discontent and Its Civilizations: Dispatches from Lahore, New York, and London* (New York: Riverhead, 2015), 43.

37 Walkowitz, *Born Translated*, 195.

38 Nicolas Bourriaud, *Relational Aesthetics*, trans. Simon Pleasance and Fronza Woods with the participation of Mathieu Copeland (Dijon, France: Les presses du réel, 2002), 43.

39 See Monika Fludernik's article "Second-Person Narrative as a Test Case for Narratology: The Limits of Realism," *Style* 28, no. 3 (Fall 1994): 445–79.

40 Walkowitz, *Born Translated*, 194.

41 Nadeem Aslam, *Maps for Lost Lovers* (New York: Knopf, 2005). All references to the Aslam novel are to this edition.

42 Waddell, *Exit*, 68. One essay that discusses the role of Brexit in *Exit West* is Shazia Sadaf's "'We Are All Migrants through Time': History and Geography in Mohsin Hamid's *Exit West*," *Journal of Postcolonial Writing* 56, no. 5 (2020): 636–47.

43 A number of critics have focused on the door motif in the novel. See, for example, Steve Almquist, "The Doors of Compression: Time, Space, and Global Backlash to Migration in Mohsin Hamid's *Exit West*," *Journal of Postcolonial Studies* 8, no. 2 (2020): 137–53, and Paula Brauer, "'Doors That Could Take You Elsewhere': Migration, Magic and Rancièrian *Dissensus* in Mohsin Hamid's *Exit West*," *Postcolonial Interventions: An Interdisciplinary Journal of Postcolonial Studies* 4, no. 1 (January 2019): 296–316. Ewa Kowal also discusses magical-realist elements of *Exit West* and their relation to the door theme in "Immense Risks: The Migrant Crisis, Magical Realism, and Realist 'Magic' in Mohsin Hamid's Novel *Exit West*," *Polish Journal of English Studies* 6, no. 1 (2020): 22–42.

44 Brauer reminds us in her reading of *Exit West* that "the magical elements' credibility is never questioned within the text." See her essay "'Doors That Could Take You Elsewhere,'" 297.

45 Mohsin Hamid, "Mohsin Hamid on the Dangers of Nostalgia: We Need to Imagine a Brighter Future," *The Guardian*, Saturday 25 February, 2017, https://www.theguardian.com/books/2017/feb/25/mohsin-hamid-danger-nostalgia-brighter-future (accessed March 14, 2022).

46 Waddell, *Exit*, xvii.

47 Waddell, *Exit*, xiii.

48 On objects and their relationships to time and "timescapes," see Kevin K. Birth's *Objects of Time: How Things Shape Temporality* (New York: Palgrave Macmillan, 2012).

49 Hamid, "Mohsin Hamid on the Dangers of Nostalgia."

50 "I was living in Lahore, an ancient city in southwest Asia," Hamid tells Anne Brice, "and I was watching other ancient cities in southwest Asia being consumed by violence and war: Kabul, Baghdad, Damascus, Aleppo. I worried about something like that happening where I lived, being forced to flee. At the same time, I was teleporting through black rectangles on a regular basis, the screens of my phone and computer, on video calls and while watching television and films." See Mohsin Hamid, "*Exit West* Author Mohsin Hamid: 'Migration Is What Our Species Does,'" interview with Anne Brice, *Berkeley News*, September 1, 2020, https://news.berkeley.edu/2020/09/01/on-the-same-page-exit-west-mohsin-hamid/ (accessed March 2, 2022).

51 Georg Simmel, *Simmel on Culture: Selected Writings*, ed. David Frisby and Mike Featherstone (London, UK: Sage, 1997), 173.

52 Simmel, *Simmel on Culture*, 174.

53 Hamid, "*Exit West* Author Mohsin Hamid: 'Migration Is What Our Species Does.'"

54 Kowal, "Immense Risks," 34.

55 Brauer, "'Doors That Could Take You Elsewhere,'" 305, passim.

56 Daniel Kehlmann, *Fame*, trans. Carol Brown Janeway (New York: Random House, 2010). In the Austrian writer's novel, even IT specialists do not trust phones (3) and computers, nor do they really understand how the devices work (5), why they fail, and so forth.

FOUR | Revenant

1 The 2011 science-fiction horror movie *The Thing* directed by Matthijs van Heijningen Jr. is a prequel to the John Carpenter film.

2 Thomas Pynchon, *Inherent Vice* (New York: Penguin, 2009), 132.

3 In Grace Lee's 2007 mockumentary horror movie *American Zombie*, certain characters retain the ability to function in human society.

4 Colson Whitehead, *Zone One* (New York: Random House, 2011). All references to Whitehead's novel are to this edition.

5 Mitchum Huehls makes a few but observant comments on the meaning—or better yet, meaninglessness—of objects in *Zone One* (see his excellent book *After Critique: Twenty-First-Century Fiction in a Neoliberal Age* [Oxford, UK: Oxford University Press, 2016], 27–8; 109–10). Less indebted to the post-critique platform, my political reading of objectuality in Whitehead's novel differs from Huehl's to some extent, as part four's second chapter makes clear.

6 Leif Sorensen refers to Whitehead's *Apex Hides the Hurt* (2006) and *Sag Harbor* (2009) in "Against the Post-Apocalyptic: Narrative Closure in Colson Whitehead's *Zone One*," *Contemporary Literature* 55, no. 3 (2014), 577.

7 In *The Democracy of Objects*, Bryant notes that "Lacan tell[s] us that 'the universe is the flower of rhetoric,' treating the beings that populate the world as an effect of the signifier" (35).

8 Bryant, *The Democracy of Objects*, 133.

9 Bryant, *The Democracy of Objects*, 133.

10 On March 22, 2011, the Dean of Students Office and the Office of Campus Activities and Programs at University of North Carolina, Greensboro, sent out a campus-wide email announcing that "hundreds of students" were expected to play "Humans vs. Zombies, a game of moderated tag," between March 28 and April 3, 2011.

11 Recent African American zombie fiction includes works by Jeff Carroll (*Rasheeda the Zombie Killer* [2016)], V. H. Galloway (*The Un-United States of Z* trilogy [2016]), and P. M. Barnes (the *Zombie Seed* series [2014–16]), to list but a few.

12 Christopher Campbell, "10 Classic Films That Would Be Better With Zombies," http://blog.spout.com/2009/02/04/10-classic-films-that-would-be-better-with-

zombies/ (accessed March 31, 2010). In his turn, Scott Roeben supplies an even funnier list of "classic novels zombified." The list has been posted by Cory Casciato at http://www.inevitablezombieapocalypse.com/2009/03/classic-novels-zombified/ (accessed December 28, 2010).

13 Mark Leyner's alter-ego protagonist casts Arnold Schwarzenegger in classic movies in *Et Tu, Babe* (1992). For a discussion of Leyner's remakes, see my book *Rewriting*, 129–42.

14 Robert Kirk is just one philosopher who has taken the zombie problem seriously. See his book *Zombies and Consciousness* (Oxford: Clarendon Press, 2005). On the zombie metaphor in economics, see Ben Woodard, "Zombie Economy," *Naught Thought*, May 17, 2007, http://naughtthought.wordpress.com/2007/05/17/zombie-economy/ (accessed April 4, 2010). The movie *Fido* also features a company named Zomcom, which controls the zombie outbreak by re-humanizing—that is, basically enslaving—the undead.

15 See Stefan Dziemianowicz's article "Might of the Living Dead: A Ghoulish Genre Gets New Life," *Publishers Weekly*, July 13, 2009: 20–4. "In some sense, every zombie film is a kind of remake," Meghan Sutherland remarks along similar lines in "Rigor/Mortis: The Industrial Life of Style in American Zombie Cinema," *Framework* 48, no. 1 (Spring 2007): 64.

16 Kyle Bishop, "Raising the Dead: Unearthing the Nonliterary Origins of Zombie Cinema," *Journal of Popular Film and Television* 33, no. 4 (Winter 2006): 201.

17 "Although they were once human, zombies have no real connection to humanity aside from their physical form; they are the ultimate foreign Other," Bishop maintains in "Raising the Dead" (201). At the same time, the critic argues that zombies "are in essence a metaphor for humanity itself" (201).

18 In Hamilton's *The Laughing Corpse* (New York: Ace, 1994), Anita Blake runs into a zombie who regains consciousness and language after eating human flesh (257).

19 Elizabeth Kostova, *The Historian* (New York: Little, Brown, and Company, 2005), 88, 144.

20 Zombies are, Sutherland writes in "Rigor/Mortis," "bodies utterly surrendered to their own physicality" (64).

21 Regarding the "body without organs," its structure, and psychosocial role, see the locus classicus in Gilles Deleuze and Félix Guattari's *Anti-Oedipus: Capitalism and Schizophrenia*, translated by Robert Hurley, Mark Seem, and Helen R. Lane with a preface by Michel Foucault (Minneapolis, MN: University of Minnesota Press, 1992), "The Body without Organs" chapter, 9–21. See too Slavoj Žižek, *Organs without Bodies: On Deleuze and Consequences* (New York: Routledge, 2004), especially 133–5, for a discussion of the issue apropos of the zombie problem in popular culture, Lacanian psychoanalysis, and philosophy. D. Harlan Wilson applies the "body without organs" model to zombie corporeality in "Schizosophy of the Medieval Dead: Sam Raimi's *Army of Darkness*," *Journal of Popular Culture* 41, no. 3 (2008), especially 514–15.

22 Slavoj Žižek, *The Metastases of Enjoyment: Six Essays on Women and Causality* (London, UK: Verso, 1994), 122.

23 On surface, depth, and the body without organs' thing-becoming, also see Wilson's "Schizosophy of the Medieval Dead," 514–15.

24 Brown, *A Sense of Things*, 45.

25 Jacques Lacan, *Le Séminaire. Livre VII. L'éthique de la psychanalyse*, texte établi par Jacques-Alain Miller (Paris: Seuil, 1986), 68.

26 Jean Baudrillard, *Fatal Strategies* (Los Angeles: Semiotext(e), 2008), 141.

27 On the cadaver as an example of "absolute" abjection, see Julia Kristeva, *Pouvoirs de l'horreur: Essai sur l'abjection* (Paris: Seuil, 1980), 11.

28 Baudrillard, *Fatal Strategies*, 141.

29 Julia de Funès, *Coup de philo . . . sur les idées reçues* (Paris: Michel Lafon, 2010), 33–5.

30 Baudrillard, *Fatal Strategies*, 141. On Baudrillard and the object's status in Western thought, see Brown, *A Sense of Things*, 179.

31 Jacques Lacan, *Le Désir et son interprétation. Séminaire 1958–1959. Publication hors commerce. Document interne de l'Association freudienne internationale et destiné a son members*. Leçon 3, 26 novembre 1958 (n. p.: n. d.), 29.

32 Kostova, *The Historian*, 90.

33 Lacan, *Le Désir et son interprétation*, 66.

34 Barbara Johnson, *Persons and Things* (Cambridge, MA: Harvard University Press, 2008), 107.

35 See Jerah Johnson, "The Concept of the 'King's Two Bodies' in *Hamlet*," *Shakespeare Quarterly* 18, no. 4 (Fall 1967): 430–4. After briefly surveying the centuries-long controversy surrounding the baffling passage, the critic concludes that "Hamlet's speech was a timely reflection of, and upon," the early modern "Two Bodies theory" of kingship, with which Shakespeare was undoubtedly familiar (433).

36 Brown, *A Sense of Things*, 63.

37 Lacan, *Le Désir et son interpretation*, 370.

38 Jacques Lacan, *Écrits*. A selection translated from the French by Alan Sheridan (New York: W. W. Norton, 1977), 287. Also see Barbara Johnson, *Persons and Things*, 212, 217.

39 Lacan, *Écrits*, 285.

40 Lacan, *Écrits*, 288.

41 Nicole Lapierre glosses on Montaigne's dictum "Nous pensons tousjours ailleurs" ("Our thinking always takes place elsewhere") in *Pensons ailleurs* (Paris: Gallimard, 2006), 11–20.

42 Lacan, *Le Désir et son interpretation*, 249.

43 Joyce Carol Oates, *Zombie* (New York: Dutton, 1995), 169.

44 Peter Dendle, "The Zombie as Barometer of Cultural Anxiety," in Niall Scott, *Monsters and the Monstrous: Myths and Metaphors of Enduring Evil* (Amsterdam: Rodopi, 2007), 48.

45 Brown, *A Sense of Things*, 171.

46 Baudrillard, *Fatal Strategies*, 142.

47 Jacques Derrida, *Specters of Marx: The State of the Debt, the Work of Mourning, and the New International*, translated by Peggy Kamuf with an Introduction by Bernd Magnus and Stephen Cullenberg (New York: Routledge, 1994), 68.

48 Derrida, *Specters of Marx*, 174.

49 On the conscience/conscienceless distinction in relation to the ghost/zombie divide, also see Sarah Juliet Lauro and Karen Embry, "A Zombie Manifesto: The Nonhuman Condition in the Era of Advanced Capitalism," *boundary 2* 35, no. 1 (Spring 2008): 93–6.

50 Derrida, *Specters of Marx*, 176.

51 Nina Auerbach, *Our Vampires, Ourselves* (Chicago, IL: University of Chicago Press, 1995).

52 Derrida, *Specters of Marx*, 176.

53 Kevin Alexander Boon, "Ontological Anxiety Made Flesh: The Zombie in Literature, Film and Culture," in Scott, *Monsters and the Monstrous*, 36. On things, ghosts, and souls, see Barbara M. Benedict, "The Spirit of Things," in Blackwell, *The Secret Life of Things*, 19, passim.

54 Paul Auster, *Sunset Park* (New York: Henry Holt, 2010), 217.

55 See Jacques Lacan's "Sortie de l'ultra-monde" chapter of *Le Séminaire. Livre VIII. Le Transfert*, texte établi par Jacques-Alain Miller (Paris: Seuil, 2001), 153–66.

56 In "Raising the Dead," Bishop holds that the human victim "recognizes" itself in the zombie assailant (203).

57 Johnson, *Persons and Things*, 164.

58 See, for example, Tomislav Z. Longinović, "Vampires Like Us: Gothic Imaginary and 'the Serbs,'" in *Balkan as Metaphor: Between Globalization and Fragmentation*, ed. Dušan I. Bjelić and Obrad Savić, 39–59 (Cambridge, MA: MIT Press, 2002).

59 Lacan, *Écrits*, 291.

60 Jacques Derrida, "Le facteur de la vérité," in *The Post Card: From Socrates to Freud and Beyond*, translated by Alan Bass (Chicago: University of Chicago Press, 1987), especially 480–2.

61 Derrida, *Specters of Marx*, 174.

62 Slavoj Žižek, "Introduction: Robespierre, or, the 'Divine Violence' of Terror," in Maximilien Robespierre, *Virtue and Terror*, introduction by Slavoj Žižek, text selected and annotated by Jean Ducange, translated by John Howe (London, UK: Verso, 2007), vii.

63 Pynchon, *Inherent Vice*, 244.

64 Pynchon, *Inherent Vice*, 334.

65 Pynchon, *Inherent Vice*, 306.

66 Jacques Lacan, *The Seminar. Book VII. The Ethics of Psychoanalysis, 1959–60*, edited by Jacques-Alain Miller, translated with notes by Dennis Porter (London, UK: Routledge, 1992), 55.

67 Lacan, *Le Séminaire. Livre VII*, 68.

68 In "A Zombie Manifesto," Lauro and Embry also talk about "negative dialectics" apropos of zombies. Unlike mine, their use of the concept follows closely Max Horkheimer and Theodor W. Adorno.

69 Lacan, *Écrits*, 53.

70 Lacan, *Le Séminaire. Livre VII*, 69, 68.

71 Lacan, *Le Séminaire. Livre VII*, 68.

72 Robert Kirkman, Tony Moore, and Cliff Rathburn, *The Walking Dead, Vol. 1: Days Gone By* (Berkeley, CA: Image Comics, 2010).

73 Robert Kirkman, Tony Moore, and Cliff Rathburn, *The Walking Dead, Vol. 4: The Heart's Desire* (Berkeley, CA: Image Comics, 2010).

74 On Freud, Lacan, and the dream as rebus, see Lacan, "The Insistence of the Letter in the Unconscious," in David Lodge and Nigel Wood, eds. *Modern Criticism and Theory: A Reader*, 3rd ed. (Harlow, UK: Longman, 2008), 195.

75 Gilbert D. Chaitin, *Rhetoric and Culture in Lacan* (Cambridge, UK: Cambridge University Press, 1996), 6.

76 Martin Heidegger, *Being and Time*: A Translation of *Sein und Zeit*, translated by Joan Stambaugh (Albany, NY: SUNY Press, 1996), 59.

77 Michael Inwood, *A Heidegger Dictionary* (Malden, MA: Blackwell: 1999), 215.

78 On *chose* ("thing") and *cause* ("cause," "reason") in Lacan, see *Écrits*, 151.

79 Inwood, *A Heidegger Dictionary*, 215.

80 Žižek, *Organs Without Bodies*, 136.

81 Bishop, "Raising the Dead," 204. On the zombie as a trope in general and, in particular, as a signifier of "our" anxieties, also see Scott, *Monsters and the Monstrous*, and in it especially Boon, "Ontological Anxiety Made Flesh," and Peter Dendle, "The Zombie as Barometer of Cultural Anxiety."

82 On the "zombies-like-us" theme, see, for instance, Bishop, "Raising the Dead," and Lauro and Embry, "A Zombie Manifesto."

83 Lacan, *Le Désir et son interprétation*, 240.

84 Kristeva, *Pouvoirs de l'horreur*, 180. On the zombie as "boundary-figure," the reader may consult too Lauro and Embry, "A Zombie Manifesto," 90.

85 Deleuze and Guattari, *A Thousand Plateaus*, 249.

86 Žižek, "Fantasy as a Political Category: A Lacanian Approach," in Lodge and Wood, *Modern Criticism and Theory*, 698.

87 Leonard Wilcox, "Don DeLillo's *Underworld* and the Return of the Real," *Contemporary Literature* 43, no. 1 (Spring 2002): 120–37. Wilcox's is the best Lacanian interpretation of DeLillo's novel to date.

88 Chaitin, *Rhetoric and Culture in Lacan*, 67.

89 Boon argues that "cultural zombies" illustrate just one zombie "category" ("Ontological Anxiety Made Flesh," 40).

90 Wilson, "Schizosophy of the Medieval Dead," 523.

91 On oral activity, language, and voraciousness, see Kristeva, *Pouvoirs de l'horreur*, 52.

92 The phallus plays a key signifying role by standing outside the signifying chain ("Le phallus . . . est élément signifiant soustrait à la chaîne de la parole, en tant qu'elle engage tout rapport avec l'autre"). On this account, see Lacan, *Le Désir et son interprétation*, 28. On Lacan, *Hamlet*, and the role of the phallus with respect to the subject's "speaking position," see Stefan Polatinsky and Derek Hook, "On the Ghostly Father: Lacan on Hamlet," *Psychoanalytic Review* 95, no. 3 (June 2008): 370.

93 Jean Baudrillard, *The Intelligence of Evil or the Lucidity Pact*, translated by Chris Turner (Oxford, UK: Berg, 2005), 21, 24.

94 On Afro-pessimism, see the useful overview by Patrice Douglass, Selamawit D. Terrefe, and Frank B. Wilderson, "Afro-Pessimism," *Oxford Bibliographies* 28 August 2018, https://www.oxfordbibliographies.com/view/document/obo-9780190280024/obo-9780190280024–0056.xml (accessed March 2, 2022).

95 On *Zone One* and the critique of postracialism, see, among other similar interventions, Grace Heneks, "The American Subplot: Colson Whitehead's Post-Racial Allegory in *Zone One*," *The Comparatist* 42 (2018): 60–79. In "'The sad aperture of the dead': Colson Whitehead's *Zone One* and the Anti-Blackness of the Book as an Object" (*Textual Practice* 35, no. 12 [2020]: 1957–72, Beth A. McCoy and Jasmine Y. Montgomery contend that the novel's basic plot and zombie theme reference primarily and extensively "slavery's dead," specifically the architecture of New York City's African Burial Ground National Monument (1957).

96 See Colson Whitehead, "Colson Whitehead's Monsters—*Zone One* (Interview)" by Jade Colbert, *The Varsity*, January 30, 2012, https://thevarsity.ca/2012/01/30/colson-whiteheads-monsters-zone-one-interview/ (accessed March 12, 2022).

97 "In some of my books," Whitehead declares in the 2012 *Varsity* interview, "race and ideas about race are a big part of the narrative; sometimes they're not. *Colossus* is just about the city; it's not about the Black city, it's about the city. *Sag Harbor*, while having a 95 percent African-American cast, isn't to me that much about race; it's just about being a teenager and tapping into universal longings and themes of disquiet and universal ideas of invention, identity-making. In [*Zone One*, race] didn't have a place in my idea of the apocalypse. It seemed like if you're in the basement of a pizza parlour and there's 10 thousand living dead above, whether the person you're trapped with is Black, a woman, Canadian, has a very funny southern accent, is not really what you're concentrating on. [What y]ou're concentrating on is 'How are we going to get out of here?'" ("Colson Whitehead's Monsters").

98 For a different take on the novel's watery imagery, see McCoy and Montgomery, "'The sad aperture of the dead,'" 1959, 1962, passim.

99 The 2013 blockbuster movie *World War Z* starring Brad Pitt was made after Max Brooks's 2006 novel *World War Z* (subtitled *An Oral History of the Zombie War*). There is also a 2013 videogame of the same title.

100 Walter Benjamin, "Traumkitsch," in *Gesammelte Schriften*, vol. II, 2, ed. Rolf Tiedemann and Hermann Schweppenhäuser (Frankfurt, Germany: 1991), 620–2. The relevant German sentences are: "Der Traum eröffnet nicht mehr eine blaue Ferne. Er ist grau geworden. Die graue Staubsicht auf den Dingen ist sein bestes Teil" (620).

101 Walter Benjamin, "Dream Kitsch: Gloss on Surrealism," in *The Work of Art in the Age of Its Technological Reproducibility and Other Writings on Media*, edited by Michael W. Jennings, Brigid Doherty, and Thomas Y. Levin, translated by Edmund Jephcott, Rodney Livingstone, Howard Eiland, and others (Cambridge, MA: Harvard University Press, 2008), 236.

102 For an excellent discussion of *Zone One*'s Benjamin epigraph and dust motif along largely different lines, see chapter 4 of Heather J. Hicks's *The Post-Apocalyptic Novel in the Twenty-First Century: Modernity Beyond Salvage* (New York: Palgrave Macmillan, 2016), 105–35. Hicks's analysis, which focuses on kitsch and the sublime, also features cogent comments on the novel's "world of things" (119–24).

103 Sorensen, "Against the Post-Apocalyptic," 590.

104 "A Quiet Storm," Wikipedia, https://en.wikipedia.org/wiki/A_Quiet_Storm (accessed March 2, 2022).

FIVE: Kinship

1 Jonathan Safran Foer, "Foreword," in Bruno Schulz, *The Street of Crocodiles and Other Stories*, trans. Celina Wieniewska, foreword by Jonathan Safran Foer, introduction by David A. Goldfarb (New York: Penguin, 2008), vii–x.

2 VisualEditions, "The making of *Tree of Codes* by Jonathan Safran Foer. Watch the last three months of production in just three minutes," https://www.youtube.com/watch?v=r0GcB0PYKjY (accessed November 29, 2017).

3 "Jonathan Safran Foer: Die Cutting a Novel," https://www.youtube.com/watch?v=WPW6hMlHQNA (accessed November 29, 2017).

4 Jonathan Safran Foer, *Tree of Codes* (London, UK: Visual Editions, 2010), 137–9.

5 Nicole Krauss, *Forest Dark* (New York: HarperCollins, 2017), 107. All references to *Forest Dark* are to this edition.

6 Harold Bloom, "The Breaking of Form," in Harold Bloom, Paul de Man, Jacques Derrida, Geoffrey Hartman, and J. Hillis Miller, *Deconstruction and Criticism* (New York: The Seabury Press, 1979), 14.

7 Christian Moraru, "Worlding Comparative Literature," in *The Bloomsbury Handbook of World Theory*, ed. Jeffrey R. Di Leo and Christian Moraru, 109.

8 Wai Chee Dimock, *Through Other Continents: American Literature across Deep Time* (Princeton, NJ: Princeton University Press, 2008), 3.

9   Dimock, *Through Other Continents*, 144.

10 Jorge Luis Borges, *Selected Non-Fictions*, ed. Eliot Weinberger, trans. Esther Allen, Suzanne Jill Levine, and Eliot Weinberger (New York: Viking, 1999), 357.

11 Blecher has been called "the Romanian Kafka" by numerous writers and critics inside and outside Romania. See, for example, Andrei Codrescu's essay "Max Blecher's Adventures," in Max Blecher, *Adventures in Immediate Reality*, trans. Michael Henry Heim (New York: New Directions, 2015), xi.

12 Dimock, *Through Other Continents*, 144–5.

13 On Kafka's "unknown family" of animals, see Walter Benjamin, *Illuminations: Essays and Reflection*, edited and with an Introduction by Hannah Arendt (New York: Schocken Books, 1985), 132. Foer draws from this place in Benjamin's essay "Franz Kafka: On the Tenth Anniversary of His Death" in *Eating Animals* (New York: Little, Brown and Company, 2009), 36–7.

14 Henry Sussman, *Idylls of the Wanderer: Outside in Literature and Theory* (New York: Fordham University Press, 2007), 162.

15 On this subject, also see Ian Thomas Fleishman, "The Rustle of the Anthropocene: Kafka's Odradek as Ecocritical Icon," in *The Germanic Review* 92, no. 1 (January–March 2017), 44. In his essay, Fleishman critiques ecocriticism and new materialist interpretations by Timothy Morton, Jane Bennett, and J. Hillis Miller. Also see Bennett's comments on Odradek in *Vibrant Matter*, 6–8, 10, 20.

16 See Jerzy Ficowski, *Regions of Great Heresy—Bruno Schulz: A Biographical Portrait*, translated and edited by Theodosia Robertson (New York: W. W. Norton, 2003).

17 Foer, "Foreword," viii.

18 Schulz, *The Street of Crocodiles and Other Stories*, 116.

19 Foer, "Foreword," viii.

20 Foer, "Foreword," ix.

21 Foer, "Foreword," ix.

22 Foer quotes from a 1904 letter Kafka sent to Oskar Pollack.

23 David A. Goldfarb, "Introduction," in Schulz, *The Street of Crocodiles and Other Stories*, xix.

24 Schulz, *The Street of Crocodiles and Other Stories*, 166.

25 Schulz, *The Street of Crocodiles and Other Stories*, 165–6.

26 Schulz, *The Street of Crocodiles and Other Stories*, 167.

27 On this vitalist energy and "vitalist materialism" in general, see Bennett, *Vibrant Matter*.

28 Schulz, *The Street of Crocodiles and Other Stories*, 167.

29 Efthymia Rentzou, "Animal," in *A New Vocabulary for Global Modernism*, ed. Eric Hayot and Rebecca L. Walkowitz (New York: Columbia University Press, 2016), 30.

30 Schulz, *The Street of Crocodiles and Other Stories*, 174.

31 Schulz, *The Street of Crocodiles and Other Stories*, 31; Foer, *Tree of Codes*, 49–50.

32 Ulrich Beck formulated his critique of "methodological nationalism" first in a 2002 article and reformulated it in "Toward a New Critical Theory with a Cosmopolitan Intent," which came out in *Constellations* 10, no. 4 (2003): 453–68.

33 Codrescu, "Max Blecher's Adventures," x.

34 Schulz, *The Street of Crocodiles and Other Stories*, 230.

35 Schulz, *The Street of Crocodiles and Other Stories*, 67; Foer, *Tree of Codes*, 92.

36 Codrescu refers to Blecher's "hyperrealism" in "Max Blecher's Adventures," x.

37 Blecher, *Adventures in Immediate Reality*, 8–9.

38 Blecher, *Adventures in Immediate Reality*, 9.

39 Blecher, *Adventures in Immediate Reality*, 9.

40 On Blecher's "body without organs," see Cezar Gheorghe's article "Max Blecher's Body without Organs," http://www.romanianliteraturenow.com/uncategorized-ro/download-and-watch-movie-john-wick-chapter-2–2017/ (accessed June 17, 2018).

41 Blecher, *Adventures in Immediate Reality*, 77.

42 Max Blecher, *Scarred Hearts*, translated by Henry Howard with an Introduction by Paul Bailey (London, UK: Old Street, 2008), 194.

43 Blecher, *Scarred Hearts*, 130.

44 Blecher, *Adventures in Immediate Reality*, 85.

45 Schulz, *The Street of Crocodiles and Other Stories*, 42.

46 Max Brod, *Franz Kafka: A Biography*, translated by G. Humphreys Roberts and Richard Winston (New York: Schocken Books, 1975), 74. Foer responds to this scene in Brod's biography in *Eating Animals*, especially 36–41.

47 Jonathan Safran Foer, *Extremely Loud and Incredibly Close* (Boston: Houghton Mifflin, 2005), 17.

48 Franz Kafka, *Parables and Paradoxes*, in German and English (New York: Schocken Books, 1976), 40–5. On Kierkegaard, Kafka, and the time-honored tradition of interpreting the Akedah story in all Abrahamic religions and philosophies, see Bradley Beach and Matthew T. Powell, eds., *Interpreting Abraham: Journeys to Moriah* (Minneapolis, MN: Fortress Press, 2014).

49 Jacques Derrida, *The Gift of Death* (Second Edition) and *Literature in Secret*, trans. David Wills (Chicago, IL: The University of Chicago Press, 2008), 71.

50 Krauss calls Kafka a "crazy uncle" in a recent interview. See Nicole Krauss, "Nicole Krauss on *Forest Dark*," Shakespeare and Company Bookshop interview, YouTube, June 28, 2018, https://www.youtube.com/watch?v=-VzQvNI0tzM (accessed March 27, 2022).

51 Epstein's missing and possibly stolen overcoat is a reference to Nikolai Gogol's classical 1842 short story "The Overcoat."

52 "[T]hinking in ways not permitted by Western metaphysics," Kabbalah pictures God "at once [as] *Ein-Sof* and *ayin*, total presence and total absence," writes Harold Bloom in *Kabbalah and Criticism* (New York: The Seabury Press, 1975), 53.

53 "The Kabbalistic concept of Gilgul," Krauss explains in an interview, "means reincarnation, also transformation. In Hebrew, it comes from the idea of a cycle or a wheel—the transmigration of the soul going round. I knew about Kafka's translation of *The Metamorphosis* into Hebrew and Yiddish as *Der Gilgul* and thought it was interesting that the Jewish reading of that story related about the soul. In the English translation we think about it as obviously physical but the Jewish reading of it is more or equally metaphysical. It made sense that the rabbi's school Epstein visits is called Gilgul. At some point, I wanted to call the novel *The Gilgul* but my American publisher argued me into the ground with that, saying you can't call an American novel by a Hebrew word." See Nicole Krauss, "Interview: Nicole Krauss," with Anne Joseph, *The Jewish Chronicle*, September 7, 2017, https://www.thejc.com/culture/features/nicole-krauss-it-s-limiting-to-describe-myself-as-a-jewish-writer-1.443952 (accessed March 2, 2022).

54 Eva Hoffe, daughter of Esther Hoffe, Max Brod's former secretary, was still, Nicole suggests, holding onto Kafka's manuscripts at the time of the novel's writing (172). Hoffe was ordered by an Israeli court in 2015 to hand them over to the National Library, and the Jerusalem establishment began to take possession of the precious archive in late 2016. See Hilo Glazer, "A Final Note From Kafka, a Trove of Manuscripts, and a Trial That Left an Israeli Heiress 'Destitute,'" *Haaretz*, April 24, 2018. https://www.haaretz.com/israel-news/. premium.MAGAZINE-a-note-from-kafka-a-trial-and-a-destitute-heiress-1.5436733 (accessed April 28, 2022).

55 Franz Kafka, "Das Paradies"/"Paradise," in *Parables and Paradoxes*, 28–9. Krauss's English version differs slightly from the Schocken edition, where the German *dauernd* is translated as "continuously " (29), closer to its actual meaning.

CONCLUSION | Composing the Contemporary

1 Bruno Latour, "Why Has Critique Run out of Steam? From Matters of Fact to Matters of Concern," *Critical Inquiry* 30 (Winter 2004): 225–48.

2 See Emmanuel Alloa and Élie During, eds., *Choses en Soi: Métaphysique du réalisme* (Paris: Presses Universitaires de France, 2018).

3 See Hans Ulrich Gumbrecht, *Production of Presence* and *Our Broad Present: Time and Contemporary Culture* (New York: Columbia University Press, 2014); Hermann's *Präsenztheorie*; and Armen Avanessian and Anke Hennig, *Present Tense: A Poetics* (London, UK: Bloomsbury, 2015).

4 See Eelco Runia, "Presence," *History and Theory* 45, no. 1 (February 2006): 1–29.

5 Robin van den Akker, Alison Gibbons, and Timotheus Vermeulen, eds., *Metamodernism: Historicity, Affect, and Depth after Postmodernism* (Lanham, MD: Rowman and Littlefield, 2017).

6 See, for example, Alexandru Matei, "Post-Aesthetics: Literature, Ontology, and Criticism as Diplomacy," in *Theory in the "Post" Era*, ed. Matei, Moraru, and Terian, 55–71; the entire issue of *Metacritic* 7, no. 1 (July 2021); and also *Post/h/um* 5, no. 1 (2019).

7 See Diana Taylor, *¡Presente! The Politics of Presence* (Durham, NC: Duke University Press, 2020), especially on the need to "come into presence" (19–23).

8 Jean Starobinski, *Jean-Jacques Rousseau. La transparence et l'obstacle* (Paris: Plon, 1957). The book was translated into English by Arthur Goldhammer as *Jean-Jacques Rousseau: Transparency and Obstruction* (Chicago, IL: University of Chicago Press, 1988).

9 Brian McHale, *Postmodernist Fiction* (New York: Methuen, 1987) 11.

10 See T. V. Reed, *The Bloomsbury Introduction to Postmodern Realist Fiction* (London, UK: Bloomsbury, 2021).

11 Matt Mullins, *Postmodernism in Pieces: Materializing the Social in U.S. Fiction* (New York: Oxford University Press, 2016). "Flattening Nature and Culture" (65) is the title of the third chapter of Mullins's book, but *Postmodernism in Pieces* as a whole is indebted to "triple o." So is Huehls's *After Critique*.

12 On postmodern reprise, see my book *Memorious Discourse: Reprise and Representation in Postmodernism* (Teaneck, NJ: Fairleigh Dickinson University Press, 2005).

13 David Foster Wallace, "Tri-Stan: I Sold Sissee Nar to Ecko," in *After Yesterday's Crash: The Avant-Pop Anthology*, ed. Larry McCaffery, 232 (New York: Penguin, 1995).

14 For an extensive discussion of "recursivity" in *Infinite Jest*, see N. Katherine Hayles, "The Illusion of Autonomy and the Fact of Recursivity: Virtual Ecologies, Entertainment, and *Infinite Jest*," *New Literary History* 30, no. 3 (Summer 1999): 675–97.

15 Maurizio Ferraris, *Manifesto of New Realism*, trans. Sarah De Sanctis, foreword by Graham Herman (Albany, NY: SUNY Press, 2014), x.

16 Moraru, *Cosmodernism*, 11.

17 Moraru, *Cosmodernism*, 36, where I credit Jean-Pierre Warner for the phrase.

18 Jérôme David, *Spectres de Goethe: Les métamorphoses de la "littérature mondiale"* (Paris: Les Prairies Ordinaires, 2011), 17.

19 Lionel Ruffel, "Introduction: Qu'est-ce que le contemporain?," in Ruffel, *Qu'est-ce que le contemporain?*, 30.

20 Amy Hungerford, "On the Period Formerly Known as Contemporary," *American Literary History* 20, nos. 1–2 (Spring–Summer 2008): 410. Hungerford mentions McGurl's work on the "program era."

246 NOTES

21 Martin, *Contemporary Drift*.

22 Nathalie Heinich, *Le paradigm de l'art contemporain. Structure d'une revolution artistique* (Paris: Gallimard, 2014), 89–92. Heinich's approach to art objects and the relations in which they are involved revisits Bourriaud's *Relational Aesthetics*.

23 Terry Smith, *What Is Contemporary Art?* (Chicago, IL: The University of Chicago Press, 2009), 196–8.

24 Vincent Descombes, "Qu'est-ce qu'être contemporain?," *Le Genre humain* 2, no. 35 (1999), 26.

25 Christian Ruby, *Devenir contemporain? La couleur du temps au prisme de l'art* (Paris: Le Félin, 2007), 25.

26 John Ashbery, "The Experience of Experience," 246.

27 Jacques Derrida, *Of Grammatology*, fortieth anniversary ed., trans. Gayatri Chakravorty Spivak, introduction by Judith Butler (Baltimore, MD: Johns Hopkins University Press, 2016), 5.

Bibliography

Adams, Rachel. "The Ends of America, the Ends of Postmodernism." *Twentieth-Century Literature* 53, no. 3 (Fall 2007): 248–72.

Agamben, Giorgio. *The Coming Community*. Translated by Michael Hardt. Minneapolis, MN: University of Minnesota Press, 2009.

Agamben, Giorgio. *Homo Sacer: Sovereign Power and Bare Life*. Translated by Daniel Heller-Roazen. Stanford, CA: Stanford University Press, 1998.

Agamben, Giorgio. *Potentialities: Collected Essays in Philosophy*. Edited and translated, with an Introduction by Daniel Heller-Roazen. Stanford, CA: Stanford University Press, 1999.

Aliu, Xhenet. *Brass*. New York: Random House, 2018.

Aliu, Xhenet. *Domesticated Wild Things*. Lincoln, NE: University of Nebraska Press, 2013.

Alloa, Emmanuel, and Élie During, eds. *Choses en Soi: Métaphysique du réalisme*. Paris: Presses Universitaires de France, 2018.

Almquist, Steve. "The Doors of Compression: Time, Space, and Global Backlash to Migration in Mohsin Hamid's *Exit West*." *Journal of Postcolonial Studies* 8, no. 2 (2020): 137–53.

Alston, Lucy Eleanor. "'Always think of the objects': Ekphrasis as Aesthetics in the Contemporary Novel." MA thesis, Victoria University of Wellington, New Zealand, 2014. http://researcharchive.vuw.ac.nz/bitstream/handle/10063/3570/thesis.pdf?sequence=2 (accessed August 3, 2021).

Anderson, Amanda. *The Powers of Distance: Cosmopolitanism and the Cultivation of Detachment*. Princeton, NJ: Princeton University Press, 2001.

Apter, Emily. "Rethinking Periodization for the 'Now-Time.'" In *Being Contemporary: French Literature, Culture and Politics Today*, edited by Lia Brozgal and Sara Kippur, 29–42. Liverpool, UK: Liverpool University Press, 2016.

Arendt, Hannah. *The Origins of Totalitarianism*. New Edition with Added Prefaces. New York: Harcourt, 1985.

Ashbery, John. "The Experience of Experience: A Conversation with John Ashbery." With A. Poulin, Jr. *Michigan Quarterly Review* 20, no. 3 (Summer 1981): 242–55.

Ashcroft, Bill. "Transcultural Presence." In Ghosh and Kleinberg, *Presence: Philosophy, History, and Cultural Theory for the Twenty-First Century*, 122–43.

Aslam, Nadeem. *Maps for Lost Lovers*. New York: Knopf, 2005.

Auerbach, Nina. *Our Vampires, Ourselves*. Chicago, IL: University of Chicago Press, 1995.

Augé, Marc. *La Communauté illusoire*. Paris: Payot and Rivages, 2010.
Augé, Marc. *Non-Places: Introduction to an Anthropology of Supermodernity*. Translated by John Howe. New York: Verso, 1995.
Auster, Paul. *Sunset Park*. New York: Henry Holt, 2010.
Avanessian, Armen, and Anke Hennig. *Present Tense: A Poetics*. London, UK: Bloomsbury, 2015.
Badiou, Alain. *The Century*. Translated, with a commentary and notes, by Alberto Toscano. Cambridge, UK: Polity, 2008.
Badiou, Alain, with Fabien Tarby. *Philosophy and the Event*. Translated by Louise Burchill. Cambridge, UK: Polity, 2013.
Bal, Mieke. "Telling Objects: A Narrative Perspective on Collecting." In Elsner and Cardinal, *The Cultures of Collecting*, 97–115.
Barad, Karen. *Meeting the Universe Halfway: Quantum Physics and the Entanglements of Matter and Meaning*. Durham, NC: Duke University Press, 2007.
Baudrillard, Jean. *Fatal Strategies*. Los Angeles, CA: Semiotext(e), 2008.
Baudrillard, Jean. *The Intelligence of Evil or the Lucidity Pact*. Translated by Chris Turner. Oxford, UK: Berg, 2005.
Baudrillard, Jean. "The System of Collection." In Elsner and Cardinal, *The Cultures of Collecting*, 7–24.
Beach, Bradley, and Matthew T. Powell, eds. *Interpreting Abraham: Journeys to Moriah*. Minneapolis, MN: Fortress Press, 2014.
Beck, Ulrich. "Toward a New Critical Theory with a Cosmopolitan Intent." *Constellations* 10, no. 4 (2003): 453–68.
Benedict, M. Barbara. "The Spirit of Things." In Blackwell, *The Secret Life of Things*, 19–42.
Benjamin, Walter. *Gesammelte Schriften*, Vol. II. Edited by Rolf Tiedemann and Hermann Schweppenhäuser. Frankfurt, Germany: Suhrkamp, 1991.
Benjamin, Walter. *Illuminations: Essays and Reflection*. Edited and with an Introduction by Hannah Arendt. New York: Schocken Books, 1985.
Benjamin, Walter. *The Work of Art in the Age of Its Technological Reproducibility and Other Writings on Media*. Edited by Michael W. Jennings, Brigid Doherty, and Thomas Y. Levin. Translated by Edmund Jephcott, Rodney Livingstone, Howard Eiland, and others. Cambridge, MA: Harvard University Press, 2008.
Bennett, Jane. "Systems and Things: A Response to Graham Harman and Timothy Morton." *New Literary History* 43, no. 2 (Spring 2012): 225–33.
Bennett, Jane. *Vibrant Matter: A Political Ecology of Things*. Durham, NC: Duke University Press, 2010.
Birth, Kevin K. *Objects of Time: How Things Shape Temporality*. New York: Palgrave Macmillan, 2012.
Bishop, Kyle. "Raising the Dead: Unearthing the Nonliterary Origins of Zombie Cinema." *Journal of Popular Film and Television* 33, no. 4 (Winter 2006): 196–205.
Blackburn, David. "'The Horologe of Time': Periodization in History." *PMLA* 127, no. 2 (March 2012): 301–7.
Blackwell, Mark. *The Secret Life of Things: Animals, Objects, and It-Narratives in Eighteenth-Century England*. Lewisburg, PA: Bucknell University Press.

Blanchot, Maurice. *The Writing of the Disaster*. Translated by Ann Smock. New Edition. Lincoln, NE: University of Nebraska Press, 1995.

Blecher, Max. *Adventures in Immediate Reality*. Translated by Michael Henry Heim. New York: New Directions, 2015.

Blecher, Max. *Întâmplări in irealitatea imediată. Inimi cicatrizate. Vizuina luminată. Corp transparent. Corespondenţă*. Edited by Constantin M. Popa and Nicolae Ţone. Preface by Radu G. Ţeposu. Craiova and Bucharest: Aius and Vinea, 1999.

Blecher, Max. *Opere. Întâmplări în irealitatea imediată. Inimi cicatrizate. Vizuina luminată. Proza scurtă. Aforisme. Poezii. Traduceri. Publicistică. Scrisori. Arhivă. Documentar. Mărturii. Iconografie*. Critical edition, introduction, notes, commentary, variants, and chronology by Doris Mironescu. Afterword by Eugen Simion. Bucharest: Academia Română, Fundaţia Naţională pentru Ştiintă şi Artă, Muzeul Naţional al Literaturii Române, 2017.

Blecher, Max. *Scarred Hearts*. Translated by Henry Howard with an Introduction by Paul Bailey. London, UK: Old Street, 2008.

Blimes, Leonid. "'An actual present alive with multiple futures': Narrative, Memory and Time in Ben Lerner's *10:04*." *Textual Practice* 34, no. 7 (2020): 1081–1102.

Bloom, Harold. "The Breaking of Form." In Harold Bloom, Paul de Man, Jacques Derrida, Geoffrey Hartman, and J. Hillis Miller, *Deconstruction and Criticism*. New York: The Seabury Press, 1979. 1–37.

Bloom, Harold. *Kabbalah and Criticism*. New York: The Seabury Press, 1975.

Bogost, Ian. *Alien Phenomenology, or What It's Like to Be a Thing*. Minneapolis, MN: University of Minnesota Press, 2012.

Boltanski, Luc, and Arnaud Esquerre. *Enrichissement: Un critique de la merchandise*. Paris: Gallimard, 2017.

Boon, Kevin Alexander. "Ontological Anxiety Made Flesh: The Zombie in Literature, Film and Culture." In Scott, *Monsters and the Monstrous*, 33–43.

Borges, Jorge Luis. *Selected Non-Fictions*. Edited by Eliot Weinberger. Translated by Esther Allen, Suzanne Jill Levine, and Eliot Weinberger. New York: Viking, 1999.

Bourriaud, Nicolas. *Relational Aesthetics*. Translated by Simon Pleasance and Fronza Woods with the participation of Mathieu Copeland. Dijon, France: Les presses du réel, 2002.

Brauer, Paula. "'Doors That Could Take You Elsewhere': Migration, Magic and Rancièrian *Dissensus* in Mohsin Hamid's *Exit West*." *Postcolonial Interventions: An Interdisciplinary Journal of Postcolonial Studies* 4, no. 1 (January 2019): 296–316.

Brod, Max. *Franz Kafka: A Biography*. Translated from the German by G. Humphreys Roberts and Richard Winston. New York: Schocken Books, 1975.

Broker, Joseph. "Involutions of the Word: Lorrie Moore and Jonathan Lethem." In *The Contemporaneity of Modernism: Literature, Media, Culture*, edited by Michael D'Arcy and Mathias Nilges, 105–18. New York: Routledge, 2016.

Brooks, Lisa. "The Primacy of the Present, the Primacy of Place: Navigating the Spiral of History in the Digital World." *PMLA* 127, no. 2 (March 2012): 308–16.

Brown, Bill. *A Sense of Things: The Object Matter of American Literature*. Chicago, IL: The University of Chicago Press, 2003.

Brown, Bill. "Thing Theory." *Critical Inquiry* 20, no. 1 (Autumn 2001): 1–22.
Brown, Bill. "Thing Theory." In Di Leo, *The Bloomsbury Handbook of Literary and Cultural Theory*, 720–1.
Bryant, Levi R. *The Democracy of Objects*. Ann Arbor, MI: Open Humanities Press, 2011.
Buncombe, Andrew. "Allied forces knew about Holocaust two years before discovery of concentration camps, secret documents reveal. Archive shows Adolf Hitler was indicted for war crimes in 1944." *Independent*, April 18, 2017. https://www.independent.co.uk/news/world/world-history/holocaust-allied-forces-knew-before-concentration-camp-discovery-us-uk-soviets-secret-documents-a7688036.html (accessed November 21, 2021).
Campbell, Christopher. "10 Classic Films That Would Be Better With Zombies." http://blog.spout.com/2009/02/04/10-classic-films-that-would-be-better-with-zombies/ (accessed March 31, 2010).
Chabon, Michael. "A Conversation with Michael Chabon." In Michael Chabon, *The Final Solution: A Story of Detection*. With Steven Inskeep. New York: HarperCollins, 2005. 5–9.
Chabon, Michael. *The Final Solution: A Story of Detection*. New York: HarperCollins, 2005.
Chaitin, Gilbert D. *Rhetoric and Culture in Lacan*. Cambridge, UK: Cambridge University Press, 1996.
Ciccoricco, David. *Reading Network Fiction*. Tuscaloosa, AL: The University of Alabama Press, 2007.
Codrescu, Andrei. *The Disappearance of the Outside: A Manifesto for Escape*. With a New Preface. St. Paul, MN: Ruminator Books, 2001.
Codrescu, Andrei. "Max Blecher's Adventures." In Max Blecher, *Adventures in Immediate Reality*. Translated by Michael Henry Heim. New York: New Directions, 2015. ix–xvi.
Cohen, Joshua. *Book of Numbers*. New York: Random House, 2016.
Colman, Adam. *New Uses for Failure: Ben Lerner's* 10:04. New York: Fiction Advocate, 2018.
Columbia University Graduate School of Architecture, Planning, and Preservation. "No Longer Art. https://www.arch.columbia.edu/exhibitions/14-no-longer-art-salvage-art-institute (accessed January 22, 2020).
Cowart, David. *The Tribe of Pyn: Literary Generations in the Postmodern Period*. Ann Arbor, MI: University of Michigan Press, 2015.
Craps, Stef, and Gert Buelens. "Traumatic Mirrorings: Holocaust and Colonial Trauma in Michael Chabon's *The Final Solution*." *Criticism* 53, no. 4 (Fall 2011): 569–86.
David, Jérôme. *Spectres de Goethe: Les métamorphoses de la "littérature mondiale*." Paris: Les Prairies Ordinaires, 2011.
Davies, Ben. "The Darkness-within-the-light of Contemporary Fiction: Agamben's Missing Reader and Ben Lerner's *10:04*." *Textual Practice* 34, no. 10 (2020): 1729–49.
Dällenbach, Lucien. *The Mirror in the Text*. Translated by Jeremy Whiteley with Emma Hughes. Chicago, IL: University of Chicago Press, 1989.
De Bruyn, Ben. "Realism 4°: Objects, Weather and Infrastructure in Ben Lerner's *10:04*." *Textual Practice*. 31, no. 5 (2017): 951–71.

De Cristofaro, Diletta. "Critical Temporalities: *Station Eleven* and the Contemporary Post-Apocalyptic Novel." *Open Library of Humanities* 4, no. 2 (2018): 1–26. https://doi.org/10.16995/olh.206 (accessed September 12, 2021).

De Funès, Julia. *Coup de philo . . . sur les idées reçues*. Paris: Michel Lafon, 2010.

DeLanda, Manuel. *Intensive Science and Virtual Philosophy*. London, UK: Bloomsbury, 2011.

Deleuze, Gilles. *Difference and Repetition*. Translated by Paul Patton. London, UK: Bloomsbury, 2014.

Deleuze, Gilles, and Félix Guattari. *Anti-Oedipus: Capitalism and Schizophrenia*. Translated by Robert Hurley, Mark Seem, and Helen R. Lane. Preface by Michel Foucault. Minneapolis, MN: University of Minnesota Press, 1992.

Deleuze, Gilles, and Félix Guattari. *A Thousand Plateaus: Capitalism and Schizophrenia*. Translation and Foreword by Brian Massumi. Minneapolis, MN: University of Minnesota Press, 1993.

DeLillo, Don. *Cosmopolis*. New York: Scribner, 2003.

DeLillo, Don. *The Names*. New York: Vintage, 1989.

DeLillo, Don. *Point Omega*. New York: Scribner, 2010.

DeLillo, Don. *Silence*. New York: Scribner, 2020.

DeLillo, Don. *Underworld*. New York: Scribner, 1997.

DeLillo, Don. *White Noise*. New York: Penguin, 1986.

Dendle, Peter. "The Zombie as Barometer of Cultural Anxiety." In Scott, *Monsters and the Monstrous*, 45–57.

Derrida, Jacques. *The Gift of Death* (Second Edition) and *Literature in Secret*. Translated by David Wills. Chicago, IL: The University of Chicago Press, 2008.

Derrida, Jacques. *Of Grammatology*. Fortieth Anniversary Edition. Translated by Gayatri Chakravorty Spivak. Introduction by Judith Butler. Baltimore, MD: Johns Hopkins University Press, 2016.

Derrida, Jacques. *The Post Card: From Socrates to Freud and Beyond*. Translated by Alan Bass. Chicago, IL: University of Chicago Press, 1987.

Derrida, Jacques. *Specters of Marx: The State of the Debt, the Work of Mourning, and the New International*. Translated by Peggy Kamuf. With an Introduction by Bernd Magnus and Stephen Cullenberg. New York: Routledge, 1994.

Descombes, Vincent. "Qu'est-ce qu'être contemporain?" *Le Genre humain* 2, no. 35 (1999): 21–32.

Di Leo, Jeffrey R., ed. *The Bloomsbury Handbook of Literary and Cultural Theory*. London, UK: Bloomsbury, 2019.

Di Leo, Jeffrey R., and Christian Moraru, eds. *The Bloomsbury Handbook of World Theory*. New York: Bloomsbury, 2022.

Dimock, Wai Chee. "Historicism, Presentism, Futurism." *PMLA* 132, no. 2 (March 2018): 257–63.

Dimock, Wai Chee. *Through Other Continents: American Literature Across Deep Time*. Princeton, NJ: Princeton University Press, 2008.

Dimock, Wai Chee. *Weak Planet: Literature and Assisted Survival*. Chicago, IL: The University of Chicago Press, 2020.

Douglass, Patrice, Selamawit D. Terrefe, and Frank B. Wilderson, "Afro-Pessimism." *Oxford Bibliographies*, 28 August 2018. https://www.oxfordbibliographies.com/view/document/obo-9780190280024/obo-9780190280024-0056.xml (accessed March 2, 2022).

Doyle, Arthur Conan. *His Last Bow: A Reminiscence of Sherlock Holmes*. Mineola, NY: Dover, 2016.

Dziemianowicz, Stefan. "Might of the Living Dead: A Ghoulish Genre Gets New Life." *Publishers Weekly*, July 13, 2009, 20–24.

Eastman, P. D. *Go Dog. Go!: P. D. Eastman's Book of Things That Go*. New York: Random House, 1989.

Egan, Jennifer. *A Visit from the Goon Squad*. New York: Anchor Books, 2011.

Elsner, John, and Roger Cardinal. *The Cultures of Collecting*. Cambridge, MA: Harvard University Press, 1994.

Eve, Martin Paul. "Reading Very Well for Our Age: Hyperobject Metadata and Global Warming in Emily St. John Mandel's *Station Eleven*." *Open Library of Humanities* 4, no. 1 (2018): 1–27.

Felski, Rita. "Context Stinks!" *New Literary History* 42, no. 4 (Autumn 2011): 573–91.

Ferraris, Maurizio. *Manifesto of New Realism*. Translate by Sarah De Sanctis, with a Foreword by Graham Herman. Albany, NY: SUNY Press, 2014.

Ficowski, Jerzy. *Regions of Great Heresy—Bruno Schulz: A Biographical Portrait*. Translated and edited by Theodosia Robertson. New York: W. W. Norton, 2003.

Fleishman, Ian Thomas. "The Rustle of the Anthropocene: Kafka's Odradek as Ecocritical Icon." *The Germanic Review* 92, no. 1 (January–March 2017): 40–62.

Fludernik, Monika. "Second-Person Narrative as a Test Case for Narratology: The Limits of Realism." *Style* 28, no. 3 (Fall 1994): 445–79.

Foer, Jonathan Safran. *Eating Animals*. New York: Little, Brown and Company, 2009.

Foer, Jonathan Safran. *Extremely Loud and Incredibly Close*. Boston: Houghton Mifflin, 2005.

Foer, Jonathan Safran. "Foreword." In Schulz, *The Street of Crocodiles and Other Stories*, vii–x.

Foer, Jonathan Safran. *Here I Am*. New York: Farrar, Straus and Giroux, 2016.

Foer, Jonathan. "Jonathan Safran Foer: Die Cutting a Novel." https://www.youtube.com/watch?v=WPW6hMlHQNA (accessed November 29, 2017).

Foer, Jonathan Safran. *Tree of Codes*. London, UK: Visual Editions, 2010.

Friedman, Susan Stanford. "Alternatives to Periodization: Literary History, Modernism, and the 'New' Temporalities." *MLQ* 80, no. 4 (December 2019): 379–402.

Friedman, Susan Stanford. *Planetary Modernisms: Provocations on Modernity Across Time*. New York: Columbia University Press, 2015.

Friedman, Thomas. *The World Is Flat: A Brief History of the Twenty-First Century*. Further Updated and Expanded. New York: Farrar, Strauss and Giroux, 2006.

Fure, Adam. "Aesthetics Postdigital." In Gage, *Aesthetics Equals Politics*, 99–125.

Gage, Mark Foster, ed. *Aesthetics Equals Politics: New Discourses Across Art, Architecture, and Philosophy*. Cambridge, MA: The MIT Press, 2019.

Gattas, Luciana. "Of Presence and Electronic Literature." In *The Bloomsbury Handbook of Electronic Literature*, edited by Joseph Tabbi, 323–34. London, UK: Bloomsbury, 2018.

Gheorghe, Cezar. "Max Blecher's Body without Organs." http://www.romanianliterature- now.com/uncategorized-ro/download-and-watch-movie-john-wick-chapter-2-2017/ (accessed June 17, 2018).

Ghosh, Ranjan. "Epilogue: Presence Continuous." In Ghosh and Kleinberg, *Presence: Philosophy, History, and Cultural Theory for the Twenty-First Century*, 186–98.

Ghosh, Ranjan, and Ethan Kleinberg, eds. *Presence: Philosophy, History, and Cultural Theory for the Twenty-First Century*. Ithaca, NY: Cornell University Press, 2013.

Gibbons, Alison. "Metamodernism, the Anthropocene, and the Resurgence of Historicity: Ben Lerner's *10:04* and 'The Utopian Glimmer of Fiction.'" *Critique: Studies in Contemporary Fiction* 62, no. 2 (2021): 137–51.

Glazer, Hilo. "A Final Note from Kafka, a Trove of Manuscripts, and a Trial that Left an Israeli Heiress 'Destitute.'" *Haaretz*. April 24, 2018. https://www. haaretz.com/israel-news/.premium.MAGAZINE-a-note-from-kafka-a-trial-and-a-destitute-heiress-1.5436733 (accessed April 28, 2022).

Goldfarb, David A. "Introduction." In Schulz, *The Street of Crocodiles and Other Stories*. xi–xxv.

Grant, Iain Hamilton. *Philosophies of Nature after Schelling*. London, UK: Continuum, 2008.

Green, Jeremy. *Late Postmodernism: American Fiction at the Millennium*. New York: Palgrave Macmillan, 2005.

Grossman, Allen. *The Long Schoolroom: Lessons in the Bitter Logic of the Poetic Principle*. Ann Arbor, MI: The University of Michigan Press, 2000.

Groys, Boris. "Exhibitions, Installations, and Nostalgia." In Terry Smith, *Talking Contemporary Curating*, 60–84.

Gumbrecht, Hans Ulrich. *Our Broad Present: Time and Contemporary Culture*. New York: Columbia University Press, 2014.

Gumbrecht, Hans Ulrich. *Production of Presence: What Meaning Cannot Convey*. Stanford, CA: Stanford University Press, 2004.

Hamid, Mohsin. *Discontent and Its Civilizations: Dispatches from Lahore, New York, and London*. New York: Riverhead, 2015.

Hamid, Mohsin. *Exit West*. New York: Riverhead, 2017.

Hamid, Mohsin. "*Exit West* Author Mohsin Hamid: 'Migration Is What Our Species Does.'" Interview by Anne Brice. *Berkeley News*, September 1, 2020. https://news.berkeley.edu/2020/09/01/on-the-same-page-exit-west-mohsin-hamid/ (accessed March 2, 2022).

Hamid, Mohsin. *How to Get Filthy Rich in Rising Asia*. New York: Riverhead, 2013.

Hamid, Mohsin. *Moth Smoke*. New York: Riverhead, 2012.

Hamid, Mohsin. "Mohsin Hamid on the Dangers of Nostalgia: We Need to Imagine a Brighter Future." *The Guardian*, February 25, 2017. https://www. theguardian.com/books/2017/feb/25/mohsin-hamid-danger-nostalgia-brighter-future (accessed March 14, 2022).

Hamid, Mohsin. *The Reluctant Fundamentalist*. New York: Mariner Books, 2008.

Hamilton, Laurell K. *The Laughing Corpse*. New York: Ace, 1994.

Harman, Graham. *Art and Objects*. Cambridge, UK: Polity, 2020.

Harman, Graham. *Guerilla Metaphysics: Phenomenology and the Carpentry of Things*. Chicago, IL: Open Court, 2005.

Harman, Graham. *Immaterialism: Objects and Social Theory*. Cambridge, UK: Polity, 2017.

Harman, Graham. *Object-Oriented Ontology: A New Theory of Everything.* London, UK: Penguin, 2018.

Harman, Graham. *Prince of Networks: Bruno Latour and Metaphysics.* Melbourne, Australia: re.press, 2009.

Harman, Graham. *The Quadruple Object.* Alresford, UK: Zero Books, 2011.

Harman, Graham. *Speculative Realism: An Introduction.* Cambridge, UK: Polity, 2018.

Hartog, François. *Regimes of Historicity: Presentism and Experiences of Time.* Translated by Saskia Brown. New York: Columbia University Press, 2017.

Hayles, N. Katherine. "The Illusion of Autonomy and the Fact of Recursivity: Virtual Ecologies, Entertainment, and *Infinite Jest.*" *New Literary History* 30, no. 3 (Summer 1999): 675–97.

Hayot, Eric. "Against Periodization; or, On Institutional Time." *New Literary History* 42, no. 4 (Autumn 2011): 739–56.

Hayot, Eric. "Literary History after Literary Dominance." *MLQ* 80, no. 4 (December 2019): 479–94.

Heidegger, Martin. *Being and Time*: A Translation of *Sein und Zeit.* Translated by Joan Stambaugh. Albany, NY: SUNY Press, 1996.

Heidegger, Martin. *Sein und Zeit.* Neunzehnte Auflage. Tübingen, Germany: Max Niemeyer, 2006.

Heinich, Nathalie. *Le paradigm de l'art contemporain. Structure d'une revolution artistique.* Paris: Gallimard, 2014.

Heneks, Grace. "The American Subplot: Colson Whitehead's Post-Racial Allegory in *Zone One.*" *The Comparatist* 42 (2018): 60–79.

Hennig, Anke. *Present Tense: A Poetics.* London, UK: Bloomsbury, 2015.

Henry, Casey Michael. *New Media and the Transformation of Postmodern American Literature: From Cage to Connection.* London, UK: Bloomsbury, 2019.

Hermann, Robert. *Präsenztheorie: Möglichkeiten eines neuen Paradigmas anhand dreier Texte der deutschen Gegenwartliteratur (Goetz, Krausser, Herrndorf).* Baden-Baden, Germany: Egon, 2019.

Hermann, Sebastian M., Katja Kanzler, and Stefan Schubert. "Historicization without Periodization: Post-Postmodernism and the Poetics of Politics." https://www.academia.edu/27364209/-Historicization_without_Periodization_Post-Postmodernism_and_the_Poetics_of_Politics [2016] (accessed May 12, 2020).

Hicks, Heather J. *The Post-Apocalyptic Novel in the Twenty-First Century: Modernity Beyond Salvage.* New York: Palgrave Macmillan, 2016.

Huehls, Mitchum. *After Critique: Twenty-First-Century Fiction in a Neoliberal Age.* Oxford, UK: Oxford University Press, 2016.

Hungerford, Amy. "On the Period Formerly Known as Contemporary." *American Literary History* 20, nos. 1–2 (Spring–Summer 2008): 410–19.

Hunter, Anna. "Tales from Over There: The Uses and Meanings of Fairy-Tales in Contemporary Holocaust Narrative." *MODERNISM / modernity* 20, no. 1 (2013): 59–75.

Hyde, Emily, and Sarah Wasserman. "The Contemporary." *Literature Compass* 14, no. 9 (September 2017): 1–19.

Inwood, Michael. *A Heidegger Dictionary.* Malden, MA: Blackwell, 1999.

Iovănel, Mihai. "Neocritique: Sherlock Holmes Investigates Literature." In Matei, Moraru, and Terian, *Theory in the "Post" Era*, 251–66.

Jagoda, Patrick. *Network Aesthetics*. Chicago, IL: The University of Chicago Press, 2006.

Jameson, Fredric. "Future City." *New Left Review* 21 (May 2003): 65–79.

Jameson, Fredric. "New Literary History after the End of the New." *New Literary History* 39, no. 3 (Summer 2008): 375–87.

Jameson, Fredric. *The Seeds of Time*. New York: Columbia University Press, 1994.

Jameson, Fredric. *A Singular Modernity*. London, UK: Verso, 2012.

Johnson, Barbara. *Persons and Things*. Cambridge, MA: Harvard University Press, 2008.

Johnson, Jerah. "The Concept of the 'King's Two Bodies' in *Hamlet*." *Shakespeare Quarterly* 18, no. 4 (Fall 1967): 430–34.

Kafka, Franz. *Parables and Paradoxes*. In German and English. New York: Schocken Books, 1976.

Kaplan, Robert D. *The Revenge of Geography: What the Map Tells Us About Coming Conflicts and the Battle Against Fate*. New York: Random House, 2012.

Katz, Daniel. "'I did not walk here all the way from prose': Ben Lerner's Virtual Poetics." *Textual Practice* 31, no. 2 (2017): 315–37.

Kehlmann, Daniel. *Fame*. Translated from the German by Carol Brown Janeway. New York: Random House, 2010.

King, Daniel. "The Rise of the Comics *Künstlerroman*, or, the Limits of Comics Acceptance: The Depiction of Comics Creators in the Work of Michael Chabon and Emily St. John Mandel." *Open Library of Humanities*, 4, no. 2 (2018): 1–22. https://doi.org/10.16995/olh.246 (accessed September 10, 2021).

Kingsolver, Barbara. *The Poisonwood Bible*. New York: HarperCollins, 1998.

Kirk, Robert. *Zombies and Consciousness*. Oxford, UK: Clarendon Press, 2005.

Kirkman, Robert, Tony Moore, and Cliff Rathburn. *The Walking Dead, Vol. 1: Days Gone By*. Berkeley, CA: Image Comics, 2010.

Kirkman, Robert, Tony Moore, and Cliff Rathburn. *The Walking Dead, Vol. 4: The Heart's Desire*. Berkeley, CA: Image Comics, 2010.

Koselleck, Reinhart. *Futures Past: On the Semantics of Historical Time*. Translated and with an Introduction by Keith Tribe. New York: Columbia University Press, 2004.

Kostova, Elizabeth. *The Historian*. New York: Little, Brown, and Company, 2005.

Kowal, Eva. "Immense Risks: The Migrant Crisis, Magical Realism, and Realist 'Magic' in Mohsin Hamid's Novel *Exit West*." *Polish Journal of English Studies* 6, no. 1 (2020): 22–42.

Krajewska, Elka. "Salvage Art Institute." http://salvageartinstitute.org (accessed January 20, 2022).

Krauss, Nicole. *Forest Dark*. New York: HarperCollins, 2017.

Krauss, Nicole. *Great House*. New York: W. W. Norton, 2010.

Krauss, Nicole. *The History of Love*. New York: W. W. Norton, 2006.

Krauss, Nicole. "Interview: Nicole Krauss." With Anne Joseph. *The Jewish Chronicle*. September 7, 2017. https://www.thejc.com/culture/features/nicole-krauss-it-s-limiting-to-describe-myself-as-a-jewish-writer-1.443952 (accessed March 2, 2022).

Krauss, Nicole. "Nicole Krauss on *Forest Dark*." Shakespeare and Company Bookshop interview. YouTube. June 28, 2018. https://www.youtube.com/watch?v=-VzQvNI0tzM (accessed March 27, 2022).

Krauss, Rosalind. "'Specific' Objects." *RES: Anthropology and Aesthetics* 46 (Autumn 2004): 221–4.

Kristeva, Julia. *Pouvoirs de l'horreur: Essai sur l'abjection*. Paris: Seuil, 1980.

Kunkel, Benjamin. *Indecision*. New York: Random House, 2005.

Kuspit, Donald. *The End of Art*. Cambridge, UK: Cambridge University Press, 2004.

Kwok, Jean. *Girl in Translation*. New York: Riverhead, 2010.

Lacan, Jacques. *Le Désir et son interprétation. Séminaire 1958–1959. Publication hors commerce. Document interne de l'Association freudienne internationale et destiné a son members*. Leçon 3, 26 novembre 1958 (n.p.: n.d.).

Lacan, Jacques, *Écrits*. A selection translated from the French by Alan Sheridan. New York: W. W. Norton, 1977.

Lacan, Jacques. "The Insistence of the Letter in the Unconscious." In Lodge and Wood, *Modern Criticism and Theory*, 186–209.

Lacan, Jacques. *Le Séminaire. Livre VII. L'éthique de la psychanalyse*. Texte établi par Jacques-Alain Miller. Paris: Seuil, 1986.

Lacan, Jacques. *Le Séminaire. Livre VIII. Le Transfert*. Texte établi par Jacques-Alain Miller. Paris: Seuil, 2001.

Lacan, Jacques. *The Seminar. Book VII. The Ethics of Psychoanalysis, 1959–60*. Edited by Jacques-Alain Miller. Translated with notes by Dennis Porter. London, UK: Routledge, 1992.

Lapierre, Nicole. *Pensons ailleurs*. Paris: Gallimard, 2006.

Lashbrook, Angela. "A Love Letter to the Modern World: On Emily St. John Mandel's *Station Eleven*." *Flavorwire*, 18 November 2014. www.flavorwire.com/489116/a-love-letter-to-themodern-world-on-emily-st-john-mandels-station-eleven (accessed September 2, 2021).

Latour, Bruno. "An Attempt at a 'Compositionist Manifesto.'" *New Literary History* 41, no. 3 (Summer 2010): 471–90.

Latour, Bruno. *An Inquiry into Modes of Existence: An Anthropology of the Moderns*. Translated by Catherine Porter. Cambridge, MA: Harvard University Press, 2013.

Latour, Bruno. *Reassembling the Social: An Introduction to Actor-Network-Theory*. Oxford, UK: Oxford University Press, 2005.

Latour, Bruno. "Why Has Critique Run out of Steam? From Matters of Fact to Matters of Concern." *Critical Inquiry* 30 (Winter 2004): 225–48.

Lauro, Sarah Juliet, and Karen Embry. "A Zombie Manifesto: The Nonhuman Condition in the Era of Advanced Capitalism." *boundary 2* 35, no. 1 (Spring 2008): 85–108.

LeClair, Tom. *In the Loop: Don DeLillo and the Systems Novel*. Urbana, IL: University of Illinois Press, 1987.

Lee, Chang-rae. *My Year Abroad*. New York: Riverhead, 2021.

Lefebvre, Henri. *The Production of Space*. Translated by Donald Nicholson-Smith. Oxford, UK: Blackwell, 2009.

Leggatt, Matthew. "'Another World Just out of Sight': Remembering or Imagining Utopia in Emily St. John Mandel's *Station Eleven*." *Open Library of Humanities*, 4, no. 2 (2018): 1–22. https://doi.org/10.16995/olh.256 (accessed September 2, 2021).

Lerner, Ben. *10:04*. New York: Picador, 2014.

Lerner, Ben. *Angle of Yaw*. Port Townsend, WA: Copper Canyon Press, 2006.

Lerner, Ben. "Contest of Words: High School Debate and the Demise of Public Speech." *Harper's Magazine*, October 2012, 60–66.

Lerner, Ben. "A Conversation with Ben Lerner." Interview by Catherine Bush. *Brick: A Literary Journal* 91 (Summer 2013): 32–8.

Lerner, Ben. "Damage Control: The Modern Art World's Tyranny of Price." *Harper's Magazine* 327, no. 1963 (December 2013). https://harpers.org/archive/2013/12/damage-control/ (accessed December 28, 2021).

Lerner, Ben. "The Future Continuous: Ashbery's Lyric Mediacy." *boundary 2* 37, no. 1 (2010): 201–213.

Lerner, Ben. "The Golden Vanity." *The New Yorker* 88, no. 16 (June 11, 2012). https://www.newyorker.com/magazine/2012/06/18/the-golden-vanity (accessed December 23, 2021).

Lerner, Ben. *The Hatred of Poetry*. New York: Farrar, Straus and Giroux, 2016.

Lerner, Ben. "An Interview with Ben Lerner Conducted by Gayle Rogers." *Contemporary Literature* 54, no. 2 (Summer 2013): 218–38.

Lerner, Ben. *Leaving the Atocha Station*. Minneapolis, MN: Coffee House Press, 2011.

Lerner, Ben. "Letter from America: Trump's measures." *Critical Quarterly* 62, no. 2 (July 2020): 7–8. https://onlinelibrary-wiley-com.libproxy.uncg.edu/doi/full/10.1111/criq.12550?sid=worldcat.org (accessed October 19, 2020).

Lerner, Ben. "People say, 'Oh, here's another Brooklyn novel by a guy with glasses.'" *The Guardian*, January 3, 2015. Interview by Emily Witt. https://www.theguardian.com/books/2015/jan/03/ben-lerner-1004-novel-books-interview (accessed May 21, 2018).

Lerner, Ben. *The Topeka School*. New York: Farrar, Straus and Giroux, 2019.

Lerner, Ben, and Ariana Reines. "Ben Lerner & Ariana Reines," *Bomb*. October 1, 2014. https://bombmagazine.org/articles/ben-lerner-ariana-reines/ (accessed August 29, 2021).

Lethem, Jonathan. *The Arrest*. New York: HarperCollins, 2020.

Lethem, Jonathan. *Girl in Landscape*. New York: Random House, 1998.

Lodge, David, and Nigel Wood, eds. *Modern Criticism and Theory: A Reader*, 3rd ed. Harlow, UK: Longman, 2008.

Longinović, Tomislav Z. "Vampires Like Us: Gothic Imaginary and 'the Serbs.'" In *Balkan as Metaphor: Between Globalization and Fragmentation*, edited by Dušan I. Bjelić and Obrad Savić, 39–59. Cambridge, MA: MIT Press, 2002.

Mandel, Emily St. John. *The Glass Hotel*. New York: Knopf, 2020.

Mandel, Emily St. John. "'How to Make a Living without Losing Your Mind': An Interview with Emily St. John Mandel" by Lesley Wheeler. *Contemporary Women's Writing* 14, no. 1 (March 2020): 1–12.

Mandel, Emily St. John. *The Singer's Gun*. New York: Vintage, 2015.

Mandel, Emily St. John. *Station Eleven*. New York: Knopf, 2015.

Martin, Theodore. *Contemporary Drift: Genre, Historicism, and the Problem of the Present*. New York: Columbia University Press, 2017.

Matei, Alexandru. "Post-Aesthetics: Literature, Ontology, and Criticism as Diplomacy." In Matei, Moraru, and Terian, *Theory in the "Post" Era*, 55–71.

Matei, Alexandru, Christian Moraru, and Andrei Terian, eds. *Theory in the "Post" Era: A Vocabulary for the Twenty-First-Century Conceptual Commons*. New York: Bloomsbury, 2021.

McCoy, Beth A., and Jasmine Y. Montgomery. "'The sad aperture of the dead': Colson Whitehead's *Zone One* and the Anti-Blackness of the Book as an Object." *Textual Practice* 35, no. 12 (2020): 1957–72.

McHale, Brian. *The Cambridge Introduction to Postmodernism*. Cambridge, UK: Cambridge University Press, 2016.

McHale, Brian. *Postmodernist Fiction*. New York: Methuen, 1987.

Meillassoux, Quentin. *After Finitude: An Essay on the Necessity of Contingency*. Translated by Ray Brassier. With a Preface by Alain Badiou. London, UK: Bloomsbury, 2016.

Méndez-García, Carmen M. "Postapocalyptic Curating: Cultural Crises and the Permanence of Art in Emily St. John Mandel's *Station Eleven*." *Studies in the Literary Imagination* 50, no. 1 (Spring 2017): 111–30.

Montgomery, Sy. *The Soul of an Octopus: A Surprising Exploration into the Wonder of Consciousness*. New York: Simon & Schuster, 2016.

Moraru, Christian. *Cosmodernism: American Narrative, Late Globalization, and the New Cultural Imaginary*. Ann Arbor, MI: University of Michigan Press, 2011.

Moraru, Christian. *Memorious Discourse: Reprise and Representation in Postmodernism*. Teaneck, NJ: Fairleigh Dickinson University Press, 2005.

Moraru, Christian. *Reading for the Planet: Toward a Geomethodology*. Ann Arbor, MI: University of Michigan Press, 2015.

Moraru, Christian. "Revisionary Strategies." In *American Literature in Transition: 1990- 2000*, edited by Stephen Burn, 199–214. Cambridge, UK: Cambridge University Press, 2018.

Moraru, Christian. *Rewriting: Postmodern Narrative and Cultural Critique in the Age of Cloning*. Albany, NY: SUNY Press, 2001.

Moraru, Christian. "Worlding Comparative Literature." In *The Bloomsbury Handbook of World Theory*, edited by Jeffrey R. Di Leo and Christian Moraru, 101–18. New York: Bloomsbury, 2022.

Morton, Timothy. *Humankind: Solidarity with Nonhuman People*. Lodon, UK: Verso, 2019.

Morton, Timothy. *Hyperobjects: Philosophy and Ecology after the End of the World*. Minneapolis, MN: University of Minnesota Press, 2013.

Morton, Timothy. "An Object-Oriented Defense of Poetry." *New Literary History* 43, no. 2 (Spring 2012): 205–24.

Morton, Timothy. *Realist Magic Objects, Ontology, Causality*. Ann Arbor, MI: Open Humanities Press, 2013.

Morton, Timothy. *Spacecraft*. New York: Bloomsbury, 2022.

Morton, Timothy. "Use the Force." In Gage, *Aesthetics Equals Politics*, 65–79.

Moss, Robert A. "Michael Chabon's *Final Solution*: An Appreciation." *The Baker Street Journal* 60, no. 1 (Spring 2010): 54–9.

Mullins, Matthew. *Postmodernism in Pieces: Materializing the Social in U.S. Fiction*. New York: Oxford University Press, 2016.

Munn, Luke. "Machine Readable Race: Constructing Racial Information in the Third Reich." *Open Information Science* 4 (2020): 143–55. https://doi.org/10.1515/opis-2020-0011 (accessed December 2, 2021).

Nagel, Thomas. "What It Is Like to Be a Bat." *The Philosophical Review* 88, no. 4 (October 1974): 435–50.

North, Michael. *What Is the Present?* Princeton, NJ: Princeton University Press, 2018.

Oates, Joyce Carol. *Zombie*. New York: Dutton, 1995.

Obrist, Hans Ulrich. "Curating as Medium." In Terry Smith, *Talking Contemporary Curating*, 114–38.

O'Dell, Jacqueline. "One More Time with Feeling: Repetition, Contingency, and Sincerity in Ben Lerner's *10:04*." *Critique: Studies in Contemporary Fiction*, 60, no. 4 (2019): 447–61.

Olson, Charles. *Collected Prose*. Edited by Donald Allen and Benjamin Friedlander. With an Introduction by Robert Creeley. Berkeley, CA: University of California Press, 1997.

O'Neill, Joseph. *The Dog*. New York: Pantheon Books, 2014.

O'Neill, Joseph. *Good Trouble: Stories*. New York: Pantheon Books, 2018.

Polatinsky, Stefan, and Derek Hook. "On the Ghostly Father: Lacan on Hamlet." *Psychoanalytic Review* 95, no. 3 (June 2008): 359–85.

Prelli, Lawrence J., ed. *Rhetorics of Display*. Columbia, SC: University of South Carolina Press, 2006.

Pynchon, Thomas, *Inherent Vice*. New York: Penguin, 2009.

Rabaté, Jean-Michel. *Crimes of the Future: Theory and Its Global Reproduction*. New York: Bloomsbury, 2014.

Ramírez, Mari Carmen. "Brokering Identities: Translating Latin America." In Terry Smith, *Talking Contemporary Curating*, 214–47.

Rancière, Jacques. *The Emancipated Spectator*. Translated by Gregory Elliott. London: Verso, 2011.

Rancière, Jacques. *En quel temps vivons-nous? Conversation avec Eric Hazan*. Paris: La Fabrique, 2017.

Ranciére, Jacques. "La pensée de la politique aujourd'hui." In *La modernité après le post-modern*, edited by Henri Meschonnic and Shiguehiko Hasumi, 41–49. Paris: Maisonneuve & Larose, 2002.

Rancière, Jacques. *The Lost Thread: The Democracy of Modern Fiction*. Translated by Steven Corcoran. London, UK: Bloomsbury, 2017.

Rancière, Jacques. *The Politics of Aesthetics: The Distribution of the Sensible*. Translated with an Introduction by Gabriel Rockhill. With an afterword by Slavoj Žižek. London, UK: Continuum, 2011.

Reed, T. V. *The Bloomsbury Introduction to Postmodern Realist Fiction*. London, UK: Bloomsbury, 2021.

Rentzou, Efthymia. "Animal." In *A New Vocabulary for Global Modernism*, edited by Eric Hayot and Rebecca L. Walkowitz, 29–42. New York: Columbia University Press, 2016.

Richardson, Anna. "In Search of the Final Solution: Crime Narrative as a Paradigm for Exploring Responses to the Holocaust." *European Journal of English Studies* 14, no. 2 (2010): 159–71.

Roberts, John. "Revolutionary Pathos, Negation, and the Suspensive Avant[-] Garde." In *The Idea of the Avant Garde and What It Means Today*, edited by Marc James Léger, 138–45. Manchester, UK: Manchester University Press, 2014.

Robespierre, Maximilien. *Virtue and Terror*. Introduction by Slavoj Žižek. Text selected and annotated by Jean Ducange. Translated by John Howe. London: Verso, 2007.

Ruby, Christian. *Devenir contemporain? La couleur du temps au prisme de l'art*. Paris: Le Félin, 2007.

Rueff, Martin. "La concordance des temps." In Ruffel, *Qu'est-ce que le contemporain?*, 93–110.

Ruffel, Lionel. *Brouhaha: Worlds of the Contemporary*. Translated by Raymond M. MacKenzie. Minneapolis, MN: University of Minnesota Press, 2018.

Ruffel, Lionel. "Introduction: Qu'est-ce que le contemporain?" In Ruffel, *Qu'est-ce que le contemporain?*, 9–35.

Ruffel, Lionel. *Qu'est-ce que le contemporain? Texts réunis par Lionel Ruffel*. Nantes, France: Cécile Defaut, 2010.

Runia, Eelco. "Presence." *History and Theory* 45, no. 1 (February 2006): 1–29.

Russo, Rhett. "Architecture, Deep and Cryptic." In Gage, *Aesthetics Equals Politics*, 269–79.

Sadaf, Shazia. "'We Are All Migrants through Time': History and Geography in Mohsin Hamid's *Exit West*." *Journal of Postcolonial Writing* 56, no. 5 (2020): 636–47.

Saiko, Yuriko. *Everyday Aesthetics*. Oxford, UK: Oxford University Press, 2007.

Saint-Amour, Paul K. "Perpetual Interwar." In *Postmodern | Postwar—and After: Rethinking American Literature*, edited by Jason Gladstone, Andrew Hoberek, and Daniel Worden, 165–77. Iowa City, IA: University of Iowa Press, 2016.

Sánchez, Canales Gustavo. "Holocaust Imagery in Michael Chabon's *The Final Solution*." *Americana: E-journal of American Studies in Hungary* 9, no. 1 (Spring 2013). http://americanaejournal.hu/vol9no1/sanchez-canales (accessed November 4, 2021).

Schina, Damiano. "'A Place for the Genuine': Ben Lerner's Poetics of Liminality." MA thesis, University Ca' Foscari, Venice, Italy, 2018. http://dspace.unive.it/handle/10579/13257 (accessed August 4, 2021).

Schulz, Bruno. *The Street of Crocodiles and Other Stories*. Translated by Celina Wieniewska. Foreword by Jonathan Safran Foer. Introduction by David A. Goldfarb. New York: Penguin, 2008.

Scott, Niall, ed. *Monsters and the Monstrous: Myths and Metaphors of Enduring Evil*. Amsterdam: Rodopi, 2007.

Shaviro, Steven. *Connected, or What It Means to Live in the Network Society*. Minneapolis, MN: University of Minnesota Press, 2003.

Shaviro, Steven. *The Universe of Things: On Speculative Realism*. Minneapolis, MN: University of Minnesota Press, 2014.

Shotter, John. "Creating Real Presences: Displays in Liminal Worlds." In Prelli, *Rhetorics of Display*, 273–89.

Simmel, Georg. *Simmel on Culture: Selected Writings*. Edited by David Frisby and Mike Featherstone. London, UK: Sage, 1997.

Skinner, Jonathan. "Visceral Ecopoetics in Charles Olson and Michael McClure: Proprioception, Biology, and the Writing Body." In *Ecopoetics: Essays in the*

Field, edited by Angela Hume and Gillian Osborne, 65–83. Iowa City: University of Iowa Press, 2018.

Smith, Alexandra. "Writing Against the Image: Teju Cole, Ben Lerner, and Aesthetics of Failure." PhD diss., University of Sydney, 2015.

Smith, Terry. *Talking Contemporary Curating*. New York: Independent Curators International, 2015.

Smith, Terry. *What Is Contemporary Art?* Chicago, IL: The University of Chicago Press, 2009.

Sorensen, Leif. "Against the Post-Apocalyptic: Narrative Closure in Colson Whitehead's *Zone One*." *Contemporary Literature* 55, no. 3 (2014): 559–92.

Starobinski, Jean. *Jean-Jacques Rousseau: La transparence et l'obstacle*. Paris: Plon, 1957.

Stefans, Brian Kim. *Word Toys: Poetry and Technics*. Tuscaloosa, AL: University of Alabama Press, 2017.

Sussman, Henry. *Idylls of the Wanderer: Outside in Literature and Theory*. New York: Fordham University Press, 2007.

Sutherland, Meghan. "Rigor/Mortis: The Industrial Life of Style in American Zombie Cinema." *Framework* 48, no. 1 (Spring 2007): 64–78.

Taylor, Diana. *¡Presente! The Politics of Presence*. Durham, NC: Duke University Press, 2020.

Teh, David. "What Is a Sovereign Object? Baudrillard and the Inexchangeable." *International Journal of Baudrillard Studies* 5, no. 1 (January 2008). https://baudrillardstudies.ubishops.ca/what-is-a-sovereign-object-baudrillard-and-the-inexchangeable/ (accessed December 5, 2020).

Toth, Josh. *Truth and Metafiction: Plasticity and Renewal in American Narrative*. New York: Bloomsbury, 2021.

Trumpener, Katie. "In the Grid: Period and Experience." *PMLA* 127, no. 2 (March 2012): 349–57.

Van den Akker, Robin, Alison Gibbons, and Timotheus Vermeulen, eds. *Metamodernism: Historicity, Affect, and Depth after Postmodernism*. Lanham, MD: Rowman and Littlefield, 2017.

Vermeulen, Pieter. "Beauty That Must Die: *Station Eleven*, Climate Change, and the Life of Form." *Studies in the Novel* 50, no. 1 (Spring 2018): 9–25.

VisualEditions. "The making of *Tree of Codes* by Jonathan Safran Foer. Watch the last three months of production in just three minutes." March 7, 2011. https://www.youtube.com/watch?v=r0GcB0PYKjY (accessed November 29, 2017).

Volta, Luigi. "'Horror' nella cultura di massa: dal mito allo *zombie*." *Quaderni di Filologia Germanica della Facolta di Lettere e Filosofia dell'Universita di Bologna* 2 (1982).

Waddell, Laura. *Exit*. New York: Bloomsbury, 2020.

Walkowitz, Rebecca L. *Born Translated: The Contemporary Novel in an Age of World Literature*. New York: Columbia University Press, 2015.

Wallace, David Foster. "Tri-Stan: I Sold Sissee Nar to Ecko." In *After Yesterday's Crash: The Avant-Pop Anthology*, edited by Larry McCaffery, 232–45. New York: Penguin, 1995.

West, Mark. "Apocalypse Without Revelation? Shakespeare, Salvagepunk, and Station Eleven." *Open Library of Humanities*, 4, no. 1 (2018): 1–26. https://doi.org/10.16995/olh.235 (accessed September 10, 2021).

Westphal, Bertrand. *La Géocritique. Réel, fiction, espace*. Paris: Minuit, 2007.
Whitehead, Colson. "Colson Whitehead's Monsters—*Zone One* (Interview)." By Jade Colbert. *The Varsity*, January 30, 2012. https://thevarsity.ca/2012/01/30/colson-whiteheads-monsters-zone-one-interview/ (accessed March 12, 2022).
Whitehead, Colson. *Zone One*. New York: Random House, 2011.
Wikipedia. "A Quiet Storm." https://en.wikipedia.org/wiki/A_Quiet_Storm (accessed March 2, 2022).
Wilcox, Leonard. "Don DeLillo's *Underworld* and the Return of the Real." *Contemporary Literature* 43, no. 1 (Spring 2002): 120–37.
Williams, Jeffrey J., and Robert Kilpatrick. "Fiction: The 1980s to the Present." *American Literary Scholarship* (2018): 297–316.
Wilmann, Fabrice. *Emily St. John Mandel's* Station Eleven. Cheltenham, Australia: Insight, 2018.
Wilson, D. Harlan. "Schizosophy of the Medieval Dead: Sam Raimi's *Army of Darkness*." *Journal of Popular Culture* 41, no. 3 (2008): 509–35.
Wisnoski, Barbara. "An Aesthetic of Everything Else: Craft and Flat Ontologies." *The Modern Journal of Craft* 12, no. 3 (November 2019): 205–17.
Wolf, Nelly. *Le Roman de la démocratie*. Saint-Denis, France: Presses Universitaires de Vincennes, 2003.
Woodard, Ben. "Zombie Economy." *Naught Thought*, May 17, 2007. http://naughtthought.wordpress.com/2007/05/17/zombie-economy/ (accessed April 4, 2010).
Wurth, Kiene Brillenburg, Kári Driscoll, and Jessica Pressman, eds. *Book Presence in a Digital Age*. New York: Bloomsbury, 2019.
Yarbrough, Stephen R. *The Levels of Ambience: An Introduction to Integrative Rhetoric*. Intermezzo. E-book: http://intermezzo.enculturation.net/09-yarbrough.htm, 2018.
Žižek, Slavoj. "Fantasy as a Political Category: A Lacanian Approach." In Lodge and Wood, *Modern Criticism and Theory*, 695–705.
Žižek, Slavoj. *The Metastases of Enjoyment: Six Essays on Women and Causality*. London, UK: Verso, 1994.
Žižek, Slavoj. *Organs Without Bodies: On Deleuze and Consequences*. New York: Routledge, 2004.

Index